Politics, Paradigms, and Intelligence Failures

Politics, Paradigms, and Intelligence Failures

Why So Few Predicted the Collapse of the Soviet Union

OFIRA SELIKTAR

M.E.Sharpe
Armonk, New York
London, England

Copyright © 2004 by M.E.Sharpe, Inc.

All rights reserved. No part of this book may be reproduced in any form
without written permission from the publisher, M.E. Sharpe, Inc.,
80 Business Park Drive, Armonk, New York 10504.

Library of Congress Cataloging-in-Publication Data

Seliktar, Ofira.
  Politics, paradigms, and intelligence failures : why so few predicted the collapse of the
Soviet Union / by Ofira Seliktar.
    p. cm.
  Includes bibliographical references and index.
  ISBN 0-7656-1464-2 (cloth : alk. paper)
  1. Soviet Union—Politics and government—1953–1985. 2. Soviet Union—Politics and
government—1985–1991. I. Title.
DK274.S375 2004
327.73047'09'048—dc22

2004002477

Printed in the United States of America

The paper used in this publication meets the minimum requirements of
American National Standard for Information Sciences
Permanence of Paper for Printed Library Materials,
ANSI Z 39.48-1984.

∞

MM   BM (c)   10   9   8   7   6   5   4   3   2   1

To my grandchildren
Yehoshua, Orly, Benjamin, and Shlomo

Contents

List of Abbreviations

ACDA   Arms Control and Disarmament Agency
ACFPC   Arms Control and Foreign Policy Caucus
ASC   American Security Council
CED   Committee for Economic Development
CFE   Conventional Forces in Europe
CIA   Central Intelligence Agency
CIS   Commonwealth of Independent States
CPD   Committee for Present Danger
CPD   Congress of People's Deputies
DCI   Director of Central Intelligence
DDI   Deputy Director for Intelligence
DIA   Defense Intelligence Agency
IMEMO   Institute of the World Economy and International Relations
IMF   International Monetary Fund
INF   Intermediate Nuclear Forces
IPS   Institute for Policy Studies
IRGD   Inter-Regional Group of Deputies
ISKAN   Institute of the USA and Canada
JEC   Joint Economic Committee
KGB   Committee for State Security
MAD   Mutual Assured Destruction
MCPL   Members of Congress for Peace through Law
MDP   Militarism and Disarmament Project
MVD   Ministry of Interior Affairs
NED   National Endowment for Democracy
NIO   National Intelligence Officer

NKVD	People's Commissariat of Internal Affairs
NPT	New Political Thinking
NSC	National Security Council
NSDD	National Security Decisions Directives
NVOI	National Voice of Iran
OPD	Office of Public Diplomacy
PDPA	People's Democratic Party of Afghanistan
PFIAB	President's Foreign Intelligence Advisory Board
SALT	Strategic Arms Limitation Treaty
SANE	National Committee for Sane Nuclear Policy
SCAM	Strategic Cost Analysis Model
SCC	Special Coordination Committee
SDI	Strategic Defense Initiative
SOVA	Office of Soviet Analysis
START	Strategic Arms Reduction Talks
WFTU	World Federation of Trade Unions
WPC	World Peace Council

Preface

On December 25, 1991, the Soviet flag was lowered for the last time over the Kremlin, ending the longest running communist experiment in the world. The seemingly sudden collapse of the Soviet Union sent shock waves around the globe. It ended the epic struggle between East and West that fueled the Cold War and left the United States as the only superpower in the world.

Unlike the communist revolution in China and the fundamentalist revolution in Iran, the demise of the Soviet empire was a positive development in terms of American national security. However, Washington's failure to foresee the events in Moscow ranks high in the pantheon of predictive failures. Indeed, this failure has been a subject of a long, passionate, and multidimensional debate. Complicating the debate are two factors. First, the collapse of the Soviet Union followed a long *crisis of legitimacy*, a process that has been hard to conceptualize, let alone measure. Second, the question of who got it right or wrong has been intertwined with the deeper issue of who "won" the Cold War. Like the inverse but methodologically similar disputes over who "lost" China and Iran, this debate has been fought along ideological and partisan lines, with conservatives claming credit for devising policies that toppled the Soviet regime and liberals arguing that the United States had no input into the collapse. The intelligence community has been criticized most harshly, but the predictive debacle has also shaken Sovietology, with the discipline dissolving in a round of acrimonious post-mortems and finger pointing.

This passionate discourse has generated a voluminous literature, most of which deals with relatively narrow segments of the process that informed American views of the changing realities in the Soviet Union. By far, the largest volume of writings has been generated by a discussion of the role of academic Sovietology in the predictive debacle, followed by that of the intelligence and foreign policy communities. However, there has been little effort to provide an *integrative and time-line-based* analysis that focuses on the complex ways in which legitimacy-driven political change in the Soviet Union was conceptualized by American political science, applied to Washington's foreign policy, and used in the predictive endeavor.

This book hopes to contribute to such an understanding by offering *the first systematic analysis of the predictive failure at the paradigmatic, foreign policy, and intelligence levels.* The theoretical part of the book discusses the social science paradigms that were instrumental in determining how Sovietology viewed political change in the Soviet Union. The applied section of the book is composed of two sequential analyses. The first part illustrates how these paradigmatic assumptions had influenced the U.S. approach to predicting and managing political change in the Soviet Union. Revisionist views, fortified by the pluralist model, comparative politics, and other vogues in political science, informed the Carter administration's liberal vision of a New Internationalist partnership with the Soviet Union. The totalitarian approach, fortified by conservative and neoconservative thinking, was behind the Reagan administration's crusade to vanquish communism. The second part describes how the Reagan challenge exacerbated the crisis of legitimacy in the Soviet Union and influenced the efforts of Mikhail Gorbachev to revamp the legitimizing framework of Soviet communism as a way of improving its competitive performance. Each of the chapters in this section is based on a chronological-thematic analysis of the developments in the Soviet Union, the politics of the predictive process in Washington, and the paradigmatic debates that shaped this process.

Although the analytical framework of this book was devised around the Soviet problematique, it can be used for the study of other instances of critical political change. As the relatively stable Cold War situation gave way to a multitude of volatile international problems, lessons from the failure to predict the demise of the Soviet empire can be used for anticipating changes that lie ahead in the Muslim world and beyond.

A study of this scope would not have been possible without access to a variety of classified documents and personal recollections. The CIA has declassified a large volume of its Soviet estimates. In addition, the National Security Archive used the Freedom of Information Act to declassify CIA and State Department documents, and the Cold War project at the Woodrow Wilson Center has amassed a large collection of relevant documents. Joining this large body of knowledge are disclosures from Soviet archives, numerous retrospective conferences and workshops of key Soviet and American players, and a large library of memoirs and books by American and Soviet leaders and intelligence officials, as well as KGB defectors. Analyzed in great detail, this information was instrumental in the reconstruction of political changes in the Soviet Union in the decade preceding its collapse and the American perceptions of this change.

Politics, Paradigms, and Intelligence Failures

Introduction

The Theory and Practice of Predicting Political Change

The collapse of the Soviet empire has often been described as one of the pivotal events in human history, comparable to the demise of Roman civilization and the ascent of Christianity. Even those who do not subscribe to such a sweeping view of history have acknowledged the enormous significance of this period. As one observer put it, "for a brief span of time, the extraordinary became an almost daily event." Another remarked that "the most quixotic optimists were repeatedly proved too cautious," and yet another described as "fantastic" any effort to foresee the developments a few years earlier (Fischer 1999, 4; Kuran 1995, 262; Hyland 1987, 7). The disintegration of the Soviet Union turned out to be an unprecedented success for American national security policy. However, the failure to foresee what lay ahead looms large in its pantheon of predictive failures, along with the communist takeover of China and the fundamentalist revolution in Iran. As with these other cataclysmic events, the round of post-mortem debates focused the limelight on the way the United States predicts and manages political change.

Prediction and effective foreign policy making are closely related. Consciously or subconsciously, policy decisions rest on predictions of the likely course of future events. One scholar noted that "even the naïve practitioner who insists that he makes every decision solely on the facts at hand operates with an implicit conception of what the future will be like" (Rothstein 1972, 159). Henry Kissinger (1981, 283–84) equated foreign policy with the ability to perceive trends, be they dangers or opportunities. In his view, officials must act on "judgments about the future that cannot be proved true when they are made." Nowhere was this dictum more evident than during the Cold

War, when momentous policy decisions and enormous expenditures were riding on assumptions about the expected course of Soviet behavior.

Given the high cost of surprise, following World War II the United States mounted an enormous intellectual effort to improve military and political forecasting. Although forecasting military-strategic as opposed to political change focuses on different dimensions of international reality, they are both susceptible to the same types of predictive errors. Logically conceived, prediction is comparable to a form of statistical inference. In every predictive episode, evidence is assessed and probability assigned to the "hypotheses" that change will or will not occur. Prognosticators run the risk of committing two types of statistical errors. They can either reject a "true hypothesis"— that is, decide that change will not take place when, in fact, change is going to occur—or accept a "false hypothesis"—that is, decide that change will take place when it will not occur. Experts have worked to eliminate both types of errors, but instances in which adverse change was not predicted have, understandably, attracted the most attention. For the same reason, there has been relatively less interest in opportunity as opposed to crisis forecasting, although such changes can be beneficial to national security (Ofri 1983).

Predictive failures range from minimal to fundamental and can be grouped in four categories. In the first two—known as residuals and errors—the actual prediction of the event is successful, but the time frame is off by a certain margin. Failure here does not necessitate any change in basic theory and/or predictive methodology. In the third category, the miss is known as an outliner—the error is large enough for the methodology and the applications to be revised, but the basic theory behind it is still viewed as adequate. In the last category, the miss is so great that, in terms of the philosophy of science, it becomes an anomaly. In such cases, the subsequent debate about the misdiagnosis leads to a major revision of the predictive process at the level of procedures and organization. More important, a fundamental failure triggers a revision at the epistemic level of knowledge, often referred to as a paradigm.

There is little doubt that the case of the Soviet empire fits the model of a fundamental failure at the intelligence level. A commentator noted that it "beggars incredulity" that the CIA "had no idea that Soviet Union was on the verge of radical change" after spending 50 percent of its budget on Soviet analysis (Perry 1992, 308).

But the failure is also paradigmatic, best understood in terms of Thomas Kuhn's analysis of revolutionary changes in knowledge. In his famous work on the structure of scientific revolution, Kuhn postulated that during routine times, agreed-upon fundamental concepts are used to analyze a situation. These deep-seated concepts, known as master theories or paradigms, dominate the field of a given intellectual endeavor and dictate the standards of inquiry. They form the "entire constellation of beliefs, values, techniques. . . shared by the members of a given community." The dominant paradigm ordains what questions will arise, what forms of explanation will be accepted, and what interpretations will be recognized as legitimate. As long as the paradigm is not challenged, its normalcy is widely accepted. But in the wake of a severe crisis, the dominant paradigm is questioned and overthrown. These paradigmatic battles, which are fought at the very frontiers of rationality, dictate how the community of practitioners looks at relevant reality (Kuhn 1970, 175).

Although Kuhn was primarily concerned with the scientific community, his work can be applied to the study of intelligence failures. The assumption here is that foreign policy practitioners use paradigms to analyze the political reality of countries in their purview. One study aptly contended that without such paradigms—a set of rules and standards for evaluating facts—"a policymaker is lost . . . all problems, approaches, facts and possible courses of action seem equally plausible" (Shafer 1988, 34). While the use of what one intelligence expert called "exception theories" for predicting crisis may work better in certain cases, there is no substation for "normal" paradigmatic theories in foretelling change (Betts 1983, 831).

Kuhn's theory notwithstanding, discerning how paradigms shape the view of changing international reality is not easy. Traditional models of foreign policy decision making do not focus on the epistemics of "understanding" that is crucial to such an endeavor. The rational choice model, the bureaucratic politics model, and the crisis behavior model have either emphasized the political, environmental, and structural dimension of policy making or have analyzed the process through which a collective understanding of a situation is reached.

The cognitive approach is closer to the issue of epistemology; a leading authority compared the belief system of foreign policy practitioners to a "set of lenses through which information concerning the physical and social environment is received" (Holsti 1962, 245). But even top researchers in the field have failed to agree on how the two elements in the "cognitive map" of actors—broad fundamentals and the more narrowly proscribed instrumental beliefs—interact in discerning changing realities. A perusal of the cognitive belief literature hints at the source of these difficulties. A dominant assumption of this model is that key decision-makers in charge of appraising the situation can readily be identified and that their beliefs and perceptions can be deduced through cognitive mapping, simulation, or other analytical devises. Yet from an epistemic standpoint, this assumption is too static and limited. Studies on how bureaucracies "think" reveal that a collective understanding of a situation is arrived at as a result of the performance of a large number of individuals who apply concepts from an "analytic community inventory." Such inventories are formed through complex and ill-defined intellectual interactions among foreign policy makers, bureaucratic experts, scholars, and journalists.

Studies of American foreign policy culture offer an alternative for tracking paradigms used in discerning political change. This large literature shows how enduring patterns of thought, symbols, and values affect foreign policy deliberation and inform perceptions of the future. Although direct empirical links between prevalent intellectual trends and foreign policy practices are hard to demonstrate, they are necessarily pervasive. One scholar used an image from Indian cosmology to describe how fundamental beliefs affect policymakers: "[t]he table at which policymakers sit is like the platform . . . on which the world stands: under it is a pyramid of arbitrary assumption, untested and indeed untestable hypothesis and imprecise measures" (Staniland 1991, 275–76). While undoubtedly true, this definition is too broad to capture the paradigmatic assumptions that underlie any given forecasting episode.

To go beyond these limits requires a more dialectically oriented psychological, sociological, and ethnographic approach. Ralph Pettman (1975), writing on the epistemology of foreign policy, argued that the search for the paradigms that determine how practitioners conceive of foreign societies should involve the *entire community of discourse on the issue at hand.* More recently, Giandomenico Majone (1989, 161–94), in his *Evidence, Argument and Persuasion in the Policy Process*, formalized this proposition. The book, which is fast setting standards for the discipline, focuses attention on the discourse of the *policy community*—defined as all those who share an active interest in a certain policy domain, that is political actors, professional analysts, interest groups, academics, and journalists. Majone argued that the discourse surrounding a given policy issue is highly dynamic and dialectic. Because a policy community is jointed loosely and its members have different professional, ideological, and intellectual commitments, the focus of inquiry should involve the entire discourse rather than select participants.

Using the discourse community as a model for understanding how forecasting of political change occurs makes it possible to combine the features of the more traditional approaches to decision making with elements of political culture and the epistemology of collective concept-use. Unfortunately, like many sociological constructs, a discourse community is a somewhat loose set of assumptions and concepts. The complexity and opacity of the process of discourse poses a considerable analytical problem. Following Majone, intelligence experts defined an epistemic community as "a coming together" of practitioners, political scientists, historians, and journalists (Fry and Hochstein 1993). Even so, the influence wielded by academics and intellectuals over policymakers is seldom direct and measurable. As James Smith (1993, 40) put it, "ideas are not a consumer good shipped from intellectual warehouses . . . to be retailed in the executive branches of Capitol Hill." Tanter and Ullman (1972, 3) asserted more bluntly that policymakers "have seldom given much heed to the writing of theorists." At the same time a plausible argument can be made that the "thinking professions" have a major, albeit indirect and diffuse, impact on policy making in the sense that they create a "climate of ideas," define the situation, and mold the belief systems of the policymakers. Over time, these ideas form an "almost rigid, congealed mass of conventional wisdom" (Etzioni-Halevy 1985, 26). Given their pervasiveness, it would be naïve to assume that practitioners could diverge significantly from such views of reality. In fact, "academic pens leave a mark . . . on policymakers" whereby "basic understanding of the world seldom differs fundamentally from social scientists" (Shafer 1988, 12).

Using the concept of a discourse community makes special sense in analyzing American perceptions of change in the Soviet Union, a field that was heavily influenced by various academic paradigms. Not coincidentally, many in the post-mortem debate castigated Sovietology for its alleged failures. Once critic asked, "how could so many have been wrong about so much for so long?" (Malia 1994, 6). Another stated that the "collapse of the Soviet Union was a catastrophe for Sovietology and, more broadly, the entire discipline of political science." He added that "never has so much money been allocated to study one country," an endeavor that occupied countless "academic and government specialists" (Pipes 1995a, 159; 1994, 6). Yet another observer pointed out that few social scientists "have been put in the position of having their model so spectacularly disproved" (Rutland 1993, 122). Still others claimed that for Sovietologists "the collapse of the USSR represented a colossal failure" (Urban and Fish 1998, 165). Comparative politics and international relations have also been severely criticized, with some observers questioning the entire theoretical foundation of these disciplines (Janos 1991; Wohlforth 1998; Tucker 1993).

Right or wrong, the paradigms developed by Sovietologists were crucial in informing views of political change in the Soviet Union. Indeed, this book is based on the assumption that a dialectic relation exists between intellectual ways of thinking about political change and the way in which such collective concepts inform politicians, foreign policy bureaucrats, and intelligence officials. To restate the Kuhnian proposition, the intellectual outlook generated in the relevant branches of knowledge had influenced the epistemology of foreign policy practitioners charged with Soviet prognostication. At the same time, the political practices of the Cold War had shaped and reshaped the intellectual paradigms. This interaction is inseparable, but for analytical purposes the elements of such a process can be isolated.

First, this study will discuss theories of political change that were popular in the two decades before the demise of the USSR. Political change in the Soviet Union, as in other revolutionary situations, was precipitated by a *crisis of legitimacy*. Such a crisis occurs when fundamental societal norms are discarded and new ones adopted. These norms and values are embedded in the *collective belief system of a society*, which can be identified by tracking the societal legitimacy discourse, or more precisely the process of legitimation and delegitimation. As norms and values change, so do their more tangible edifices such as political processes and institutions. Successful prediction of impending change must involve an early identification of changing collective beliefs and especially the indices of delegitimation.

In spite of its obvious advantages as an "early warning system," legitimacy is not an easy tool to use. As one observer noted, "the concept of legitimacy is simple in principle but notoriously slippery in application" (Rigby 1983, 9). Francis Fukuyama (1992, 15), who coined the term "the end of history" to describe the collapse of the Soviet empire, maintained that legitimacy "is a relative concept that exists in people's subjective perception." Unlike indicators of performance, legitimacy norms are amorphous and illdefined. Scholars have been deeply divided over the question of how, why, and when societies embrace and drop political norms. A major cause of this disagreement stems from the fact that, in analyzing how norms of legitimacy change, social scientists rely on different ontological and epistemic assumptions about societal reality and embrace a sharply divergent view of human nature. These root assumptions form the base of paradigms through which political change is discerned, whether observers are aware of them or not. In turn, paradigms generate predictive formulas about the cause, the timing, and direction of political change. Since paradigms are themselves normative in character, they dictate what norms and values *should be considered legitimate.* Locked into their respective paradigms, observers tend to project their own sense of legitimacy onto the belief systems of the society they analyze. What is more important, these normative projections tend to inform their predictions of when and how political change will occur and what direction it will take.

Second, this study will discuss the paradigms and political science models that underlay the field of Sovietology. In the first two decades after World War II, the study of the Soviet system followed the totalitarian model. Although the totalitarian model depicted the USSR as sui generis, it had a complex relation to the then dominant developmentalist paradigm, which was formulated to chart political change in the Third World. Alternatively known as modernization theory, developmentalism postulated that all societies are ultimately destined to evolve into a Western-type democracy with a market economy. In this view, the totalitarian and brutally coercive Soviet regime was considered to be an aberration in the process of modernization and was expected eventually to disappear from the stage of history.

The failure of the underdeveloped world to follow the prescriptive path of the West, as well as the war in Vietnam, discredited the tenets of developmentalism and popularized a neo-Marxist critique of modernization theory. Known as dependency or *dependencia*, the new paradigm acknowledged that linear progress takes place, but asserted that, ultimately, societies would legitimize an enlightened, egalitarian distributive justice system. Although dependency theory was initially developed to analyze change in Latin America, the notion that egalitarianism rather than a market economy is mankind's destiny enhanced the legitimacy of socialism. In an unrelated push for a strong comparative orientation in political science, a new generation of Sovietologists had portrayed the Soviet Union as the functional equivalent of a Western pluralistic society. With the totalitarian model rapidly falling into disrepute, some observers took to predicting that the West and the Soviet Union would ultimately converge into a type of democratic egalitarianism. Even those who did not buy into the convergence thesis believed that the Soviet system had shed its totalitarian-era coercion and become legitimized by the population at large.

Scholars who used the newly popular rational choice theory to study the Soviet system challenged this perceived legitimacy. Rational choice theorists pointed out that what was seen as popular acceptance of the regime was in fact an adaptive posture by individuals scared into masking their true beliefs. Such insights jelled into the neoconservative critique of the pluralistic paradigm, which also incorporated elements of the totalitarian model. Neoconservative critics posited that the communist system is not reformable and that, ultimately eroded by a progressive crisis of legitimacy, the Soviet Union would collapse.

Third, this book will analyze how these paradigms affected American foreign policy toward the Soviet Union and were, in turn, affected by changing international realities. Since the discourse community approach is based on cross-fertilization between practitioners and larger intellectual trends, it was only natural that the totalitarian model would became part of the Cold War attempt to contain communism. However, the war in Vietnam made containment too costly, prompting the Nixon administration to engage in the process of détente whereby the revisionist vision of a pluralistic Soviet Union gained some traction. However, it was only after the Carter administration embraced New Internationalism, a mix of New Left egalitarianism and neo-Wilsonian moralism, that this vision was fully incorporated into American foreign policy. But neoconservatives adamantly opposed the notion that the Soviet Union was poised to liberalize domestically and moderate its expansionist foreign policies, igniting a firestorm in the discursive community. They were vindicated by the Soviet invasion of Afghanistan, which discredited New Internationalism and ushered in Ronald Reagan, who used elements of the neoconservative critique to delegitimize and destabilize the Soviet Union. As Soviet communism entered what would become its last decade of existence, contending paradigms led academic observers and their counterparts among foreign policy and intelligence practitioners to draw diametrically divergent conclusions about the health, longevity, and direction of change of the Soviet empire.

The organization of this book reflects the above research strategy. Chapter 1 provides a theoretical framework for analyzing the process of legitimation and delegitimation of a collective belief system. Chapter 2 describes how the totalitarian model, the revisionist-pluralistic model, and rational choice theory applied these constructs to offer contrasting views of change in the Soviet Union. Chapter 3 details how different paradigmatic insights affected the efforts of the Nixon, Ford, and Carter administrations to fashion a policy of détente. Chapter 4 analyzes the attempt of the Reagan administration to apply specific tenets of the neoconservative model in order to delegitimize the Soviet system and expedite its demise. Chapters 5, 6, and 7 use a thematic-chronological account of the politics of the predictive process during the three stages of the "Gorbachev revolution" between 1985 and 1991. In conclusion, Chapter 8 provides a systematic analysis of the predictive failure at the paradigmatic, policy, and intelligence levels, and offers some suggestions for improving political forecasting.

1

Theories of Political Change and Prediction of Change

Methodological Problems

Starting with Aristotle and Plato, the search for principles that underlie political change has been a staple of Western philosophy. This quest has been made especially perplexing because of the seemingly inexplicable nature of political change. One scholar wrote that "ideologies stand for centuries and then one day the temples are empty" (Boulding 1962, 281). Much of this change is precipitated by a crisis of legitimacy, defined as an alternation in the core values of the collective belief system of a society. Socrates speculated that alternations in legitimacy formulas precede political change, setting off a long quest to uncover how communal norms crystallize into a collective belief system and a corresponding political structure, only to be eroded by further changes. Discovering the indices of legitimation and delegitimation is especially important to the predictive endeavor since it can signal to observers that the legitimacy of a given regime is "eroding below . . . some danger line" (Rothchild 1979, 48). However, analyzing legitimacy has been problematic, prompting Samuel Huntington (1991, 46), a leading authority on political change, to note that legitimacy "is a mushy concept that political scientists do well to avoid." Indeed, there are a number of problems that face students of legitimacy. As Claus Mueller put it, the task is comparable to "a surgical probing for that which is unseen, but nevertheless crucial for survival" (quoted in Bialer 1986a, 418).

**Methodological Problems of Tracking Changes
in a Collective Belief System**

Tracking legitimacy norms poses considerable methodological problems. Most important is the unit of analysis problem—namely, the question of who are the ideational bearers of the collective belief system. Ontologically, the answer divides political science into macrosociologial *holism* and microsociological *individualism*. The former holds that a society is whole and cannot be reduced to the sum of its individual parts; the latter postulates that a social collective is the sum total of individual beliefs. A related question deals with the kind of knowledge that should be used to probe for political beliefs. Epistemologically, the division runs between *positivism*, an assumption that the only admissible knowledge is based on scientific methods of investigation, and *antipositivism*, which holds that such knowledge is essentially subjective, relativist, or spiritual.

Thinkers as diverse as Karl Marx, Emile Durkheim, and Karl Mannheim (1955, 264–311) have subscribed to the holistic approach. Macrosociologists have insisted that the collective belief system should not be confused with the arithmetic sum of "individual consciousness" of a group. However, they are less clear as to what the appropriate unit of analysis should be. One view conceives of the "belief carrier" as an abstract, almost metaphysical "supersocietal entity" resembling the "general will" of the Enlightenment. Marxists and some neo-Marxists hold that a self-appointed intellectual vanguard should represent the "general will."

Reacting to the methodological muddle of holism, the rival school of ontological individualism is committed to the view that beliefs of individual members of a group are the only legitimate unit of analysis. Among its earliest proponents were behaviorally oriented political scientists such as Almond and Verba (1965, 13), who defined a collective political belief system as the "particular distribution of orientations toward political objects among the members of the nation." In other words, the statistically derived psychological modalities of a given population could be used to discern patterns of political change.

In spite of its popularity, ontological individualism has not escaped serious criticism. One prevalent complaint is that microsociologists neglect the distribution of power in a society (Converse 1987; Frey 1985). The inadequacies of both approaches have bred the *interactionist* perspective. Interactionism is based on the assumption that neither the group nor the individual can be accorded "unqualified primacy," and both are "mutually constitutive" in the ongoing process of creating social reality. Interactionism can be traced to the work of George Simmel and George Herbert Mead, who argued that societal belief systems constitute complex symbolic sets and should be seen as a product and a determinant of individual beliefs generated through continuous social interaction (Burrell and Morgan 1985, 69–78; Seliktar 1986).

The interactionist perspective had recast the quest for the ideational bearers of the collective. In this view, changes in legitimacy norms can be best discerned by following the *discourse* of a society. Proponents of the interactionist tradition argue that tracking the group discourse provides the best measure of changes in its collective belief system. Among other things, they advise to look for "concrete language practices to identify the actors and parameters of discourse" (Shapiro, Bonham, and Heradstveit 1988).

The Dimensions of a Collective Belief System:
Existential Imperatives as Validity Claims

Much of the insight into discursive practices comes from anthropological studies. Linton (1945) postulated that in order to survive, a group legitimizes parts of its perceptional-ideational beliefs into an all-encompassing worldview. Such a collective belief system forms the parameters of social order in a given society at a given period of time. The discursive perspective holds that norms of legitimacy are internalized by group members and translated into actions through a repetitive performance of roles. In due course these roles crystallize into structures—institutions and processes—that shape and bind the collective through an endless stream of politics. The widely used concept of regime—meaning a set of governing arrangements that include networks of rules, norms, and procedures—reflects this idea most closely.

Douglas (1992, 43, 133–34) has posited that in the process of a normative debate societies work out their existential imperatives. The three dimensions that require some type of consensus are rules for gaining membership, principles for establishing an authority system, and rules for distributing wealth. The discourse produces *normative validity claims*, namely "reasoned elaborations" intended to persuade individuals that they need to obey the principles of political practice (Matheson 1987; Misztal 1996, 251). These validity claims are used to build the three axes of the collective belief system. The first axis is horizontal and comprises the principles of group boundary—criteria for granting membership and acquiring territory—known as *group membership/territorial* legitimacy. The second axis is vertical and denotes the principles upon which the authority system rests, defined as *authority system* legitimacy. The third axis is diagonal and articulates the principles of *distributive justice* that bind group membership and authority system together.

Membership/territorial legitimacy has evolved from the *Gemeinschaft* community where validity claims were based on kinship in *Gesellschaft* association that ties members through a "feeling of interdependence" and a "community of fate." Nationalism, which puts the loyalty to the nation-state above primordial attachments, has become increasingly popular in the past few centuries. As long as a relatively homogenous group occupies a well-defined national territory, few challenges to membership/territorial legitimacy occur. However, in cases of *polycentric nationalism*, where disparate ethnic groups reside under one national roof, tensions are never far from the surface. A dominant group may treat members of other groups as inferior or try to "homogenize" them by suppressing more primordial expressions. Religious divisions have added vast complications to the membership formula, especially when religion is used to relegate minority groups to second-class citizenship. The genesis of a polycentric state plays an important part in generating challenges to national validity claims. Dutter (1990) noted that if coercion was used to incorporate a group, this "primordial encroachment" typically reinforces a sense of "ethnohistorical grievances" that are perpetuated in its collective memory. By the same token, ethnic entrepreneurs, that is politicians who manipulate ethnic sentiments, often exploit such grievances as a way of attaining power.

Authority system legitimacy comprises a set of validity claims that justify the creation of a system of controls over a group residing in a defined territory. Since controls involve an exercise of power, validity claims help to ensure members' compliance. According to one definition, this type of legitimacy is "the foundation of such governmental power as is exercised both with a consciousness on the government's part that it has a right to govern and with some recognition by the governed of that right" (Kirsch 1982, 111). Max Weber's analysis of authority system legitimacy is well known. He identified three pure types of validity claims: (1) rational grounds—a belief in the legality of rule; (2) traditional grounds—based on the sanctity of traditions and the legitimacy of those who exercise authority according to certain traditional tenets; and (3) charismatic ground—resting on the commitment to a certain individual and the order revealed to him. Weber's taxonomy has generated an enormous critical literature, not the least because of the ambiguity surrounding rational legitimacy. To those who have maintained that rational legitimacy translates into a civic or contractual agreement, legitimation involves popular sovereignty as discharged in periodic elections. But others felt that authoritarian regimes, which have not institutionalized democratic procedures of choice, should be also considered legitimate, a stand that was sanctioned by Weber himself (Herz 1978; Berki 1982; Epstein 1984).

In the absence of universally binding guidelines, political scientists have adopted two approaches. One, which includes the writings of a large number of historians and traditional political scientists, has been based on a variety of *subjective* and highly intuitive criteria for estimating legitimacy in any of the three dimensions. The resulting disagreements among these observers have filled pages of academic publications. Largely as a reaction, behavioral scientists proposed a functional definition of a regime's legitimacy based on an *objective* compatibility between the collective belief system of a society and governmental "outputs" (Jackman 1976; Perlmutter 1980; Dixon and Moon 1986). Yet in spite of the strong faith of behavioralists that a value-free evaluation of authority system legitimacy is possible, precious little consensus has emerged. One of the critical questions is how to define illegitimate regimes. In his classic taxonomy, Richard Rose (1969) contended that regimes that are very low on public support and high on coercion should be considered "repudiated" or illegitimate. Although Rose did not include communist regimes, many of the Sovietologists used this type of reasoning to brand the Soviet Union as an illegitimate system. To confuse matters further, the disagreements on how legitimacy of a communist authority system should be evaluated had become intertwined with issues that pertain to distributive justice.

Distributive justice is part of a larger domain of social justice, defined as a series of principles for assigning particular things to particular individuals (Galston 1980, 5). Distributive justice is focused on the more limited question of "who distributes to whom, in virtue of what criterial characteristics, by what procedures, with what distributive outcomes" (Lane 1986). To satisfy the requirements of social justice, distributive schemes have been based on a number of validity claims. Three pure types can be identified: (1) ascriptive-traditional claims that underpin traditional economies; (2) utilitarian-productive claims that underline market economies; and (3) egalitarian principles that inform communist economies.

Ascriptive claims, based largely on birthright, have been prevalent in traditional societies whose constitutive domain was noneconomic. Following the emergence of economics as the constitutive domain in modernizing societies, efficiency rather than birth generated a utilitarian-productive validity claim used in distributive justice. As a result, economically meritorious individuals, defined as those who possess scarce factors of entrepreneurship and skill, were deemed worthy of receiving a share of resources commensurate with their contribution. Although the market economy has been highly efficient in generating wealth, it has created large inequalities among social classes and "boom and bust cycles" to which the poorer strata are particularly vulnerable.

It was left to Karl Marx, in his well-known critique of capitalism, to argue that general principles of justice demand an egalitarian distribution of resources. At a later stage of communist economy, Marx envisioned a distribution based on human needs, a notion that various neo-Marxist thinkers developed more than a century later. To ensure that the principles of egalitarian distributive justice are not violated, Marx urged the abolition of private property and the creation of a command economy run by the state on behalf of its citizens. Such a centralized economy was expected to generate sustained and even growth, thus providing material benefits to all and eliminating the cyclical recessions of capitalism. Following the Bolshevik revolution of 1917, the popularity of egalitarian validity, once considered an unworkable utopia, had gained steady appeal in the West. Indeed, as will become apparent, egalitarian distribution came to be increasingly applied to evaluations of authority system legitimacy, much to the detriment of capitalist democracy.

Changing the Collective Belief System:
The Process of Delegitimation

The legitimation discourse serves as the arena for an exchange of symbolic and substantive arguments in favor of accepting or rejecting validity claims in the three legitimacy dimensions identified above. However, efforts to predict possible change by tracking an amorphous and ongoing discussion pose several difficulties. The first pertains to the locus of the discourse. Much of the research on political communication reflects the habits of equating discursive practices with Western-style rational and institutionalized political procedures (Nimmo and Sanders 1981). Critics have pointed out that such a perspective trivializes the role of cultural, nonrational, symbolic, and mythical elements. Still, following broader intellectual trends can be confusing, since there are precious few rules of recognition that would allow observers to determine well in advance which of the cultural ideas circulating in the communal discourse will alter an important legitimacy formula. To remedy this, Turner and Killian (1972) articulated an "emergent norms" theory, which holds that normative challenges emanate from individuals or groups and "chain out" to larger and larger segments of the population.

Another problem pertains to the identity of the participants in the legitimation discourse. Theoretically, all members should be counted among the "ideational bearers" of their respective society. In reality though, crucial elites form "ideational clusters" that have a disproportional impact, a fact well recognized by the numerous studies of political elites. Less scrutinized are nonpolitical leaders such as writers, students, and other free-floating intelligentsia. Such elites, especially if they turn confrontational, can challenge extant legitimacy norms and the political institutions that are built around them (Said 1978; Coser 1964; Brinton 1965, 39). One taxonomy grouped people into "members," "contenders," and "challengers"; another identified "ruling," "accepting," and "opposition" groups (Tilly 1978, 52; Moshiri 1985, 188). More recently, the "second pivot" theory has gained recognition. It refers to a process whereby an elite splits into two pivots. The "second pivot" forms a change-oriented counterelite that is prepared to collude with likeminded outside elements in order to establish itself as the "sole pivot" (Rowen and Wolf, Jr., 1990a; Shtromas 1988). Whether the collective belief system would change in any particular direction along the three axes—

membership/territory, authority system, and distributive justice—depends on the complex interplay among all these actors.

In order to discern how such changes take place, the process of delegitimation needs to be analyzed. Since the discursive perspective involves both holistic and microsociological factors, a discussion of the systemic and individual level is in order.

System-Level Mechanisms

The system level analysis is most closely associated with Talcott Parsons's (1951) structural-functional approach to the study of political change. In essence, Parsons and his followers like David Easton (1953, 1965) adopted the mechanistic-deterministic properties of Newtonian physics to describe a closed and orderly political system where change was measured in linear terms. Some critics warned that social organizations, like other living organisms, are better represented by an open system analogue. However, the behavioral fever that gripped the discipline in the 1960s put a premium on linear-deterministic models of change and the high predictability that they offered (Von Bertalanffy 1956; Burrell and Morgan 1985, 65–67). Almond (1966), the then incoming president of the American Political Science Association, commented that such exactitude in studying political development was "exhilarating."

With the decline of behaviorism in the 1970s, alternative, nonlinear ways of modeling political change made their ways into the discipline. One promising analogue came from thermodynamics, which includes the concept of entropy. Growing entropy in the system indicates an increase in disorder. This disorder, which is normally prolonged but subterranean, is not noticed by observers, leading one historian to describe it as the "lost moments of history" (Trevor-Roper 1988). At a certain point, known as the "threshold of stability," the system reaches a "bifurcation point," that is, a stage in which it has to choose between two spatial distribution paths. In political terms, such a bifurcation results in a stochastic choice between diametrically opposed directions (Prigogine and Stengers 1984, 106; Cnudde 1973; Ward 1983).

Another promising analogue is based on catastrophe theory, which accounts for sudden and dramatic changes in the behavior of a system that previously functioned in a continuous and smooth way. Mathematical modeling indicates that, as a result of unnoticed stimuli, the behavioral surface reaches a cusp where the system becomes destabilized or even chaotic. Although chaotic systems are essentially unpredictable, they can be described by a number of laws, the most important of which is the "butterfly effect." Accordingly, even some very small events can send the system into an avalanche, producing enormous changes (Tucker 1996). A variant of this theory has been popularized as the tipping point theory. Based on the work of Thomas Schelling, a tipping point is reached when a critical mass has formed, suddenly leading a large number of people to engage in behavior that they had formerly avoided. In tipping point theory, political change is analogous to an epidemic in which change taking place at the margins of the system is not linear but geometric and bursts into the open in one dramatic moment. Once the momentum builds up, the tipping point becomes a "place when the unexpected becomes expected, where radical change is more than a possibility" (Gladwell 2000, 9–10, 14; Kuran 1995, 250).

Individual Level Mechanisms

Although less abstract, the analysis of political change at the individual level is by no means well understood. The literature offers three explanatory traditions. The first is loosely based on Emile Durkheim's notion of *anomie*, which is said to affect individuals in transitional states. Anomic stress affects emotional homeostasis, defined as people's ability to cope with demands of daily life. Anomic stress creates ambiguities in what is a legitimate need satisfaction; when disoriented individuals fail to meet their confused expectations, they proceed to delegitimize collective norms (Homans 1961, 214–19). The second is derived from work on social stratification known as *normative strain* analysis. Economic changes undermine the usefulness of certain roles, while "promoting" others. When the political status of the redundant role bearers is not adjusted accordingly, it triggers powerful demands to change the validity norms that underpin the collective belief system. Neil Smelser (1962) and other theorists explained that the French middle classes delegitimized the ascriptive-aristocratic distributive justice system and the monarchy that derived its legitimacy from it, triggering the French revolution.

The third explanatory perspective is based on cognitive dissonance theories. These theories assume that individuals feel uncomfortable when they are faced with two dissonant elements. In order to reduce the feeling of discomfort, a person may eliminate the sources of dissonance by adjusting beliefs, information, and feelings (Festinger 1957). Rescher (1969), a pioneer in social forecasting, argued that when new values are introduced in the societal discourse, people either adjust their beliefs or reject the discordant norms. Still, this process is neither automatic nor quick. Converse (1964), in his seminal work on mass beliefs, found that most people harbor contradictory and dissonant beliefs. Comparative studies indicate that some cultures have a high tolerance for contradictions between beliefs and daily praxis (Ajami 1981). Attribution theory has revealed that people's propensity to cling to initial opinions, attitudes, and theories is quite substantial, leading to "belief perseverance." Worse, authorities can manipulate individual beliefs through a combination of socialization and coercion. In totalitarian and certain authoritarian regimes, the discrepancies between stated values and reality are vigorously ignored or "explained away" by the regime.

Despite these difficulties it is possible to combine insights from the three explanatory perspectives to offer an understanding of how delegitimation occurs at the individual level. Studies demonstrate that when making decisions, individuals use a mechanism known as *validation*, which links beliefs about reality with the behavioral outcomes of these beliefs. Validation, in turn, is filtered through the sense of eudaemonics, a Greek term that means a sense of well-being. Social scientists have argued that well-being is a multivariate concept: *it simultaneously depends on the state of self, the well-being of the reference group, and some general notion of what well-being should be* (Strumpel 1972, 1977). In spite of its notorious fuzziness, there are certain elements that affect eudaemonically driven validation. Declining economic performance has a negative and fairly universal impact on individuals and normally results in an urge to change the distributive justice norms of a given society. Historically, failures of capitalism had resulted in delegitimizing the validity claims of a market economy and a move toward more egalitarian–socialist views. But eudaemonics can also affect the evaluation of an authority system. In what is perhaps the best known example, the economic failures of the Weimar Republic prompted the delegitimation of democracy and the onset of Nazi totalitarianism. By the same token, good economic performance can legitimate a fascist regime, as a pioneering study of Spanish legitimacy under Franco demonstrated. The Franco regime had enjoyed a fair amount of legitimacy as long as it had delivered economic benefits (McDonough, Barnes, and López Pina 1986). Moreover, the same study as well as other research showed that the three axes of legitimacy—group, authority, and distributive justice—are intertwined in people's minds.

The very complex nature of eudaemonic considerations, coupled with the not entirely predictable way in which individuals delegitimize norms, casts doubt on linear theories of change. Evidently, the numerous ways in which people can alter the legitimacy formulas account for the "choices" that the system makes. Since personal feelings operate "under the radar," these discrete decisions become known only when they reach a critical mass, manifested either in realigning elections or revolutionary upheavals.

Activating the Process of Delegitimation:
Trigger Conditions of Change

In order to facilitate prediction, it is important to identify the trigger conditions for such legitimacy-altering events. The literature reveals a number of explanatory traditions, which, not surprisingly, reflect the continuing debate between macrosystemic and individual level views of political change. The older theories have used the Parsonion-Eastonian notions of input-output to argue that when a system becomes incapable of responding in a satisfactory manner to new demands, a crisis of legitimacy develops. Change is said to occur when the system reaches a "ceiling condition" beyond which it cannot take effective action (Apter 1974, 110; Parvin 1973). Other theories are derived from the psychological "frustration-aggression" model, which stipulated that social or economic frustration could lead to politically aggressive actions. The popular J-curve theory of Davies (1962) held that people's expectations rise during periods of economic prosperity. When economic fortunes decline, such expectations cannot be met, leading to frustration. Gurr (1968, 1970, 1973) used the concept of relative deprivation to argue that frustration sets in when there is a discrepancy between the value expectation of individuals and the system's capability. However, in spite of its enormous popularity, the relative deprivation theory has failed to produce universal measures of discontent. Critics pointed out that the process of *collectivization of discontent* is influenced by a complex and interactive pattern of comparisons, including *temporal* comparison (between past and present), *social* comparisons (with other members of the national group), and *vertical* comparison (with other societies).

Reacting to these problems, a new generation of theories focused on structural factors of delegitimation. Shaped by the Marxist notions of structural change, Barrington Moore (1966) and his disciple Theda Skocpol (1979) rejected the notion that human agency in the shape of ideological beliefs has any impact on change. In Skocpol's opinion, the crucial triggers are structural —the weakening and progressive incapacitation of the administration and the military machine of the state. This theory, along with other unadulterated structuralist theories, was discredited by the Iranian revolution. Skocpol's many critics chastised her for claiming that revolutions do not depend on "subjective factors" such as belief, expectations, or attitudes (Kuran 1991, 15). The fundamentalist upheaval in Iran ushered in yet another generation of theories that saw ideas as a major trigger of change. In what became the standard for these theories, one scholar wrote that the focus on culture is essential because "it provides an ideational foundation for structure and institutions" (Kimmel 1990, 190).

While enormous energy has been expended on testing the various theories of change, relatively little attention has been devoted to the discursive practices that precede an impending crisis. A major reason for this neglect stems from the fact that much of societal discourse proceeds at the symbolic level. Foreign observers are hard-pressed to understand symbolic meanings that are permeated by condensed references to indigenous cultural events. Students of symbolic politics have warned that ignoring what often seems esoteric and "irrational" in foreign cultures can impede the understanding of the process of delegitimation. Research on predictive failure has found that American experts often discard "irrational" information, which does not conform to Western standards of "hierarchical, unidirectional truth" (Michael 1985; Maruyama 1973, 1974). A related problem in deciphering societal discourse pertains to the linguistics of deceit, deception, and bad faith. *Semantic prevarication* has been assiduously practiced by totalitarian regimes that try to control the flow of information and shape perceptions of reality (DiPalma 1991). Spontaneous outbreaks of prevarication occur at the societal level as well. Whether originating in scraps of bona fide news or stemming from deliberate lying or forgery, sensationalism and gossip spread fabrications and conspiracy theories around. The latter are particularly common in societies afflicted with powerful historical traumas. The so-called "emic," that is, native explanation of causality in political reality, is rooted in particularistic chains of causation that make little overt sense to foreign researchers who track communal communication. Dismissing them as "irrational" may obscure vital elements in the legitimation discourse, as the case of the Iranian revolution demonstrated (Anderson 1986; Sexton 1986; Pipes 1997; Seliktar 2000, 14–16).

Another important strategy involves tracking of signs of anomie. To Durkheim's well-known list of indicators should be added other types of asocial behavior: drunkenness, breaches of sexual norms, venality, and personal and political corruption. Corruption is especially delegitimizing to an authority system because it promotes a sense of normlessness in daily life. At the same time, in certain societies corruption is an established social norm, making it hard for observers to decide whether it is "tearing down the system" or simply part of the native culture (Johnson 1966, 120; Faris 1955, 467–71; Codevilla 1992, 407).

Finally, analyzing political affairs and scandals can be helpful in discerning impending changes. Methodologically, such occurrences should be viewed as nonroutine power struggles that center around core norms of the political system. For instance, corruption scandals reflect a growing reluctance to regard public positions as remunerative means of personal enrichment. At a deeper level, this may indicate a growing acceptance of legal-rational legitimacy that calls for a separation between the private and public spheres. In closed societies like the Soviet Union, the study of witch hunts and purges is particularly promising. Since such purges are akin to medieval persecutions against those who challenge the sacred dogma, the "unmasking" of the offenders provides an inside view of changing norms. Another fruitful avenue involves the examination of sanctioned and nonsanctioned debates among intellectuals and academics. As will be made clear, the reforms of Mikhail Gorbachev were preceded by a seemingly obscure academic debate about communist economics during which Marxist dogma was criticized (Furhman 1988).

As challenges to the official belief system multiply, a society can enter a period of *liminality* where "all previous standards and modes are subject to criticism" (Pilskin 1980, 13). Whether such challenges can lead to the transformation of the collective belief system and the regime that rests on it depends on an array of mechanisms that bolster the durability of extant norms. Studies have repeatedly found that, on the whole, collective norms are quite durable. Even harder to undermine are the political structures built around them. In the words of one scholar: "To fail to accord legitimacy, to delegitimate an established institution or process runs contrary to many natural psychological processes" (R.E. Lane 1979, 68).

The Durability of Legitimacy: Personal and Systemic Factors of Maintenance

Extensive research efforts have failed to provide a clear picture of how norms of legitimacy operate as a mental construct. After decades of study, Apter's (1965, 391) old comment that "legitimacy is too complex, related as it is to personal identity, and ultimately, to individual needs for meaning and purpose" is still relevant. At the core of the problem are two conflicting views of how people form and maintain feelings of legitimacy. In their classic study, French and Raven (1959) argued that legitimacy is something sentimental; it derives from a sense of obligation and duty toward the group and the authority system, but is independent of performance factors. Easton (1965, 273) added that legitimacy is experienced by individuals as a "strong inner conviction of the moral validity of the authority system." Experts have assumed that such feelings form early in life and crystallize into *diffuse support* for the political system (Frasier 1974).

The opposing view is based on the much quoted study of Hollander and Julian (1970), who found that feelings of legitimacy are strongly related to the performance of the system. This so-called *functional legitimacy* is bolstered by insights from rational choice theory, which shows that people's perceptions of legitimacy are derived from a complex calculus of costs and benefits associated with accepting or rejecting a regime and the validity claims on which it is based. On the positive side are psychic and material rewards that stimulate the feelings of legitimacy. On the negative side are fear of coercion and punishment that can dissuade a person from rejecting collectively sanctioned norms and the constructs that top them (Mueller 1979; Wrong 1980;

Tyler 1990). Indeed, observers have speculated that what seems like legitimacy may actually be a simulated hypocrisy or submission that stems from
extreme coercion. Persistent fear can create a sense of helplessness and hope-
lessness, prompting an individual to persist in feelings of legitimacy because
"there is no acceptable alternative" (Rigby 1982, 4). Whether such negatively
conferred consent is acceptable in evaluating the legitimacy of a given regime
has been a subject of a fierce and ongoing debate (Pakulski 1986; Rothschild
1979; Johnson 1966, 15; Barner-Barry and Hody 1995, 1–2).

Given the lack of consensus, it is probably safe to assume that neither
general sentiments nor self-interest nor fear of coercion can explain how
individuals maintain the belief that their political universe is legitimate.
Boulding (1962, 79) postulated that in forming a view of what is legitimate,
individuals are guided by a mix of three perceptual systems: an *integrative
system*, based on a diffuse sense of support; a *threat system*, based on coercion; and an *exchange system*, based on utilitarian-functional considerations.
A study of the growth and decay of norms found that people use complex
strategies to determine when to delegitimize norms. Violating internalized
norms is psychologically painful even when material benefits are involved,
but fear of punishment also plays a large role in the calculus. *Social proof*,
that is, clues derived from observing others, is a major factor in deciding
whether to maintain or discard beliefs (Axelrod 1986).

In democratic regimes the integrative system is dominant, followed by
the exchange system. Indeed, obedience motivated by a belief in legitimacy
of the political system is the least costly way for maintaining societal order
since it involves few rewards and avoids the high cost of coercion. In totalitarian regimes, the threat system plays a large role; it punishes those who
deviate from the norms and serves as a potent deterrent to others. Since there
is little intrinsic support for the regime, the exchange system is also important. As noted in the Spanish study, the legitimacy of Franco's government
was partially bolstered by the economic rewards associated with the regime.

Empirical support for the existence of such a tripartite scheme is possible
to obtain only in open societies, where elections and survey technology provide a continuing update on any changes in the three axes of legitimacy. It is
a truism that measuring the level and mix of legitimacy considerations in
closed societies is difficult if not impossible. The Soviet case was especially
daunting because the regime blocked any efforts to assert its true legitimacy.
As a result, the extent of support for the Soviet authority system, its egalitarian distributive justice system, and its multinational membership structure
could be treated only macrosociologically—that is, *as a probability that appropriate attitudes had existed because of the remarkable stability of the
Soviet empire.* Such a macrosociological approach gives enormous latitude

to scholars and lay observers when they speculate on the legitimacy of a system. An expert on legitimacy argued that social scientists make a *judgment*, "not a report about people's belief in legitimacy," when "concluding that a power relationship is legitimate" (Beetham 1991, 13). In making this judgment observers tend to project their own normative expectations on the legitimizing discourse of the society they study. Such expectations are subtle but powerful because they shape the field of inquiry and dictate research strategies. A respected scholar of international relations noted that the bias introduced by normative projection resists any scientific scrutiny, making the term "objective" in political science a dubious proposition (Gaddis 1992–93). Most important, as the Soviet case proves, judgments about the legitimacy of the system have influenced the predictions of change.

Legitimacy of the Soviet Union: The Theory and Politics of a Concept

Before the emergence of the United States as a superpower following World War II, the foreign policy and academic community showed little interest in the study of the future. But by the onset of the Cold War, Washington was gripped by anxiety about the Third World, where the Soviet Union was thought to have aggressive designs. The Truman administration enlisted a large number of academics to study economic and political change in order to ascertain what type of societies would be least susceptible to communist penetration. Going beyond the original mandate and spurred by such seminal figures as Max Milikan and Walt W. Rostow, this collective effort generated the developmental paradigm, alternatively referred to as modernization theory.

Part of the behavioral movement in American political science, developmentalism drew on nomothetic knowledge that sought to formulate general laws of political behavior. Ontologically, it assumed that reality is external to individuals and can be broken up into discrete parts made up of concrete events that are amenable to statistical treatment. Based on these assumptions, developmental theorists generated a number of universal laws of political change. Societies were said to move from "primitive" (underdeveloped stages) to more advanced forms patterned on the secularized, democratic Western nation-state. Underlying the laws of modernization were a number of assumptions about legitimacy. With regard to authority systems, developmentalists expected people to embrace a preference for the type of civic-rational legitimacy that has underpinned liberal democracies in the West. In their influential study, *The Civic Culture*, Almond and Verba (1965) demonstrated that societies progress from parochial culture, to subject culture and, ultimately, to a Western-style civic culture. Deutsch (1953) argued that, in a parallel process, groups discard tribal-ethnic loyalties in favor of a more inclusive form of membership known as a nation-state.

The same logic of linear transition was applied to changes in formulas of distributive justice. Rostow (1964), the author of the developmental bible, *The Stages of Economic Growth*, postulated that as societies move along the traditional–modern trajectory, ascriptive validity claims would be delegitimized in favor of market meritocracy. Nudging traditional societies along the path of modernization was seen as a crucial task for American foreign policy, especially because large societal inequalities in the Third World provided a fertile ground for communist agitation. Those who hoped to deny the Soviet Union such an advantage were encouraged by the pioneering work of Kuznetz (1955), who demonstrated that inequality declines with the rise in the level of economic development.

Although the developmental paradigm dealt mostly with Third World countries, it had some implication for predicting change in the Soviet Union. Inspired by the work of Hannah Arendt on German totalitarianism, early studies of the Soviet Union viewed the USSR as a totalitarian state without popular legitimacy. These studies predicted that such a "repudiated" system would go the way of Nazi Germany and Fascist Italy. Many observers also doubted that a command economy could survive the inefficiency built into it. This forecast was based on the Austrian school of economics of Friedrich von Hayek and Ludwig von Mises, who argued that such inefficiencies were related to the "lack of an entire range of information indispensable for the economic rational allocation of production factors" (Staniszkis 1984, 563). These and other economists asserted that information scarcity, coupled with the absence of other market mechanisms such as capital and the failure to consider decapitalization (depreciation of capital and assets) as costs, would eventually undermine the socialist economy. So confident was Rostow that all societies would evolve into a market economy that he subtitled his work an anticommunist manifesto.

Still, not all experts were persuaded that planned organization of production is unworkable, leading to a lively scholarly exchange. The prominent British historian Edward H. Carr (1962, 39) asserted that socialist planning was being slighted by "old fashioned democrats whose conception of democracy is rooted in the derelict philosophy of laissez-faire." Joseph A. Schumpeter (1950, 191–93), a leading economic philosopher, went so far as to argue that socialist systems are more efficient because people value egalitarianism rather than the market and its inequalities. The liberal economist John Kenneth Galbraith (1967, 332) professed his belief that planning has significant advantages over market processes.

While academics debated, international reality was confounding the developmental paradigm. The assumption that inequality would fade away as countries move up on the developmental ladder was hotly contested by a host of new studies (Lenski 1966; Azar and Farah 1981; Elsenhans 1983). Moreover, most of the underdeveloped countries had failed to transit to capitalism or liberal democracy as envisaged by Washington. Beginning in the 1960s, an unmistakable drift toward socialism and authoritarianism had surfaced in Asia, Africa, and Latin America.

With modernization theory progressively discredited, the new paradigm known as *dependencia* (dependency) took root in political science. Heavily influenced by Marxist and neo-Marxist concepts, dependency scholars put market legitimacy and, indeed, liberal democracy as envisioned by Rostow's stages of development on the defensive. Rather than considering Western democracies and capitalism as a source of progress worth emulating, they regarded them as roots of the Third World's "peripheral" position and economic backwardness. Dependency theorists posited that true development could be achieved only by undermining the hegemonic ideology of capitalism. They condemned the American-European view of "economic growth first, redistribution later" and confidently predicted that socialism, not capitalism, would be the ultimate destiny of humanity. Thus, to the doubts of whether the Western path of development is a desirable one was added the deterministic view that it is not a possible one (Coleman 1977, 7–8; M. Brown 1985).

What helped Marxist and neo-Marxist scholars to propagate their paradigm were its core assumptions, a somewhat incongruent mix of *radical structuralism* and *radical humanism*. Ontologically, radical structuralism is positivistic and nomothetic, making it possible for its practitioners to develop their own laws of political change. Radical structuralists expected underdeveloped countries to shed their dependency status and reach a socialist "golden age." Cuba was most often mentioned as a possible model, followed by China or even Vietnam (Cardoso and Faletto 1979, 173–77; Packenham 1992, 30; Fagen 1978, 299). Radical humanism was based on a subjective ontology of nominalism that was assisted by antipositivist epistemology and buttressed by a voluntaristic rather than deterministic view of human nature. Methodologically ideographic, radical humanism relied heavily on subjective states of consciousness and emphasized the role of the scholar as both an interpreter and a shaper of political reality. In contrast to behavorialists who worked hard to separate scholarship and politics, neo-Marxists followed the Gramscian imperative that scholarship is an "agent of struggle" to be applied to the discursive venues of society with a view of changing prevalent norms of legitimacy (Packenham 1992, 15, 225). Galbraith (1985, 298) provided a blueprint for such action. He urged his academic colleagues to use their skills to change the prevalent paradigm by putting forward "seemingly implausible suggestions for reform. As they gained adherents, these suggestions would emerge as human needs and finally human rights."

Initially, neo-Marxist scholarship was limited to the fringes of American political science, but within a decade the new paradigm penetrated the mainstream. In a subtle but powerful shift, the behavioral tradition of value-free science was replaced by social advocacy. In an extraordinary about-face, Easton (1969) admitted that "behaviorism conceals an ideology based upon empirical conservatism" and called for a focus on "contemporary needs." This call fell on the receptive ears of a new generation of social scientists. As early as the 1920s, studies had found that social scientists were more left-leaning than the general population. The war in Vietnam exacerbated this trend, creating a strong New Left cohort in academia. Helped by the expansion of the universities in the 1960s and 1970s, the number of leftist professors in social science departments had increased dramatically (Lipset 1959; Ladd and Lipset 1973, 21; Lipset and Ladd 1972a, 1972b; Lipset and Dobson 1973; Ladd and Lipset 1971, 1975; Wynn 1972; Lipset 1982; Rothman and Lichter 1996; Hollander 1992, 153–54). Working outside academia were radical scholars and public intellectuals such as the group associated with the Institute for Policy Studies (IPS), founded by Marcus L. Raskin and Richard J. Barnet in 1963. Championing egalitarianism, the IPS took a lead in criticizing American capitalism and extolling socialism.

These younger scholars exhibited a deep commitment to egalitarian norms and a concomitant distaste for American capitalism, which they accused of inauthenticity, social injustice, aggressiveness, repression, and causing a declining quality of life (Hollander 1992, 49–54). The perception that egalitarian norms are more legitimate than other forms of distributive justice gained considerable boost when John Rawls published his philosophical treatise *A Theory of Justice* (1971). This immensely influential work asserted that economic growth should be regulated so as to maximize the well-being of the poorest member of society. Although Rawls was not a socialist per se, his egalitarian creed, which spread rapidly in the social sciences, imposed an important normative limit on what should be a *morally acceptable level of inequality*. Rawls's work spurred a large research effort to prove that American voters consider equality of outcomes more legitimate than the market principle of equality of opportunity. A number of studies demonstrated that people vote *sociotropically*, that is, out of preference for a more equitable distribution of income even if their self-interest is negatively affected (Deutsch 1975; Jasso and Rossi 1977; Jasso 1980; Florig 1986; Kinder and Kiewiet 1979; Suraska 1988).

In yet another vote of no confidence for the market economy, a large volume of research was devoted to finding evidence of the "coming legitimacy crisis of capitalism." Jurgen Habermas (1975), a neo-Marxist German philosopher who became highly influential in the United States, argued that once capitalism runs out of "payoffs," people will delegitimize it and embrace socialism. A number of highly pessimistic studies on the "overload" of Western democracies added academic respectability to the notion that validity claims of a market economy were being repudiated. Some found that capitalism had created a "cold society" that encourages "Machiavellian types," and others described alienation, the quest for self-respect and meaningful existence, and dissatisfaction with material values of capitalism (R. Lane 1978, 1979; Strumpel 1977; Erikson 1986; King 1975; Birch 1984).

Forecasting the impending decline of capitalism became a major preoccupation of leftist social scientists and historians. In the words of Bogdan Denitch (1979, 8), the "general optimism [about capitalism] . . . is replaced by an increasingly fashionable pessimism." Economist Robert Heilbroner declared that socialism is "the expression of a collective hope for mankind" (quoted in Taubman 1974). IPS's Raskin (1983, 244) urged that in the name of fairness, "stringent limits are to be set on wealth and that poverty is to be abolished." Even those who did not agree with the forecast that "capitalist nations will pass into the trashcan of history" felt that the United States would end up "on the wrong side" of history if more egalitarian norms were not adopted (Manning 1976). The new thinking was extremely effective in changing the public discourse on wealth and poverty in America. Although there was little change in the actual distribution of wealth, poverty became a major political issue, spurring the Great Society welfare reforms (Majone 1989, 148–49).

With a growing emphasis on economic equality, human needs, and other neo-Marxist themes, a slow but fundamental shift in the perceived legitimacy of nondemocratic regimes took place. The new orthodoxy called for a distinction between right- and left-wing authoritarian regimes. The former were labeled "reactionary" and "coercive" whereas the latter were described as "progressive." In what was a fairly typical position, a leading expert on developing countries stated that Third World regimes that promote "substantive economic and social egalitarianism" should be considered legitimate, even if they do not practice democracy (Packenham 1973, 275–76). It became equally common to argue that liberal democracy was only one of the many forms of legitimate participation. The influential scholar Johan Galtung (1976) argued that human needs cannot be confined to a simple parliamentary-style mode of participation but should reflect the deeper process of "conscious formation" and elements of "confrontation and struggle."

Such assessments were accompanied by a marked scholarly disenchantment with the quality of the American polity. No less an authority than Barrington Moore (1966, 507–8) pointed out that Western liberalism had begun to "display many symptoms of obsolescence." Another leading scholar argued that there was a "doctrinal tension" between democracy and capitalism and worried that the market economy might be repudiated on moral grounds (Lane 1986). Still another asserted that the democratic system masks great inequities and serves only the interests of the few (Parenti 1983).

It is within this intellectual context that a revisionist approach to the legitimacy of the Soviet Union became popular. As opposed to the totalitarian model, which emphasized coercion, the new model leaned toward a more expansive view of communist legitimacy. The leading Soviet scholar Robert Tucker (1961) was among the first to note that the Soviet system enlisted "masses of people" into various political meaningful, albeit guided, activities. As will be demonstrated in the next chapter, the revisionist impulse spurred a large body of work that created the impression that many features of the Soviet system were functional equivalents of Western pluralism. By the mid-1970s, it became commonplace in mainstream Sovietology to argue that the Soviet system involved a good deal of citizens' participation in the political system, bolstered by robust interest group inputs. One revisionist enthusiast claimed that Soviet leadership was almost closer to the spirit of the pluralistic model of American political science than the American one (Hough 1973; 1977b, 10).

The perceived superiority of egalitarian principles of distributive justice spurred a new look at the communist economy as a source of legitimacy. A number of neo-Marxist scholars interested in applying Weber's criteria to communist regimes developed the theme of paternalistic legitimacy. In exchange for job security, social amenities, and an equitable distribution of wealth, citizens in communist countries were said to be happy to accept the "centrally defined and guaranteed life strategies" offered by the regime (Denitch 1979; Feher 1982; Rigby 1982). Implied in this positive evaluation of egalitarianism was a prediction of global political change based on a gradual convergence of the communist and capitalist systems. According to this scenario, the Soviet and American systems were destined to converge, making social democracy the only historically inevitable choice. As Irving L. Horowitz (1977, 361), one of the convergence theorists, noted, there was already a common consensus that the ultimate "moral goals" of the United States and the Soviet Union were "roughly parallel." In his view, both countries represented an extension of the philosophy of "Enlightenment and Christian rationalism" (Wolfe 1971, 1978).

With the upgrade in the legitimacy of the Soviet Union came a fresh interpretation of its foreign policy. Revisionist scholars, some of whom were associated with the IPS, blamed the Cold War on American capitalism rather than Moscow's expansionism. They declared that capitalist society—based on a grossly inequitable distribution of wealth and income—had to fight the "ascendancy movement of change." These and other historical revisionists posited that American fears of the Soviet Union were either highly exaggerated or invented to feed the "American military complex" and big corporations (Williams 1969, 5; Kolko 1969, 5; Kolko and Kolko 1972, 3; Baran and Sweezy 1966, 184; Raskin 1979, 32–34; Barnet 1971). Raymond L. Garthoff (1978), a well-respected Soviet expert, claimed that those who believed in Soviet aggressive intentions were politically motivated. Over time, such views became quite common among mainstream scholars.

Not all academics shared in the new revisionist view of the Soviet Union. Zbigniew Brzezinski and his conservative colleagues such as the Harvard historian Richard Pipes had continued to assert that the Soviet system lacked legitimacy. But, as will be clear in the next chapter, they were often attacked or dismissed as "émigré scholars." Paul Hollander (1992, 9–10, 29), who authored a number of studies on the subject, explained that revisionism was part of a broader trend of anti-anticommunism among academic and intellectuals. This "adversary culture" intelligentsia was said to be driven by a powerful sense of alienation and anti-Americanism.

With much of the debate on communist legitimacy taking place within the confines of the highly politicized community of Soviet experts, little notice was given to the growth of rational choice theory as the new paradigm in political science. Although largely ignored as a tool for the study of communism, rational choice theorists provided a novel way of looking at the legitimacy of the Soviet regime.

Rational Choice Theory and Soviet Legitimacy: Coercion and Preference Falsification

Rational choice theory postulates that individuals maximize the expected values of their payoffs as measured by utility scales. The emphasis on expected rather than actual utility is related to the fact that most decisions are made under conditions of uncertainty. Maximizing behavior takes place at the individual rather than collective level, making it imperative for rational choice theorists to explain collective outcomes by modeling individual decisions. When making decisions, individuals are said to calculate the costs and benefits of these decisions within a certain set of opportunities and constraints. As the set changes, so does the calculus of the individuals.

In focusing on opportunity sets, rational choice theorists have provided important insights into the process of legitimation and delegitimation of communist regimes. To begin with, compliance is generated by the knowledge that the regime approves all benefits, including employment, housing, travel, and scarce consumer goods. Since dissent may trigger the withdrawal of approval, altering dramatically one's "life chances," open defiance of norms is rare. The cost of such an act can be very high, including loss of a job, political harassment, or imprisonment, while the benefits are doubtful because of the overwhelming control power of the authorities. Such a calculus is said to result in the so-called *learned helplessness* behavior, which stipulates that when neither fight nor flight is an option, individuals will simulate feelings of legitimacy for the regime.

In a pioneering work, Timur Kuran argued that the apparent legitimacy of the Soviet regime was a product of *preference falsification* practiced by its citizens, defined as a decision to conceal true beliefs and adopt behavior expected by the regime. Even after the more severe forms of Stalinist punishment—imprisonment, torture, and execution—were abolished, people could still be penalized for failing to participate in a whole array of events, including party meetings, celebration of holidays, or officially sanctioned demonstrations against "capitalism and imperialism." On the exchange side of legitimacy, there were rewards for joining the party or spying on others. Since preference falsification is so pervasive, it generates *pluralistic ignorance*, that is, a lack of awareness of how widespread the resentment of the regime really is. In the Soviet Union these acts of insincerity created a "pervasive culture of mendacity" where individuals "applauded speakers whose message they disliked, joined organizations they disliked, and signed defamatory letters against people they admired" (Kuran 1991, 26; 1995, 110, 123, 125). Vladimir Shlapentokh (1985), a Soviet scholar who immigrated to the United States, provided detailed empirical evidence of how preference falsification worked to create a society in which individuals learned to cultivate a public as opposed to a private persona. Aleksandr Solzhenitsyn and East European dissidents such as Vaclav Havel argued that "living a lie" became the vital glue that held the legitimacy system together. Communist authorities contributed to this type of political culture through their efforts to create an in illusion of *societas perfecta*, a perfect socialist society where consensus and good had triumphed over the capitalist contradictions and class warfare (Flis 1988; Pakulski 1986; Connor 1975).

When public preferences are at such odds with private ones, following the public discourse for signs of delegitimation is very difficult. Because of the subterranean nature of alterations in private preferences, opposition to regime norms may spread without any apparent change in the public status quo. Yet sooner or later an event or a series of events can bring enough individuals to express their preferences in public and unleash a long latent bandwagon. By its very nature, such processes are nonlinear, akin to the sudden systemic eruptions discussed above and essentially unpredictable.

As Kuran (1991, 20) noted, "neither private preferences nor the corresponding thresholds [for changing them] are common knowledge. So a society can come to the brink of a revolution without anyone knowing it." Another expert warned that in analyzing communist states it would be "basic mistake" to project "Western patterns of incrementalism on a system prone to abrupt reversals" (Groth 1990, 19).

While rational choice theory provides important tools for discerning early signs of delegitimation, few among the revisionist scholars were ready to embrace them. It was left to the critics of the revisionist-pluralistic paradigm to apply some of these insights and conclude that the Soviet Union was headed toward a crisis of legitimacy. However, this was a minority view in a field that, during the crucial decade that preceded the ascent of Mikhail Gorbachev, was fragmented and politicized. As the next chapter will demonstrate, different observers had reached diametrically different conclusions about the stability, durability, and legitimacy of the Soviet Union and the belief system that gave it birth.

2

Oligarchic Petrification
or Pluralistic Transformation

*Paradigmatic Views of the Soviet Union
in the 1970s*

Faced with the prospect of Soviet expansion following World War II, the United States embarked on a vigorous policy of containment of its erstwhile ally. In what became the opening salvo of the Cold War, the Truman administration asked the foreign policy and academic communities to provide insights into the workings of the communist system and to suggest the most effective ways to change its international behavior. Answering the call, George Kennan, a high-ranking State Department official, contended in his famous long telegram of 1946 that, if contained by the West, the communist system would ultimately fail. While policymakers focused on implementing the policy of containment, academics were busy building a theoretical understanding of the communist state. The resulting totalitarian model viewed the Soviet Union as an essentially illegitimate regime that had maintained stability through a mix of paltry material inducements and a large dose of coercion as epitomized by Joseph Stalin. The portrayal of the Soviet empire as an illegitimate entity repudiated by civilized society and its own population went beyond simple academic discourse. As noted by observers, "it furnished an enemy image that helped justify enormous defense expenditures and American intervention" all over the globe (Urban and Fish 1998, 167).

However, following the reforms of Stalin's successor Nikita Khrushchev, and, more importantly, as disenchantment with American involvement in Vietnam began to spread, the totalitarian model was displaced by a number of theories that took a more benign view of the Soviet Union. The revisionist model was based on the assumption that Soviet citizens, far from being terrorized into submission, had legitimized communist rule through a patrimonial social contract. In exchange for an egalitarian and guaranteed division of material rewards, they voluntarily gave up on certain liberties and freedoms. With coercion taken out of the equation, the improved Soviet image, like its totalitarian predecessor, served an important function in legitimizing the budding policy of détente. To quote the same observers, it "helped to destigmatize the Soviet Union, thus facilitating public and elite acceptance of détente" (Urban and Fish 1998, 167). Although much of the debate over the respective merit of the two models focused on their foreign policy implications, the diametrically different concepts of legitimacy embedded in them painted a drastically divergent path of political change.

The Totalitarian Model: Oligarchic Petrification and Final Doom

Conducted against the background of the Cold War, early research on the Soviet Union embraced the totalitarian model, which, as noted, was first articulated by Hannah Arendt in her work on Nazi Germany. In the early 1950s Carl J. Friedrich organized a conference on totalitarianism sponsored by the American Academy of Arts and Sciences that compared Nazi Germany, Italy, and the Soviet Union. Subsequently conceptualized in a book that Friedrich co-authored with Zbigniew Brzezinski (1956), the totalitarian view of the Soviet Union received a wide hearing, with many Soviet experts using the indicators of totalitarianism—elaborate ideology, a single mass party, monopoly on communication, centrally controlled economy, and coercion—in their work. According to the totalitarian logic, in the absence of popular legitimacy, extraordinarily high levels of coercion had sustained the system, a fact amply documented by Brzezinski (1956) in his work on the phenomenon of Stalin's permanent purge.

Within a few years the Friedrich-Brzezinski model became a staple in Soviet studies. The highly respected work by Merle Fainsod, *How Russia Is Ruled* (1964), and other writings were unanimous in stressing that terror, far from being a Stalinist aberration, was crucial to the working of the system. As Hazard (1960, 203) noted, even in the post-Stalinist period there were few restrictions on the security police, no independent judiciary, and severe limitations on individual or group activity. The totalitarian model and its variants asserted that the Communist Party, which laid claim to infallibility, used its monopoly of communications to paint a picture of Soviet society as "the best of all possible societies" and a "world of harmony and cheerful collaboration" (Meyer 1965, 91). Since any attempt to question this dogma was severely punished, Soviet citizens had to develop strategies for coping with the resulting cognitive dissonance. Thus one popular technique entailed a double-level mentality whereby individuals were socialized to foster a public as opposed to a private persona. Indeed, the deformation of language in the political discourse made cynicism and mistrust of authority endemic (Smith 1976, 10, 105; Barghoorn 1966; Gilison 1968; Connor 1975; Bell 1976, 244). Cynicism was also said to be a reaction to the compulsory participation in public rituals, all of which were designed to manufacture a sense of unanimous support of the regime. Accordingly, events ranging from May Day celebrations to meetings of the Supreme Soviet were choreographed to exude "unanimity, solidarity and strength" (Kaiser 1976, 159).

Although the totalitarian model was mostly descriptive, its inner logic included a trajectory of change. Brzezinski (1966) predicted that the Soviet Union, unable to maintain indefinitely a doctrinaire dictatorship over an increasingly modern society, would gradually petrify and collapse. In an edited volume on the subject, Brzezinski (1969) elaborated upon the notion of petrification and degeneration, while some of the other contributors raised the possibility of evolution in a different, albeit not clearly specified, direction. At the heart of Brzezinski's argument was the view that the party oligarchs, eager to stay in control, would fail to relinquish enough power to enable the communist system to modernize and progress. Although Brzezinski (1976) and like-minded scholars did not provide a specific time framework, they steadfastly maintained that the Soviet Union was headed toward a collapse (Cocks et al., 1976).

In making the argument for degeneration, these theorists argued that the Soviet Union was suffering from a legitimacy deficit in a number of important dimensions, starting with membership legitimacy. In what was at the time a fairly isolated point of view, Brzezinski (1970) insisted that the "happy family of nations," a reference to the growth of a new, inclusive Soviet identity, promoted in the official Soviet discourse, was a sham covering a growing nationalist resentment in the republics. Brzezinski (1971) complained that American scholars minimized or ignored the "critically important" issue of nationality in the Soviet Union, a development that, in his view, was mimicked by the U.S. government. Initially, Brzezinski was almost alone in asserting that the lack of nationalist legitimacy in the republics would make it impossible for the Soviet elite to liberalize or decentralize the regime.

Eventually, a small number of scholars came to support Brzezinski's line of argument. According to one of them, in spite of the 1971 Party Congress declaration that a "new historical community of people—the Soviet people" had evolved in the country, ethnic and linguistic resistance to Soviet rule was on the increase. Another wrote about the "precariousness of stability in Soviet society," (Rakowska-Harmstone. 1974, 1)which was threatened by centrifugal national forces (Kaiser 1976, 174; Szporluk 1972). A study of the Baltics found no evidence that the communist idea of *sblizhenie* (coming together of nationalities) had worked in the republics (Vardys 1975). Summing it all up, the noted Harvard historian Richard Pipes (1975, 3) contended that, against Marxist-Leninist expectations, nationalism in the Soviet Union failed "to dissolve in the acid bath of modernity."

An important part of the totalitarian petrification theory dealt with economic legitimacy. Some Soviet experts and economists questioned the notion that legitimizing a fully egalitarian system is desirable, let alone possible, leading them to describe the communist experiment as a "utopia" or a "grand illusion." Drawing on the arguments of Hayek and von Mises, they pointed out that in the absence of market mechanisms an economy does not have enough information to make efficient pricing and capital allocation decisions (Nove 1961, 311). Rostow (1965, 162–63) went so far as to call communism a "disease of transition" in his stages of development. There were equal misgivings about the possibility that human beings could truly accept an egalitarian regimen of work and rewards. The Yugoslav dissident Milovan Djilas (1969, 205) coined the term the "new class" to describe officials in the party and state bureaucracy, known as the *nomenklatura*, whose extensive system of privileges made a mockery of official equality. Some of the earliest work on corruption in the Soviet Union detailed the ways in which the nomenklatura used its position for personal gain (Landy 1961; Staats 1972; Brzezinski and Huntington 1971, 425; Kaiser 1976, 177). Indeed, a pathbreaking study found that, official ideology notwithstanding, by the early 1970s, Soviet society boasted considerable differences of "power, income status and opportunity" (Lipset 1973a, 356; 1973b; Lipset and Dobson 1973; Yanowitch and Fisher 1973).

Even if egalitarianism was achievable, the totalitarian model cast doubt on the capacity of a highly centralized command economy to cope with technological change. Noting that America was becoming a "technetronic society" driven by the impact of technology and electronics, Brzezinski (1968; 1970, 150–53; 1971) asserted that the centralized Soviet economy would be disadvantaged in the age of technology. The "obsolescence of planning" was also discussed by the futurist Alvin Toffler (1970, 448–49), who explained that planning reflected the time bias of the industrial age. Other observers debated the so-called Soviet dilemma—unleashing scientific creativity or losing political control. These scholars predicted that, faced with what one of them described as "contradictory demands of centralized political control on the one hand and economic efficiency on the other," Soviet leaders would become paralyzed by their own system (Taubman 1974, 377; Amann 1977–78; Thomas and Kruse-Vaucienne 1977–78).

Closely related to the issue of technology was that of human capital. Brzezinski (1966, 5) was among the first to claim that the Soviet economic system, with its rigid controls and egalitarian *dictat*, could neither find nor nourish talent. On the contrary, the frequent purges, the stifling of creativity and initiative, and bureaucratic immobilism had created a "negative selection" of mediocrity. This resulted in a culture in which "conformity, caution and currying favor with superiors counts more . . . than individual initiative." Brzezinski (1966, 5) found it difficult to imagine that reforms in the Soviet Union could generate a "significant burst of innovation and adaptation." Ironically, Georgi Arbatov (1992, 242), the head of the Soviet Institute of the USA and Canada (ISKAN) and a long-time regime spokesman, subsequently confirmed Brzezinski's argument, writing that the Soviet system was an example of reverse Darwinism in which the best were selected in order to "cut off their heads."

While based on a careful analysis of the workings of the communist system, the totalitarian model fit the ideological atmosphere of the Cold War. With McCarthyism setting the tone of much of the debate, it was easier to portray the negative features of the Soviet reality than to list the positive ones. As one of the Soviet specialists admitted, the forecast of Soviet doom was very much in line with the American desire to see the Soviet empire disappear (Meyer 1993, 169). However, as the backlash against McCarthyism and the war in Vietnam gave way to anti-anticommunist sentiment in academic-intellectual circles, the oligarchic petrification model came under intense scrutiny. It was only a matter of time before Sovietology produced a more liberal appraisal of the USSR.

The Revisionist Model: Pluralistic Transformation and Final Convergence

Even before the political climate in the United States shifted away from its strident anticommunism, some of the leading Soviet experts began to display unease with the totalitarian model. In their view, totalitarian petrification could not explain the liberalizing reforms of Khrushchev and other developments that followed the death of Stalin. In a 1961 meeting of the American Political Science Association, Robert Tucker called for a "more effective theoretical apparatus" to study communist change, a view shared by Raymond A. Bauer, Alex Inkeles, and Clyde Kluckhorn from the Harvard Project on the Soviet Union. Inkeles in particular urged researchers to determine whether the Soviet Union had moved beyond its centralized, coercion-driven modus operandi.

Inkeles's pleas were eagerly answered by a growing numbers of academics. Tucker (1963, 11) spoke of the Soviet Union as a "mobilization society" or "guided democracy," where there was "mass popular participation in the continuing revolution of national revival." Kassoff (1964, 560) developed the theme of an "administered society," which he defined as "totalitarianism without terror." Rigby (1964) coined the term "crypto-politics" to describe the real policy disagreements behind the monolithic façade of the system. Löwenthal (1970) postulated that with increased development, the Soviet Union would exchange its utopian totalitarianism for a more pluralistic and realistic model of society and economy. Mayer (1965, 468) used the analogy of a corporation to describe the Soviet system, stating at one point that the USSR was a "modern corporation writ large." The Canadian political scientist Gordon H. Skilling (1966, 1970) introduced the then radical notion of group conflict as a guiding principle of Soviet politics, inspiring younger generations of Soviet scholars. In what was considered a trailblazer at the time, Skilling and Franklyn Griffith (1971) produced a detailed analysis of interest groups in the Soviet Union.

While all these authors alluded to increased pluralism in the Soviet system, Jerry F. Hough is normally credited with developing the pluralistic model. In a widely discussed response to Brzezinski, Hough (1972) categorically rejected the oligarchic petrification thesis and posited that the Soviet Union was evolving toward institutional pluralism. In this and subsequent works, Hough (1973, 1974) rejected the dichotomy between totalitarianism and democracy and argued that the Soviet Union had exhibited functional equivalents of democratic pluralism in the sense that bureaucrats and other "intermediate actors" exercised considerable latitude in decision making.

In attempting to discredit the view of the Soviet Union as a petrified structure held together by coercion, Hough and other revisionist Sovietologists painted a dramatically different view of its legitimacy. The revisionists found that political participation and political opinion in the USSR produced meaningful inputs into the system. Using detailed membership statistics, Hough (1976; 1977a, 14; 1977b, 116, 120; Hough and Fainsod 1979, 297) found impressive rates of face-to-face and small-group participation, and showed that the rate of membership growth in formal groups had surpassed the rate of growth in the population. He also pointed out that there was an increase in participatory bodies and a robust discussion in the press read by an "attentive public." Hough even implied that some basic policy decisions, including foreign policy ones, were made in response to shifts in public attitudes. As for the degree of individual freedom of expression, it was permitted when, in his words, it pertained to "advocacy of incremental change" and when "phrased carefully." A subsequent study of political culture found some support for the thesis that the overall level of participation had increased (White 1979, 89).

Pluralists and other revisionists painted an optimistic picture of the legitimacy that the egalitarian principles enjoyed. As a matter of fact, Hough (1972, 39) chastised his colleagues for failing to acknowledge the efforts of Soviet leadership to move the income distribution of the country in "the direction of equality." After comparing the ratio of average earnings of the top 10 percent of Soviet employees to that of the bottom 10 percent, Hough concluded that egalitarian norms had been greatly advanced under Leonid Brezhnev, who assumed power in 1964 (Hough and Fainsod 1979, 265). Another study stressed the "upward social mobility for the economically lowest classes, especially in comparison to the previous regime" (Groth 1974, 311). Coming on top of steady employment and subsidized goods and services, this type of egalitarianism was said to provide the basis for a new legitimizing formula between the communist authority and the people.

Developed by a group of scholars intent on applying Weberian concepts of legitimacy to the communist system, the new theory postulated that citizens of the Soviet empire had exchanged political freedoms for social and labor security. To reward people for political compliance, the regime provided "broad guarantees of full and secure employment, state controlled and heavily subsidized prices for essential goods, fully subsidized human services and egalitarian wage policies" (Cook 1993, 1). This new formula was said to derive from Khrushchev's efforts to replace Stalin-era coercion with a more exchange-oriented form of legitimacy. In this context Khrushchev's famous promise to catch up and surpass America economically was construed to mean that, henceforth, communist legitimacy would become eudaemonic and goal oriented, most specifically by providing material and social rewards to its members.

Once formulated, the social contract view of legitimacy, also known as patrimonial legitimacy, was widely embraced by academic experts. Gilison (1972, xi) noted that contemporary Soviet society "is built upon a solid foundation of regime support." A 1977 conference on Legitimation and Delegitimation of Regimes produced some of the most enthusiastic testimony to this effect. David Lane (1979, 193) expressed confidence that there was no crisis of legitimacy in the Soviet Union because "the values and beliefs of the working class are generally congruent with those of the political elite." Soviet citizens were also said to appreciate the "centrally defined and guaranteed life strategies" offered by the authorities (Denitch 1979; Feher 1982; Rigby 1982; Holmes 1993, 15).

The German Democratic Republic (GDR)—which according to pluralist theorists boasted a high standard of living—was considered a real showcase for the communist-style social contract. One theorist stressed that the economic performance of the GDR, as "measured by the rate of growth of output, has been roughly as good as that of the Federal Republic of Germany" (Keren 1976, 85). Another contended that the GDR's "status as one of the world's leading industrial powers" imbued its citizens with considerable pride, not the least because it was "wrought by their own labor" (Baylis 1972, 49). Even those who normally did not share the pluralist perspective did not escape its intellectual reach. The author of a study of political culture in the Soviet Union insisted that there was a "fairly high level of popular consensus" with regard to the regime (Barghoorn 1974, 273). He also found that, in general, the process of communist socialization had worked quite well in inculcating features of Soviet morality such as emphasis on obedience, respect for authority, and hard work.

Lending credence to the patrimonial legitimacy theory were observers who emphasized the traditional authoritarian culture of Russia. One stated that the country's history "instilled in the Russian political mind an exceptional high level of appreciation for stern, autocratic, overwhelming powerful authority" (Barghoorn 1973, 31). Another claimed that, unlike the American democratic model, the Soviet model appealed to people who appreciate collective action to accomplish "programs of social and economic development" (Larson 1978, 128). Yet another wrote that the Soviet masses did not "demand legality, representative institutions and freedom," because they considered them "unfamiliar and exotic concepts." He rated the chances for the emergence of a Western democracy "very slight," adding that "the Soviet soil seems no more hospitable to such an outcome today than it was in 1917" (Connor 1972, 50; 1975). Richard Barnet (1977, 51), from the Institute for Policy Studies, went so far as to suggest that the centuries old Russian tradition of "mobilization from the top" made it difficult for Soviet authorities to allow free circulation of ideas.

Such positive evaluation of communist legitimacy extended to the performance of the command economy. According to Leonid Brezhnev, who replaced Khrushchev in 1964, by the early 1970s the Soviet Union had reached a stage of "mature socialism," which was poised by dint of universal laws of development to overtake capitalism as the dominant mode of production. While revisionist scholars did not embrace this forecast, it was not uncommon among them to note that the growth rate of Soviet GNP was about to exceed that of the United States, giving credence to Khrushchev's boast that Russia would overtake the United States. Many economists came to share a 1974 assessment that the "longtime ability of the Soviet economy to function without private ownership" indicated its viability (quoted in Shlapentokh 1998). Economist Paul Samuelson asserted in 1977 that it was "a vulgar mistake to think that most people in Eastern Europe are miserable" (quoted in Harries 1991, 19). Laura D'Andrea Tyson, a future chairman of the Council of Economic Advisers in the Clinton administration, reviewed favorably the Romanian and Yugoslav economies (Miller and Damask 1993). Hough (1973) declared that Russia was on the way to becoming a true meritocracy capable of husbanding its human capital. In his view, Soviet officials had an orderly Weberian-type career pattern based on performance and technocratic skills.

The same positive assessments contributed to the convergence theory mentioned in the previous chapter. Convergence prognosticators emphasized that the American and Soviet societies were destined to converge within the "framework of democratic socialism" patterned on the Scandinavian model. Fueling this vision was the more generalized hope that "rationality, tolerance, decency and freedom will inevitability triumph" in the Soviet Union and elsewhere (Meyer 1970, 323, 337). Although convergence theory had only a moderate following among mainstream Sovietologists, the revisionist model, which implied that the Soviet system was moving toward technocratic, Weberian-style rationality, bolstered the credibility of convergence advocates (Breslauer 1992).

By design or default, the consensual-exchange view of legitimacy embedded in the social contract model helped to dispel the old image of repressive totalitarianism. Nowhere was this more evident than in Hough's rewrite of Fainsod's classic study. In the newer version, renamed *How the Soviet Union Is Governed*, terror and coercion were hardly mentioned. In fact, Hough asserted that in the new Soviet Union the KGB performed an important "educational role" by attempting to persuade dissidents that they were mistaken. Neither was dissent given any prominence. Hough devoted only one paragraph to the subject, noting the difficulties of measurement and the "fuzzy boundary between legitimate protest and illegal dissent" (Hough and Fainsod 1979, 281, 305). Revisionist-pluralistic literature paid even less attention to national, ethnic, and religious dissent, a development that did not square well with the new formula of consensual legitimacy.

While the revisionist model was primarily applied to analyzing future change in the Soviet system, it had important implications for the study of the past. Whereas traditional historians regarded the October revolution as a coup carried out by a marginal and highly unrepresentative group with a totalitarian bent, revisionist historians held the view that the Bolsheviks were successful because their belief system was shared by the Russian masses, making communism a true popular movement. Sheila Fitzpatrick (1974, 1978) took the lead in arguing that the Bolshevik revolution was essentially a spontaneous cultural revolution with virtually no central authority instruction to local activists. Hough (1978) backed up this position by noting that "one need not be a Marxist to recognize" that many workers and peasants felt genuine resentment toward the better-off classes.

In a variant of this argument, Lenin was depicted as driven to adopt a more repressive stance by the pressure of radicalized masses. Revisionist historians such as Stephen Cohen (1973) treated Stalinism as an unfortunate aberration, arguing that, had Nikolai Bukharin, rather than Stalin, won the Kremlin power struggle in the 1930s, the Soviet Union would have evolved in a more liberal direction. Cohen also found that New Economic Policy (NEP) instituted in the 1920s was imbued with "toleration of social diversity . . . emphasis on social harmony . . . and the rule of law" (quoted in Charen 2003, 92). Others downplayed the severity of Stalin's purges by arguing that the number of deaths in the Gulag was in the thousands rather than the millions, as traditional scholarship had asserted. Even the publication of Aleksandr Solzhenitsyn's *Gulag Archipelago* did not fluster the revisionists. In the view of one political scientist: "absolute judgments [about the morality of the system] are luxuries that few but great writers can afford" (Sharlet 1974, 71).

By the mid-1970s, revisionist scholarship and the pluralistic model had come to virtually monopolize mainstream Sovietology. This process was also fueled by a wave of writings that sought, as noted, to rewrite the history of the Cold War. A 1972 survey of the Association of Historians of American Foreign Relations revealed a high level of familiarity with revisionist studies (Braeman 1983). In a telling sign of the times, an author who opposed that approach characterized his stance as a "dissenting view" (Odom 1976).

Observers pointed to a number of factors that accounted for the remarkable spread of revisionism. One pertained to the growing popularity of comparative studies in political science. In order to use the new comparative tools, Soviet experts had to discard the totalitarian model that viewed the Soviet Union as sui generis. Meyer (1970, 231) warned his colleagues about the "methodological trap concealed behind the assumptions of uniqueness" and chastised "political scientists in the West" for failing to apply "to the Communist world the rich store of concepts developed for the comparative study of politics" (quoted in Bunce and Echols 1979, 43). To do so, these normalizers had to reject the notion that the Soviet Union was a unique system "standing outside history" (Shlapentokh 1998, 191; McNeill 1998).

Among the normalizers, Hough has been singled out for his prodigious effort to provide a comparative view of the Soviet system. Writing about the Brezhnev tenure, Hough (1977a, 7) found it "striking" that many of his policies could be explained "in the light of the hypothetical requirements of 'electoral' politics." He added that to "a careful student of the Soviet political process . . . the most striking characteristic of this American pluralistic literature . . . is the extent to which many of the phenomena it highlighted seem to have their counterparts" in the Soviet system" (Hough 1977b, 9). As for political conflicts, Hough found them to be almost as compartmentalized in the Soviet Union as they were in the United States and limited to a small group of actors. He admonished American scholars for forgetting that "most of the statements about the political institutions in the Soviet Union are true of any parliamentary system with a disciplined majority system." While acknowledging the disparity of power between leaders and rank-and-file in the Soviet Union, Hough noted that Robert Dahl had argued that power distribution in the United States was far "from perfect" (Hough and Fainsod 1979, 207, 263, 525, 547). Another comparative Sovietologist contended that "even the slightest penetration into the legitimizing doctrines supporting the Soviet and the British system reveals that they are both built upon concepts of representation." He also argued against the common practice of juxtaposing the "sovereign" British Parliament with the "powerless" Supreme Soviet, because the former had become increasingly purely symbolic (Gilison 1972, xi).

Pluralism also profited from the spread of behaviorism that underlay the comparative perspective. In his 1966 presidential address to the American Political Science Association, Gabriel Almond, one of the champions of comparative behaviorism, announced that the new approach would use statistical methods to generate universal laws of development (Almond 1966). As already noted, Almond was highly enthusiastic about the new "science" of politics, a view that resonated with an increasing number of Soviet experts. Two books, *Communist Studies and the Social Sciences: Essays on Methodology and Empirical Theory* (Fleron 1969) and *The Behavioral Revolution in Communist Studies* (Kanet 1971), which offered a variety of new scientific methods to study communism, became the virtual Bible of behaviorally oriented Sovietologists. The logical positivism and the air of objectivity that behaviorism exuded appealed particularly to the younger generation of Soviet experts, who had little patience for past ideological and historical disputations. The new science promised to elevate Sovietology above what was seen as the "subjective, instinctive, prejudiced folklorist" approach to the field (Laqueur 1994, 102). Jumping on the behavioral bandwagon could bring handsome professional payoffs as well. Using the "standard language of political science" and statistical methods opened up publishing opportunities in the most prestigious publications in the discipline (Urban and Fish 1998, 167).

Last, the more general embrace of egalitarianism and neo-Marxism discussed in the previous chapter was highly providential for Soviet revisionism. One observer pointed out that in the historical debate among "egalitarians" and market proponents, inequality was increasingly defined as a failure to achieve equality of outcome rather than equality of opportunity (Connor 1979a, 13). Another scholar claimed that Marxist terminology became a "vocabulary of choice" in the West, radicalizing Sovietology (Gleason 1995, 131). The disdain for what neo-Marxist critics defined as Western procedural democracy was quickly transmitted to Soviet studies and was coupled with the value-free judgment of comparative politics. In what was not an uncommon criticism, some observers contended that a procedural definition of democracy was a product of Anglo-American culture and that equal hearing should be given to the Bolshevik emphasis on economic rather than political freedoms (Rutland 1993, 112). This type of intellectual relativism was particularly popular because, as found in one study, by the 1970s most Sovietologists were left-liberal politically. Many of them were attracted to the "high ideals" of a socialist society of brotherhood, social justice, and community and gave less importance to freedom of expression and political choice (Hollander 1981, 173, 420). For instance, the IPS scholar Richard Barnet (1977, 51) declared that "Western critics tend to focus on intellectuals" and others "for whom procedural freedoms are essential to their craft," but ignore the fact that "the vast majority of Soviet citizens would probably choose substantive freedoms over procedural freedoms."

Veneration of economic security was part of the larger movement to delegitimize capitalism. While only hardcore Marxist scholars regarded profits and all nonlabor income as tribute rather than exchange, many others were highly critical of the market economy. As already noted, capitalism came to be associated with exploitation, alienation, delinquency, and a host of other social ills. Todd Gitlin (1978, 239), a well-known sociologist, railed against the "exploitative conditions of work and family in the world of organized capitalism." In his book *The Cultural Contradictions of Capitalism*, Daniel Bell (1976, xi, 238), an eminent scholar, echoed the Habermasian theme of crisis of legitimacy of late capitalism. The highly respected political scientist Robert Dahl (1970, 130) depicted Yugoslavia as a model country where the "old dream of industrial democracy was translated into reality." A series of articles in the forecasting journal *Futures* bemoaned the alienation and powerlessness of people in the West and predicted "emancipation from employment" and a decline in preoccupation with growth (Holroyd 1978; Marsh 1979; Pym 1980).

Many scholars sought an alternative to the concept of totalitarianism because of its negative connotations for Soviet legitimacy. In his memoirs, Skilling (2000, 170–1), who was briefly a member of the Communist Party, related how his search for a more positive definition of the Soviet system led him to the group conflict approach. In his words, such a view was designed to "avoid the spirit of the Cold War and the demonization of the Soviet and Eastern European systems." Skilling revealed that his co-author, Franklyn Griffith, contemplated withdrawing from the project because of doubts about the appropriateness of using the group concept. Other revisionist scholars were less candid or less self-conscious about their motives. However, as one scholar observed, "driven by their distaste for the Cold War" and the fear of nuclear disaster, they portrayed the USSR in a favorable light to "prove that they were just like us" (Rutland 1993, 113). Another critic concurred, adding that during the Cold War, American academics and intellectuals were "compelled to defend the Soviet Union warts and all" (Ticktin 1998, 78).

The dominance of the pluralist perspective unleashed protest from the adherents of the totalitarian model and experts who found pluralism unsatisfactory for explaining the increasingly problematic tenure of Brezhnev. Due to his prominent role in the pluralist movement, Hough bore the brunt of their criticism. Although few went so far as to describe him as being to "some extent a freak, even among oddball Sovietologists," he was accused of overstating his case for pluralism in an "extreme way" (Conquest 1993, 93). Hough was charged with being an "apologist in the academic world for the Soviet system," and for whitewashing Stalin's terror (Miller and Damask 1993, 259; Fukuyama 1993). Critics were particularly upset by his rewrite of Fainsod's book, which excluded terror, forced labor, heavy-handed indoctrination of the population, and other factors that could cast doubt on the legitimacy of the regime. Others took offense at what they perceived as his deliberate attempts to blur the distinctions between the Soviet Union and the West, mainly by turning the pluralist theory of David Truman into the "governing paradigm for the study of the Soviet Union" (Armstrong 1993, 74). They found Hough's definition of pluralism—"that legitimate political process must take place within an institutional framework"—nebulous in the extreme and construed in a way to suggest that "pluralism was legitimized in the USSR" (Brown 1979, 107).

Scholars such as Richard Pipes (1977), Robert Wesson (1976, 150), John Patrick Diggins (1973, 1993, 298), Robert Conquest (1993, 97), Lewis S. Feuer (1978), and others accused revisionist Sovietologists of neo-Marxist bias (Tiersky 1977). They complained about "university Marxists," alienated from the American ethos and drawn to an egalitarian utopia. In the words of Conquest, "many second rate academics" radicalized by Vietnam and suffering from a "Pavlovian reflex" of rejecting their own system made a "fetish of the word socialism." These tenured academics were said to be busy peddling a "failed theory" to "captive college audiences." Conservative critics blamed the "maimed sense of reality" or "epistemological naiveté" of revisionists for their failure to see the disintegration of the Soviet empire. Summing up such sentiments, one critic noted that "the very word 'capitalism' ... or money had a bad odor of greed and selfishness," while socialism had a connotation of "unselfish action" (Wesson 1976, 150). Interestingly enough, Soviet scholars who studied American Sovietology seemed to agree with this conclusion. One of their reports suggested that this body of work revealed more about the authors than about the Soviet Union (Taubman 1974).

Perhaps the harshest critique was reserved for the methodological objectivism and statistical exactitude of many of the studies inspired by the pluralist model. As one critic put it, the "pseudo-scientific orientation" associated with Frederick Fleron and Roger Kanet was "the heaviest millstone around the collective neck of Soviet specialists" (Eidlin 1979, 134). Another scholar attacked a "few superficial Sovietologists," whom he described as "entrepreneurs rather than researchers," for voicing "slavish obeisance" to comparative conceptualization (Armstrong 1971; 1973; 1993, 173). Writing in 1976 Adam Ulam, a leading Soviet historian, cautioned against the "passion for abstract models" to the neglect of the "living reality" of the Soviet Union (quoted in Krancberg 1994, 15). Subsequent commentary emphasized that the "myopic obsession" with official data often went hand in hand with an openly expressed desire to avoid judgment (Conquest 1993, 94). Another charge involved the allegedly indiscriminate use of statistical methods. As two critics put it, comparative methods were being employed for the "analysis of voting, accounts of political participation, and discussion of public opinion in a land in which no real elections ever occurred, no meaningful participation was possible, and public opinion could scarcely be known" (Urban and Fish 1998, 167). Malia (1992a, 101) wrote that the language of pluralist methodology worked to sanitize totalitarian brutality, portraying purges as "struggles between center and periphery."

Critics also blamed model-driven revisionist scholarship for excessive emphasis on formal inputs and outputs of the system, leaving little room for the more anecdotal type of knowledge that would have revealed the real working of Brezhnev's Russia (Bunce and Echols 1979). According to some observers, the "disconnect" between the political scientists' work and reality was deliberate, driven by a pattern of intellectual pride—"a sort of insensitivity to Soviet real life and politics" (Krancberg 1994, 11). In a rush to emulate the value-free hard sciences, the experts lost "contact with the subjects of their inquiry"—the Soviet people and their misery. Testimony of citizens was dismissed as "anecdotal" and thus unworthy of attention (Pipes 2000b, 47). Some conservative scholars argued that their revisionist colleagues—with their lack of feel for Russian culture and history and their love of abstract models—were more easily manipulated by official Soviet deception (Wesson 1976, 153–54; Krancberg 1994, 4). As one observer put it, such a combination of "ignorance, wishful thinking, favorable predisposition and sometimes manipulation" created a serious Western misperception of communist countries (Hollander 2000, 177).

Sustaining what one critic described as a "Pollyannish hypercredulity" was made easier because revisionist social scientists had, by and large, ignored literature, memoirs, and the work of émigrés and dissidents (Laqueur 1985, 280). Antirevisionist scholars charged that this tendency was nourished by a "determination" to overlook any information that could cast doubts on the pluralist models (N. Eberstadt 1988, 72; Hollander 2000, 177). As noted, in the intensely politicized atmosphere of Soviet scholarship, émigré scholars had become suspect and the label "émigré scholarship" was often used as a euphemism for bias. Pipes and Brzezinski were often targeted and their writings portrayed as efforts to "propagate anti-Communist stereotypes" (Beardsley 1973, 79). According to one expert, the political rivalry in the discipline left most émigré scholars "out in the cold" and deprived Sovietology of their insights (Rutland 1993, 112). At the same time, due to travel and study restrictions imposed by Moscow, researchers had little exposure to life under communism. For instance, out of the eighty-seven Soviet area studies doctoral dissertations written between 1976 and 1987, only seven were written by researchers who had actually studied in the Soviet Union. Those who were admitted were often manipulated by the authorities, who tried to steer them into providing a positive image of the regime (Rutland 1993; Pipes 2003, 125–27).

Moving on to consider the consequences of such bias and ignorance, critics accused revisionist scholarship of failing to detect signs of delegitimation and progressive dysfunctionality of the system under Brezhnev. According to one of them, "the symptoms of Soviet structural decomposition were hidden behind a smokescreen of false pretenses" where conflict and tension "vanished in models of a conflict-free, self-regulating social system" (Krancberg 1994, 5). Joining the chorus of criticism were two groups of newcomers to the debate about the "real" Soviet Union. The first group consisted of scholars who drew their inspiration from rational choice theory. As indicated, when applied to the analysis of behavior under communism, rational choice studies showed how seeming compliance and participation were part of adaptive posturing rather than a reflection of the diffuse loyalty crucial for genuine legitimacy. The other group consisted of French academics and intellectuals such as Jean-François Revel, Hélène Carrère d'Encausse, and Emmanuel Todd, who adopted a neototalitarian approach following the revelations about the Gulag. French neototalitarians were among the first to warn about the impending collapse of the Soviet empire. A few Soviet and East European scholars and dissidents augmented the ranks of what became a neoconservative critique of revisionism (Hollander 2000).

Revising the Revisionist View of the Soviet Union: Oligarchic Degeneration and Ideological Assertion in the Late Brezhnev Period

For scholars looking for early signs of delegitimation, the latter part of Brezhnev's rule provided a veritable cornucopia of indices. Undoubtedly, the most noticeable malfunction occurred in the standard of living of the citizens, eroding the eudaemonics that would have been required for patrimonial legitimacy. Although camouflaged by official statistics, certain trends stood out. Starting in the late '60s and early '70s, there was a rise in early deaths and infant mortality. Two demographers working for the U.S. Bureau of the Census provided rigorous data on declining health standards and climbing mortality rates (Davis and Feshbach 1980). Journalists and visitors published more anecdotal evidence, with one describing "Third World" Russian hospitals with little medical care and patients relying on food brought by relatives (Kaiser 1976, 100). Other studies drew a bleak picture of an overburdened housing and transportation system that could not keep up with the increased demand. In particular, housing shortages were described as the most severe "material hardship borne by the people" (Crouch 1990; Morton 1979). Based on this evidence, the London *Times* pointed out in 1981 that the Soviet Union had still not met its own housing standard of 1928 (Kirkpatrick 1990, 11). Abel Aganbegyan (1988a, 26), a leading Soviet reformist economist, subsequently confirmed that lack of housing created serious social problems in the society, contributing to family disintegration and delinquency.

Amplifying the health and infrastructure problems was the ecological degradation documented in a number of studies. Although the full extent of the ecological disaster did not become known until the collapse of the Soviet Union, these early studies linked health problems to pollution and other hazards (Volgyes 1974; Singleton 1974; Shabad 1979). Adding to environmental woes were occasional disasters involving the production of nuclear, biological, and chemical weapons, references to which circulated in the dissident press (Smith 1990, 101). Following glasnost-era accounts, an authoritative American study argued that these health and ecological problems amounted to "ecocide" (Feshbach and Friendly 1991).

Another line of research focused on the dysfunctionality of the command economy and the distortions generated by central planning. Other studies painted a picture of severe food and consumer goods shortages. Agriculture was seen as the main problem and came to be known as the "Achilles' heel" of the Soviet Union. Detailed analysis revealed that since 1970 investment in agriculture accounted for about one-fifth of the GNP, but between 1971 and 1979 outputs rose by only 0.9 percent, necessitating large grain imports. The large layout in agriculture with almost nil returns contributed to what was described as the "crisis index" of the Soviet economy (Millar 1977; Lee 1995, 165; Crouch 1990, 57). These rigorous studies were supplemented by anecdotal testimony from journalists and travelers. An American college professor who visited Russia numerous times wrote about the food shortages in

Moscow and despaired over the poverty and backwardness of the country-side. He questioned anyone who believed that the Soviet Union could catch up, let alone overtake the United States as predicted by Khrushchev (Byrnes 1977–78). Viewed through the prism of eudaemonics, this economic down-turn had ominous implications for conditional patrimonial legitimacy. The authorities had a difficult time providing material benefits at the level needed to maintain the social contract. As Löwenthal (1976, 87) argued, the Soviet regime "could be only temporarily and precariously legitimated by economic performance." He added that in the absence of "legitimacy based upon insti-tutional procedure," declining standards of living could spell big trouble.

Indeed, signs of delegitimation as manifested by individual behavior were abundant. A number of studies of Soviet workers pointed to widespread ab-senteeism and drunkenness. There were even accounts of more overt forms of labor unrest (Gidwitz 1982). Withdrawal of labor and sabotage of machin-ery and outputs were not uncommon but harder to document because of pau-city of official accounts. According to rational choice theorists this type of activity was typical among workers who could not readily strike or openly express their frustration with the system. In rational choice parlance, this is known as the "infrapolitics of subordinate groups"—that is, an effort to obscure intentions by taking cover behind an apparently meaningful pro-cess. Helped by the official mendacity at the top, Soviet citizens developed "highly elaborated sophisticated procedures to imitate useful activity." Summed up in the popular saying "they pretend to pay us, we pretend to work," such behavior resulted in low productivity rates and manufacturing of shoddy goods (Scott 1990, 199, 220; Pereira 1999, Shlapentokh 1989, 11; Laqueur 1994, 55).

According to the critics of the revisionist model, labor disaffection was part of a larger phenomenon of societal delinquency, alienation, and anomie, especially as measured against the standards of the New Soviet Man, an ideal that the Soviet authorities had sought to inculcate in the population since the revolution (Bockmuhl 1986, 130). As described by Stanislav Strumilin (1964, 99), a leading Soviet expert on socialization, the commu-nist moral code listed moral rectitude, hard work, self-reliance, and lack of selfishness among its top characteristics. Other requirements demanded a high sense of public duty, intolerance of action harmful to public interests, camaraderie, and dedication to the collective good. An "uncompromising attitude toward injustice, parasitism and money grabbing" rounded out the new communist citizen. These values were said to contrast with the avarice, materialism, and alienation that plagued capitalism (White 1999, 25).

However, according to a number of studies, Soviet behavior in the late Brezhnev period deviated sharply from this ideal. Voluntarism was on the decline and delinquency and deviance—defined as theft, property damage, prostitution, and alcoholism and drug abuse—were pervasive. Rape was the most frequent social crime, and even murder, including infanticide and child killings, was on the rise. Particularly worrisome to the authorities was the huge increase in drunkenness, a major factor in the decline of levels of health and productivity. That delinquency was most frequent among workers and youth was a reflection of the regime's inability to socialize the "masses" and create the New Soviet Man (Connor 1972, 2; Feifer 1973, 150; Connor and Gitelman 1977, 113; Katz 1971; Powell 1973; Schwartz 1973; White 1999, 7; Chalidze 1977, 123, 133).

Perhaps even more delegitimizing was the widespread corruption of the communist system. As noted in the theoretical chapter, corruption is particularly corrosive to the legitimacy of the authority system because it creates a sense of normlessness, defined as an expectation that socially unapproved behavior is required to achieve life goals. Critical observers asserted that corruption in the Soviet Union stemmed from three closely interrelated factors. First, the command economy had resulted in permanent and severe shortages of goods and services. According to economist Gregory Grossman (1977), such pervasive deficits had created a black and gray market, collectively known as the second economy. The second economy ranged from underground entrepreneurs running large-scale operations to small-time actors who sold goods or provided services, often by moonlighting from their official jobs. Grossman calculated that in the latter part of the 1970s some 50 percent of personal income in the Soviet Union came from the second economy. Subsequent Soviet disclosures under the glasnost policy estimated that some 20 million people worked *na levo*, "on the left" or on the side. The volume of service businesses alone in the second economy reached some 30 percent of the state service sector (Staats 1972; Kramer 1977; Kaiser 1976, 53, 88–89; Smith 1990, 266).

Second, the underground economy flourished because stealing and embezzlement from the state were exceedingly easy. Raw materials were diverted by truck drivers and finished products were sold on the black market after being recorded as damaged or lost in transit. Fish taken by poaching approached the tonnage of the legal catch from Soviet internal waters. Murders of game, forestry, and other officials in charge of overseeing state property were common. In retail, scales were tampered with and cheaper goods substituted to the detriment of the consumers. The pilfering of state property was so widespread that the Ministry of Internal Security created the Department for the Struggle Against Plundering of Socialist Property (Chalidze 1977, 105, 158–87; Feifer 1976, 42; Wesson 1976, 238; Smith 1976, 81–101; Connor 1972, 145–61).

Third, the centrally planned economy with its stiff production quotas mandated by the five-year plans forced mangers to engage in "creative" bookkeeping. False reporting, inflating labor force and inventories, avoidance of specific procedures, and other forms of corner cutting were pervasive. Even honest managers had to occasionally resort to such tactics in order to fulfill their quotas. Much of it was helped by the widespread custom of bribery (*blat*), a technique also used to obtain goods and services from the system. Bribes were given to secure favorable court rulings, influence police and college admission decisions, and to obtain degrees and other bureaucratic favors. In the words of one expert, by the 1970s the Soviet Union had become a "kleptocratic state," where public office was used for private gains (Kramer 1977). Another observer pointed out that because of its pervasive nature, corruption amounted to a "criminalization of ordinary existence" (Boyes 1990, 6; Staats 1972; Simis 1977–78; 1982, 34, 180–205; Topol and Neznansky 1983).

While most Soviet citizens had partaken in an array of illegal and corrupt practices, it was the corrupt nomenklatura that stood to profit the most. Far from being the dedicated public servants envisaged by the communist moral codes, many of them had become affluent, if not spectacularly rich. In some of the Asian republics, the widespread corruption amounted to what experts called a "tribute" system in which officials used their positions to receive kickbacks or extort payments for services rendered by the state. As such, it resembled the medieval Russian system of *kormlenie* wherein the central government allowed appointed officials to rule a province for a time in order to enrich their own coffers by whatever means they could (Odom 1992, 81). In the communist era, this "massive and ubiquitous corruption at the district level" had forged close ties between party officials and the criminal world that ran sectors of the second economy. Indeed, in the popular view the term "mafia" became associated with the government (Simis 1977–78; 1982, 72, 95; Smith 1990, 91). Even when not taking direct bribes, members of the nomenklatura could count on furthering their interests through nepotism (*kumovstvo*), which reached epidemic proportions in the Asian republics. Political and personal patronage was another common way to get ahead. In 1975 and 1976 the Soviet sociologist Aleksandr Levikov published a number of articles showing that promotions were based on personal and family ties and political loyalty rather than professional qualifications (Laqueur 1994, 61; Simis 1985).

The creation of this Bolshevik nouveau-riche class was greatly facilitated by the special privileges accorded them by the state. Since the communist oligarchy had claimed egalitarian legitimacy as a basis for its rule, starting with Lenin a whole array of special advantages were created behind the official façade of egalitarian austerity. By the 1970s, the special privilege system functioned as a second moneyless economy for the elite. Its members enjoyed special hospitals, stores, vacation houses, and preferences in housing and car allocations. Top officials were provided an array of domestic help. Although there had developed a large subeconomy catering to the elite, the authorities went to extreme lengths to hide the privileged life-style of the partocracy. For instance, the large apartments of the party elite were camouflaged behind the façade of ordinary high-rises, and special hospitals were hidden in residential areas (Connor 1979a, 250; Kramer 1977; Simis 1982, 35; Smith 1976; Zemtsov 1985, 97; Novikov and Bascio 1994, 26).

Given the massive scale of corruption and privilege, antirevisionist scholars argued that the commitment to revolutionary egalitarianism was undermined "implicitly but systematically" (Daniels 1978). A comprehensive study of social and economic inequality found that the Soviet Union was deeply divided society with an almost castelike social system. At the top of the social pyramid were top party officials and their children, followed by the lesser nomenklatura (Yanowitch 1977, 58–59). Another study concluded that "patterns of [Soviet] inequality . . . can easily be paralleled with reports from American and other Western sociological work" (Yanowitch and Fisher 1973, xxii; Lipset 1973a). Subsequent revelations confirmed these findings and fleshed out the account of life of the "new class," whom one commentator termed a Soviet aristocracy, a "life peerage associated with honors" (Zemtsov 1985; Arbatov 1992, 225).

Adding to these signs of delegitimation was the growing national discontent in the republics. Hélène Carrère d'Encausse, a demographer and Soviet expert, detailed the intensity of religious and national feelings in the republics in her 1978 book *L'Empire éclaté,* which was published under the prophetic English title *Decline of an Empire* (1979). A symposium of the Center for Strategic and International Studies in 1976 reached pretty much the same conclusion. Richard Pipes, one of the participants, forecasted a national upheaval in the next five to ten years. Pipes was also among the first to note that the Russians, often called to subsidize the less-developed Asian republics, had began to question the benefits of the empire. A small but growing literature on "imperial discontent" made the same arguments (Linden and Simes 1977; Zwick 1979; Azrael 1978).

To those who searched for signs of discontent, the "external empire" in Eastern Europe did not look any better. As a matter of fact, a serious deficit of legitimacy there had been documented since the wave of anticommunist upheavals in Hungary, Poland, and East Germany in the 1950s. The leading Polish philosopher and dissident Leszek Kolakowski (1971, 90–91) warned that efforts to enforce the communist utopia in the face of a radically different reality were "grotesque" and would lead to "monstrous deformation" of society. Naimark (1979, 553) called the accounts of legitimacy in the GDR an "egregious distortion" of reality, adding that mainstream literature did not mention the fear, apathy, and resentment of the population held behind the Berlin Wall and a heavily fortified border. A number of articles found that, fearing the deepening crisis of legitimacy, the Soviet Union felt compelled to subsidize the poorly performing economies of its satellites, creating a strain on its own dwindling resources. The so-called "empire strikes back" literature of the late 1970s argued that this practice transformed Eastern Europe from a Soviet asset to a Soviet liability (Marer 1974; Bunce 1985).

By combining these various indicators the neoconservatives were able to conclude that the Soviet empire had entered a severe crisis of legitimation. Evidence in support of this view came from Soviet dissidents like Andrei Amalrik, Roy Medvedev, and Aleksandr Solzhenitsyn. Amalrik (1970), in *Will the Soviet Union Survive Until 1984?*, discussed the demoralizing effects of the regime's coercive grip and predicted the national disintegration in the Soviet Union. Medvedev's book, *Let History Judge: The Origins and Consequences of Stalinism* (1972), painted a picture of corruption and venality among the spreading bureaucracy and the sullen disaffection of the masses.

Many East European intellectuals and dissidents, including Czech playwright Vaclav Havel, as well as the French neototalitarian scholars, embraced these views. Borrowing the terminology of Habermas, they and others argued that the system was ultimately doomed because of internal contradictions built into communism. In 1978 Kolakowski called Marxism the "greatest fantasy of our century"; others deplored its moral degradation and the discrepancy between word and deed, or what Solzhenitsyn called the culture of the Lie (quoted in Hollander 2000, 188). In this view, failure to provide the material incentives required by patrimonial legitimacy and the cohabitation of egalitarian norms with widespread privileges had made the communist system precariously fragile. In what turned out to be a prescient analysis, the French intellectual Emmanuel Todd warned in a 1976 book that the Soviet Union would collapse within a decade or so. Based on such forecasts, Bernard Levine wrote in the *Times* of London of August 1977 that "a new Russian revolution is inevitable" because the "thirst for freedom and decency in the countries of the Soviet empire cannot remain much longer unshaken" (Larson 1978, 108; reprinted in the *National Interest* 1993, 64).

Predictions of communist demise focused attention on the role of political inertia, according to which the "morally corrupt, threadbare Soviet leadership," was unable to adapt because of "fear of change" (Wesson 1976, 237). Indeed, according to rational choice theory, party officials were expected to use their authority to maximize their private benefits and shun changes that would jeopardize them. Some experts pointed out that, far from being the enlightened ruler of the pluralistic paradigm, Brezhnev oversaw a system in which his family and his protégés were primary beneficiaries of the system of nepotism and corruption (Jacobs 1978). The regime's immobilism was also blamed on Brezhnev's physical and mental debility following his collapse on December 24, 1974, during President Ford's visit to the Soviet Union. Although kept as a state secret, the illness turned the aging Brezhnev, a poorly educated man whose main reading was the magazine *Circus*, into a progressively senile dictator dedicated to fostering his personality cult. Former Soviet ambassador to Washington Anatoly Dobrynin (1995, 476) and other insiders confirmed that in the last few years of his life the Soviet leader barely functioned and was only indirectly involved in policy making (Volkogonov 1998, 302–18; Ligachev 1993, 148). Brezhnev's love of honors and decorations became the butt of popular jokes like the one describing his routine as "morning, gives medals, afternoon receives medals." Other jokes reflected the make-believe reality that Brezhnev's rule had created and especially the vast discrepancy between "what people see and what they hear" (Collins 1998, 179; Strayer 1998, 53; Dobbs 1997, 84–85).

Brezhnev's long leadership drift was amplified by the aging Politburo, which some scholars described as suffering from a number of pathologies like devolution of power to subordinates, failure to make prompt decisions, denial that problems existed, priority given to unity maintenance over decision making, and minimal work output. For instance, it was widely known that, following Brezhnev's illness, the Politburo decided to limit their chief's workload. Soon after, other Politburo members adopted the new regimen of three or four abbreviated workdays a week (Shoup 1989; Ligachev 1993, 148). Analysts who followed these developments concluded that the leadership could not make the decisions necessary to address the nation's economic problems, which were routinely swept under the rug by manufactured statistics. As one observer noted, "statistics were cheerfully manufactured to support Brezhnev's contention that the Soviet Union had already reached the stage of 'advanced socialism'" (Kaiser 1991, 59). As predicted by Brzezinski, technological innovations were delayed out of fear of the decentralization and democratization that they would entail (Wesson 1976, 101; Jacobs 1978). Georgi Arbatov (1992, 213, 214), a regime insider, would later write that the Brezhnev Politburo found it too complex and painful to "shake" the Stalinist model of economy and that in spite of the fact that many in the leadership knew about the statistically fabricated reality, nothing was done.

Still, some leaders apparently realized the erosion of the system's legitimacy, but the regime's response to the evolving crisis made things worse. First, in order to preserve the façade of socialist legitimacy, the authorities had renewed their drive to weed out all dissent. The KGB, headed by Yuri Andropov, had progressively moved against national, ethnic, religious, and political dissent. Jews who wanted to emigrate to Israel, and other ethnic or religious minorities who tried to assert their rights, did not fare well. Political dissidents were punished most harshly. Although the Stalinist regimen of mass executions and deportations to Siberia was abandoned, a whole array of more sophisticated methods was adopted, including social isolation, organized slander, and confinement to psychiatric hospitals, a method credited to Andropov himself. Accounts of these official misdeeds had circulated in the *samizdat* literature and were later confirmed by regime insiders who also noted that the Communist Party paid a high price in terms of the elite and public demoralization that followed (Arbatov 1992, 231).

Second, the declining domestic prestige of the regime had generated an ideological retrenchment in foreign affairs. In this view, Brezhnev's weakness and the aging cohorts in the Politburo made it easier for the ideologues to push for Soviet expansion abroad. Chief among them was the Soviet military, whose raison d'être was linked to the ethos of defending and spreading socialism. Ideology also served as a rationale for claiming a large share of national resources for the military and the military-industrial complex, whose higher echelons were among the most privileged in the country. Upon retirement, this group was given such lavish perks that they were known as the Paradise Company. Pipes (1976) and others argued that Brezhnev presided over the largest arms buildup in Russian history, turning the country into a heavily armed fortress (Coleman 1996, 57; Pozner 1992, 160–61).

The International Department (ID) of the Central Committee of the Communist Party, which was responsible for Moscow's relations with the Third World, housed another large group of ideologues. Its head, Boris Ponomarev, a veteran Stalinist official and a protégé of the Politburo's chief ideologue Mikhail Suslov, was among the most ardent advocates of using military and economic aid to spread socialism in underdeveloped countries. The huge military outlays for conventional and nuclear weapons and the strain of promoting socialism were subjects of an agonizing "guns vs. butter debate" among the leadership. In 1975 the Politburo decided to cut investment rather than make substantial cuts in either defense or current production; future economic growth was thus sacrificed (Rush 1982–83).

According to neoconservative scholars, taken together these developments contradicted the revisionist-pluralistic literature in some important aspects. They showed that far from enjoying popular legitimacy, the system presided over an alienated and cynical citizenry that had found sophisticated ways of evading the coercive reach of the state. Moreover, instead of becoming normal, rational, and pragmatic, the Soviet Union had continued to be guided by

Marxist dogma, especially in foreign policy. Most important, as Odom (1998, 389) pointed out, the military dimension of the economy was overlooked because of Western subconscious inclination to see socialism in "Fabian terms of concern with equity and social justice." Odom and others contended that lost in this benign Fabian view was the fact that Soviet socialism was true to its revolutionary character in which pursuit of international class struggle took priority over domestic welfare.

Still, the detailed portrayal of ideological retrenchment amid general degeneration had little impact on mainstream Sovietology. As mentioned, many of the antirevisionist writings came from dissidents or émigré scholars who were held in particularly low esteem among American experts. The fact that many of these studies exposed corruption and deep class differences was not helpful in gaining a hearing among scholars eager to present the Soviet Union as a society with a viable economy and egalitarian society. The schism between pro-American East European intellectuals disenchanted with socialism and their Western counterparts dedicated to advocating egalitarianism struck one commentator as "ironic" (Feuer 1976). Another observer recalled how the American Historical Association rejected out of hand his motion to support Soviet historians who labored under the threat of retaliation to provide an accurate picture of life in their country. To such critics, this was a sign that revisionist scholars were not interested in a reality that could undermine their paradigm (Miller and Damask 1993). Igor Birman (1980a; 1980b; 1981), an émigré Soviet economist who wrote extensively about the pathologies of communism, complained that his work, along with the hundreds of publications of other émigré scholars, was ignored because "nobody in the West wanted to listen."

In rejecting the neoconservative view, mainstream Sovietologists were apparently also guided by methodological considerations. As will be clear from the previous chapter, the legitimacy discourse is replete with nuanced and symbolic expressions of disaffection that are hard to measure empirically. Much of this type of evidence, including the numerous jokes about the regime, was relegated to the anecdotal category. The official statistics used by revisionist scholars led them to conclude that Soviet workers had participated in large numbers in various organizations and, far from being alienated, were actually "incorporated" in the regime. The occasional alienation, attributed mostly to nonskilled labor, was explained by changes in technology which both in the USSR and the West "required workers to be involved in routine production" (Lane and O'Dell 1978, 41, 44). An analysis generated by a conference on labor organized by the Kennan Institute for Advanced Russian Studies in 1977 was equally positive. The author stated that "there is every reason to believe that the basic political perceptions of the workers' stratum are generally positive and pro-system. In the sphere of material expectations wants have been met" (Connor 1979b, 317).

The widespread corruption and its implications were largely ignored by mainstream Sovietology, leading one observer to wonder why "this enduring aspect of Soviet society" had attracted so little attention (Staats 1972). Grossman (1977, 39) warned his colleagues that corruption throws "serious doubts . . . on the recent attempts in the West to reconstruct and interpret the size distribution of personal income in the USSR," or more generally Western "quantitative notions about the Soviet Union." But this and other misgivings about the potemkinization of the Soviet Union went equally unheeded (Smith 1976, 17). A study that set out to test the Amalrik scenario found no evidence of a legitimacy crisis as measured by value consensus, degree of satisfaction with the economic status quo, alienation, and egalitarian distributive justice (Hahn 1978).

Even if antirevisionist analysis had been better integrated into mainstream Sovietology, it is doubtful whether a more unified understanding of where the Soviet Union was headed would have emerged. A leading Soviet expert who reviewed a large number of studies on "stability and change" identified at least five possible future scenarios. Not surprisingly, the dividing line among the prognosticators followed their view of the legitimacy of the communist system. The adherents of the totalitarian model and its neoconservative and neototalitarian variants were convinced that the "authoritarian structures offend the human spirit and will ultimately prove incapable of eliciting legitimacy and compliance," while advocates of pluralism were more optimistic (Breslauer 1978; 1976, 70). Amann (1986), who later named these Group A and Group B theories, found that the former represented the view that the Soviet Union was essentially unredeemable and would collapse, whereas the latter asserted that the Soviet Union was moving in a more liberal and democratic direction.

Under normal circumstances the paradigmatic battles waged by scholars would have been confined to the academy. However, in the supercharged atmosphere of the Cold War, the academic debate was intimately related to the larger U.S. foreign policy discourse on the Soviet Union. In the words of one commentator, "much of the controversy . . . over what is and is not happening in the Soviet Union is really about what direction American policy should take. The focus is less on ascertaining Soviet reality than vindicating one or another side of an intramural American quarrel" (Codevilla 1988, 23–24). Which view of the Soviet Union to adopt became a crucial issue when the monolithic hostility of the Cold War gave way to the divisive debate in the United States about superpower relations during the period of détente.

3

Paradigms and the Debate on Relations with the Soviet Union

Détente, New Internationalism, and Neoconservatism

As long as containment guided American foreign policy, the revisionist model made little impact on the discourse in Washington. However, the high cost of the war in Vietnam prompted a rising chorus of voices to question the wisdom of the policy of containment. In search for a new international formula, the Nixon administration developed the détente policy, in which the pluralistic vision of Soviet Union gained some traction. Still, it was only during the Carter presidency that the revisionist model became fully integrated into New Internationalism, the liberal-idealist foreign policy of his administration. Such a high-level embrace of the idea that the Soviet Union was progressively liberalizing its domestic and foreign policy provoked a conservative backlash, fueled by Soviet intervention in Third World conflicts.

The Realpolitik View of Détente: Securing American National Interests from a Declining Position of Power

When Richard Nixon narrowly defeated Hubert Humphrey in 1968, the new Republican administration faced a number of challenges. The war in Vietnam was inconclusive, and relations with the Soviet Union were at a standstill. The old containment formula that divided the world into "good" and "evil" states was eroding, and there was increasing questioning of America's own moral standing. Bereft of ideological simplicity, let alone the idealism of the earlier era, the Nixon administration had to fashion a new approach to international relations, a task that fell to Henry Kissinger, Nixon's national security adviser. Kissinger, who was highly critical of Wilsonian idealism in American foreign policy, was a disciple of the realist school of international relations. At the core of his realpolitik philosophy was the view that moral considerations should not determine foreign policy, a notion that enabled Kissinger to argue that the United States needed to engage the Soviet Union in a process of détente. Underlying détente was the premise that the power of the United States had diminished and that, without eliminating the stick of deterrence, Washington had to offer Moscow the carrot of normalization and economic cooperation as a way of curbing its appetite for global domination. Although the Nixon administration did not buy into the thesis of a pluralistic transformation in the Soviet Union, it was hoped that Moscow would tone down its revolutionary rhetoric and, more important, slow down its arms race and refrain from fomenting regional conflicts to spread socialism.

The centerpiece of the détente policy was a nuclear arms agreement, to be followed by a normalization of relations based on the principle of linkage. In 1972 the administration signed the Strategic Arms Limitation Treaty (SALT) and then moved to relax its trade policy with the Soviet Union. In taking these steps, Nixon also hoped to assuage domestic opposition to the war in Vietnam and control the growing Watergate scandal.

Among the most powerful critics of the administration were numerous New Left groups, the liberal wing of the Democratic Party led by George McGovern, and a younger generation of foreign policy intellectuals and practitioners that came to dominate the Council on Foreign Relations and other venues of discourse. It was among these new foreign policy elites, bolstered by the changing academic paradigm, that the anti-anticommunist stand was most pronounced. The Congress, which by 1974 boasted many "Vietnam class" legislators, provided a powerful backing for such emerging sentiments. The leftist congressional lobby—Members of Congress for Peace Through Law (MCPL), later renamed Arms Control and Foreign Policy Caucus (ACFPC)—supported arms limitation, a more equitable global economic order, and the abolition of war (Seliktar 2000, 43–47).

The end of the war in Vietnam and the resignation of Nixon did not dramatically change this equation, leaving Nixon's successor, Gerald Ford, with limited political resources to pursue the linkage policies of détente. Under the influence of the leftist lobbies, which made curtailing American intelligence activities their main focus, Congress embarked on an investigation of the Central Intelligence Agency (CIA). The highly critical reports of the Senate committee under Senator Frank Church and its House counterpart resulted in the establishment of a permanent congressional intelligence oversight in 1975. Encouraged by their victory, the leftist lobbies pressed for an intelligence charter that would have curtailed many of the CIA's covert operations.

Congress was equally decisive in limiting the ability of the Ford administration to counter Soviet involvement in regional conflicts as epitomized by Angola. Following the revolution that toppled the dictatorship of Portugal in April 1974, the Soviet Union sponsored the Marxist Movement for the Liberation of Angola (MPLA) which fought against the Western-oriented National Union for the Total Liberation of Angola (UNITA). When the Ford administration, which charged Moscow with undermining the détente-mandated linkage, asked Congress to approve aid for Angola, it was strongly rebuffed. At the end of 1975 Congress voted to bar American aid, forcing the bitterly disappointed Ford to sign into law the so-called Clark-Tunney Amendment on February 4, 1976. Not surprisingly, Republicans charged that the "McGovernite" Congress was sending a strong signal that the United States was willing to let the Soviet Union undermine the linkage policy (Kissinger 1999, 801).

Whatever meaning the Republican administrations ascribed to détente changed dramatically when Jimmy Carter won the election in 1976. Taking credit for the Democratic victory were various leftist groups, revisionist scholars, and the liberal wing of the Democratic Party. In their hour of triumph, the leftist coalition vowed to replace what it viewed as the cynical Nixon-Kissinger realpolitik with a new and more moral foreign policy that became known as New Internationalism.

The New Internationalist View of Détente: Superpowers Working Together for a Moral Universe

The ideological foundation of New Internationalism was a mix of neo-Wilsonian idealism, egalitarianism, and anti-Americanism. This unique New Left vision of international relations rejected the concept of power as the guiding principle of foreign policy and emphasized peaceful relations and goodwill among nations. The claim that power had contributed to conflicts between states led New Internationalists to denounce deterrence as an acceptable principle of international relations. The "ban power" crusade was driven by a generation of academics and activists bitterly opposed to the Vietnam War. In the words of one observer, this intellectual campaign "legitimized the notion that power is bad and American power is the worst" (Billington 1987).

The companion emphasis on distributive justice put a premium on getting the United States to move to the "right side of history." As one New Internationalist put it, "the United States should be identifying with those groups or governments that are . . . working toward equality of social and economic justice and personal freedom" (Gurtov 1974, 213). New Internationalists also insisted that regional conflicts should be decoupled from global superpower competition. They stressed the indigenous causes of local conflict, asserting that they were caused by "conditions of injustice and human degradation" rather than Soviet meddling (Dellums 1983). Finally, the New Internationalists wanted to make American foreign policy more humane and less militaristic. The IPS-affiliated Militarism and Disarmament Project (MDP) advocated substantial limitation on arms sales to American allies and a freeze on sales to countries run by right-wing dictatorships like Iran. The MDP, along with the Coalition for a New Foreign Policy, the Peace Through Law Educational Fund, and the ACFPC, urged a drastic reduction in the American arsenal, including the B-1 bomber, the Trident missile system, and the neutron bomb. The development of the neutron bomb, first proposed by the Nixon administration, was strenuously opposed by Moscow, which made it the linchpin of its peace campaign in the United States and Europe (Dumbrell 1993, 210–11; Bell 1980, 31).

Key to the new international relations philosophy was the revisionist view of the Soviet Union as a progressively pluralistic society with little appetite for international expansionism. Indeed, many of the early revisionist scholars were associated with the IPS, which took a lead in propagating these themes through an intensive outreach to Congress and the media (Powell 1987, 10–26; Isaac 1983; Isaac and Isaac 1983, 108–40). They and others posited that American fears of the Soviet Union were highly exaggerated or invented to benefit the American military-industrial complex and big corporations. Soviet policies in the Third World were described as "essentially defensive," aimed at weakening American "monopoly" (Barnet 1971; 1977, 63; Raskin 1979, 32–34; Kaldor 1978, 42). Even such respected mainstream experts as Raymond Garthoff (1978) chided those who "assume the worst" when estimating Soviet foreign policy intentions. Quite naturally, New Internationalists were among the most enthusiastic advocates of normalizing relations with Moscow, with a special emphasis on economic and technological exchange.

Whether beholden to the McGovernites or guided by his own moral vision of international relations, President Carter incorporated many New Internationalist themes into his foreign policy. Vice President Walter Mondale and a number of second- and third-tier foreign policy appointees had ties to the IPS and other New Left lobbies. In a major speech, Carter proclaimed himself cured of the "inordinate fear of communism," adding that in pursuing containment the United States violated her own principles by supporting dictatorships and alienating "progressive forces" around the globe. In his view, the threat of conflict with the Soviet Union faded in face of questions of justice, equity, and human rights. The president denounced Kissinger's policy of blaming regional conflicts on Soviet machinations and testified to his satisfaction with Moscow's global conduct. Secretary of State Cyrus Vance was also sympathetic to the task of building a more just international order. He told *Time* magazine that Carter and Soviet president Brezhnev had "similar dreams and aspirations." To show its newly found resolve to delink regional conflicts from bilateral relations, the administration studiously overlooked Soviet and Cuban involvement in Angola, Mozambique, and the Horn of Africa. Vance was convinced that such decoupling would be helpful in negotiating a second SALT agreement (Seliktar 2000, 51; Gershman 1980, 13; Dumbrell 1993, 192–93; DeJames 1994; Gates 1996, 71). These ideas delighted the New Left. IPS's Barnet (1977, 173) praised the administration for "correctly" seeing that global division between the rich North and the poor South "pose a far greater challenge to the survival of the American way of life than the Kremlin's master plan whatever it may be."

Carter was equally eager to adjust other aspects of American foreign policy to New Internationalist standards. He announced a limit on arms sales and denounced the human rights violations of right-wing allies of the United States, including the pivotal shah of Iran. He also moved to reorganize the CIA, which he had previously called "a disgrace," according to strict guidelines. Although the intelligence charter favored by Mondale and the anti-intelligence lobby led by IPS failed to pass Congress, Carter gave it a new lease on life in his Executive Order 12036. Carter's CIA director, Stansfield Turner, curbed human intelligence and covert action in favor of the morally "clean" technical intelligence, leading one CIA insider to argue that the president wanted to turn the "often ugly" business of espionage into a "morally uplifting experience." Turner's reforms were also designed to abolish the "cult of secrecy" that Carter and the New Left had so vociferously denounced (Bearden and Risen 2003, 64; Cline 1981, 272).

In incorporating so much of New Internationalism, the former governor of Georgia went further than any contemporary president in redefining the principles of American international conduct. However, promoting what one observer called "a new system of world order based upon international stability, peace and justice," proved more difficult than Carter had envisaged (Rosati 1987, 42). For one thing, not all of the foreign policy appointees in his administration shared the benign view of the Soviet Union. Foremost among them was Carter's national security adviser Zbigniew Brzezinski, who used his position to try and implement an ambitious anti-Soviet agenda. Acting upon his long-standing view that the Soviet Union enjoyed little legitimacy among its constituent nationalities, the national security chief sought to launch a number of overt and covert measures to foment unrest in the republics. Brzezinski was equally assertive in trying to exploit the crisis of legitimacy in Poland along the lines advocated by the "empire strikes back" literature. Most important, Brzezinski planned to use the human rights campaign of the administration to challenge the legitimacy of the Soviet regime among its own people (Brzezinski 1983a, 148–50).

Although the administration implemented some cultural measures advocated by Brzezinski, including the strengthening of Radio Liberty and Radio Free Europe, his initiative was bitterly opposed by the State Department and ran into roadblocks in the CIA. According to one insider, the bureaucracy was "gagging" at the thought of destabilizing the Soviet empire, an initiative that was outside "the parameter of the rules of the game as it has been played for many years." Turner's crusade against covert action, coupled with Carter's drive to open a new and more cooperative page in relations with the Soviet Union, was hardly helpful (Gates 1996, 71, 90–93; Andrew 1995, 433). Carter's New Left constituency was particularly outraged at what they saw as Brzezinski's visceral anticommunism and his strategy of dismantling the Soviet Union through "decapitation and balkanization" (Raskin 1991, 197–98).

The very public infighting within the administration between the New Internationalists in the White House and State Department on the one hand and Brzezinski and the hard-liners in the Department of Defense was hurtful to Carter's internationalist vision. However, far more threatening to his version of détente was the behavior of the Soviet Union.

The Soviet View of Détente: Improving the "Correlation of Forces"

The Soviet idea for détente originated in the June 1969 International Conference of Communist and Workers' Parties where Brezhnev proposed a program that would "intensify the struggle against capitalism and imperialism" while simultaneously "conducting a struggle for peace." At the 1976 Party Congress Brezhnev repeated his assurance that "détente does not in the slightest abolish and cannot abolish or alter the laws of the class struggle." Observers noted that these seemingly contradictory goals could be easily reconciled within the overall Marxist view of the inevitable triumph of communism. In the historical competition with capitalism, the "correlation of forces"—a complicated web of military, economic, and propaganda elements—would ultimately turn in Soviet favor. Though convinced of this historical inevitability, the regime hoped to bolster the correlation of forces by parlaying a more peaceful posture into economic and technological help from the West. In essence, Brezhnev was reviving Khrushchev's old efforts to appeal to the West through a series of initiatives focused on peaceful coexistence to fashion a new détente program (Barghoorn 1976, 126; Crouch 1990, 68; Coleman 1996, 188; Gibney 1960, 9).

As conceived in Moscow, détente was a way to continue the class struggle while decreasing the danger of a nuclear conflagration. The opening to the West had a number of additional advantages. Moscow hoped to use its extensive propaganda network to influence the foreign policy debates in the United States and in Europe. The KGB's Department of Special Measures, which dealt with propaganda and misinformation, was elevated in status and became known as Service A in the First Directorate (Snyder 1995, 93; Bittman 1990). The Institute of the USA and Canada (ISKAN), which was established by Yuri Andropov soon after he took control of the KGB in 1967, played a leading role, supplemented by the various fronts such as World Peace Council (WPC), World Federation of Trade Unions (WFTU), and others. According to Soviet defector Vladimir Sakharov, the propaganda drive was designed to enhance the "peace loving image" of Moscow and contrast it with the Vietnam-tarnished one of Washington (Sakharov and Tosi 1980, 96). Georgi Arbatov (1973, 305), the high-profile ISKAN director, was quite confident in his assessment that the Soviet Union was going to win the "war of ideas." Among other things, he boasted that "Soviet [economic] growth has captured the imagination of the world." Arbatov was particularly successful in legitimizing his country in the United States, at one point securing an introduction by Senator J. William Fulbright for his book (Ebon 1987, 232). By its own reckoning, Moscow scored a major victory when its peace campaign in 1977 forced President Carter to cancel plans to develop a neutron bomb (Tyson 1981, 156).

Détente also provided a cover for efforts to expand Soviet influence in Africa and other developing regions. Ambassador Dobrynin (1995, 361, 468, 473) revealed that the Politburo strongly believed that the Soviet Union should utilize regional conflicts to "perform our international duty to other people." In his view, this ideological stand was deeply ingrained; when discussing foreign policy issues, Soviet leaders used the ideologically laden language of the official press and seemed to believe in their own rhetoric. Ignoring the American desire for linkage, the Soviet leadership "was proud to be assisting the struggle of subject peoples toward their liberation" and socialism. Dobrynin noted that the repeated warnings of the Soviet embassy in Washington "fell on the deaf ears of the morally self-righteous." Other insiders concurred with this conclusion. Arbatov (1992, 170) wrote that the leadership kept repeating "that peaceful coexistence did not mean an end to the ideological struggle." Eduard Shevardnadze (1991, 84, 87) argued that the "doctrine that ideological struggle between the social and political systems is inevitable" reigned supreme in Moscow, adding that any agreement with the "bourgeoisie" or "imperialists" was seen as a necessary evil, a tactical maneuver to gain time. It was subsequently revealed that, starting in early 1970, Soviet economists assured the Soviet leadership that the "final stages" of capitalism had begun. Brezhnev, who was eager to "give history a push" in the socialist direction, stepped up the arms race and Third World expansion. In the mid-1970s Service A became highly active in Angola, Mozambique, Ethiopia, South Yemen, Afghanistan, and Nicaragua. As for détente, the Soviet leadership persuaded itself that the process was irreversible (Fischer 1999, 15; Bittman 1990; Crouch 1990, 56).

The failure of Congress to take a stand on Angola strengthened the hand of the ideologues against Foreign Minister Andrei Gromyko as well as Ambassador Dobrynin (1995, 362; 404–5), who tried to persuade his superiors that Washington took a global view of détente. In fact, the Clark-Tunney Amendment had contributed to what the ambassador and other insiders described as the "Angola syndrome." Having suffered no consequences because of their actions there, the Politburo proceeded to interfere in the Horn of Africa, the Middle East, and ultimately in Afghanistan. As Arbatov (1992, 195) noted, "we were unable to resist temptations to become involved in the complex internal affairs of other countries. After Angola, we went boldly down the path of intervention."

Jimmy Carter's tenure in the White House did little to cure the Angola syndrome. Gromyko deemed Carter "painfully naïve" for thinking that he could work with the Soviet Union in honest partnership (Shevchenko 1985, 401). But the Soviet leadership was alarmed by Carter's human rights crusade and highly annoyed by Brzezinski, who was perceived as an ardent anticommunist and cold warrior. However, the efforts of Congress, Secretary Vance, and other liberal foreign policy actors to isolate regional conflicts from bilateral relations reassured Moscow that the core of the détente policy was not in jeopardy. Indeed, this stand discredited the continued efforts of the Soviet embassy in Washington to persuade Moscow to abstain from involvement in the war between Somalia and Ethiopia and its meddling in Yemen. Dobrynin (1995, 404–6) explained that even though the Foreign Ministry was not happy with these developments, Gromyko had no control over Suslov, Ponomarev, and Andropov, who pushed to support "vanguard parties" in the Third World. The case for intervention was also taken up by a number of top generals headed by the minister of defense Marshal Andrei Grechko and his successor Marshal Dmitri Ustinov, who were "emotionally pleased" by "showing the flag in remote areas" and thus defying America. The ailing Brezhnev was persuaded that such assertions of Soviet "global power" would, in the final analysis, not harm détente. Whatever protestations Washington offered were dismissed as routine propaganda attacks in the continuous "natural" ideological struggle between the West and communism (Collins 1998, 171; Andrew and Gordievsky 1990, 554; Kitrinos 1984; Albright 1991). Gates (1996, 82, 170) later commented that Vietnam, Watergate, and the economic crisis following the 1973 oil embargo must have emboldened the Soviet Union to improve its "correlation of forces." He described as "naïve" the view that Moscow would not take advantage of the situation. Gates added that it was ironic that "members of the U.S. Congress, Secretary Vance, others in the administration, and various pundits" were stressing the importance of not turning local or regional conflicts into global conflicts, when it was already a "done deal."

Even if Moscow could justify its Third World actions by denying that détente involved linkage, it was harder to explain the expansion of the Soviet nuclear arsenal in contravention of the spirit if not the letter of the SALT agreements. In the most visible step, in 1976–77, the USSR began deploying the SS-20, a powerful intermediary missile that had seriously upset the NATO balance in Europe. Secretly, the Soviet military reinterpreted the concept of strategic parity embedded in the agreements with Nixon as a license to demand all types of weapons that the American military possessed and to even surpass them in quantity. A similar interpretation of parity was applied to conventional weapons, setting off another round of the arms race.

Subsequent accounts revealed that the Soviet military-industrial complex drove much of this expansion. The Ministry of Defense and the Ministry of Defense Industry were only accountable to Brezhnev who, as the general secretary of the party, was also the commander in chief and the chairman of the Defense Council. Brezhnev, a long-standing champion of the military-industrial complex and a self-anointed authority on military matters, approved many of the top-secret military projects brought before him. It probably helped that before becoming defense minister, Dimitri Ustinov had spent most of his career in the armament industry. Without any internal debate on the economic or foreign policy implications of these projects, the military and industrial leaders received a virtual blank check to expand. As Brezhnev's health progressively declined, the institutional autonomy of the military-industrial complex greatly increased. Dobrynin disclosed that for the most part, when discussing nuclear matters in Washington, the Soviet embassy was "completely ignorant" about the expansion programs at home (Dobrynin 1995, 474–75, 474; Shevardnadze 1991, 58; Coleman 1996, 57; Larabee 1988).

Secrecy and ambiguity extended to the issue of first strike doctrine. In the 1960s and early 1970s, Soviet military writings implied that nuclear war was a "rational instrument of policy" and that "strategic superiority was obtainable and desirable." However, in 1977 Brezhnev in a speech in the city of Tula denounced such thinking. The "Tula line," apparently endorsed by the

Chief of Staff Nikolai Ogarkov, was aimed at reassuring the United States that the Soviet Union would never initiate a nuclear strike, a fact that was confirmed in 1994 by two high-ranking Russian generals who were involved in nuclear planning. Soon after, though, the mercurial Ogarkov seemed to balk at the no-first-strike doctrine, a stand expressed in his increasingly strident public pronouncements (Larabee 1988; Dobrynin 1995, 475; Herspring 1990, 131; Azrael 1987, vi).

Moscow's interpretation of détente posed a major challenge to the New Left and its allies in the Carter administration. They redoubled their efforts to portray the Soviet Union as a liberalizing, normalizing, and peace-loving nation operating well within the parameters of acceptable superpower relations. Behind this increasingly anxious search to find the right phraseology to describe Moscow's action was the fact that the administration had found itself under growing attack by neoconservative critics.

The Neoconservative View of Détente: Outmaneuvering
the United States

The challengers of détente fashioned their argument along the lines of the totalitarian model and the antirevisionist literature. While accepting the Nixon-Kissinger position that American national security was compromised by the anti-Vietnam backlash, neoconservative critics vehemently opposed the notion that Moscow had given up its expansionist strategy. What changed, in their opinion, was not Moscow's ultimate goal but its tactics, which had become progressively more sophisticated in manipulating the foreign policy discourse in the West. Recalling Lenin's old adage about capitalists "selling the rope" that the communists would use to hang them, critics charged the KGB, the International Department of the Central Committee, and ISKAN with cultivating academics, intellectuals, and other opinion leaders in the United States and Europe. Described as a middle-ground stratum—between diplomatic and clandestine operations—these contacts were credited with nurturing numerous fellow travelers and agents of influence. In Moscow's internal parlance, many of them became "termites"—that is, anti-anticommunists helpful in propagating "Soviet friendly" themes (Rositzke 1975; Tyson 1981, 30). Arbatov, the head of the USA and Canada Institute, was said to be particularly adroit at manipulating Americans. In the words of Kissinger, Arbatov was especially "subtle in playing the inexhaustible masochism of American intellectuals who took as an article of faith that every difficulty in U.S.-Soviet relations had to be caused by American stupidity and intransigence" (quoted in Powell 1987, 338).

Using data collected from an investigation of Soviet subversion and deception programs in the United States, neoconservatives accused some far left lobbies, including church, peace, and antinuclear groups, of acting as Soviet fronts. The IPS, which through its affiliates was highly active in the anti-CIA campaign, was singled out for particular criticism. Senator Strom Thurmond contended that the tax-exempt institute supported global revolutions. Brian Crozier (1979), the director of the conservative London-based Institute for the Study of Conflict, noted that the "IPS is a perfect front for Soviet activities which would have been resisted if they were to originate openly from the KGB." Arnaud de Borchgrave's thinly disguised novel about the IPS, *The Spike*, made the same claim. These and other critics pointed out that IPS had particularly close ties to Arbatov's ISKAN (Braley 1984, 588; de Borchgrave and Moss 1980, 167; Tyson 1981; Rees 1983).

What worried the neoconservatives most was the fact that the Soviet Union, through its network of ideological allies, could impact congressional deliberations on issues ranging from the CIA charter to the Angola amendment. Stopping short of accusing individual legislators of being "propaganda assets" of the Soviet Union, critics claimed that Moscow was actively trying to penetrate Congress. High on their list of suspicious activities were Ponomarev's efforts to establish quasi-formal relations with Capitol Hill, or as one critic put it, "to co-opt" Congress (Hubert 1989, 117, 143; Tyson 1981, 28; Rees 1983).

From the neoconservative perspective, the most alarming outcome of the Soviet propaganda campaign was the spirit of appeasement that had allegedly permeated the foreign policy culture in the United States. In a programmatic article, "Making the World Safe for Communism," Norman Podhoretz (1976, 33), a leading neoconservative intellectual, decried the "new liberal position" of dismantling America's military assets and adopting the rhetoric of "fighting social injustice." Others complained that the culture of appeasement had spread via the media into the popular domain (Garson 1996, 183).

While some critics of détente focused on subversive tactics, others took a broader view of why the American foreign policy establishment underestimated the Soviet commitment to militarism and expansionism. At the heart of their argument was the notion that many in the foreign policy community were either "mechanical pragmatists" or "integrationists"; both groups were said to make light of the aggressive expansionist ideology of communist rulers. In contrast, neoconservatives took pride in being "essentialists"— that is, believers in the essentially ideological roots of Moscow's expansionism. True to his credentials, Richard Pipes emerged as a leading proponent of the view that it was the dominant academic paradigm that colored Washington's failure to appreciate Soviet aggressive intentions. Pipes charged that, far from being the domain of the leftist lobbies, underestimating the

Soviet Union was embedded in the intellectual habits of the academic and intelligence community. According to Pipes (1986, 29; 1981, 74) the CIA, like any other intelligence community, "reflects the habits of thought of the elite from whose ranks it is recruited and on whom it depends for intellectual sustenance." As a result, its analysts shared the American academic penchant "for philosophical positivism, cultural agnosticism and political liberalism." The intelligence community's perceptions of the "vices and virtues" of the Soviet Union were a reflection of the "American academic writings on the Soviet Union," especially in political science and in journalism. Pipes accused the professors and their journalistic followers of producing faddish and unrealistic accounts of Soviet politics and failing to make a distinction between capability and intentions (Pipes 2003, 137–43).

Pipes was not the first to charge the CIA's Soviet estimates with logical positivism and ethnocentric mirror imaging. In fact, Klaus Knorr (1964) used the term "philosophical disposition" to explain why American intelligence assumed that the Russians would not deploy strategic weapons in Cuba. More significantly, in two important articles in 1974 the respected analyst Albert Wohlstetter (1974a, 1974b) denounced the intelligence community for underestimating the Soviet nuclear arms race and questioned the premise of mutual assured destruction (MAD) on which American nuclear policy was built. But Pipes went further than other critics did by attacking the very premise on which MAD was based. Academic strategists had arrived at the concept of MAD by applying game theory to elucidate the dynamics of binary competition. Since the model assumed that both sides "evaluate the rewards of certain outcomes equally," the United States and the USSR were said to be mutually deterred by their nuclear buildup (Dalby 1990, 124; Plous 1985).

Calling these civilian strategists "philosopher kings," Pipes charged that their methodology had a fatal flow. It eliminated from "serious considerations many experiences which have traditionally been regarded as of critical importance for strategy and warfare" including ideology, tradition, religion, and national ethos (Pipes 1981, 77; 1986). In a stab at the reluctance of academics to consider violence as a mode of international existence, Pipes added that the notion of being threatened "has acquired an almost class connotation." With "sophisticated elites" in America refusing to accept the fact that the "Soviet elite regards conflict and violence as normal and natural regulations in human affairs," the United States found itself mirror imaging its peaceful vision onto the enemy (Pipes 1977, 25). Vehemently denying that the Soviets operated within the MAD framework of rationality, Pipes asserted that Moscow used détente as a cover to pursue its goal of strategic superiority and socialist expansion. General William Odom (1998, 390), another critic of MAD, held that a majority of military Sovietologists perceived the Soviet Union through "Western preconceptions." Such mirror imaging led them to "fundamentally misunderstand" the fact that Soviet Union could not follow the deterrence theory of military stability without abandoning the "ideological foundation of their state's legitimacy and purpose." As Ken Booth, an author of a study on American strategic thinking and ethnocentricity, found "widespread intellectual conceit in the profession" that bordered on "solipsism and narcissism" (Booth 1979, 137; Lee 1995, 157).

Joining outside critics of MAD was a high-ranking insider, General George Keegan, assistant secretary of air force intelligence. Uneasy about SALT I and the pending SALT II negotiations, Keegan was convinced that the Soviet Union was manipulating public opinion while at the same time overtaking the United States in strategic weapons. To him, the Soviet military buildup was an indicator that Moscow was poised to seek world domination, which the CIA refused to see. In 1975, in response to Keegan's pressure, the intelligence community tried to reach a consensus on Soviet motives. But Fritz Ermath, the national intelligence official who wrote the report "Understanding Soviet Strategic Policy," concluded that the United States "did not really know what the Soviets really wanted or intended." The report was a major admission of "analytic weakness and overall analytic confusion," adding to the concerns raised by Wohlstetter, Pipes, and others (Ranelagh 1987, 662–63).

Misgivings about the nuclear arms race were part of a larger neoconservative critique of the way the CIA estimated the strength of the Soviet military buildup, calculated as a percentage of its economy. Efforts to measure trends in Soviet military priorities as reflected in allocation of economic resources dated to the early 1950s. At a minimum, there was a need to estimate the growth of Soviet national output and its component, to compare the size of the Soviet and U.S. economies, and to assess the absolute and relative changes in Soviet military spending. Given the extreme secrecy and unreliability of statistics, estimating the Soviet GNP was a formidable endeavor. Even more vexing was the question of how to translate the workings of a nonmarket economy into Western economic concepts.

A major debate in the intelligence community surrounding these issues revealed considerable differences of opinion. In the end, two schools of thought for estimating Soviet military spending emerged. The so-called residual method was based on the assumption that much of the Soviet military budget was hidden in other outlays. By netting the civilian components from these outlays, the total military budget was established. The rival method of direct costing, better known as the building block approach, tried to identify all military-related activities and estimate their cost in rubles and dollars to provide the total defense budget. The building block method, known as Strategic Cost Analysis Model (SCAM), required a large research apparatus to produce a two-step analysis. First, the entire Soviet military establishment and armament production programs had to be broken down into cost-generating entities. Second, appropriate prices had to be applied to these entities, first in rubles and then in dollars. Because of deficiencies of the Soviet price system, the CIA had used an adjusted cost standard valuation developed by the RAND Corporation. The dollar valuation, which was added later, was deemed particularly helpful in conveying the size of the military budget to Congress and U.S. military planners. American analogues that were appropriately "Sovietized" were used to fill information gaps (Becker 1994; Schroeder 1995; Firth and Noren 1998, 12–14, 16, 21; Prados 1982, 245–46).

SCAM's methodology was challenged by a number of critics, including William Lee, a military analyst who used the residual method; Steven Rosefielde, a deputy assistant secretary of defense for intelligence in the Nixon administration; and others who felt that the CIA had underestimated Soviet military expenditure. In the early 1970s the Defense Intelligence Agency (DIA) switched to an alternative method of evaluating the cost of Soviet defenses, which produced considerably higher figures than the CIA estimate of 6 percent of Soviet GNP. When Major General Daniel Graham, an outspoken critic of the CIA's methodology, became the director of the DIA in 1974, he mounted a public campaign against the CIA estimate (Rosefielde 1982, 1; Ranelagh 1987, 619–22).

Graham, who was known for his anticommunist zeal, was helped by a number of fortuitous developments. In 1974 Nixon's secretary of defense, James Schlesinger, who during his tenure as the CIA director was skeptical of the 6 percent figure, asked for a paper on the Soviet military burden. Like other conservative critics, Schlesinger noted that Soviet society was too highly militarized to warrant such a low ratio, but a draft of the so-called "burden paper" restated that military expenditure was "about 6 percent of the GNP" in 1972. Graham vehemently protested, and the revised April 1975 version of the report added that for the Soviet leaders costs seem to have not been a "major factor in their military decision" and were "unlikely to constrain them in the future" (Firth and Noren 1998, 54–55).

The CIA's confidence in its methodology was further undermined by a number of revelations from the Soviet Union. In 1972 Brezhnev was reported to have told a closed forum that "one out of three rubles" of the Soviet budget was spent on defense. Soon after, an émigré who worked in Gosplan (the Soviet economic planning agency) revealed that Soviet military expenditure for 1970 was about one-third of the budget and 12.5 percent of the GNP, a fact that was confirmed by a smuggled copy of the Politburo's Statistical Handbook. The émigré also revealed that most of the costs of military procurement were accounted for under civilian production (Lee 1995, 36; Nitze 1989, 400).

With external attacks and rising internal doubts, CIA director William Colby appointed a joint CIA-DIA study group. In a major victory for the DIA, in February 1976 the CIA revised its estimates of Soviet military spending to about 10 to 15 percent of the GNP. By its own admission, the CIA's underestimation was caused by a failure to research the ruble price of military hardware. The report acknowledged that, "in retrospect, it is evident that the estimates of the mid- and late 1960s failed to convey an adequate sense of the determination of the Soviets to build up sizeable forces and warfighting capabilities." It also conceded that the "Soviets adopted ambitious strategic force goals and moved steadily forward without much concern that the U.S. might feel it necessary to step up its own programs in turn" (Ranelagh 1987, 622; Firth and Noren 1998, 56; Haines and Leggett 2001, 285–86).

The upward revision created a firestorm in the discourse on the Soviet Union. Critics denounced the CIA for caving in to political pressure. They charged that the Agency was responding to the demands from the Defense Department and the DIA to make Moscow look more militaristic. Economist Franklyn Holzman (1980, 1989), a professor at Tufts University, published an analysis to show that the dollar costs used by the CIA to estimate the cost of Soviet weapons had created an upward bias, making the real rate of military expenditure to GNP lower, not higher. Still, the neoconservatives who had previously complained that the CIA misrepresented the Brezhnev statement and tried to discredit the Soviet émigré saw their cause vindicated. They were soon granted an even more important victory.

In August 1975, George W. Anderson, Jr., the chairman of the President's Foreign Intelligence Advisory Board (PFIAB), wrote to President Ford to suggest a competitive analysis of the CIA's Soviet estimate. In spite of the objections of Colby, Robert F. Ellsworth, the recently appointed deputy secretary for defense with responsibility for intelligence, endorsed the competitive exercise on January 26, 1976. Howard Stoertz, the Agency's national intelligence officer for the Soviet Union, headed Team A. Team B was led by Richard Pipes and included such known Agency critics as General Graham, Paul Nitze, and Paul Wolfowitz from the Arms Control and Disarmament Agency (ACDA). In a report presented to the PFIAB at the end of the year, Team B criticized the CIA for concentrating too heavily on Soviet military capabilities to the neglect of intentions. As for the latter, the report accused the Agency of underestimating Moscow's willingness to fight a nuclear war, a failure attributed to mirror imaging and other "unproven and unrealistic assumptions" about Soviet behavior. In addition, Team B found that the Soviet Union was intent on achieving global domination through a combination of economic leverage and military might. Most important, Team B members contended that Moscow's defense expenditures would not be guided by concerns over the negative impact of military outlays on the health of the economy (Pipes 1986; Ranelagh 1987, 623; Reich 1989; Jeffreys-Jones 1989, 212).

MAD aside, Team B challenged the wisdom of using a highly empirical and quantitative methodology to evaluate the complex and elusive Soviet economy. Although much less publicized, other critics shared similar misgivings about what one study called the "problem of false precision" (Berkowitz and Richelson 1995, 40). Interestingly enough, Gertrude Schroeder (1968), the senior author of the CIA consumption comparison, had earlier questioned her agency's comparison between Soviet and U.S. GNP. While serving as an attaché in Moscow in 1967, Schroeder described the hardships of daily Soviet life, concluding that "our measurements of the position of Soviet consumers in relation to those of the United States" were biased in favor of the Soviets. She also argued that the ruble–dollar ratio was set far too low for most Soviet consumer goods, which, because of their shoddiness, could not be compared to Western ones. Based on his estimates, Grossman (1977, 39) demonstrated that the huge distortions created by the second economy called "into question Western quantitative notions about the Soviet Union." British economist Philip Hanson argued that efforts to calculate precise ratios were part of an American "cultural deficiency." In his words, "the notion that you can generate a number though it might be wiser not to, is un-American and un-governmental" (quoted in Becker 1994, 317). Years later, Arbatov (1992, 214) would concede that the Soviet statistics and the way they were collected were geared toward supporting the "existing system and the existing model of economic management" at the cost of misrepresenting reality.

Although Team B was ultimately destined to change the discourse on the Soviet Union, its short-range impact looked less promising. President Carter disbanded the PFIAB, apparently because he believed it to be a "political ploy" to force his administration into a more conservative direction. By selecting Paul Warnke, a leading New Internationalist with ties to IPS and the release of the Pentagon Papers to head the ACDA, Carter showed little concern for the conclusions of Team B. Indeed, the appointment of the controversial Warnke, who abolished the agency's Verification and Analysis Bureau and fired Paul Wolfowitz, coupled with the disbanding of the PFIAB, outraged the critics of détente. Soon after, Paul Nitze founded the Committee for Present Danger (CPD), which included many Team B members, along with prominent intellectuals and conservative politicians like Ronald Reagan. *Commentary* and *The Public Interest*, magazines that became bastions of the rapidly growing neoconservative movement, took a lead in highlighting concerns about Carter's foreign policy, and the American Enterprise Institute provided a major scholarly base for the group. In 1978 *Commentary* published a scathing attack on the American academy, the media, and the CIA for misreading and ignoring Soviet reality and especially its economic decline. Some critics went so far as to allege that the CIA overestimated Soviet GNP in order to hide the high rate of military expenditure (Prados 1982, 250; Steinfels 1979, 5–7; Sorman 1985, 81).

In addition to a general critique of what was described as Carter's appeasement of Moscow, neoconservative critics targeted a number of specific policies of the administration. First, they charged that the large number of New Internationalist appointees were either responsive to Soviet propaganda, or worse, helped Moscow with its efforts to subvert American foreign policy. Carter's decision to cancel the development of the neutron bomb, his efforts to withdraw American troops from South Korea, demilitarize the Indian Ocean, and cut military budgets were viewed as major victories for the Soviet propaganda program (Seliktar 2000, 43–57).

Second, they accused the administration of tolerating repressive left-wing regimes while coming down hard on right-wing allies of the United States. High on their list of complaints was Assistant Secretary of State for Human Rights Patricia Derian, a former civil rights activist with deep roots in the leftist network, who pushed to "disassociate" the United States from right-wing regimes like Iran. Conservatives were equally dismayed with Andrew Young, Carter's appointee to serve as U.S. ambassador the United Nations. Young, who once noted that Western-style political freedoms were a "luxury" for poor people, had also advised Americans not to get "paranoid" about Cuban forces in Angola, which, in his view, were "helping to provide order and stability" (Gershman 1978, 20; 1979). In what became a celebrated piece of neoconservative writing, Jeane Kirkpatrick (1979) accused the administration of a double standard on human rights. Kirkpatrick and others were alarmed that the human rights crusade, while doing little to dent communist legitimacy, was destabilizing the more fragile right-wing regimes, notably Iran.

Third, neoconservatives were adamantly opposed to Carter's efforts to lift restrictions on exports of goods and technology to the Soviet Union. The initial move was made by Nixon, who signed the Export Administration Act in 1969, an initiative that was advocated by the Committee for Economic Development (CED), a group of business and academic supporters of détente. Borrowing a page from the pluralist paradigm, the CED argued that technological transfer through "peaceful trade" would strengthen the moderate forces in the Soviet Union and give them a stake in détente. However, Richard Perle, an assistant to Senator Henry Jackson and a leading neoconservative figure, argued forcefully that technological transfers would only strengthen Moscow's hand in global competition. One critic called such sales America's "national suicide," and another pointed out that the Soviet Union was not ready to modify its behavior. The writer Aleksandr Solzhenitsyn, who passionately urged the use of trade sanctions and the end of unilateral concessions to improve the Soviet human rights record, backed critics of technological transfer. When the Soviet Union put a number of prominent dissidents on trial, neoconservatives tried, largely unsuccessfully, to force Carter to suspend the sale of a computer system and oil drilling equipment (Kissinger 1999, 649; Sutton 1973, 19–20; Goldman 1987; Wood 1978; Gershman 1979; Wesson 1980, 81).

Fourth, neoconservatives charged Carter and Turner, who was writing his own estimates, with manipulating the CIA reports to suit the administration's Soviet policy. David S. Sullivan (1980), who was fired by Turner because of a disagreement over an estimate, accused the Agency of bending over "to downplay the Soviet military buildup." Sullivan, who also accused the Agency of succumbing to Soviet deception, became a major voice among a group dedicated to exposing the alleged bias of the CIA, a stand that was given even more weight when General Keegan resigned in 1977 to publicize his view on Soviet aggressive intentions (Ranelagh 1987, 662–63). The Association of Former Intelligence Officers, which was founded by David A. Phillips in 1975, also became involved in the controversy. In a conference on intelligence requirements for the 1980s organized by conservative intelligence experts, participants suggested that the "value free" intelligence approach of the Agency was responsible for the benign view of the enemy (Jeffreys-Jones 1989, 212; Godson 1980).

To an agency already demoralized by congressional investigations and the Carter-Turner reforms, the pressure from the left and the right could not have come at a worse time. Donald R. Burton (1983), chief of the Military Economic Analysis Center who was in charge of the CIA revision, wrote that the Soviet estimate became so politically contentious that the Agency could not satisfy those who thought it was either too high or too low. Gates (1996, 562) expressed similar sentiments, writing that the "liberals . . . argued that CIA overestimated Soviet military power and the conservatives argued just as stridently that we underestimated." External agitation fed into the internal division in the CIA, long polarized over how serious the Soviet deception and disinformation problem was. Even the Directorate of Intelligence, which had a well-established reputation for "comity and academic reserve," became affected. The Office of Soviet Analysis (SOVA) was the locus of a bitter controversy over Soviet intentions in Angola and more broadly in the developing world. Melvin A. Goodman, the officer in charge of analyzing Soviet Third World policy, argued that Moscow could not sustain a long overseas engagement and would not try other adventures. Goodman's views were pitted against Gates's judgment that the Soviet Union was bent on exporting socialism regardless of social and economic costs (Epstein 1978; Perry 1992, 314).

Indeed, it was Moscow's conduct in the Third World that provided more ammunition to Carter's foreign policy critics. By 1977 the Committee on the Present Danger gained a wider hearing for its notion that conflicts in Africa and Asia were not indigenous but fomented by the Soviet Union (Dalby 1990, 102). This so-called "arc of crisis" theory, which was taken up by Brzezinski as well, along with much of the neoconservative critique, received a huge boost after the Soviet invasion of Afghanistan.

Afghanistan and the Triumph of Neoconservatism

With so much riding on the view that regional conflicts were indigenous in nature, the Carter administration chose initially to ignore the increasing Soviet and Cuban involvement in the Horn of Africa and Yemen. When Katangan rebels, supported by Cubans in Angola, launched an incursion into the Shaba province of Zaire in 1977, the head of North-South Affairs on Carter's National Security Council urged restraint in the name of détente. The State Department studiously overlooked Castro's efforts to create a Marxist federation in the Horn of Africa and compared Cuban involvement in Angola and Mozambique to French backing of Chad (Seliktar 2000, 51; Crocker and Lewis 1979). Using the "right side of history" argument, Secretary of State Vance explained that "change was and is sweeping through Africa, and those who identify with it will be able . . . to influence its directions" (quoted in Dumbrell 1993, 192–93). The same policy was applied to the conflict between pro-Western Somalia and Marxist Ethiopia, which was armed by the Soviet Union and Cuba. When the shah of Iran offered to ship arms to Somalia, Washington advised him that the United States government "could not endorse third party transfers of American military equipment" (Ledeen and Lewis 1981, 55–56, 95).

The Carter administration seemed equally dismissive of efforts by its predecessors to secure a friendly regime in Afghanistan. After coming to power in 1973, Prince Mohammed Daoud Khan, who had initially helped to shift the country into the Soviet sphere of interest, moved in a more Western direction. Daoud's foreign policy course prompted the Afghan communists—the People's Democratic Party of Afghanistan (PDPA)—to increase agitation against the regime. In spite of growing tensions in Afghanistan and a visible Soviet involvement, the White House, bound by the theory of indigenous revolutions, showed little apprehension.

However, by the fall of 1977 National Security Adviser Brzezinski became alarmed at what he saw as Moscow's transgressions against détente.

He warned about Soviet consolidation in Ethiopia and South Yemen and began pushing for a Rapid Deployment Force, a topic that was taken up by a Special Coordination Committee (SCC) in December. The SCC also dealt with the deteriorating situation in Iran, where forces hostile to the monarchy, supported by many of the shah's opponents in the United States, were destabilizing the regime. Although much of the anti-shah protest was domestic, the administration could not be oblivious to the Soviet role. It had been known for a while that Moscow had considerable interest in getting rid of the Pahlavi regime. The shah's help in putting down the communist rebellion in the Dhofar province in Oman in 1975, along with his anti-Soviet activity in Africa, was a sore point. Iran headed the so-called Safari club, a group of conservative countries, including Saudi Arabia, that was dedicated to stopping communist expansion. Most important, the shah was personally involved in helping Daoud to execute his pro-Western strategy. In retaliation, the KGB activated the National Voice of Iran (NVOI) based in Baku, which broadcasted under the guise of an independent station in Iran, and the Soviet embassy in Teheran printed *Navid*, the organ of the Iranian communist party, the Tudeh. Both NVOI and *Navid* spread virulent anti-American propaganda and often employed blatant disinformation (Rubin 1980, 214; Moss 1978).

Still, Brzezinski was not able to prevail upon Vance and others in the administration who refused to censure the Soviet Union for breaking the rules of détente. Even when, in April 1978, the PDPA, with the help of Moscow, overthrew Daoud and established a communist regime in Afghanistan, the State Department did not protest. According to Theodore Eliot, the then ambassador to Kabul, Vance feared that severing ties with the new regime would only drive it deeper into the Soviet embrace (Scott 1996, 41–42; Ledeen and Lewis 1981).

Diplomatic license notwithstanding, the notion that the new communist regime of Noor Mohammad Taraki was somewhat independent of Moscow was a serious misrepresentation of reality. In fact, KGB agents were involved in the bloody coup in which Daoud, his entire family, and some 7,000 officers and officials were murdered. Moscow, represented by Ambassador Aleksandr Puzanov, was also closely involved in the running of the Taraki regime, which announced a sweeping revolutionary program. It was also the KGB that helped Taraki to conduct a bloody vendetta against Islamic fundamentalists and ethnic leaders who objected to the rapid social changes wrought by the revolution.

But it was only on June 1, 1978, that the intelligence community briefed Carter on the new Soviet estimate entitled "Soviet Goals and Expectations in the Global Arena." The report detailed direct Soviet military assistance and the use of proxies in a large number of Third World countries and provided a "somber assessment" of Moscow's overall goal of global expansion. De-scribed by Gates (1996, 74–75) as a "cold shower," the briefing hurt the standing of the New Internationalists in the administration. On August 15 a Policy Review Committee chaired by Vance took note of the growing Soviet influence in the "arc of crisis" in Asia and Africa. On August 24 Carter signed a Presidential Review Memorandum that called for containment of the So-viet Union along the "arc," a strategy urged by Brzezinski and the Depart-ment of Defense.

But the administration, badly divided between the cautious Vance, who was deeply invested in the SALT II negotiations, and the more assertive Brzezinski, could not agree on a plan of action. In any event, the spiraling crisis in Iran paralyzed the Carter team, with Brzezinski pushing for a mili-tary intervention to save the shah and the New Internationalists eager to bid goodbye to a regime that was high on their target list. Ironically, the Soviet Union had turned its new base in Afghanistan into a center of anti-shah ac-tivity, with KGB and Soviet military intelligence agents freely crossing the border hidden among the flood of Afghan refugees (Moss 1978). The frantic last-ditch efforts of the U.S. administration to establish a moderate and pro-Western successor regime in Iran failed, leaving the shaken Carter to face the staunchly anti-American Muslim fundamentalist leader Ayatollah Ruhallah Khomeini, who took over on February 1, 1979.

The profound geopolitical change in the Gulf region triggered by the fun-damentalist revolution in Iran dealt a severe blow to Carter's hope of leading the world into a new era of global cooperation and goodwill. To the neoconservative critics who had warned all along that Carter's human rights campaign would destabilize the Pahlavis, the bloody Khomeini regime was proof of the bankruptcy of Carter's international vision. This vision was all but undermined when, after an alarming increase in anti-American hostility in Iran, on November 4, a group claiming to represent revolutionary students attacked the U.S. embassy in Teheran and seized its entire staff. In spite of considerable pressure, the Iranian government held the hostages captive for 444 days, thus greatly contributing to the failure of Carter's bid for reelec-tion. Although the Soviet role in the embassy seizure had not been pivotal, it is known that some among the attackers had contacts with Soviet agents (Seliktar 2000, 169–71).

But it was the situation in Afghanistan that utterly undermined hope for a constructive détente policy. In the summer of 1978 the opposition to the Soviet-backed Taraki government erupted in a number of largely uncoordi-nated revolts in the provinces and there was episodic fighting in the capital, Kabul. On February 14, 1979, U.S. ambassador Adolph Dubs was killed, thus ending official American presence in the country. Meanwhile, personal and factional tensions in the ruling PDPA mounted. Babrak Kamal, the leader of the Parchan faction of the party, was banished, ending up in Moscow. Hafizuallah Amin, an associate of Taraki, became prime minister on March 28, although Taraki retained the post of president of the Revolutionary Council. On September 14, Amin seized all power and, on October 9, Taraki was murdered on Amin's orders.

Worried about the stiffening resistance to the regime, Amin tried to broaden his base of support by appealing to Pakistan and the United States. Unwilling to see a communist government unravel, the Soviet Union invaded Afghanistan on December 24, and on December 27 Amin was killed by agents from the Alpha group, the KGB's special forces created by Andropov in 1974. The special forces, for whom this was the first major operation, also purged many of Amin's followers and helped to install Babrak Kamal as the new leader of an orthodox communist government in Kabul (Andrew and Mitrokhin 1999, 389–91).

Going beyond mere tactical surprise, the Soviet invasion of Afghanistan left the Carter administration and the entire New Internationalist camp in turmoil. In particular, it embarrassed some leading experts who just months prior to the invasion had assured their readers that there was little evidence to support the impression of an expansionist Soviet leadership, as Robert Legvold (1979), the head of the Soviet Project at the Council on Foreign Relations, asserted. Equally discomforted were SOVA analysts who had ruled out future Soviet adventurism. Although there were some voices among the radical New Left who considered the invasion a legitimate application of the Brezhnev doctrine, or even a "defensive act," they were drowned out by a majority of observers who viewed Moscow's move as an egregious breach of the operating rules of détente.

Moreover, the action belied the assumptions of the revisionist model of the Soviet Union on which the New Internationalist version of détente had rested. Subsequent disclosures made it clear that the Politburo decision-making process bore no resemblance to the allegedly rational and pragmatic foreign policy model touted by some pluralist scholars. Far from being responsive to public sentiments, the decision to invade Afghanistan was taken by a small number of senior Politburo members on December 12. The KGB's Andropov, who believed that Amin was a CIA agent poised to take Afghanistan back into the Western orbit, dominated the meeting. Defense Minister Ustinov supported Andropov, but even the normally cautious Gromyko did not raise serious objections. According to Dobrynin, Gromyko underestimated the possible reaction of the Carter administration and the potential damage to détente. As in the case of Angola, Washington's failure to censure Soviet interference in Afghani internal relations and its hasty retreat following the murder of Dubs gave the hardliners in the Politburo a virtual carte blanche. Ironically, it was the general staff, which was apprehensive about inserting regular troops into a civil war fought in a difficult mountainous terrain, that emerged as the only dissenting voice. On December 26, Brezhnev rubberstamped the decision during a meeting with Andropov, Ustinov, Gromyko, and Konstantin Chernenko, a close associate of the ailing leader (Dobrynin 1995, 437–39; Gelman 1984, 170; Andrew and Gordievsky 1990, 574, 578; Greenstein and Wohlforth 1994, 35; Solovyov and Klepikova 1983, 180–83; Ekedahl and Goodman 1997, 184; Arbatov 1992, 197).

Faced with the collapse of his foreign policy, on December 28, Carter sent a message to Brezhnev demanding the immediate withdrawal of Soviet troops. On December 31, in a confession born of what some critics described as "crushed naiveté," Carter admitted that Afghanistan had made a dramatic change in his opinion of the Soviet goals. If Carter expected to garner some public support because of his fast learning curve, Ronald Reagan's victory in the November 1980 was a humiliating political rebuff. More important, like the war in Vietnam, which undermined the containment doctrine, Afghanistan discredited New Internationalism and the foreign policy elite that propagated it. Carter's own security adviser reflected this view when he accused the Democratic Party of moving "excessively to the left" and of becoming "excessively preoccupied with what might be called the do-gooder agenda in international relations." Brzezinski also infuriated the Democrats by seemingly blessing the hard-line Alexander Haig, Reagan's choice for secretary of state (Brinkley 1998, 93). Commenting on the "rise and fall" of this New Left elite, one observer noted that Carter's perception of the Soviet Union was not "a product of his naiveté but rather reflected the conventional wisdom of most government officials, academics, experts and others specializing in foreign affairs" (Gershman 1980, 13). Waiting in the wings to replace them were the neoconservatives who had greatly contributed to Reagan's victory and were poised to shape his vision of international relations.

4

The Reagan Administration and the Soviet Interregnum

Accelerating the Demise of the Communist Empire

Interpreting his victory as a mandate to rewrite American foreign policy, President Reagan moved rapidly to unveil a plan to vanquish the Soviet empire. At its center was an assumption that communism was an illegitimate and coercive system that could be destabilized and undermined by increasing its maintenance costs. However, the ambiguities of the long interregnum process in Moscow provided no clear confirmation that such a task was feasible or, indeed, prudent given the danger of a nuclear conflict. With a split between the anticommunist crusaders and the pragmatists in the administration growing, the forecasting process became increasingly politicized, a development that reignited the debate between the two contending paradigms in Sovietology.

The Neoconservative Paradigm in Action: The Administration's Blueprint for Delegitimizing the Soviet Union

Even before President Ronald Reagan took the oath of office in January 1981, the contour of his policy toward the Soviet Union was outlined by the Committee of Santa Fe and a transition team that included members and supporters of the Committee for Present Danger (CPD). Essentially, both teams agreed that the United States should go beyond containment and try to defeat the Soviet empire, which was viewed as internally brittle and susceptible to a concerted American effort to delegitimize and collapse it. The so-called "feet of clay" argument was made by Richard Pipes (1984c) and other transition team members, including Angelo Codevilla (1992, 378), an intelligence expert. According to this view, the Soviet Union had degenerated in the late '70s to a "premodern" and highly corrupt state that was vulnerable to external manipulation. The reports recommended a long list of policies that would subvert the communist regime and lead to its ultimate demise. To ensure that such policies would be given vigorous attention, Reagan appointed more than thirty members of the CPD to his foreign policy team, including Richard Allen, William Clark, Jeane Kirkpatrick, Paul Nitze, and Richard Perle. William Casey became the director of Central Intelligence and Richard Pipes was picked to serve as the Soviet expert on the National Security Council (NSC) (Scott 1996, 19). Although less of an ideologue, Secretary of State Alexander Haig was known to be a foe of communism.

At the very heart of the administration's philosophy was the belief that the international environment had changed in favor of the United States, a development that could be used to undermine the Soviet "correlation of forces." Unlike the New Internationalists, who worried that the United States was on the "wrong side of history," the neoconservatives resurrected Friedrich Hayek and Ludwig von Mises to argue that the international economy was irrevocably moving toward a market-oriented future. In one of the earliest expositions of this theme, a group at the conservative Hoover Institution predicted that the coming globalization and the spread of technology had given the United States a competitive edge over its rival (Duignan and Rabushka 1980). The Presidential Commission on Industrial Competitiveness reached the same conclusions, emphasizing that the United States and its economic allies like Japan, Taiwan, and South Korea had an advantage in terms of the "ingenuity factor," the rapid adaptation to changing conditions in an integrated global economy. Conversely, the rigid, semi-autarkic socialist economies were judged to have little success in a world where international exposure had created an "absolute productivity standard" and which put a premium on competitive specialization (Porter 1990, xii, 8; Homer-Dixon 2000, 21).

To capitalize on the new trends, CIA director Casey commissioned a number of "vulnerability studies" of the Soviet Union. The new director, who had little regard for the earlier Soviet estimates produced by the CIA, put Herbert Meyer, a former economic editor of *Fortune*, and Henry S. Rowen, a former president of RAND, in charge of the alternative estimates. David Wigg, Casey's White House liaison, was in charge of tracking Soviet hard currency flows and foreign exchange. These and other specialists reported that the Soviet Union was an "economic basket case," rapidly running out of foreign currency reserves and selling large quantities of gold to finance its growing dependence on foreign technology (Schweitzer 1994, 41, 64, 114). Economist Judy Shelton (1989, xi–xiii), who worked for Martin Anderson, a senior fellow at the Hoover Institute and a domestic adviser to Reagan, reached pretty much the same conclusion (Persico 1990, 284, 295).

The team's analysis of East European economies illuminated another trouble spot in the communist empire. To those who showed a keen interest in the vulnerabilities of the system, the Polish debt crisis of the early 1980s was a virtual red flag. The debt was accrued by the massive spending spree of Edward Gierek, who imported foodstuffs and consumer goods in a vain effort to fight a legitimacy crisis. Unable to pay off the debt, Warsaw turned to Moscow, which refused to cover the debt. That Moscow failed to deploy its "financial umbrella" over Poland, which was nearly bankrupt and in political turmoil, signaled to the Reagan team that the Soviet Union was no longer capable of bailing out its troubled external empire. Indeed, the hard currency debt of the Soviet Union and its satellites had increased nearly tenfold in one decade, reaching some 66 billion dollars in the beginning of the 1980s (Cohen 1986, 180; Dallin and Lapidus 1987). From the point of view of the administration, Moscow's struggle to keep up the inefficient economies of its Third World allies was another sign of potential vulnerability. John Hardt, a specialist at the Congressional Research Center, found that billions of rubles' worth of discounted oil and agricultural and industrial products went to Cuba, Afghanistan, Ethiopia, and other revolutionary venues (Flint 1980).

Using this and other data, the administration developed a formula for estimating the cost of the Soviet empire. Charles Wolf, Jr. (1982; 1983, v–vi, 43–46, 51), a close associate of Rowen's and one of the researchers involved, calculated that in the 1971–80 period the "total and component" costs of empire went up from $13.6 billion to $46.5 billion, an average annual growth of 8.7 percent. Representing some 2.7 percent of the Soviet GNP, this figure was well above the annual rate of growth of the Soviet economy. Using rational choice theory, Wolf argued that Moscow's willingness to incur the cost of maintaining and expanding its empire could be tempered if the United States would increase the "costs of imperial activity." As Casey (1989, 22) noted, the Soviet economy was "gasping" under its inherent inefficiencies and its burden of economic and military expenditures. Meyer asserted that the Soviet empire had "entered its terminal phase," giving him and others the confidence that the administration could destabilize the Soviet economy and society (Pemberton 1998, 157; Garthoff 1994, 163–64). To accelerate the communist demise, the administration developed a four-pronged attack plan.

The first prong was based on an economic warfare project against the Soviet Union. To begin with, the Casey team estimated that the post-1973 oil price increase greatly benefited Moscow, with each one-dollar-a-barrel increase adding annually $1 billion in hard currency to its coffers. These oil revenues helped the Soviet Union to finance revolutionary expansion in underdeveloped countries, increase aid to its client states, and bail out the politically distressed Eastern European satellites. To reverse this trend, Casey pressured Saudi Arabia—a key OPEC player—to lower oil prices by, among other things, increasing oil production. It was estimated that a $10 drop in the price of a barrel of oil would deprive the Soviet treasury of $10 billion a year. In one of the ironic twists of history, Casey's plan mimicked the successful Soviet effort in the 1970s to persuade OPEC to raise its prices (Schweitzer 1994, 105; Epstein 1986; Greenwald and Slocombe 1987; Sakharov and Tosi 1980, 279).

Another part of economic warfare involved efforts by the administration to manipulate international finances and trade in order to compound Soviet difficulties. Focusing on Polish debt, the Reagan administration tried to convince Western bankers that "sovereign risk," a term denoting a country's default on its debt, was a real possibility in the Soviet bloc. American efforts resulted in a considerable tightening of credits to the Soviet Union and, more importantly, to its European satellites, forcing Moscow to step in as a financial guarantor of last resort. The administration also sought to restrict Soviet access to Western technology and technological know-how. Building on the CIA's K Project, Casey strove to block Soviet access to Western technological markets and confounded its vast technological espionage program by restricting visas to foreign scholars and feeding scientific misinformation (Schweitzer 1994, 46–47, 83, 132, 187). A number of National Security Decisions Directives (NSDD) signed by President Reagan provided a legal mandate for these operations. NSDD-32, NSDD-66, and NSDD-75 authorized the government to "wage a protracted economic warfare" against the Soviet Union and "exacerbate the Soviet economic problem in order to plunge it into a crisis." Affirming that Soviet aggressiveness had "deep roots in the internal system," the administration planned to use this crisis in order to promote a "process of change in the Soviet Union toward a more pluralistic political and economic system" (Simpson 1995, 62–63, 68, 80, 255; Pemberton 1998, 156; Oye 1987).

The second prong, known as Project Democracy, involved political warfare to exploit the economic, ethnic, and political tensions in the Soviet Union and the Soviet bloc. At the center of this program was the National Endowment for Democracy (NED), created in 1983 to promote democratic freedoms, human rights, and free markets in communist states. The quasi-governmental NED was part of a broad strategy of public diplomacy that also included the Office of Public Diplomacy (OPD) and the U.S. Information Agency, headed by Charles Z. Wick, a Hollywood entrepreneur and personal friend of Reagan. Concluding that ideas became important in the growing global communications network, the public diplomacy program targeted East European audiences through the reinvigorated Radio Liberty and Radio Free Europe. In a less publicized part, the NED and other agencies sought to aid ethnic, religious, and political dissidents in the Soviet Union and the satellites. In his May 1982 NSDD-32 President Reagan ordered covert economic and political action to "strengthen indigenous forces for freedom in the region." Around the same time the RAND corporation prepared a number of studies on the delegitimation process in Eastern Europe, including disaffection among soldiers and workers. These papers also outlined plans for "institutionalization of dissent" in the Eastern bloc (Pemberton 1998, 156; Andrew 1995, 468; Rowen 1989).

In what turned out to be the model for such activities, the Reagan administration helped the Solidarity movement to undermine the legitimacy of the communist regime in Poland, long considered the weakest link in the Soviet empire. In November 1981, Secretary Haig noted that the "peaceful revolution" in Poland, if consolidated, would hurt Moscow's power in Eastern Europe. When, on December 12, General Wojciech Jaruzelski imposed martial law in Poland, the Reagan administration responded with a list of sanctions against the Soviet Union (MacEachin 2000, 4–11). On June 7, 1982, Reagan met with Pope John Paul II and Casey met with Archbishop Luigi Poggi, a leading Vatican diplomat. The president would later write that the events in Poland "were thrilling," giving the White House the hope that they might spread across Eastern Europe like a "contagion" (Reagan 1990, 301). In due course, a covert program that involved the NED, AFL-CIO, and the administration furnished Solidarity with money and equipment to publicize its cause. By early 1985 the United States was spending some $5 million a year to keep Solidarity afloat. That this was money well spent was confirmed when Solidarity's leader Lech Walesa was awarded the Nobel Peace Prize in October 1983, posing a moral threat to the Soviet hold on Eastern Europe (Gates 1996, 450; Pemberton 1998, 157).

The third prong was designed to increase the cost of Soviet Third World involvement. In what was a virtual reversal of roles, the United States stepped up its help to a large number of anticommunist insurgencies in Latin America, Africa, and Asia. In preparation for what became known as the Reagan Doctrine, the president asked Casey to identify anticommunist national liberation movements that the United States could support. By the mid-1980s Washington supported some thirteen such insurgencies, including the mujahedeen in Afghanistan. Commenting on how effective such efforts were in increasing Soviet costs, Casey emphasized that this reversal of roles was a new and promising phenomenon in international relations. Haig put it more bluntly, stating that the Soviets had to be persuaded that "their time of unresisted adventurism in the Third World is over" (Menges 1990, 6–7; Scott 1996, 18, 20; Lukes 1989).

The fourth prong entailed a massive buildup of both conventional and strategic weapons. As noted, neoconservative critics had long warned about Soviet military superiority and complained about the inadequacy of American response under Carter. Intelligence reports in the early 1980s argued that, in spite of economic problems, the Soviets showed no signs of cutting back on their extensive program of strategic modernization, which included land-based ICBMs, intermediate range SS-20s, submarine-launched ballistic missiles, and other weapons. Since the administration accepted the Team B argument that Moscow had developed a first strike doctrine, an American buildup made strategic sense. At its center was the Strategic Defense Initiative (SDI), a strategic shield around the United States that had been advocated by the physicist Edward Teller, the Joint Chiefs of Staff, and Project High Frontiers, a group of conservatives that included the outspoken anticommunist General Daniel Graham. The project, which was dubbed Star Wars, was also supported by the American Security Council (ASC) and the Coalition for Peace Through Strength, two groups established to counter the left-leaning Coalition for Peace Through Law. On March 23, 1983, in a speech entitled "Defense and National Security," Reagan laid out the SDI initiative (Graham 1995, 102–97; Teller 2001, 528; Oberdorfer 1992, 25; Shultz 1993, 256).

By deciding on a large military buildup topped by the SDI, the Reagan administration hoped to achieve more than just a defense of the United States. The technologically sophisticated and costly military program was also aimed at further squeezing the hard-pressed Soviet economy. As Robert Gates (1996, 539), who became Deputy Director for Intelligence (DDI) in 1982, put it, the Soviet leaders, "already panting hard as they tried to keep pace with current and prospective U.S. military developments . . . were left breathless by one U.S. military initiative after another." Accordingly, the United States planned to develop weapons that were "difficult for the Soviets to counter, impose disproportionate cost, open up new areas of major military competition and obsolesce previous Soviet investment" (Huntington 1983, 94). It was subsequently disclosed that the Star Wars project rigged a crucial 1984 test as part of a deception campaign to persuade the Soviets to spend billions of rubles to match the American initiative (Weiner 1993). In this sense, the American "warriors of disinformation," as one book called them, borrowed a page from Soviet efforts at nuclear deception (Snyder 1995, 1; Ziegler 1997).

While most of the items in the program to destabilize the Soviet Union were secret, President Reagan intensified his public effort to delegitimize communism. In his first presidential press conference, on January 29, 1981, Reagan declared that since 1917 all Soviet leaders had sought to promote revolution, adding that they considered it "moral to lie and cheat for the purpose of advancing communism" (Reagan 1990, 267).

In May, in a speech at Notre Dame University, the president responded to Khrushchev's taunt that socialism would bury the West. He declared that the United States would not only contain communism but also transcend it, turning the communist experiment into a "sad, bizarre chapter in human history whose last pages are now being written." Reagan repeated the same theme in a June 1982 speech before the British Parliament, where he predicted that "the march of freedom and democracy . . . will leave Marxism-Leninism on the ash heap of history as it has left other tyrannies, which stifle the freedom and muzzle the self expression of people." In his March 8, 1983, speech to an evangelical convention in Orlando, the president called the Soviet Union an "evil empire" and urged people to "pray for the salvation of all those who live in totalitarian darkness" (Pipes 1995b, 157; Fitzgerald 2000, 154; Anderson 1988, xxxii; Reagan 1990, 570).

In spite of the harsh and undiplomatic vocabulary, Reagan's speeches were carefully calibrated for effect. Jack Matlock, a Soviet specialist on the NSC and an ambassador to Moscow, admitted that the "purpose was to delegitimize the system." Martin Anderson (1988, xxxiii) wrote that Reagan deliberately threw the Soviets off balance by striking at the "soft underbelly of the Soviet political system, its moral mooring." Turning the tables on communism, the president promised to lead a democratic revolution that would "foster the infrastructure of democracy—the system of a free press, unions, political parties, universities—which allows people to choose their own way" (Dallin and Lapidus 1987, 221).

Reagan's bold gamble to expedite the demise of the Soviet empire stirred up a heated controversy in the foreign policy community. Reaction was swift and predictable. Conservatives and neoconservatives lauded the president and wholeheartedly agreed that, in the words of Podhoretz (1981, 40), the conflict between the United States and USSR was a conflict between two civilizations, or rather between "civilization" and "barbarism." Many in the conservative camp were encouraged when the journalist George Feifer (1981) published an article in *Harper's* that depicted the depth of economic disarray and predicted the "end of the socialist dream." To quote one observer, Feifer's devastating portrayal of decay amounted to uncovering of the "real Russia" (Buchanan 1982).

However, liberals, beholden to the tenets of New Internationalism, decried Reagan's policy as misguided and dangerous. Speaking in 1982, Democratic senator Christopher Dodd declared that the United States was "on the wrong side of history." Social scientist Alan Wolfe (1982, 241) dismissed the conservative assumption that capitalism was bound to win. In a book about the "American impasse," he affirmed that the "theoretical beauty of market-based models was eliminated." The Sovietologist Stephen Cohen (1986, 17) explained in a 1983 article that Reagan's foreign policy was driven by Sovietophobia. A Reagan biographer called the president's "devil history of the Soviet Union" "predictable and primitive ideology," a sentiment shared by other liberal commentators (Dugger 1983, 355, 373).

The Council on Foreign Relations created a special study group to warn against Reagan's Soviet policy. Strobe Talbott (1984b, 74–75), one of the participants, scorned the "unprecedented assertion" that the United States "had the ability to effect crucial changes" in the Soviet system. Talbott was particularly hard on Richard Pipes, the intellectual father of the anti-Soviet crusade as epitomized in NSDD-75. Talbott described him as the "principal theoretician" of the view that "the Soviet Union could be tamed if not dismantled." He called this theorizing "idiosyncratic, extremist and very much confined to the fringes of government" (Pipes 2003, 193). Historian Arthur Schlesinger, Jr. (1983, 5) declared that the president's approach represented a "mighty comeback" of messianism. These and other observers warned that Reagan's unprecedented break with past foreign policy tradition would make the Soviets more belligerent and strengthen the hard-liners. Talbott (1984b, 7) quoted the Soviet expert Seweryn Bialer who, upon return from a trip to the Soviet Union, wrote in an editorial that he had found "combative, angry people in Moscow." As the Brezhnev era was coming to a close, the developments in Moscow were to provide a reality check for both sides.

The Brezhnev-Andropov Transition: The View from Moscow

By the early 1980s Brezhnev's health problems, which according to accounts included leukemia, a heart condition, emphysema, arteriosclerosis of the brain, and a number of strokes, had severely reduced his physical and mental capacity. Sleeping pills for his chronic insomnia and addiction to prescription drugs had resulted in slurred speech, attacks of chronic fatigue, and temporary paralysis. General Dmitri Volkogonov (1998, 302–18), a former head of the Soviet army's political administration, revealed that the Soviet chief had problems with speaking and other cognitive functions. In addition to the doctors who treated him, Brezhnev put his faith in Dzhuna Davitashvili, an Assyrian faith healer from the Caucasus who was popular in elite party circles (Solovyov and Klepikova 1983, 172–73, 258; Dobbs 1997, 6–7, 8, 84; Doder 1988; Dobrynin 1995, 476).

In spite of a Herculean effort to stage-manage Brezhnev—special escalators were installed to climb steps, and speech writers were instructed to avoid long words that he could not pronounce—his public appearance attested to his increasing frailty. On numerous occasions he was seen disoriented or clinging to his colleagues for support. In March 1982, after a visit to Tashkent, Brezhnev suffered a stroke, and in a September appearance in Baku, after his notes became mixed up, he started to read the wrong speech in full view of a national television audience. At his last function, celebrating the anniversary of the revolution on November 7, he stood almost paralyzed on top of the Mausoleum. To compensate for such shortcomings, Brezhnev had continued to receive awards and medals and his ghostwritten literary work was nominated by the Writers' Union for the Lenin Prize and glowingly reviewed by leading writers (Felshman 1992, 107–8; Solovyov and Klepikova 1983, 236–35, 259; Arbatov 1992; 1973, 254; Doder 1988, 96; Volkogonov 1998, 324).

With Brezhnev progressively incapacitated, the system, which lacked an orderly mechanism for transfer of power, reached a stage of almost total immobilism. Politburo meetings were reduced to 15–20 minutes to accommodate Brezhnev's short attention span, and important projects were either rubber-stamped by the not-always-coherent general secretary or postponed. In the highly centralized decision-making system, regional officials had to travel to Moscow, where their access was limited to a "window of opportunity" dictated by the fact that many Politburo members were part of the "ruling gerontocracy" with a median age in the late seventies. Some, like the 78-year-old prime minister Nikolai Tikhonov, dozed through longer sessions or kept only a skeletal workweek. Many officials were part of the so-called Dnepropetrovsk Mafia, close associates and cronies of Brezhnev who had a reputation for inefficiency or corruption. To avoid competition, Brezhnev had favored gray and mediocre personalities, leading one observer to dub the system the "survival of the blandest." Emblematic of this category was Chernenko, a drab apparatchik, and General Nikolai A. Shchelokov, under whose leadership the Interior Ministry reached "unprecedented levels of corruption." The inner circle advanced their careers by catering to Brezhnev's pathological vanity rather than attending to state business (Gorbachev 1996, 134; Yeltsin 1990, 69, 142; Solovyov and Klepikova 1983, 62, 231; Arbatov 1992, 251, 253; Dobbs 1997, 5–6, 109; Ligachev 1993, 148).

Reagan's vigorous anticommunist campaign compounded the burdens of the dysfunctional system. Already in 1979 the Central Committee commissioned a special comparative analysis of the Soviet and American economies that showed that the gap between the outputs of the two countries was widening at a "nonlinear rate." By the early 1980, billions of petrodollars disappeared, due to lower oil prices and the depletion of natural resources, making it harder to cover budgetary shortfalls at a time when consumer shortages were becoming more acute. Adding to the difficulties was the intractable agricultural sector, whose inefficiency drained the treasury of foreign currency needed to import grains. The catastrophic lack of infrastructure—the Soviet Union, with an area of some 300,000 square miles, had fewer paved roads than Texas—rounded out a picture of decay and degradation in transportation, housing, health, and the environment. Perhaps the most staggering problem was posed by the technological backwardness of the country, which had virtually no computer industry and little in terms of information technology. The Central Committee plenum on technology, planned for the late 1970s, was postponed a few years in a row, casting doubt on whether the party was ready to launch the long-heralded technological revolution.

Even the enfeebled Brezhnev and his septuagenarian colleagues understood that the deteriorating quality of life eroded the remnants of the social contract. Although the 26th Party Congress, which took place on February 23–March 3, 1981, still glorified "mature socialism," Brezhnev delivered an unusually somber report. He hinted that the "correlation of forces" was turning against the Soviet Union, leading to an official conclusion that the period under review had been "rough and complicated" (Crouch 1990, 56). The widespread pubic discontent over food shortages in the winter of 1981–82 prompted the party to promise a Food Program followed by an announcement, in June 1982, that the government would increase production of consumer goods. However, the Food Program, launched with great fanfare, soon petered out and efforts to shift spending into consumer programs had run into fierce opposition from the military and the military industry.

In fact, Reagan's challenge to the regime stung the military, already unhappy with the economic problems and the failure to keep up with the micro-electronic revolution. The continuing slowdown of the economy had reduced the expansion in machine building on which the armament industry depended, making the proposed shift to consumer goods even more threatening. In the summer of 1981, Chief of General Staff Nikolai Ogarkov took his dispute with Brezhnev public, warning about the American arms buildup and demanding more spending on the military. However, the Politburo, concluding that consumer shortages had caused the legitimacy crisis in Poland, pushed through a Five-Year Plan that seemed to assign a higher priority to light industry. Ogarkov responded with more alarmist publications about the danger of war, a sentiment that was apparently shared by the upper echelons of the armed forces. Moving to confront the unprecedented dispute, during a consultation with the military chiefs on October 27, 1982, Brezhnev promised to meet "all the needs of the military" to counter American rearmament programs. Although there were rumors that Brezhnev planned to use his concessions to fire Ogarkov, the insubordinate chief of staff was still in power when the general secretary died on November 10 (Doder 1988, 99–100; Gelman 1984, 179–80; Azrael 1987, vii; Herspring 1990, 206).

That a fierce guns vs. butter debate could take place amid a deep systemic crisis did not surprise a growing number of internal critics of the Brezhnev regime who gradually congealed into the "second pivot" reformist elite. Unlike the better-known dissidents who openly challenged the party, members of this group worked on the margins of the legitimate intellectual establishment. Many of them were young academics employed by the various institutes of the USSR Academy of Sciences, including the prestigious Institute of the World Economy and International Relations (IMEMO) in Moscow and the Institute of Economics and Organization of Industrial Production in Akademgorodok near Novosibirsk. Often described as "havens of official dissent" or "oases of creative thinking," these institutes had access to foreign publications and, over time, developed a fairly good understanding of Western economy. Some received classified material from the KGB-controlled Progress Publishing House, which translated Western social science literature (Strayer 1998, 65; Arbatov 1992, 236; Suraska 1998, 24–25).

Abel Agenbegyan, the head of the Novosibirsk institute, and his associate, Tatyana Zaslavskaya, took an early lead in reviving the idea of a "socialist market economy" first articulated by the economist Yevsei Liberman, an adviser to the short-lived economic reforms of Prime Minister Aleksei Kosygin in the 1960s. Liberman advocated light industry, incentives for economic efficiency, and decentralization as a means of promoting technological development. The USSR State Committee on Science and Technology—dubbed the Soviet RAND and headed by Dzherman Gvishiani, the son-in-law of Kosygin—promoted equally unorthodox ideas. In the early '70s, Agenbegyan took a huge risk when, during a secret conference, he informed Kosygin that his reforms were failing and that the Soviet Union was suffering from hidden inflation obscured by official statistics. In 1978 Agenbegyan used a novel econometric model to warn that the Soviet "society is on the verge of collapse" (Smith 1990, 10; Aron 2000, 484; Sheehy 1990, 134).

Collectively, the Novosibirsk team, Gvishiani's economists, and other unorthodox thinkers developed a comprehensive critique of socialist economy and society. Echoing the Austrian school, they blamed the lack of market feedback for the inefficient allocation of resources and linked the absence of incentives to low productivity. In her pioneering work on human capital, the sociologist Zaslavskaya (1990, 105, 106) argued that the socialist ideal of "egalitarian leveling," which severs the relation between a person's contribution and remuneration, hampered the "development and realization of human abilities." Zaslavskaya posited that efforts to institute what she described as a utopian scheme of distributive justice, coupled with state paternalism, resulted in a society permeated by hypocrisy, mendacity, and corruption, and populated by alienated and apathetic individuals who had lost even the most basic economic habits. Building on these themes, Agenbegyan wrote in an October 1981 article that the absence of work ethics and endemic alcoholism had produced an intolerable drag on the Soviet economy (Novak 2000, 94; Smith 1990, 10).

Another group of relatively junior officials came to realize the shortcomings of communism while touring or serving abroad. The comparison between West and East planted seeds of doubt about the superiority of their system. Ruslan Khasbulatov (1993, 6), a future leader in the Gorbachev revolution, revealed that after returning from Canada, which was affluent, clean, and neat, he could not accept the official party line that the West was "decaying" and the USSR was prospering. Aleksandr N. Yakovlev, Moscow's ambassador to Ottawa, became another pro-Western convert through this type of "demonstration effect." Yakovlev, who had been "exiled" to Canada for challenging official orthodoxy in 1972, concluded that the remarkably well functioning Western system was a result of the market economy. Less-known reformist figures emerged among the *mezhdunarodniki*, literally, internationalists, who worked as international policy analysts, journalists, diplomats, and publicists representing the Soviet Union in the West. Ironically, this small army created by Moscow to understand and manipulate the West, ended up undermining the "certainty of the system." Unlike the poorly educated, xenophobic Brezhnev generation, these Westernized liberals sought to replace the class-based view of international relations with the philosophy of "universal human values," laying an early foundation of what became subsequently known as New Political Thinking. Pro-Americanism "became part of their social identity" and a symbol of rejection of the Soviet system (English 2000, 70–72, 121, 147; Andrew and Gordievsky 1990, 624; Shiraev and Zubok 2000, 26).

Though quite comprehensive, the critique of the "institute academics," the *mezhdunarodniki*, and others who were exposed to the West would have amounted to little without the backing of more influential reformist elite. Coming up the party ranks in the 1960s and 1970s, this group was comprised of relatively junior regional party officials like Mikhail Gorbachev, Boris Yeltsin, Yegor Ligachev, and Eduard Shevardnadze, among others. They were part of a larger political cohort known as *shestidesiatniki*, literally, those who came of age in the 1960s, after Khrushchev's secret speech denouncing Stalin. Although socialized into the traditional communist mold and conformist on the surface, these "young Turks" had become disenchanted with the inefficient, corrupt, and highly secretive system. They watched in dismay as "Brezhnev and the other senile leaders . . . had become symbols of the decay, decline and erosion of the system," to quote one of them (Volkogonov 1998, 326). Volkogonov and others confessed to feeling ashamed of "our state, of its half-dead leaders, of the encroaching senility," and outraged by the corruption and thievery (Dobbs 1997, 26). Shevardnadze (1991, 123), who served as the KGB boss and the first secretary in Georgia, was appalled at the level of corruption in his republic. Yeltsin, who started his career as an engineer in charge of a home-building *kombinat* in Sverdlovsk, was well aware of the rampant vandalism and thievery on construction sites across the country. Yeltsin also recalled his loathing of the privileges accorded to the nomenklatura and the "obsequiousness and obedience" demanded from officials in turn for preferential treatment, which lead to the "sycophancy" surrounding Brezhnev (Aron 2000, 39, 77–79; Yeltsin 1990, 155, 157–58; 2000, 73–74).

The highly secretive system that shielded the Brezhnev leadership bothered many of these cohorts. Gorbachev (1996, 133, 203–4) revealed that, in an effort to protect himself from criticism, Brezhnev turned large parts of the economy, including the military industry and foreign trade, into "closed zones" of secrecy. The lack of information was so acute that even senior Politburo members did not know the full picture. The statistical bodies—State Committee on Statistics (Goskomstat) and the State Planning Committee (Gosplan)—often used incompatible data, and all efforts to realistically appraise the situation "were nipped in the bud." Overall, the amount of official data had steadily declined, with problems like crime and substance abuse being "solved" by simply "discontinuing information about them" (White 1990, 66–68).

Individually and collectively, members of this loosely knit network of would-be reformers reached a conclusion that the potemkinization of Soviet life and the resultant discrepancy between "word and deed," as Shevardnadze (1991, 27, 87, 123) put it, was built into the system. In this view, the endemic corruption and other problems of the economy were equally systemic, bred by a political culture in which "deception and fraud are elevated to the highest honor." Shevardnadze, who began experimenting with economic reforms in Georgia, discussed these issues with Gorbachev. They would later agree that "everything is rotten. It has to be changed." When Gorbachev was made party secretary for agriculture in 1979, he began meeting with a number of social scientists, including Zaslavskaya. By his own admission, Gorbachev (1996, 148–50) was deeply impressed when he visited Yakovlev in Canada in October 1981. Yakovlev subsequently revealed that Gorbachev told him that under the condition of dictatorship and absence of freedom, the country "will perish" and complained about the "stupidity" of deploying the SS-20 missiles (Zaslavskaya 1990, xi; Kreisler 1996; Ekedahl and Goodman 1997, xi).

Much as the "young Turks" desired to change the system, they would have never made it into positions of power and influence without the help of

Andropov. The much older KGB chief did not fit the category of "second pivot" elite, but during his long years as the chief spymaster he formed some negative impressions of the communist system. Under his leadership the KGB became the repository of the best statistical data on the Soviet empire, some of which came from a secret economic department he had created. These and other materials made Andropov aware of the true extent of economic stagnation and the related problems of corruption, absenteeism, alcoholism, and health and environmental degradation. The KGB's large quantitative economic model showed that the "correlation of forces" in political, military, and economic terms had turned in the West's favor by the late 1970s (Kaiser 1991, 57, 97; Lee 1997, 97).

Not unlike the reformist elite, Andropov understood the effects of the potemkinization and corruption on the legitimacy of the regime. The KGB's secret opinion polls and sociological research, much of it using Western methodology, indicated the depth of anomie and deviancy, especially among the youth. This research indicated that even the Young Pioneers' vaunted model, Pavlik Morozov, who had denounced his father as a kulak during Stalin's collectivization drive, was held in deep contempt (Shlapentokh 1988, 5; Crouch 1990, 84; Lewin 1991, 86–88). Andropov was also worried about the revival of religion, in the Muslim and Christian republics alike. Viewed against the background of the Polish crisis, the flammable relationship between religion and nationality alarmed the KGB chief, who was also well aware of the brisk spread of Protestant sects. That such a religious resurgence could take place after decades of official atheism and religious persecution was sobering to Andropov, who, according to a Polish source, conceded that the Soviet Union had a "church problem" (Lane 1978; Crozier, Middleton, and Murray-Brown 1985, 289; Shultz 1993, 124).

Ranking highest on Andropov's list of ills was corruption, especially in the Asiatic republics, whose system by the early 1980s had turned into "feudal socialism." As noted by one observer, the KGB chief had to confront the "accursed problem of authoritarian and totalitarian regimes: control over its ruling class" (Holmes 1993, 223). Starting with the so-called "caviar scandal" in 1979, the KGB arrested and demoted senior officials, among them Sergei Medunov, the first secretary of the Krasnodar region, and moved against party bosses of Georgia, Azerbaijan, and other Asian and Transcaucasian republics. Andropov was behind a secret Central Committee resolution in September 1980 to mount an anticorruption campaign and pushed for more vigorous measures at the 26th Party Congress. The campaign intensified in November 1981 when newspapers carried exposés about a multimillion-dollar embezzlement scheme in Georgia and the theft of a large quantity of meat in Minsk. Most incendiary was the announcement, on December 27, that stolen diamonds were found in the possession of a famous performer and a close friend of Brezhnev's daughter, Galina Churbanov (Doder 1988, 53).

There is no doubt that Andropov, a man of modest personal tastes, was appalled at the excesses of the Brezhnev regime. However, Andropov had also turned corruption into a weapon in his increasingly bold succession struggle against Brezhnev loyalists. Many of the officials targeted were either part of the Brezhnev network or, like the Asian bosses, were known to have given lavish presents to Brezhnev, his family, and his cronies. In addition to Galina, who was implicated in the diamond scandal, Brezhnev's son-in-law Yuri Churbanov was accused of corruption and malfeasance. What made the attack on the Brezhnev family especially poignant was the fact that on January 19, 1982, General Semyon Tsvigun, deputy chairman of the KGB and Brezhnev's brother-in-law, was found dead in his office—an alleged suicide. In March, Aleksei Shibayev, chairman of the Soviet trade unions and a Brezhnev protégé, was fired for misuse of funds, which, according to rumors, were used to build private dachas and fund sexual orgies (Aron 2000, 114; Solovyov and Klepikova 1983, 269; Doder 1988, 62; Knight 1988, 88–89, 92–93).

In fact, according to some sources, toward the end of his life Brezhnev lived in increasing fear of Andropov. The KGB chief was rumored to be behind the public mishaps that Brezhnev suffered in Tashkent and Baku. Andropov was regularly informed about Brezhnev's health by his physician, Dr. Yevgeni Chazov, the head of the fourth directorate in the Ministry of Health in charge of members of the Politburo. Over Chazov's objections, Andropov insisted on a grueling schedule of public appearances for the Soviet leader, which featured the final and fatal four-hour lineup on top of the Mausoleum. Indeed, Andropov's reputation for ruthlessness was already well established after two potential Brezhnev successors in the Politburo—Fyodor Kulakov and Pyotr Masherov—died under mysterious circumstances in 1978 and 1980. Others were disgraced by scandals. In 1978, First Deputy Prime Minister Kiril Mazurov was suddenly dismissed, possibly because of secret KGB files that were given to Brezhnev. The reputation of Gregory Romanov, the party boss from Leningrad, was tarnished because of an incident at the wedding of his daughter in 1979 that was allegedly manufactured by the KGB. Romanov had been a protégé of Kosygin and Suslov, who had made him a full Politburo member and showcased him before foreign delegations visiting Moscow. Andrei Kirilenko, a prominent Politburo member, was a victim of persistent rumors that he was senile. He was finally disgraced in 1982 when his son-in-law, a high-ranking official, was accused of defecting to England and his stepson was charged with embezzlement while working for the Soviet trade mission in Switzerland (Doder 1988, 66, 83; Azrael 1989,

26; Felshman 1992, 97; Solovyov and Klepikova 1983, 162–65, 231–33; Solovyov and Klepikova, 1986, 30).

It is impossible to establish with full certainty whether the KGB chairman was behind all these events. What matters, rather, is that the entire trajectory of the succession struggle left Andropov facing the aging Chernenko as the only real contender for power. Andropov's chances were greatly enhanced when, in May 1982, he was made the secretary of the Central Committee. Still, according to the Moscow rumor mill, a Brezhnev ally, General Shchelokov, in a desperate effort to stop Andropov, tried to arrest him on September 10, a plot that was foiled by the KGB. Building on his alliance with Marshal Ustinov and Foreign Minister Gromyko and the alleged blackmail of other Politburo members, Andropov was elected as the first secretary a few hours after the announced death of Brezhnev on November 11, 1982 (Solovyov and Klepikova 1983, 257; Hazan 1987, 136).

The Brezhnev-Andropov Transition: The View from Washington

For the Reagan administration, which set out to undermine the legitimacy of the Soviet Union, analysis of the developments in Moscow was at a premium. CIA director William Casey, who distrusted the Agency, ordered a major reshuffling of the Soviet division. In his capacity as the new DDI, Robert Gates tried to bolster what he regarded as "flabby complacent thinking" of the analytical branch (Perry 1992, 225; Gates 1989, 114; Codevilla 1992, 237; Ranelagh 1987, 689).

To what extent such prodding helped is not clear, but overall the CIA's secret reports and public testimony to the Joint Economic Committee (JEC) of the U.S. Congress in 1981 and 1982 painted a fairly accurate picture of the Soviet economy and society. Listing "constrained" raw material and energy resources as well as demographic problems, one report predicted an average GNP growth of 2 percent or less and concluded that the disproportionately high military burden would undermine the system's ability to satisfy the population. The guns vs. butter dilemma faced by the Soviet leadership was discussed in another analysis, which stated that military expenditure diverted funds from "critically needed resources in agriculture, industry and transportation." In his October 9, 1981, testimony to the JEC, Henry Rowen emphasized that "the [Soviet] economy is in a great deal of difficulty," depicting the Soviet leadership as having a "very serious problem." Rowen described a "cynical population" that had lost its expectation that standards of living would improve in the next decade. A number of papers provided a detailed description of nationality problems, including the dramatic increase in Muslim populations and its implication for the future stability of the Soviet Union (Haines and Leggett 2001, 301–3; MacEachin 1996, no. 23; CIA Documents, PA81–10199, ER81–10021, SOV81–10003X; NF81–10012).

The continuing woes of the Soviet economy dominated reports in 1982. The Agency predicted that the diminishing labor pool would force Brezhnev into increasingly "politically painful choices" and expressed little faith in his economic reforms, which were described as steps on the "treadmill." CIA analysts also deemed the Food Program to be a failure and predicted that the continuing imports of food would further deplete Moscow's foreign currency reserves. In what looked like a vindication of the administration's plans to restrict credits, the Agency warned of a growing Soviet dependency on Western trade and a coming "credit crunch" (CIA Documents, SOV82–10017; SOV82–10068; SOV82–10145; SOV82–10130; SOV-82–10018).

As the succession struggle in Moscow intensified, the CIA published a number of leadership assessment papers, including the comprehensive "Soviet Political Succession: Institutions, People and Politics" of April 1982. The report correctly identified the corruption scandals and discussed the generational differences in the Politburo, but the Agency had little inkling of Andropov's machinations and his chances were not rated high. A prior report had named Chernenko or Kirilenko as most likely candidates to succeed Brezhnev. As for the younger leadership—Gorbachev, Romanov, and Moscow party boss Viktor Grishin—SOVA expected a return to a neo-Stalinist orthodoxy rather than liberalization (CIA Documents, SOV82–10063X; Haines and Leggett 2001, 302). Still, Casey, who relied on outside sources, had picked Andropov as the most likely successor (Andrew 1995, 469).

Limited by its analytical parameters, the Agency was hardly in a position to capture the subterranean and often esoteric legitimacy discourse of the "second pivot" elite. While Rowens's testimony could be construed as forecasting a coming crisis of legitimacy, the warning was too general and the corruption scandals—normally a sign of impending changes in validity claims—were not given much prominence. There were even fewer tools in the CIA's analytical apparatus to plumb the depth of delegitimation that the communist system had suffered among the population and parts of its own elite. It was left to academic commentators to provide a more systemic view of the problem.

However, the competing paradigms in Sovietology produced differing assessments of the last two years of Brezhnev's tenure. The totalitarian theorists and their intellectual disciples viewed the glass as half-empty, focusing on the continuous legitimacy crisis at the national, authority, and economic levels. The French scholar Hélène Carrère d'Encausse (1982, 234, 246–47, 312, 329, 335, 340) wrote about the "anachronism," contradictions," and "sclerosis of the system," and noted that the party, which had tried to legitimize its power as "bearers of social progress" and ended as "socialist barons," had lost its legitimacy. In line with the Soviet reformers, d'Encausse argued that national, religious, and individualist values had sprouted in spite of the "Pavlik Morozov" ethos of collectivist socialization. Echoing the preference falsification theme in rational choice theory, she warned against judgments based on external display of pro-regime behavior and predicted the imminent collapse of the Soviet empire. Wesson (1980, 76, 101–31), reached a similar conclusion, emphasizing that some problems, especially minorities, "represent an unsolved and probably unsolvable problem for the Soviet state." The émigré lawyer Konstantin Simis (1982), utilizing his experience in the Soviet Ministry of Justice, published a comprehensive exposé on corruption in the Soviet Union and its delegitimizing effect on the system.

More limited accounts discussed a litany of problems, including low productivity, alcoholism, high mortality rates, and even hunger. One study showed that the command economy was so target-driven that it even imposed "death quotas" on hospitals, dictating the number of people who were expected to die there (Davis and Feshbach 1980; Clayton 1980; O'Hearn 1980; Treml 1982; Feshbach 1982; Gidwitz 1982; Balzer 1982; Gray 1981). A growing body of work indicated that national sentiments fueled by religion or a sense of relative deprivation were on the rise in the republics. All this evidence led one observer to speculate whether the Soviet Union was the "last of the empires." Still, many of the experts were not sure whether the Soviet successor generation, socialized in the rigid party mold, would be willing to make the necessary changes (Vardys 1980; Hahn 1981; Karklins 1981; Bahry and Nechemias 1981; Seton-Watson 1980; Laqueur 1981).

The neoconservative view received some unexpected support from a number of studies that took issue with Hough's thesis that there was meaningful participation in the Soviet Union. Stating that "we saw . . . nothing like free, spontaneous political action either possible or contemplated," one study suggested that the Communist Party was confronted with a "serious crisis of identity" (Hill, Dunmore, and Dawisha 1981, 216–17; Little 1980; Theen 1981; Unger 1981; Moses 1981). The émigré scholar Vladimir Shlapentokh (1989, 79, 92, 92, 93) rounded out this picture by providing a detailed analysis of Soviet anomie. Perhaps most interesting was the change of heart by Robert Tucker, one of the early critics of the totalitarian model. In a high-profile article in *Foreign Affairs*, Tucker (1981–82, 415) called Russia a "swollen state" and a "spent society," noting that the nomenklatura class "live in a relatively closed world of privilege" that contrasted so sharply with that of ordinary citizens that "they could be almost living in different countries."

As always, East European dissidents were much bolder, declaring that the

Soviet Union was in the throes of a systemic crisis that could be only addressed by political freedoms and a market economy (Kolakowski 1980). In a prominent article, Solzhenitsyn (1980) accused American Sovietologists of whitewashing the Soviet reality of poverty, terror, and inhuman cruelty and claimed that his compatriots despised the communist system, which exploited them to the point of "near extinction."

Practitioners of revisionist paradigms were not convinced that these problems amounted to a legitimacy crisis. Seweryn Bialer, a prominent Sovietologist, wrote that the "Brezhnev period will probably go down in history as the most successful period of Soviet international and domestic development," and that it enabled the leadership to pursue both guns and butter. As for the economic difficulties, he described them as "stringent times" that by no means reached the level of a systemic crisis. On the contrary, the "Party's role enjoyed widespread legitimacy." Bialer also took issue with Reagan's policy, arguing that it was "unrealistic to expect to inhibit Soviet growth" by escalating the arms race (Bialer 1980a; 1980b; 1981, 999; 1983a; 1983b, 39; Bialer and Gustafson 1992, 5). While acknowledging serious shortcomings, other observers felt that the system was not in imminent danger (Nove 1980, 17; 1982; Cohen 1980). Revisionist-oriented social scientists also had a greater faith in the popular legitimacy of the regime. White (1980, 339), who reviewed a large number of socialization studies, found no evidence "that the Soviet political education and lecturing system has in some sense been a failure." Disputing Solzhenitsyn, Dallin (1980, 195) claimed that the party had secured "the basic acquiescence and support of at least significant parts of the population which share in their country's pride over achievements . . . [and] many have been effectively socialized into believing what they are taught."

As if to bolster the claim of popular legitimacy, a much celebrated social history of the Russian revolution published by Oxford University Press argued that much of it was a spontaneous outbreak of a cultural struggle of working-class and militant atheistic youth and that "violence based on class resentment and prejudice was not an officially sanctioned part of the Cultural Revolution." Local activists were said to occasionally "desecrate the church or insult local 'class enemies' like the priest and schoolteacher." A *Newsweek* review described the book as "an admirable effort to rescue from politics the greatest upheaval of modern times and reclaim it for history" (Fitzpatrick 1982, 125, 131–32; 1984).

As for the crisis of legitimacy in the republics, political scientists like Hough (1982a) felt that Western preoccupation with the Central Asian republics was "probably exaggerated," but conceded that the Soviet Union would have to face the problem "probably within a decade." Olcott (1982) argued that, in contrast to Western assertions, Soviet leaders "find little threat in current Muslim revival." Lapidus (1984, 578) felt that the expectations of Western observers of ethnic destabilization were exaggerated because "the Soviet regime imposes severe constraints on the political mobilization of ethnicity."

Directly or by implication, much of the academic debate amounted to a referendum on the wisdom and effectiveness of Reagan's policy toward the Soviet Union. As expected, conservatives found that "squeezing" Moscow and increasing its "opportunity cost" was effective in terms of creating difficulties in technology transfers, trade, and foreign currency deficits. Still, many of them warned that, although devoid of internal legitimacy, Soviet leadership would not be easily swayed from pursuing its ideological mission of empire building. Pointing to the KGB's propaganda campaign, they warned that the USSR used deception to evade arms control and split NATO (Laqueur 1980; Pipes 1980; Wolf 1982; Coffman and Klecheski 1982; Bertsch 1980; Rush 1982–83; Andelman 1982; Wädekin 1982).

Some critics of the Reagan administration policy expressed doubt that U.S. efforts to manipulate events in the Soviet empire could succeed. Commenting on the notion that the Solidarity-driven democratization in Poland would encourage other satellites, Hough contended that in "the real world" such a "maximalist scenario" had a quality of "wishful thinking." He added that it was "almost impossible to imagine a national level Solidarity with any real political or even economic independence being established soon" (Hough 1982b 4, 63, 165). Bialer was skeptical that the deteriorating economy would give Washington leverage, noting that "it is unrealistic to believe that American policies can achieve a fundamental reorientation of Soviet policymaking." He stated that the United States did not have "sufficient leverage to impose such costs" without the help of its allies. On the contrary, these and other observers felt that Reagan's policy of strong-arming Moscow would "make more difficult attempts to channel Soviet domestic and international policies in a desirable direction" (Bialer and Afferica 1982–83, 264; Bialer 1983b, 39). In other words, they worried that the U.S. administration would jeopardize the prospects of the more liberal elite in its struggle with military and other hard-liners. Decrying the danger to détente, some commentators urged the United States to treat the Soviet Union as an equal. Hough, one of the advocates of this approach, pointed out that Moscow "has the right to support 'progressive' forces around the world." He argued that Washington should show no more fear of "Soviet verbal support of third world revolutions" than we fear to give "verbal support to third world . . . democracies" (Hough 1980, 163–66, 167–68; Labedz 1980, 41; Simes 1979–80, 41; 1980; 1980–81; Legvold 1980; Posen and Van Evara 1980; Holloway 1982).

Although the competing paradigms produced radically different views of the legitimacy crisis, they both missed Andropov's stealthy ascendancy. For the record, Hough (1982a) argued that Andropov was the most qualified candidate, while others linked him to the corruption scandals. His chances were not rated high because there was no historical precedent of a KGB chief who assumed the reigns of power (Ploss 1982; Schapiro 1982). As Brown (1982, 236) put it, "while not ruling him out of contention, being in KGB probably does more harm than good to his chances." Two Soviet journalists who wrote a book about Andropov noted that he "mixed the cards of Western Kremlinologists who . . . had a hard time catching on to the Byzantine style and cloakroom intrigue at the Kremlin" (Solovyov and Klepikova 1983, 223). Two other critics added that Western observers often underestimated the "power and influence of [KGB's] security and intelligence chiefs" (Andrew and Mitrokhin 1999, 550).

Even more confounding to Soviet watchers was the fact that the KGB chief, who was fighting pro-Western dissidents, would reach out to a "second pivot" elite that shared some of the same ideas. Hough was one of many experts who asserted that a pro-Western label would not only bring official repercussions but delegitimize such people in the eyes of "many Russians" who viewed them as "traitors" dedicated to serving American interests (Hough and Fainsod 1979, 569; Hough 1982b, 67).

With little inside knowledge about the crisis of confidence among the Soviet leadership, most commentators stuck to the linear progression model of forecasting. This type of prognostication posited that the "future Soviet system [will reflect] the present pattern of institutionalized power relationships" and "the basic social policies and relationships of welfare-authoritarianism" (Ryavec 1982; Gray 1981). Radical change was virtually ruled out, although some scholars warned that, given the severity of the economic problems, the new leader would have to "establish new criteria of legitimacy" (Simes 1981–1982; Mitchell 1982; Hyland 1982; Breslauer 1980; Staar 1980; Odom 1981; Mills 1981, 611).

Operating outside the field of Sovietology and largely ignored, a number of futurologists called attention to nonlinear models of change. To recall, nonlinearity is triggered by unpredictable turbulent "bursts" in the system caused by either unexpected events or "eventful men." The latter were defined as people "whose actions influenced subsequent developments along a quite different course than would have been followed if these actions had not been taken" (Ramage 1980, 272; Braillard and de Senarclens 1980). Even if Sovietologists had been more open to the suggestions of these futurologists, deciding whether Andropov would turn into such an "eventful man" was anything but easy. With interest in this question at an all-time high, both the

U.S. administration and other Kremlin watchers turned their attention to Andropov's tenure and the next phase of the transition battle.

The Andropov-Chernenko Transition: The View from Moscow

Wasting little time on the transition process, the new general secretary signaled his willingness to change the system. As already noted, Andropov understood that in order to regain legitimacy, the party had to renegotiate the badly frayed social contract, starting with the pervasive lawlessness among the ruling classes. On December 11, 1982, the Politburo condemned the "moral degradation" of the nomenklatura and followed up with a decree that listed a number of measures designed to fight corruption. The Department for Combating the Embezzlement of Socialist Property and Speculation was strengthened and a special party unit to oversee "political agencies" was created. In the resulting housecleaning a large number of officials were replaced, with the purges hitting especially hard a number of Asian republics. One high-profile case involved the popular but corrupt Sharaf Rashidov of Uzbekistan and General Nikolai Shchelokov from the Ministry of Interior, whose son was also arrested and deported to Siberia for alleged black market activities. The KGB's Lefortovo prison was filled with bureaucrats from the Central Committee and other high-ranking officials, some of whom were subjected to Stalinesque show trials. In November 1983, Yuri K. Sokolov, the director of a food emporium in Moscow, was sentenced to death for embezzlement and foreign currency speculation (d'Encausse 1993, 16–20; Rutland 1991; Doder 1988, 178, 200).

To be sure, Andropov had continued to use the anticorruption campaign to discredit the Brezhnev legacy, purge entrenched Brezhnevites in the party and state bureaucracy, and settle personal and political scores. Sokolov was a close friend of the Brezhnev family and of Viktor Grishin, the Moscow party boss and a prominent Brezhnevite. Shchelokov, a poster boy for corruption, was, as noted, also involved in the anti-Andropov plot. But the new leader was genuinely determined to rid the Soviet Union of systemic corruption, a fact attested to by his choice of protégés who had a reputation for personal probity. In addition to Gorbachev, whom Andropov groomed as an heir apparent, they included Ligachev, who was appointed to head the key Department of Organizational Party Work Committee; Nikolai Ryzhkov, who was made a secretary of the Central Committee in charge of economics; and Shevardnadze, whose anticorruption model in Georgia Andropov hoped to institute nationally.

By reaching out to the "young Turks," Andropov also signaled his resolve to revamp the archaic techniques of political mobilization whose credibility among the population at large, and especially among the young, had plummeted. Among his propaganda appointees was Fyodor Burlatsky, a political scientist and editor; Georgi Shakhnazarov, a futurologist; and Aleksandr Bovin, an *Izvestia* columnist, all of whom shared a penchant for a Western-style public relations approach to politics. They and others were charged with tackling symptoms of Soviet anomie such as political apathy and alcoholism. Special attention was devoted to low productivity, which Andropov considered a "national Achilles' heel," and its correlates such as absenteeism, pilfering, and sabotage (Smith 1990, 186). In April 1983, some 150 officials came to a seminar in Novosibirsk where Zaslavskaya argued that only a decentralized economy would fight inertia and immorality, and improve motivation and productivity. Her paper, dubbed the "Novosibirsk Report," was presented at a meeting of Central Committee and Gosplan officials, along with other proposals. Andropov agreed with the Novosibirsk group that the Brezhnev-era *uravnilovka*, or leveling of wages, should be phased out, and he seemed to have given his blessing to an American-style "managerial revolution," which was advocated by ISKAN's Arbatov. However, in what was an apparent reflection on his inner contradictions, Andropov had also acted on his belief that coercive measures were needed to tighten social and labor discipline. In terms of the legitimacy matrix, the new leader sought to add coercion to Brezhnev's exchange-oriented legitimacy mix (Hanson 1992, 55–56; Doder and Branson 1990, 49; Ligachev 1993, 45; Doder 1988, 111; Solovyov and Klepikova 1983, 281; Sheehy 1990, 135).

The ideological plenum in June 1983, which aired many of these themes, empowered Andropov to make significant changes in the Soviet economy. There was even a renewed push to convene the long-delayed plenum on scientific-technological issues. To prepare for the reforms, Andropov asked Gorbachev (1996, 215–16), along with Ryzhkov and other economic specialists, for an "objective evaluation of the national economy." The team found numerous irregularities in the top secret state budget, "latent, suppressed inflation," and huge deficits that were masked by a variety of accounting gimmicks, including illegal borrowing from the savings accounts of ordinary citizens. The real per capita income was "among the lowest of the socialist countries, not to speak of developed Western nations." Worse, Gorbachev and his colleagues suspected that defense expenditures, often hidden in the rubric of "other expenses," had grown at a rate of some one-half to two times higher than the increase in national income. These figures could not be confirmed because "only two or three people" had access to the data and Andropov refused a full disclosure. Only after becoming general secretary in 1985 was Gorbachev able to calculate that the military expenditure was not 16 percent of the budget as stated but close to 40

percent, making it 20 percent of the GNP, well above the published 6 percent. Of the 25 billion rubles slated for scientific research, 20 billion went to
military R&D (Shane 1994, 43–44).

Whatever the exact numbers, Andropov and his loyalists understood that
large military outlays were hampering plans to modernize the economy. Although Andropov might have encouraged Ogarkov to criticize Brezhnev as
part of his strategy to gain power, the chief of staff was taken aback when,
during a November 1982 Central Committee plenum, Andropov denounced
the "misguided" emphasis on military economy. In response, Ogarkov seized
upon Reagan's military buildup to argue for an increased allocation of resources. Ogarkov also pressed for a hard-line stand on the deployment of
Pershing II missiles in Europe—a NATO response to the SS-20—and the
American counteroffensive in Eastern Europe and the Third World. However, the economic deterioration, accelerated in 1983 by a drop in oil prices
engineered by the Reagan administration, turned the Andropov faction wary
of empire building. Most dramatically, Gorbachev and other modernizers
questioned the wisdom of Brezhnev's deploying Soviet missiles. Significantly,
Andropov was among senior Politburo members who ruled out a military
intervention in the Polish crisis in 1981 and later argued that building socialism in Eastern Europe would depend on the "work of the people." Karen
Brutents, the then expert on Asia and Africa in the Central Committee's International Department, noted that Soviet investment in promoting socialism
did not automatically guarantee "revolutionary success" (Azrael 1987, viii,
26, 33; Doder and Branson 1990, 153; Patman 1999, 588).

However, it was the SDI that brought the debate between the military and
the modernizers to a head. According to a number of insiders, the leadership
interpreted Reagan's Star Wars speech as evidence that the United States
could win a nuclear war. This and the fact that the Soviet Union had no
effective response to a costly and technologically advanced weapon system
made the debate agonizing. The military, supported by Defense Minister
Ustinov, pressed for permission to develop a response to the SDI, but the
understanding was that only a "cheaper" technology would be considered
(Evangelista 1999, 238; Dobrynin 1995, 528; Herspring 1990, 210–14).

Although the debate did not translate into an automatic victory for the
hard-liners, the entire leadership was genuinely concerned about Reagan's
military initiatives. On June 16, 1983, Andropov told the Central Committee
that there was an "unprecedented sharpening of the struggle between East
and West." Five days later, KGB residents in the United States and NATO
countries were ordered to intensify Operation RYAN (Raketno Yadernoe
Napadeniia—Nuclear Missile Attack), a 1981 KGB-GRU mission to uncover evidence of an American nuclear attack plan (Pry 1997, 128). This

was followed by another urgent message on August 12. Soviet anxiety reached a peak during a November NATO exercise code-named Able Archer, which was designed to practice nuclear release procedures that could be used in a surprise nuclear attack. Ironically, the Soviets' own contingency plans included a surprise nuclear attack on the West under the cover of a training exercise. In between, the shooting down of a Korean airliner by the Soviet air force on September 1 brought the relations between the two countries to a new low. President Reagan denounced the Soviets in harsh terms, triggering a hard-line response by Ogarkov. On September 28 Andropov delivered an "apocalyptic warning" about the future, and later that fall the Soviet delegation walked out of the Geneva arms control talks in protest over the U.S. missile deployment. In fact, the Euromissiles represented a personal setback for Andropov, who authorized a KGB propaganda campaign aimed at thwarting their deployment. Modeled on the effort to stop Carter from developing the neutron bomb, it exploited the large mobilization of antinuclear and peace groups in Europe and the United States that had been consolidated into the Nuclear Weapons Freeze Campaign in 1981. For good measure, the Soviets sought to scare Western public opinion by using the IPS and other sympathetic outlets to spread the word that the Pershing deployment would force Moscow to adopt a "launch and warning" strategic posture (Andrew 1995, 60, 472, 475; Andrew and Mitrokhin 1999, 392; Chatfield 1992, 153–69; Doder 1988, 91).

Since he had set out to revive the sagging legitimacy of the Soviet system, Andropov's reversal into a classical Cold War posture was puzzling. Some insiders suggested that, in the unfinished power struggle, the military and its civilian backers like Grigory Romanov, who was in charge of the military industry, took advantage of the challenge posed by Reagan and raised the level of national alarm. Such saber rattling made it harder to fire the increasingly insubordinate Ogarkov and forced Andropov into defending the military's interests. Others, including Gorbachev and Volkogonov, argued that Andropov, in spite of his brilliant analysis of Soviet problems, was too much a product of the communist system to make a drastic break in either foreign or domestic policy. In addition, distrust, which came naturally to generations of Soviet leaders, was inflamed by Reagan's anticommunist rhetoric. Although the Soviet Union had habitually engaged in this kind of propaganda against the United States, Moscow proved, in the words of Dobrynin, "extremely thin-skinned" when the shoe was on the other foot. Either way, in 1983 the Politburo revised upward by some 50 percent its planned military expenditure for the 1980–85 period. Support for Third World revolutions was made more selective, but "viable" regimes were still assured financial aid, including millions of rubles to Syria, Yemen, and the PLO. Support for global terrorism was not curtailed either, preserving USSR's status as a "nursery of worldwide terrorism" for such groups as the PLO. (Gorbachev, 1996, 153; Volkogonov 1998, 353, 359; Dobrynin 1995, 512, 527; Arbatov 1992, 258; Shevchenko 1985, 313, 243; Lee 1995, 171; Cline and Alexander 1984, 76ff; Solovyov and Klepikova 1983, 125; Sterling 1981, 271–85).

Even if Andropov had wanted to change course, his failing health made it harder for the new regime to assert authority. The general secretary started kidney dialysis in February 1983, and his condition may have been aggravated when the distraught wife of General Shchelokov allegedly attacked him in March. After an August vacation Andropov vanished from public view and, in September, was hospitalized in the elite Kuntsevo hospital. Although Andropov made some "phantom appearances" staged from his sickbed, in November *Izvestia* published a veiled article criticizing his absence, attributed to a journalist aligned with the opposition. The factional struggle for succession intensified, with some Brezhnevites rallying behind Chernenko and the military backing Romanov, who publicly vowed that the nation would "equip the army and the navy with everything necessary." For his part, the dying leader was busy placing loyalists in positions of power and trying to advance the chances of Gorbachev (Solovyov and Klepikova 1986, 10–11, 19, 33; Hazan 1987, 85, 98; Doder 1988, 123; Doder and Branson 1990, 85; Volkogonov 1998, 381).

When Andropov's death was announced on February 10, 1984, little of his ambitious plan to bolster the legitimacy of the regime had been realized. Although Andropov's fight against corruption made him personally popular, nascent reforms to increase economic performance were sabotaged by the bureaucracy and ethnic sentiments had intensified. From his days in the KGB, Andropov was well aware of center–periphery tensions, a fact he had acknowledged in a somber address on the problems of nationalities. Secretly, the secretary general worried about the explosive population growth of the Muslim republics and of national and religious dissent, which the KGB attributed to Reagan's subversion. Ironically, the horizontal disintegration of the empire was accelerated by Andropov's efforts to weed out corruption in the republics. When the practitioners of Asian "feudal socialism" were replaced by Russian officials, nationalist feeling was inflamed. More important, the anticorruption crusade turned local bosses into "ethnic entrepreneurs," a term coined by rational choice theory to describe politicians who turned to ethnic support in order to retain power. In other words, Andropov's "clean government" drive taught local politicians that, after decades of looking to Moscow, they now had to mobilize ethnic sentiment to advance their careers (Andropov 1990; Barner-Barry and Hody 1995, 67–73; Dutter 1990; Olcott 1990, 4; 1985; Ekedahl and Goodman 1997, 25).

Whether Andropov would have made more radical changes had his health been better is far from obvious. What was clear was that other top leaders did not share his perception of a legitimacy crisis when they elected the seventy-two-year-old Konstantin Chernenko as the new general secretary. The many ambiguities of the Andropov tenure and the unresolved succession struggle made it even harder for American observers to follow the developments in Moscow.

The Andropov-Chernenko Transition: The View from Washington

With so much of the Reagan agenda invested in undermining communism, deciphering the personality of Andropov was at a premium. Although the KGB launched an elaborate campaign to portray its former chief as a closet liberal, the White House remained extremely cautious in pronouncing judgment. As a matter of fact, a behind-the-scenes struggle had developed between the so-called the pragmatic "dealers" in the State Department and the ideological "squeezers" in the Department of Defense and the National Security Council (Horelick 1989–90). The former, lead by George Shultz, who replaced Haig as secretary of state, and Richard Burt, an assistant secretary for European affairs, were skeptical that the Soviet Union could be "brought to her knees" and wanted to engage Moscow in arms negotiation and cultural exchanges. In fact, Shultz (1993, 274, 276) was advocating a mixed policy of pressure and rewards and argued that the U.S. position on regional conflicts should be evaluated on the basis of their merits. To bolster this position, Shultz met with Gates (1996, 289) and Casey to assess Andropov's policy and, more generally, to find out "where the Soviet Union was headed." Gates informed the secretary of state that internal problems would make Andropov more willing to deal with the United States (Dallin and Lapidus 1987).

However, to ideologues like Secretary of Defense Casper Weinberger, Richard Perle, his assistant secretary for international security, William Clark, the national security adviser, CIA director Casey, and Richard Pipes, Shultz's plan looked like the old détente policy. They asserted that broad-based contacts would legitimatize Moscow and argued that Andropov was a traditional politician who presided over a huge deception scam designed to bolster the Soviet "correlation of forces" by preying on public opinion in the West. Herbert Romerstein, a former staffer at the House Intelligence Committee, was made head of Counter Soviet Disinformation at the USIA in charge of combating communist disinformation and forgeries (Romerstein and Breindel 2000, viii). A large body of research, some of which was funded by conservative foundations, discussed Soviet disinformation and deception practices, including the use of peace fronts and agents of influence (Shultz and Godson 1984; Epstein 1982; Brennan 1983; Tyson 1981; Ferguson 1983). Soviet defector Vladimir Sakharov confirmed that the KGB and some of the institutes had engaged in ideological warfare (Sakharov and Tosi 1980, 82–88). These and other sources emphasized Andropov's efforts to thwart the deployment of Pershing II and otherwise confound Reagan's armament program (Evans and Novak 1981, 199; Leavit and Orren 1983; Isaac 1983). In yet another attempt to show that the Andropov tenure brought no change, a Reagan-appointed General Advisory Committee on Arms Control and Disarmament produced a 300-page report on Soviet violations of the SALT agreements, among them the construction of the Krasnoyarsk radar station. According to the committee, before becoming chief of staff, Marshal Ogarkov had been in charge of the deception program, and Andropov had backed such efforts (Lee 1997, 3, 20–21; Gray 1984).

The hard-liners were also intent on proving that Andropov did not terminate Moscow's offensive efforts like biological and chemical weapon programs or cease to train terrorists, either directly or using proxies like East Germany, as detailed in a book by Claire Sterling (1981), the CIA liaison officer to Congress (Gelman 1984, 209). Casey ordered SOVA to investigate the terrorist link, but the Agency could not corroborate the allegations. Casey accused the analytic branch of neglecting the "dirty realities" of Soviet global subversion and was, in turn, blamed for twisting the intelligence reports in a bid to exaggerate Moscow's role. Ironically, glasnost-era revelations showed that even after all the pressure Casey applied on the CIA, the estimates were "too cautious" (Gates 1996, 206).

The exchanges between the two camps became so bitter that Shultz (1993, 498) described it as a "miasma of distrust." According to Pipes (2000, 46–47), Haig had been told by State Department experts that it was "crazy" to think that the United States could "bust" the Soviet Union by using economic sanctions and Shultz received "similar advice." Both sides sought to make their views public, leading to allegations that Burt leaked inside information to Strobe Talbott (1984a), who wrote an exposé on the foreign policy divisions in the administration. For his part, Casey sought to use the negative intelligence on Andropov to enhance the credibility of his anticommunist crusade. As Gates (1996, 286) put it, "Casey had his own foreign policy agenda" and considered the estimating program to be a "powerful instrument in forcing the pace in the policy arena."

Caught up in these internecine battles was the CIA's annual estimate of Soviet military expenditure, whose credibility as a tool for measuring Soviet intent was tarnished by the 1976 adjustment. In November 1982, SOVA was

asked to provide some data for a speech by Reagan, who sought public support for an increase in American military spending. In February 1983, the
Agency, in a reversal of its 1976 correction, announced that there was a
considerable slowdown or even a plateau in the increase of Soviet military
procurements. In September Gates testified to the JEC that the Politburo had
switched its priority to civilian production. The report was met with strong
resistance from Casey and Weinberger and further intensified the debates
over the CIA's methodology. On the left, Holzman (1982) repeated his charge
that the Agency was inflating the estimate to legitimize Reagan's buildup.
On the right, Rosefielde (1982, 252) accused the Agency of using "false
science" to minimize the degree of militarization of the Soviet economy. He
even implied that Soviet counterintelligence, in a bid to present a peaceful
image, manipulated the CIA estimate (Firth and Noren 1998, 75–77; Lee
1995, 171).

Adding another angle to the debate was the émigré economist Igor Birman
(1980a; 1980b; 1981, x, 199, 211), who had long criticized the CIA for
overestimating the health of the Soviet economy. In a series of detailed analyses that echoed much of the internal discourse in Moscow, Birman claimed
that the Soviet Union was plagued by extremely serious problems and that
the budget writers had used statistical gimmicks to mask considerable inflation. He confirmed Gorbachev's then still secret allegations that the government had tapped into people's savings to balance the budget. However,
Birman's efforts to meet with Gates were rebuffed and Donald F. Burton
(1983), the head of the CIA's Military Economic Analysis, did not refer to
Birman's charges when he publicly responded to the critics on the left and
right (Sciolino 1991a). For his part, Gates (1996, 318) later admitted that
the CIA's estimates "understated the full cost of the Soviet military—and
consequently also understated the burden it imposed on the Soviet economy
and society."

With the politicization of the quantitative estimate increasing, it was left
to the more descriptive SOVA reports to convey the depth of the domestic
crisis under Andropov. Ranging from analyses of ferment in the republics to
civil unrest, the reports provided a remarkably accurate portrayal of the problems facing the new leader. The assessment of the Soviet economy, including agriculture, was particularly negative. The CIA projected very low rates
of growth in the 1980s and predicted that in spite of reducing its foreign
currency debt, the Soviet Union would face continuous pressure on its foreign currency because of soft oil prices and pressure to import. Still, the CIA
did not expect Andropov to dismantle the command economy or make other
radical changes to increase labor incentives. SOVA analysts were also convinced that Andropov would be unwilling to impinge on the defense and

industrial investment in order to increase the output of consumer goods. The Agency, well aware of Andropov's health problems, named Gorbachev or Romanov as likely successors, but did not expect the younger elite to deviate radically from the path of orthodox socialism (CIA Documents, SOV83–10062, SOV83–10212, SOV83–10113, SOV-10147, SOV83–10103, SOV83–10124, GI83–10038, SOV83–10086CX; MacEachin 1996, nos. 12 and 13; National Security Archives no. 00571).

In contrast to the CIA's factual assessments, the Andropov reign provided the academic community with an opportunity to discuss the larger issues of legitimacy and change. Catching up to d'Encausse, an increasing number of studies emphasized the growing legitimacy crisis in the republics and warned of the "Central Asian problem" (Gitelman 1983; Clem 1983). There was also more focus on the Soviet economy, with most observers arguing that Andropov faced a considerable challenge in repairing the social contract or taking on the manifold economic ills (Smith 1983; Hardt and Gold 1983).

In spite of this increasing consensus on the ills of the economy, paradigmatic considerations still colored the analysis of legitimacy crisis. Conservatives and neoconservatives maintained that the Soviet Union was facing a systemic crisis and that the Soviets' singular focus on the military would eventually ruin the country. Brzezinski (1983b; 1984, 6) was among a number of observers who came to see the Soviet Union as an "Upper Volta with missiles." He contended that its one-dimensional military power was not adequate to maintain global domination. One commentator speculated that, at best, Andropov would be able to "hold the line." Others warned that, faced with a degenerating economy and lack of legitimacy, Andropov and his successors might resort to Stalinist repression at home and military adventurism abroad. To quote one of them: "modern dictatorships have powerful instruments . . . to postpone the day of reckoning for a very long time" (Odom 1983, 18; Laqueur 1983b, 16; Luttwak 1983).

More liberal scholars challenged these conclusions. Cohen (1986, 17, 22–25) argued that regardless of "important inadequacies," the economic system was still delivering a decent standard of education, health, and welfare. He attributed the talk of systemic crisis to "Sovietophobia." Bialer (1983a, 7, 65; 1983b, 39) noted that in spite of Brezhnev's failures to solve many problems, he prevented them from "becoming a source of systemic failure." He insisted that the Soviet economy, "administered by intelligent and trained professionals, will not go bankrupt" and that the leadership "will not face a systemic crisis that endangers its existence" (quoted in Hollander 2000, 172). Nove (1983, 1), who had become something of a booster of socialism, while listing the many economic problems, was nevertheless convinced that the "basic assumptions of liberal capitalism are ceasing to be true." He offered a blueprint for "feasible socialism" as a way to transform the Soviet system. These and other like-minded commentators were confident that Andropov would be able to shore up communist legitimacy, warning the pessimists not to "underestimate the system's reformist potentials and popular support," as Cohen (1986, 25) put it.

Not surprisingly, the question of popular support for communism had continued to preoccupy many scholars. In an effort to test Hough's pluralist legitimacy theory, some studies found that Soviet citizens either actively supported the regime or passively acquiesced to its rule. But others, using data from internal Soviet debates, concluded that official figures on participation were inflated and that a "great deal of public activity is nominal or is carried out on work time" (Adams 1983; White 1983; Rigby 1983; Remington 1983, 22). Hollander (1983, 58), who reviewed a number of books on workers, labor, and labor unions, some written by Soviet experts, noted that these insiders provided a devastating picture of corruption and malaise as opposed to the "bland generalization and abstract concepts" of Western scholarship. Polish scholar Aleksandra Jasinska-Kania (1983) repeated the assertion that an inverted Habermasian crisis of legitimacy could explain the situation in Poland and, by extension, in other communist regimes (Korbonski 1983).

Buried in the interminable debates among academics was a subtle shift in the reigning pluralistic paradigm. Chastened by the extent of malaise revealed in the wave of émigré publications, and under increasing attack for representing Brezhnev's tenure as the "golden age" of Soviet communism, some leading revisionists developed doubts about their theories. Skilling (1983, 24–25) conceded that his work "implied a greater participation by interest groups than was warranted." Hough (1983b, 49, 57) said that he had "bowed to editorial pressure" to coin the term "institutional pluralism," and professed to regret the field's "obsession" with models. Still, Hough reiterated his point that "in any meaningful sense" there "is some societal autonomy" in the Soviet Union and even found that Andropov's rapid ascent was part of the rationalization of the process of Soviet governance. Rejecting the notion that the military and the KGB supported Andropov, Hough (1983a) chose to see the election as an example of the "institutionalization" of the post of the general secretary. For Hough and many of his colleagues such alleged manifestations of Weberian rationality offered a promise of a true transformation of the regime after the newly discovered irrationality of the Brezhnev years.

As before, much of the analysis of Andropov's tenure served as a referendum on Reagan's policy. Leftist commentators decried the "myth of national security" and repeated the charge that the administration's military buildup was aimed at enriching the military-industrial complex (Parenti 1983, 95–96). Adding fuel to the flames of controversy was the journalist Andrew Cockburn (1983, 76), who published a book claiming that the Soviet threat was vastly overestimated. He attacked the "superhawk" CPD and warned that, if not checked, Reagan's exaggerations could lead to a new war.

Others criticized what they viewed as the president's cynical use of human rights tactics and what was described as the "democracy intervention network" epitomized in Project Democracy. Although Barnet (1983, 40–50) conceded that Andropov's persecution of intellectual and religious dissidents indicated a "moral weakness," the IPS scholar felt that it was not "in the same class . . . as the wholesale slaughter" that was taking place in the West-allied right-wing dictatorships. Reagan's "evil empire" rhetoric and the activities of the NED alarmed even less ideologically motivated commentators. While acknowledging that the Soviets had used such inflammatory language all along, Caldwell and Legvold (1983, 20) blamed the president for a decline in "superpower civility."

To restore such civility, these and others critics urged the administration to cease "crypto-warfare" and increase trade relations with the Soviet Union. They cautioned that, at worst, economic strong-arming would encourage a hard-line backlash in Moscow and, at best, would not affect Soviet economic development. Bialer repeated his view that the United States could do little to change Soviet behavior, asserting that any such hope was "simply fallacious and spawns maximalist and unrealistic objectives." He further argued that in spite of declining growth, the Soviet economy had reached a level of production "that would support its empire" (Bialer and Afferica 1982–83, 262; Bialer 1983b).

It was left to the conservatives to express faith in American ability to alter the path of Soviet communism. Defending the administration, Wolf (1983, vi) tried to prove that increasing the cost of empire maintenance would create an intolerable drag on the Soviet economy. He also urged the establishment of an American information program aimed at informing the Soviet elite of the real cost of the empire, thus prompting an internal debate in Moscow. Luttwak (1983, 21) made much the same point, noting that there was an increasing pessimism in Moscow about imperial survival. Laqueur (1983a, 1983b) blamed his liberal colleagues for refusing to acknowledge that there was a real ideological conflict between the two superpowers and chastised them for belittling the administration's efforts to undermine communism. Neoconservatives were bolstered when the prominent economist and onetime Soviet adviser to the Carter administration, Marshall I. Goldman (1983), published a book arguing that the Soviet crisis was an indication of the failure of the Soviet economic system. The book was apparently so controversial that "truth squads" of scholars traveled to local meetings of the American Association for Slavic Studies to denounce it (Mitchell 1989).

As news about Andropov's illness spread, analysis of Andropov politics turned into speculation about his successor. Most observers predicted a generational transition, although they were divided over whether Romanov or Gorbachev would be picked (Hough 1983a; Brown 1983; Ruble 1983). When Chernenko was elected, Kremlin watchers correctly assumed that the new leader represented the last gasp of the Brezhnevite generation.

The Chernenko-Gorbachev Transition: The View from Moscow

The behind-the-scenes maneuvering that brought Chernenko to power on February 11, 1984, confirmed the view that Brezhnev's generation was in demise. After a lifetime of serving as Brezhnev's aide, the elderly Chernenko had few admirers in the Politburo. He was considered a parvenu, a "country bumpkin," a "clerk," a "tremendously average man" (Doder 1988, 210). Dr. Yevgeni Chazov disclosed his precarious health condition, including heart problems, emphysema, and cirrhosis of the liver, to the Politburo, but a number of considerations favored the dean of the gerontological set. Shaken by Andropov's efforts to change the system, the "old guard" decided to let biology run its course. Some had personal interest in mind. Gromyko, who had supported Andropov, wanted to regain control over foreign policy, and Tikhonov felt threatened by the economic proposals of the "young Turks." As one observer described it, by opting for Chernenko, they "chose to return to Brezhnevism without Brezhnev" (Solovyov and Klepikova 1986, 41; Arbatov 1992, 286; Hazan 1987, 213; Volkogonov 1998, 429).

At the same time, Andropov's efforts on behalf of Gorbachev were not lost in the shuffle. The younger man became a de facto second-in-command to Chernenko, whose health began to falter in the summer. The KGB, headed by Andropov ally Viktor Chebrikov, might have been a guarantor of this arrangement, seconded by Marshal Ustinov, whose disdain for Chernenko was well known (Sheehy 1990, 165; Hazan 1987, 107; Groth 1990). Whatever the behind-the-scenes agreements, the built-in contradictions of the "co-chairmanship" became evident almost immediately.

To begin with, the Politburo became the scene of serious disagreements over the economy. While Chernenko and Prime Minister Nikolai Tikhonov were ready to continue with old-style remedies such as a grandiose plan for land reclamation, Gorbachev pressed for new ideas. While Andropov was still alive, Gorbachev had commissioned more than 110 policy papers, including an analysis of Lenin's New Economic Policy. Under his influence, on May 17, 1984, the Central Committee passed a resolution to "surmount drunkenness and alcoholism." On the same day, Gorbachev told a gathering in Leningrad that the fiction of plan fulfillment needed to be exposed, along with the fact that the machinery in industry was outdated and that Soviet citizens spent most of their salaries on shoddy consumer goods. In August Aganbegyan echoed these themes in two surprisingly candid articles. Gorbachev also unsuccessfully pressed Chernenko to schedule a plenum on technology, telling Ligachev (1993, 48) that those who postponed the plenum again were thinking "only about their own political ambition" (Hazan 1987, 164; Kaiser 1991, 68–69; Smith 1990, 77).

Under normal circumstances, the military would have been Gorbachev's natural ally in his fight against the old guard. Ogarkov and top army officers had long lobbied the party leadership to modernize the economy in order to absorb Western technology, actually coining the term perestroika. However, Ogarkov's demand that the Soviet Union keep pace with Reagan's buildup, including a Russian version of Star Wars, would have been detrimental to a meaningful economic reform. It was apparently this argument, coupled with Ogarkov's very public advocacy of a nuclear first strike and other "Bonapartist" tendencies, that led to his dismissal on September 5. There was also some fear that, if left in his post, Ogarkov would have tried to replace the ailing Ustinov as defense minister. Marshal Sergei Akhromeyev, an Andropov loyalist who shared the modernizers' conviction that the basis of Soviet power was the economy, was chosen to replace Ustinov (Novikov and Bascio 1994, 68; Bova 1988; Solovyov and Klepikova 1986; Bialer 198b, 302–3; Herspring 1990, 218).

While Ogarkov's demotion dealt a blow to the hard-line faction of Romanov, it did not end the Kremlin power struggle. Furious backroom maneuvers had sent Romanov's and Gorbachev's fortunes seesawing until the end of November. The deadlock was apparently broken when Gorbachev was picked to deliver the keynote address at the December 10–11 ideological plenum. Departing from Marxist orthodoxy, Gorbachev argued that the economic slowdown was systemic, necessitating changes in "production relations." He decried the conservatism and inertia of the country and warned against squeezing "new phenomena into the Procrustean bed of moribund conceptions" (quoted in Doder 1988, 246). Gorbachev made more news during his speech to the British Parliament on December 18, when he previewed themes of New Political Thinking (NPT) by insisting that universal human values should be put above class conflict. Gorbachev also declared that war was an unacceptable method of resolving disputes and pleaded for a stop to the nuclear arms race and for Soviet integration into Europe (Brown 1996, 78–79; Kaiser 1991, 75–79; Gorbachev 1996, 161).

There is little doubt that Gorbachev's fortunes against Romanov were boosted by the foreign policy setbacks suffered by Moscow at the hands of the Reagan administration. As noted, Andropov failed to prevent the deployment of Pershings in Europe in December 1983. Without a ready response to the seemingly successful SDI tests, the collective leadership was worried about the deteriorating status of the Warsaw Pact versus the newly energized NATO forces, a development that prompted Gromyko to ask the Pope to speak out against the nuclear race. Most important, after Reagan was reelected in November 1984, there was a growing realization in the Politburo that the Soviet Union would need to fashion a more flexible international diplomacy (Weigel 1999, 500; Andrew and Gordievsky 1990, 589–90).

The death of Marshal Ustinov on December 20 reconfigured the struggle to succeed the dying Chernenko once again. After losing a direct challenge, Romanov plotted to support Moscow's party boss Viktor Grishin in hope of creating a deadlock between the two factions, which would have made him a compromise candidate. For his part, Grishin tried to present himself as the heir apparent to Chernenko by appearing at the side of the severely ill leader, who was periodically wheeled out to deliver short speeches. Ligachev (1993, 65–67) charged that these machinations amounted to a serious form of abuse of the dying Chernenko. In any case, the Romanov-Grishin ploy failed. The KGB fought back by spreading more rumors about Romanov's alleged corruption, philandering, and alcoholism, and tying Grishin to the food emporium corruption scandal. The economic situation was also demanding some fresh ideas. Ligachev (1993, 58) recalled that the winter of 1984–85 was unusually cold, pushing the national economy to the verge of collapse, a crisis that was compounded by the barely functioning Prime Minister Tikhonov.

When Chernenko's death was announced on March 12, 1985, Gorbachev had already been chosen by the Politburo to serve as the new Soviet leader. In addition to Gromyko and KGB's Viktor Chebrikov, whose support was crucial in the Politburo, Gorbachev had a majority of provincial party secretaries on his side. It was clear that the selection represented a generational transition and a mandate for change of the ossified system. Gorbachev himself later noted that the death of so many of the old guard was "symbolic," adding that the "very system was dying away, its sluggish senile blood no longer contained vital juices" (Doder 1988, 256; Boldin 1994, 61–63; Ligachev 1993, 72–79; Yelstin 2000, 127–28; Solovyov and Klepikova 1986, 128; Gorbachev 1991, 131; 1996, 168).

However, few at that time, including the new leader, could have guessed the monumental transformation that was in store. Analyzing the rapidly paced transition drama posed a special challenge to American observers.

The Chernenko-Gorbachev Transition: The View from Washington

The appointment of Chernenko did little to settle the increasingly bitter debate in the Reagan administration between those who wanted to crusade against the Soviet empire and those who wanted to return to a modified détente posture. The forthcoming presidential election, in which the nuclear threat was expected to play a major role, helped the moderates to convince Reagan that a return to traditional arms negotiations was in order.

Although the Soviet effort to derail the Euromissiles failed, the peace movement in the United States scored some major points. In June 1983, the IPS, in conjunction with the Soviet Institute for the Study of USA and Canada, sponsored a disarmament conference in Minneapolis. The National Committee for a Sane Nuclear Policy (SANE), Educators for Social Responsibility, and Physicians for Social Responsibility were among the many groups accusing the administration of conducting a reckless nuclear policy. William Arkin, the director of nuclear weapons research at the IPS, launched a major public relations campaign to demand a nuclear freeze, a move that had sympathizers among the left-leaning Congress members. One of them, Senator George McGovern, went so far as to express regret that Andropov, whom he called one of the "most intelligent leaders," had died during the administration of "one of the most ill-informed and dangerous men ever to occupy the White House" (quoted in Hook 1985). On November 21, 1983, PBS aired the movie *The Day After*, depicting the aftermath of a nuclear attack, which attracted a huge audience; terms like "nuclear winter" entered public discourse. An administration insider admitted that the nuclear freeze movement posed a "serious challenge" to the U.S. strategic modernization plan (Gates 1996, 276; Powell 1987, 313; Leighton 1991, 146–52).

Coming on top of secret intelligence that revealed the dangerous escalation in nuclear tensions surrounding Able Archer, the nuclear freeze campaign convinced Reagan to side with the pragmatists in his administration. Two of the chief crusaders on the NSC—William Clark and Richard Pipes—were replaced with the more pragmatic Robert McFarlane and Jack Matlock, and Shultz was given more leeway in seeking new contacts with Chernenko through the unofficial Dartmouth Group headed by Brent Scowcroft. High on the secretary's agenda were START (Strategic Arms Reduction Talks), which replaced SALT, and the INF (Intermediate Nuclear Forces) negotiations. Although true believers like Weinberger and Casey retained the president's ear, the reshuffle signaled a subtle move away from the original blueprint to vanquish the Soviet empire and into a more traditional détente-like agenda (Reagan 1990, 594; Shultz 1993, 472, 478; Pemberton 1998,

158–59). Still, both sides had to wait for the succession struggle in Moscow to take its course. Chernenko's state of health was the subject of intense speculation in Washington, eclipsed only by the interest in his potential successor and the projections of economic performance.

True to its analytic character, the CIA focused most of its attention on the Soviet economy. A February 1984 estimate projected a low 2 percent growth in GNP for the remainder of the decade and the same percentage growth in military outlays. The document noted that in order to stimulate growth, the Soviet Union needed to increase productivity, but rated the chances for necessary reforms as low. A more detailed July analysis dealt with the policy implications of Soviet economic problems. The SOVA analysts predicted that economic shortages would not precipitate "sustained and widespread unrest" among the population. At the same time, they felt that citizens' support for the regime "should be vulnerable to information that reinforces the perception that living standards are not what the public believe they ought to be." The poor economy was also expected to curtail Moscow's ability to help Third World countries and handicap its response to a high-technology military race with the United States (CIA Documents, SOV84–10017, SOV84–10104, SOV84–10114, GI-84–10182). Other reports noted the financial constraints on Moscow's ability to help Eastern Europe, but overall did not envisage a collapse of the economy, which was said to be 55 percent of the U.S. GNP. As for the contentious question of the ratio of military expenditure to GNP, the CIA put it at some 15 percent (Firth and Noren 1998, 130).

Having fewer methodological constraints than the CIA, the academic community utilized the Chernenko interlude to engage in a wide-ranging debate about the legitimacy, durability, and changeability of the Soviet enterprise. For the theoretically oriented scholars, the clarion call to rethink the basis of communist legitimacy was served by Polish workers, who, in conjunction with the Roman Catholic Church, fought for Western-style democracy and a market economy. In the words of one student of Polish politics, this development "embarrassed" and "distressed" many of his colleagues, whom he accused of double standards and "asymmetry of indulgence" toward the Soviet Union (Garton Ash 1984, 122). With increasing turmoil in other parts of Eastern Europe, he and other observers came to question the real meaning of communist legitimacy, a move that was also reflected in a new round of debate about rationality of patrimonial legitimacy.

One of the debate's originators and a leading revisionist, T.H. Rigby (1984, 219) admitted that the concept of legitimacy might suffer from a "diversity of usage" and that this diversity was incorporated in "our concept of legitimacy of beliefs about the subjective attitudes of both rulers and ruled." This was a roundabout way of saying that evaluating the legitimacy of the communist regimes was an exercise in subjectivity (Lane 1984; Brown 1984; McAuley 1984). But antirevisionists hammered the theme that Soviet workers, in whose name the revolution was made, had to put up with sixty-five years of hardship and only a mixture of coercion and reflexive docile behavior kept them from rebellion (Schapiro 1984).

Paradigmatic assumptions had also underlain the evaluation of economic performance and its potential to drag the Soviet Union into a systemic crisis. Upon returning from a visit to the Soviet Union sponsored by ISKAN, John Kenneth Galbraith (1984) found the Soviet economy to have made "great material progress" and commented on the "appearance of solid well-being of the people on the streets." The noted economist explained that the Soviet Union succeeded because, "in contrast to Western industrial economy" it "makes full use of its manpower." Bialer (1984, 295, 298) believed that, with some adjustments, the Soviet economy would be able to "muddle through" until the end of the decade when a major "socio-economic crisis" could be expected.

For those who expected the Soviet economy to muddle through, the administration's attempts to squeeze Moscow were of dubious value at best and dangerous at worst. Using an econometric model, two researchers concluded that "the West cannot force the Soviet economy far off its preferred growth path" (Brandsma and Hallett 1984). Others did not need sophisticated methodology to maintain that neither the arms race nor the curtailment of trade and scientific exchange would change Soviet behavior. What was more, a leading Soviet expert warned that aggressive American tactics could trigger a hard-line backlash and the election of a "strong and ruthless leader" (Nye 1984; Gaddis 1983–84; Simes 1984a, 25; 1984b).

It was left to Pipes (1984a, 1984b) and other conservatives to restate their position that the Soviet Union was in the throes of a deep systemic crisis and that American efforts to manipulate Soviet behavior made perfect sense. This view was supported by a number of studies that listed problems ranging from epidemic levels of alcoholism to the increasing burden of supporting the far-flung Soviet empire (Burks 1984; Wesson 1984, 195; Kushnirsky 1984; Kux 1984; Zamostny 1984; Singleton 1984; Goodman 1984; Feldbrugge 1984). While suggesting that the economy could not "muddle through" for much longer, conservative observers were not optimistic that the ruling elite would be willing to transform the system. Indeed, Wesson argued that the illegitimate totalitarian regime is "difficult to shake" and that "economic failure" does not generate an "alternative authority" bent on reforming the system (Wesson 1984, 195). More to the point, Pipes (1984a, 48–49; 1984b) stressed that the communist system could not be transformed and would eventually collapse. Noting the internal contradictions of communism, including the emergence of a "parasitic" and self-serving nomenklatura class, Pipes concluded that "totalitarian regimes are by definition incapable of evolution."

Given that by the end of 1984, Gorbachev and other "second pivot" leaders were gaining an upper hand in Moscow, such predictions seemed too doctrinaire. By comparison, revisionists were more nimble in adjusting their paradigmatically driven forecasting to the new reality. After warning that Reagan's policies would help hard-liners to win power, they quickly embraced the notion that the ascendancy of a reformist elite was all but inevitable. Moreover, following a decade of defending the centralized and egalitarian economy, they were eager to point out that reformist circles represented by Gorbachev were ready to decentralize the system and even encourage small-scale private ownership (Nove 1984; Cohen 1984). Indeed, a win by Gorbachev would have represented a vindication of the revisionist theory that communism could be transformed rather than vanquished. Even more important, these Sovietologists expected the new generation to "perform the final act of convergence" by creating a liberal democracy with "socialist values" (Suraska 1998, 142). As Gorbachev took the reins of power, they and the entire American foreign policy community were keen to determine whether the new leader was an "eventful man" intent to move communism in a new direction or just a "creative" Bolshevik using new techniques to improve the sagging "correlation of forces."

5

Acceleration

Tinkering Around the Edges, 1985–1986

Having determined that the slide in performance of the economy was closely linked to a crisis of communist legitimacy, Mikhail Gorbachev was eager to find ways to refurbish the social contract and thus improve the competitiveness of the Soviet system. As the new leader embarked on a course of relatively mild reforms, he encountered a growing resistance from the orthodox opposition in his party. Gorbachev's policies had also confounded the Reagan administration, where the once single-minded determination to vanquish communism had to be adjusted to a more complex reality.

Revisiting Communist Legitimacy: In Search of a New Formula

With the legitimacy formula used since the Bolshevik revolution virtually bankrupt, Gorbachev urgently needed to find a new way to bind the people to the party. Although little noticed at the time, Gorbachev's thinking, based on the theoretical work of his intellectual associates and especially Aleksandr Yakovlev, who was made the head of IMEMO in 1984, represented a switch from the deterministic Marxist notion of class consciousness to a more eclectic understanding of human motivation and behavior. At its core was the theory of Antonio Gramsci, who rejected Lenin's concept of centralism buttressed by force in favor of a more consensual, humanistic view of the political system. This so-called Gramscian legitimacy called for "organic centralism" based on authenticity, voluntarism, humanism, and group dynamics (Levesque 1997, 33; Kubalkova and Cruickshank 1989, 63–70; Novikov and Bascio 1994, 39–41). A new formula was needed because, as Gorbachev admitted, many theoretical aspects of socialism had "stagnated on the level of the 1930s and 1940s." Worse, "animated discussions and creative thinking vanished" and were replaced by "authoritarian assessments and considerations" that were extolled as "unimpeachable truth." Recalling how thousands came to say farewell at the funeral of the Italian communist Enrico Berlinguer, which he had attended in June 1984, Gorbachev wrote that this was a "thought-provoking lesson about a different political culture." He contrasted this spontaneity with the mechanistic and show-like quality of Soviet events, "celebrations and jubilees" where people were commanded to participate (Felshman 1992, 129; Leonhard 1987–88, 403; Gorbachev 1996, 159).

Equally compelling in the new formula was the emphasis on the welfare of the individual as a key legitimizing principle of socialism. Going beyond the theoretical, Gorbachev's focus on eudaemonics was formed by traveling around the country and reading letters sent to him by citizens. According to insiders, the new leader was deeply troubled by the extreme hardship suffered by ordinary people, especially as contrasted with the privileged position of the nomenklatura. While visiting oil fields in Siberia in September 1985, Gorbachev was shaken by the squalor in which workers and their families lived (Boldin 1994, 193; Dobbs 1997, 133–37). His chief adviser, Yakovlev, articulated this feeling publicly when he stated that "for seventy years a system had been built" that was a priori indifferent or "even hostile to real human beings." In this system, the "human being means nothing, has nothing, and cannot get the most elementary things without humiliation" (quoted in Aron 2000, 127).

From the point of view of legitimacy, two additional initiatives made eminent sense. The first involved the resumption of the anticorruption drive of Andropov. In a speech to the Central Committee on April 25, 1985, Gorbachev signaled his determination to get rid of corrupt officials and practices alike. He lashed out against the "mafia," the codename for corrupt bureaucracy, and demanded an increased responsibility of the cadres. A *Pravda* article assailed the apparatchiks, accusing them, among other things, of sexual libertinism and of using their vacation lodges for sexual orgies. Verbal volleys were followed by a widespread purge of party officials including regional and republican bosses. Among those fired were the Kazakh party chief, Dinmukhamed Kunayev, and scores of lesser figures in the "Muslim mafia." As for the second economy, Gorbachev promised to eradicate the so-called "black" income and restore general order and discipline (Boyes 1990, 34–35; Moskoff 1993, 69–72; Shlapentokh 1988, 9–10; Galeotti 1997, 55; Aslund 1989, 26).

Coming in second was the antialcohol initiative, which was unveiled on May 16. According to a smuggled document in 1983 there were 40 million alcoholics in the USSR and the figure was projected to grow to 80 million by

2000, which would have constituted 65 percent of the workforce. In a presentation to the Central Committee, Novosibirsk scientists argued that a situation where "more than half of the adult population consists of alcoholics and drunkards" (Bukovsky 1986) who can barely function represents a greater risk to national security than Pershing missiles. Nikolai Ryzhkov, who replaced Tikhonov as prime minister in 1985, observed that the "country was drinking itself into the ground" (Solovyov and Klepikova 1986, 216). In his memoirs Gorbachev described the situation as "catastrophic," adding that it drastically reduced life expectancy and cost the economy 80–100 million rubles annually. Gorbachev blamed his predecessors for tacitly encouraging drinking because it generated huge receipts for the state and siphoned off monies that consumers could not otherwise spend on chronically short goods (Gorbachev 1996, 220–21; Aron 2000, 126).

To improve the standard of living of the long-suffering population, the new leader promised to increase economic performance, starting with a transformation of the system of social and labor relations. However, the scope and direction of the economic reform were subject to intense internal debate. The Novosobirsk team, which contended that collective group consciousness is inferior to self-interest in stimulating a work ethic and creating economic efficiency, positioned itself to the right. Tatyana Zaslavskaya and like-minded intellectuals were given front-page space to advance a host of once heretical notions about the relation between individual initiative, material incentives, and private property. Yakovlev admitted that, by injecting some market mechanisms into the command economy, the reformers hoped to duplicate a reverse form of Roosevelt's New Deal strategy. If accepted, such "grafting" would have replaced the hallowed principle of social equality as measured by outcomes with what was essentially a market-oriented formula of equality of opportunity. Zaslavskaya and Abel Aganbegyan, who served as economic advisers to Gorbachev, advocated a number of economic reforms that would have linked pay to productivity and introduced a market-based pricing system. On the left were Yegor Ligachev and other orthodox members of the Politburo, who argued against economic liberalization, with Ryzhkov occupying the middle ground (Aslund 1989, 26; Doder 1988, 301; Easter and Gruber 1989; Aganbegyan 1989, 1, 67, 150; Zaslavskaya 1990, 67; Sheehy 1990, 256).

Even without the left-wing opposition, Gorbachev showed little initial inclination to pursue radical economic transformation. In spite of his deep knowledge of the systemic ills of the Soviet Union, the general secretary had only a limited understanding of the modern economy. He believed that socialism could be improved upon by dispensing with the coercive features of the political system and stimulating productivity through a mixture of incentives, voluntarism, and even social emulation. To quote one observer, Gorbachev believed that "if you trusted people, created opportunities for political participation . . . people would be grateful, work harder, and would make socialism work" (Reddaway 1990, 127).

Under the slogan of *uskorenie* (acceleration) of the economy, Gorbachev unveiled a series of measures aimed at introducing rationality and accountability into the socialist production system, with a special emphasis on technocratic streamlining and technological innovation. Having been persuaded by his advisers and visiting Americans, including the futurologist Alvin Toffler, that the modern economy was based on a free flow of information, Gorbachev signaled a willingness to liberalize information policy in the economic realm. He also advocated an "integral economic and management system" as a way to improve efficiency and productivity of the economy and increase consumerism. Paving the way for a new social contract, party planners announced that by the year 2000 both productivity and output would double so that shortages in housing, health, transportation, and other public services could be fully addressed. Gorbachev made it clear that the Soviet Union needed to revitalize its economy if it wanted to retain its place in the international order. Speaking at the Smolny Institute on May 17, 1985, he hammered the theme that the Soviet Union must bring its economy up to "Western levels of efficiency and quality" (Doder 1988, 278–79) Aslund 1989, 27–28; Shane 1994, 68, 75; Sakwa 1990, 268–69).

As expected, the 27th Party Congress held between February 25 and March 3, 1986, served as a platform for unveiling the new legitimacy formula and its economic underpinnings. Speaking thirty years to the date after Khrushchev gave his "secret" speech denouncing Stalin, Gorbachev declared that communism was no longer expected to triumph over capitalism and implied that "mature socialism" was not necessarily an appropriate concept for charting the Soviet future (Doder and Branson 1990, 207; Robinson 1995, 105; Migranyan 1989, 105). Restating the Gramscian concept of humanistic socialism, Gorbachev spoke at length about "unfettering of [the] human mind and abandoning routine and fixed patterns." To underscore the importance of the human factor, the Party Congress called for the development of an interdisciplinary study of "man, science, and society" (Rawles 1996, 107; Levesque 1997, 33).

In yet another departure from orthodoxy, Gorbachev reminded Party Congress delegates that the party should be more accountable to society and questioned the morality of party privileges. Corruption of the apparatus and the need for "house cleaning" became a major theme, but speakers differed about the extent and speed of the necessary "moral purification." With orthodox communists highly uncomfortable with accountability, Boris Yeltsin emerged as the most strident critic of the party's privileged status, making him a pivotal figure among the reformers (Parker 1991, 86; Shlapentokh 1988, 13).

However, it was the debate about the economy that created the most uproar. Breaking with the habit of embellishment and self-congratulation, Gorbachev revealed the depth of Soviet retardation in science and technology and the general economic degradation. He called for an "economic reform" or even a "radical economic reform," which, if implemented, would have amounted to an embryonic socialist market. Among the new proposals was a reorganization of agriculture, with farmers slated to receive a stable procurement plan and permission to sell surplus produce. As for industry, a more market-oriented pricing mechanism was proposed that would reflect "quality, efficiency, [market] balance and demand." A flexible trading system was to be developed and enterprise management was to be based on "real economic accounting" and "self-financing." While some of the "young Turks" were disappointed by the timid nature of Gorbachev's economic vision, orthodox communists including Yegor Ligachev reacted with alarm. Much to the astonishment of those who were accustomed to the staged congresses of the past, the televised debate became personified by the sharp exchange between Yeltsin and Ligachev (Aslund 1989, 26–27; Shlapentokh 1998; Kort 1993, 301; Lockwood 2000, 121).

While most dramatic, the Party Congress was only one of the many signs that efforts to change the validity claims of the collective belief system would not be easy. For starters, Gorbachev faced stiff resistance from the nomenklatura, whose privileged position was threatened by the demand for accountability and the market-like competitiveness dictated by some of the new proposals. Complaining about sabotage of his reforms and determined to fight the opposition, Gorbachev intensified the wholesale purge of political opponents and recalcitrant middle-level bureaucrats. Still, by the summer of 1986 it became clear even to the optimistic Gorbachev that active resistance and traditional inertia threatened his vision. In a September speech he implied that future reform would be impossible without breaking the entrenched resistance of the Communist Party (Aslund 1989, 31; Oberdorfer 1992, 213).

The new Kremlin team also encountered unanticipated difficulties from citizens, especially with regard to the antialcohol campaign. Ligachev and Mikhail Solomentsev, an old-fashioned Politburo member, were put in charge of the campaign and used hard-line command tactics to restore sobriety. They closed, almost overnight, two-thirds of the liquor stores, triggering a huge increase in the moonshine industry and a shortage of sugar. The campaign backfired after hundreds of thousand of people were arrested and thousands more died from drinking commercial and industrial alcohol substitutes. Gorbachev (1996, 220–21) subsequently admitted that the "command method" of waging the campaign was wrong and Yeltsin (1990, 127) charged that the campaign had vastly expanded the black market.

Indeed, in a country where the second economy involved millions of people, these and other highly publicized steps to punish what was described as "unearned income" created even more popular discontent. According to reform economist Nikolai Shmelyov, by 1986 the volume of illegal consumer services amounted to some 30 percent of the state service sector (Smith 1990, 266). On May 28, 1986, *Pravda* and *Izvestia* published a decree on measures to strengthen the struggle against unearned income. By increasing the penalties rather than privatizing the services, Gorbachev alienated the *chastniki*, the private operators, their families, and other potential allies of his reforms (Moskoff 1993, 69–72; Ioffe 1990).

Going beyond the law of unintended consequences, the reform drive had encountered a core contradiction of communism—the need for more openness to stimulate efficiency and the strict control of the public discourse necessary for the preservation of the authority system—first identified by Hayek and von Mises. For much of its existence, the party had protected its legitimacy by restricting the amount of information on the working of the system and embellishing its record as the guardian of the common good. Although the resulting distortion of reality had demoralized and alienated the citizenry, the mixture of coercion and elaborate falsification perpetuated the validity norms on which the party based its claim to authority. Acting to increase openness, or *glasnost*, as he called it, Gorbachev knocked a huge hole in this mechanism by simultaneously lifting many of the restrictions on political discourse and forswearing the use of coercion. Although Gorbachev had toyed with the idea of glasnost since 1974, he did not realize that the newly enriched public discourse on economic reforms would discredit some of the most hallowed concepts of communist legitimacy (Laqueur 1989, 45).

First to receive intense scrutiny were issues of distributive justice. The long-standing claim that communism could satisfy popular welfare better than any other system was officially exposed as a sham. Glasnost increased awareness of such hitherto taboo issues as poverty, homelessness, and backwardness, with press accounts putting the number of those living below the poverty line at some 40 million, or a quarter of the population. Experts pointed out that if a more realistic figure for estimating poverty-level income was adopted, that number would have risen to about 40 percent (White 1999, 73–74). Daily accounts of corruption and the privileged life-style of the elite undermined whatever little credence the party's claim of egalitarian distribution of wealth still enjoyed. Encouraged by Gorbachev's attacks on the

"mafia," this intense scrutiny resulted in a rapid articulation of public grievances and a deepening division between party members and the rest of the
population. Polls taken since mid-1985 revealed that this "hastily conceptualized" but intensely felt cleavage produced extreme populist hostility toward the party (Remington 1993, 278). As one insider put it, the reforms
exposed the "real secret of 'real socialism,'" namely that communist ideology served as a cover for "a privately owned corporation represented by the
party and government apparat—the actual owner and disposer of the national wealth" (Yegorov 1993, 72). Not coincidentally, a sociological study
found that party-nominated officials in the administration, top officials in
distributive and service sectors, and workers with unjustified privileges, along
with participants in organized crime, showed the most opposition to
Gorbachev (Zaslavskaya 1990, 186).

Closely related to these delegitimizing revelations was the open debate
about the party's poor performance in managing the economy and environment. As if to dramatize these issues, the explosion at the Chernobyl nuclear
power plant on April 26, 1986, triggered a virtual "radiophobia" across the
Soviet Union. After initially hesitating, the government adopted a full disclosure policy, which revealed not only the extent of the human and environmental toll of Chernobyl but the malfunctioning of the entire Soviet system.
Although this was little appreciated by Western observers, Chernobyl had a
powerful effect on the collective belief system at both the elite and popular
level. Eduard Shevardnadze (1991, 175–76, 181) who became Gorbachev's
foreign minister, wrote that the disaster was a metaphor for "what was ill
with society," overshadowing a long list of grave ecological calamities like
the shrinking Aral Sea and the increasing pollution of the Black Sea.
Gorbachev (1996, 189; 1987, 221) added that Chernobyl exposed all that
"was wrong with the system," including its "closed nature and secrecy," com-
placency, and breaking of rules. Filtered through the esoteric meaning of the
collective discourse, Chernobyl was doubly symbolic: it was a symbol of the
failure of the command and administrative system, and a symbol of physical
retribution against the system. Described as a turning point for the Gorbachev
reforms, Chernobyl proved to be even more cataclysmic at the mass level.
The lingering fear of the authorities was replaced with the existential fear of
ecological collapse, stimulating a nascent impulse of political activism
(Palazchenko 1997, 49; Rutland 1998; Dobbs 1997, 159, 164–65; Volkogonov
1998, 434).

Working in tandem with the exposure of injustice and incompetence was
the larger notion of political transparency and accountability. Although
Gorbachev tried to limit his glasnost campaign to the economic realm, it triggered a debate on political freedoms and their dark side, political coercion. In

what was a virtual deluge of glasnost-driven publications, the party's totali-tarian history was publicly aired for the first time. The long-suppressed novel by Boris Pasternak, *Dr. Zhivago*, was published, followed by Anatoly Rybakov's *Children of the Arbat* and Anna Akhmatova's poem "Requiem." By the time Vasily Grossman's *Life and Fate* appeared, comparing Stalinism with Nazism became more prevalent (Doder and Branson 1990, 151; Crouch 1990, 69; Kort 1993, 308).

Yuri Afanasyev, a leading reformist intellectual appointed in 1986 as the rector of the State History and Archives Institute, used his position to shed a more factual light on Stalin's purges. The new estimates soon surpassed the old figure of some 4 to 5 million people killed during the peak years of 1936–39 cited by dissident historian Roy Medvedev (1972, 249). According to Olga Shatunovskaya, a clerk who worked for the Central Committee dur-ing the Khrushchev era, some 19,800,000 people were arrested between 1935 and 1941, of which 7 million were executed. Long suppressed evidence also surfaced of the mass graves in Kolpashevo in the Siberian province of Tomsk, which served in the 1930s as the torture chambers of the NKVD, the fore-runner of the KGB. Although by 1986 arrests of political offenders dropped dramatically and Gorbachev released in December the most famous political dissident, Andrei Sakharov, from his exile, the revelations had a devastating effect on the legitimacy of the communist authority system. After some sev-enty years of building a collective memory in which consensual support for the party featured very prominently, the coercive factor in the legitimacy mix was given its true due (Ligachev 1993, 254–68; Remnick 1994, 115–16; Parker 1991, 155).

An even more dramatic effect of Gorbachev's combination of glasnost and decline in coercion played itself out at the level of group legitimacy. There is no evidence to indicate that Gorbachev believed in the myth of the happy family of nations assiduously nurtured by Soviet propaganda. He was seasoned enough to realize that the legitimacy of Russian communists to rule over a vast empire rested on the increasingly hard-to-support Marxist-Leninist assumption of socialist supremacy. At the same time, Gorbachev, like many among the Russian elite, was not sensitive enough to nationalist sentiments in the republics. To quote one commentator, this Marxist "blind spot" resulted in "underestimating the power of nationalism and ethnicity as a militant psychic force in modern political consciousness" (Manuel 1992, 10). Shortly after coming to power, Gorbachev gave a speech in Kiev, Ukraine, in which he referred to the country as Russia, and on other occasions he spoke disparagingly of the corrupt culture in the republics. He chose the highly public venue of the 27th Party Congress to denounce some of the republics as "parasites" that were convinced that the "Soviet Union exists to support them." When, on December 16, 1986, the corrupt Kazakh party boss Kunayev was replaced with the ethnic Russian Gennady Kolbin, the Kremlin was caught by surprise by the ethnic riots that followed in Alma-Ata, the capital of Kazakhstan. Gorbachev was hardly more prepared for the nationalist animosity unleashed by his efforts to remove the Ukrainian leader Vladimir Shcherbitsky, who was accused of corruption and human rights violations (Doder and Branson 1990, 375; d'Encausse 1993, 5, 23–27; Kort 1993, 313; Suraska 1998, 76–77; Rigby 1990, 229–30).

To the extent that the new team considered a replacement strategy for strengthening Soviet legitimacy in the periphery, it was based on the surprisingly liberal notion that economic reforms and glasnost would turn the pseudofederation held together by force into a genuine federal community based on enlightened self-interest. Certainly, before the Alma-Ata riots, which forced Gorbachev to replace Kolbin with a Kazakh, Nursultan Nazerbayev, there was little understanding in the Kremlin of the centrifugal forces that worked to exacerbate the long-simmering ethnic animosities. But even after the disturbances, Gorbachev stuck to his opinion that the only way to handle the problem was through cooperation because "repression was useless" (Brown 1996, 254; McCauley 1998, 71–73).

Whether a cooperative strategy could overcome the built-in nationalist tensions was doubtful. The bulk of the problems could be traced to Stalin's large-scale national engineering in the 1920s, through which republican borders were created and re-created with little attention to primordial claim. In addition, entire ethnic groups were moved around, especially in the Asian republics, which became the dumping grounds for those like the Volga Germans, Crimean Tatars, Chechens, and Meskhetians, whom the regime suspected of nationalist loyalties. A more voluntary movement of population enhanced this forced ethnic mixing, with millions of ethnic Russians migrating to the republics in the service of the party or in search of job opportunities. By the mid-1980s the fifteen union republics, twenty autonomous republics, eight autonomous oblasts (provinces), and ten autonomous krai (territories) were fertile ground for ethnic grievances of mind-boggling complexity. One associate of Gorbachev described the internal borders created by Lenin and Stalin as "senseless" and claimed that 70 percent of them were potential sources of dispute. Kazakhstan with 17 million people was a case in point. Kazakhs constituted 41 percent of the population, Russians 38 percent, and the rest was composed by some one hundred ethnic groups, including Germans, Chechens, Koreans, and Chinese. With the decline of the coercion that kept this patchwork empire glued together, ethnic conflicts proliferated. In a preview of things to come, in June 1986 several thousand Tajiks attacked what were described as "foreigners" from the Caucasus who lived in the capital of Dushanbe (Yegorov 1993, 105; Barner-Barry and Hody 1995, 89; d'Encausse 1993, 97; Rashid 2002, 59).

Glasnost made it possible to air ethnic and religious grievances, distancing local identities from the Soviet one. In the Muslim republics the discourse focused on the brutal crushing of the Basmachi rebellion (1920s–30s) against the Soviet-imposed collectivization and the persecution of Islam. In the Baltics, there was a nascent outcry against the forced integration of the republics into the Soviet Union and the persecution of the Catholic Church. A debate on ecological problems following Chernobyl added a contemporary dimension to the sense of historical injury. The spreading antinuclear protest in the European republics was clearly mingled with ethnic resentment against the Russians. In Uzbekistan and Turkmenistan there was a growing outcry against the ecological disaster created by Moscow's huge irrigation schemes supporting the cotton industry. As a consequence of the irrigation system, the Aral Sea had shrunk to 51 percent of its original area and the air and soil pollution had contributed to an alarming increase in birth defects, illness, and infant mortality (Hosking 1990, 60–61).

Gorbachev's economic reforms added impetus to the centrifugal momentum. Easing central control over enterprises had redefined economic decision making by undermining the old mechanism of central planning and centralized channels of supply. Sensing an opening, regional officials demanded that a planning and supply network be established at the local level, giving national entities more power and accelerating the horizontal disintegration of the empire. Mimicking the top brass, ethnically based labor unions increasingly voiced their own grievances, often directed against Russian coworkers (Suraska 1998, 39–40; Bahry 1991).

The range of dynamics, which served to delegitimize the Soviet identity in the non-Russian periphery, fit theories of imperial demise or even decolonization, as some observers suggested. In all such cases, "the physical boundary of the regime's authority exceeds the psychological boundary of its legitimacy" (Dutter 1990, 314). Less theoretically predictable was the growing Russian ambivalence toward the empire. The glasnost discourse publicized the long-suppressed animosity and prejudice of Russians toward other citizens of the Soviet Union, especially the darker-skinned Caucasians and Asians. In a telling incident during the 8th USSR Writers' Union Congress in the summer of 1986, one Russian author published a story containing references to "fat, greasy-cheeked Georgian children," prompting the Georgian delegation to demand an apology. Inadvertently, Gorbachev himself contributed to negative stereotyping by railing against the corruption, laziness, and inefficiency of the Caucasians and Asians, once comparing the clan system in Azerbaijan to a "malignant growth" (Borovik 1991, 53; Gorbachev 1996, 144).

However, the growing doubts about the Soviet empire went beyond mere ethnic prejudice. Glasnost made it clear that contrary to the logic of center–periphery relations, Russians derived few benefits from most of their republics. On the contrary, as Gorbachev alluded, Russians found themselves subsidizing the less efficient "parasitic" ones. Russians were also much less well off than the citizens of the Baltic republics, whose economies were bolstered by the supply of cheap Russian oil and raw materials (Strayer 1998, 78). Even those who did not agree with the pan-Slavic nationalism of Aleksandr Solzhenitsyn, who urged shedding parts of the empire, including the "onerous burden of the Central Asian underbelly," expressed a growing doubt about the financial sacrifice required by Moscow to keep its large periphery. In what looked like a mirror image of the psychological distancing that took hold in the non-Russian republics, many influential Russians came to doubt whether large swaths of what was once considered an "undisputed part of the Great Soviet Motherland" were worth their upkeep (Conquest 1988, 19, 25, 140, 377; Rashid 2002, 51).

As will be apparent from the theoretical discussion, the dynamics generated by Gorbachev's resolve to adopt a Gramscian legitimacy formula impacted the collective belief system. Glasnost made a growing number of people aware of the opinion of others, thus nullifying the effects of preference falsification and the resulting political apathy. The decline in coercion made hitherto risk-averse citizens engage in authority-challenging behavior. Still, delegitimation is a relatively slow form of social learning and the process is ambiguous and diffuse enough to lull even astute leaders into believing that their policies are on the right track. Indeed, in launching his reform, Gorbachev was prepared to encounter a certain amount of resistance. But he failed to understand that it was the attempt to remove foreign policy from the legitimizing equation of communism that would pose one of the greatest threats to his plans.

Domestic Reforms and Gorbachev's Foreign Policy: Clouding the Vision for a Global Class Struggle

As interpreted by generations of Kremlin leaders, the global class struggle was one of the legitimizing principles of Soviet communism, making the military the guardian of the revolution and also its key beneficiary. Although the huge expenditure on the military was justified by what Marxism billed as an objective and scientific reading of history, ontologically, the class crusade was part and parcel of an idealistic ideology. It justified an approach to economic management whereby political goals were pursued in violation of economic rationality. At its apex stood the dual economy system in which the military and the military-industrial sector were given a quantitatively and qualitatively disproportional share of resources. By the time that Gorbachev came to power, the exhausted command economy could no longer support such expenditures, especially as the Reagan offensive increased dramatically the cost of doing foreign policy business.

What is more, Gorbachev and his economic advisers realized that the very essence of international relations had changed in a world where economics rather than military prowess alone dictated hegemony. In what was perhaps the ultimate irony, the Gorbachev team paid homage to Reagan's blueprint for an anticommunist crusade by adopting much of its analysis. Gorbachev was quick to point out that the Soviet Union was encircled not by invincible armies but by "superior economies" (Doder and Branson 1990, 207). In an April 1985 meeting of the Central Committee, Gorbachev declared that Soviet claims to world leadership would lose their credibility without a major economic revival. Gorbachev's foreign minister, Eduard Shevardnadze, would later complain that the "bloated size and unrestrained escalation of . . . the military . . . was reducing us to the level of a third rate country." Pushing the "Upper Volta with missiles" imagery even further, he declared that the Soviet Union held the first place in world military production but the sixtieth place in standard of living (Hazan 1987, 214; Shevardnadze 1991, 54).

As Gorbachev and his "young Turks" saw it, in order to revitalize the Soviet economy and restore the faith in the workability of socialism, the prominence of the military sector in the overall economy had to be downgraded. Gorbachev (1996, 401) was quick to acknowledge that "perestroika and the fundamental reforms . . . would have been impossible without the corresponding changes in Soviet foreign policy." However, in a collective belief system built on military ethos and the fight against a capitalist enemy, such a reconstruction demanded a new basis for foreign policy legitimacy.

Building on New Political Thinking (NPT), Gorbachev's foreign policy appointees such as Anatoly Chernyaev, a senior foreign policy aide, and Georgi Shakhnazarov, a senior adviser, drew on Gramsci to fashion a new foreign policy model. In Gramscian terminology, communist weakness vis-à-vis capitalism demanded a strategy of counterhegemony based on a number of adjustments such as recognition of an interdependent world and an emphasis on universal rather than class concerns. In the opinion of Gorbachev, this "Grotian Marxism" was especially imperative because nuclear weapons posed an "objective limitation" to class confrontation in the international arena. Gorbachev (1996, 402) wasted little time in announcing that the Soviet Union hoped to join the General Agreement on Trade and Tariffs and other quintessential institutions of an integrated global economy. He explained that in a world of mutual interdependence, "progress is unthinkable for any society which was cut off from the world by impenetrable state frontiers and ideological barriers." Still, Gramsci's insistence that counterhegemony was tactical in nature and would ultimately guarantee a socialist victory provided Gorbachev with a way to sell his reforms to the more orthodox elements in the leadership. By claiming that his formula would give the country a much-needed *peredyshka*, a breathing space, to start the race again, he hoped to ameliorate the opposition of the military elite and hard-line members of the Politburo (Hosking 1990, 139; Sakwa 1990, 350).

To implement NPT and give the economy a break, Gorbachev needed to revise three crucial areas of Soviet foreign policy, starting with the role of nuclear weapons. Describing the deployment of the SS-20s as an "unforgivable adventure" embarked upon because of "pressure from the military-industrial complex," Gorbachev (1996, 443) signaled his determination to weigh the "political and strategic consequences" of any future development of strategic systems and especially a response to the SDI. After commissioning a number of studies and consulting with Evgeny Velikov, a nuclear physicist and vice-president of the Academy of Sciences, Gorbachev became convinced that a Soviet response would be both too costly and not timely enough. According to Ambassador Dobrynin (1995, 620), Gorbachev was told that it would cost some 500 billion rubles to respond to Star Wars, but American sources had disputed this sum, stating that just to reconfigure the Soviet missile system would have cost around a trillion dollars (Lee 1997, 108).

Faced with a quandary and under strong pressure from the military, Gorbachev decided to use a mixture of public posturing and traditional diplomacy to stop the SDI threat. Immediately after coming to power, Gorbachev signaled his willingness to resume high-level contacts with Washington. Since the Politburo decided that expressing concern over Star Wars would only encourage the United States, Gorbachev took to asserting that the Soviet Union was not afraid of the SDI and that its military had already developed an effective response. He repeated this message during the Geneva summit meeting in November 1985 where he told President Reagan that "we have already developed a response" that "will be effective and far less expensive than your project." "If America remains deaf" we "shall accept the [SDI] challenge" (Gorbachev 1996, 407; Greenstein and Wohlforth 1994, 11–12; Levesque 1997, 24). Even though Geneva did not produce a breakthrough, Gorbachev was hard-pressed to try again at the Reykjavik summit on October 10–12, 1986. At what was described as one of the most dramatic encounters between the two superpowers, the Soviet delegation offered far-reaching concessions in "every area of arms control" in exchange for scrapping the SDI. When Reagan declined, the summit broke up, leaving Gorbachev with little to show for his extraordinary gamble (Gates 1996, 408; Haass and Williams 1988; Larabee 1986–87).

The second area targeted for reassessment was Soviet policy in the Third World. As already noted, unease about the cost of supporting movements of national liberation had surfaced even before the death of Brezhnev in 1982. Shortly after, the Institute of World Economy and International Relations and other progressive think tanks began to argue that "uncritical attempts to replicate the Soviet model of economic development" in underdeveloped countries were "premature" or even "misguided." Indeed, in a dramatic break with dependency theory, which, as noted, blamed underdevelopment on international capitalism, Soviet experts encouraged their socialist Third World clients to solve their economic problems through integration into world markets (MacFarlane 1992, 127–59; Brzezinski 1990, 215).

While the Gramscian formula made waging class warfare in the Third World questionable on theoretical grounds, the new Kremlin used the more pragmatic argument of cost to support its contention that economically nonviable clients were a drag on the Soviet Union. In this view, Moscow's support in the "struggle for national liberation" in Latin America, where the Reagan administration had mounted a successful counteroffensive in Nicaragua and El Salvador, was highly burdensome. Topping the concerns was Afghanistan, especially after the United States began supplying the mujahedeen with highly effective Stinger missiles. In April 1985 the Politburo reviewed its Afghan policy with a view to seek a way out, followed by a December decision to withdraw with dignity, a euphemism for striking a reasonable deal with the United States. This message was conveyed to the U.S. administration by various emissaries, but Washington was not responsive. Gorbachev brought up the subject during the Reykjavik summit in the hope of persuading Reagan to cease his help to the mujahedeen. The president declined. In November 1986 the Politburo finally reached the decision to get out of Afghanistan. In addition to the economic and military burden, the unpopular war, which Gorbachev described as a "bleeding wound," was blamed for draft dodging, drug addiction, and general demoralization among youth (Doder and Branson 1990, 223; Greenstein and Wohlforth 1994, 36; Shevardnadze 1991, 58; Ekedahl and Goodman 1997, 188–89; Phillips 1989).

Perhaps the most painful area of revision was Soviet relations with its external empire in Eastern Europe. Following the decision to refrain from intervention in Poland, the debate about the future of Moscow's East European satellites had intensified among the top leadership. During his first speech as general secretary, Gorbachev departed from the customary emphasis on "socialist internationalism," a code word for a homogenous commitment to a Soviet-style economy on the part of the satellites. To Gorbachev, already

concerned about the price of bailing out the inefficient East European economies, the potential cost of repressing the spreading unrest was too high to
contemplate. After almost two years of advising his East European colleagues
to reform or face domestic collapse, in November 1986 he told a gathering
of leaders that Moscow could not keep them in power any more. The message, which spelled the official end of the Brezhnev doctrine, followed a
highly secret decision to give up Eastern Europe on the grounds that "we had
the example of Afghanistan before us" (Remnick 1994, 234; Crow 1995;
Brzezinski 1990, 129–30; Kwitny 1997, 554).

Gorbachev's efforts to reform foreign policy provoked a powerful reaction. As a group, the military felt the most threatened by the switch to
Gramscian legitimacy with its vision of universal human values and more
harmonious relations between socialism and capitalism. Even such relative
liberals as General Dmitry Volkogonov, an ally of Yeltsin, were upset by
what they perceived as Gorbachev's undue "pacifism." Other senior cadres,
including the Main Political Administration of the Soviet army, tried to interpret New Political Thinking in a way that would accommodate class struggle.
The military was also taken aback by the attack on the "Ogarkov legacy"
that Gorbachev launched during the 27th Party Congress and by his announcement of the minimalist-sounding new Soviet doctrine of "military sufficiency."
Even more perturbing than ideological changes was the real possibility that a
more rational and less centralized economy would eliminate the preferential
budgetary treatment of the military since the revolution. Indeed, during his
first formal meeting with the high command in July 1985, Gorbachev discussed the need to restructure the military into a more lean and efficient
organization (Brown 1996, 223; Odom 1992; Bathurst 1993, 99; Doder and
Branson 1990, 206).

Keeping an equally anxious watch on the new leadership was the KGB.
Its chief, Viktor Chebrikov, was initially among Gorbachev's strongest supporters, a posture rewarded by a speedy elevation to a full member of Politburo in April 1985 and the honor of delivering the keynote address during
the November 6 commemoration of the revolution. But Chebrikov grew progressively uneasy when he realized that the reforms would go well beyond
the parameters envisioned by Andropov. The KGB chief and his top associates were even more tone deaf to Gorbachev's conciliatory foreign policy,
constantly accusing "Western subversion" and "Zionist sources" of fomenting unrest among Soviet nationalities and religious minorities (Garthoff 1996;
Popplewell 1991; Azrael 1989, 30–35; Shane 1994, 107).

According to a number of defectors and others familiar with Soviet intelligence, well before Reykjavik the KGB leadership began to realize that its
influence over Gorbachev was dwindling. In a bid to slow down the process

of normalization of relations with Washington, the KGB's First Chief Directorate under Vladimir Kryuchkov apparently engineered an incident whereby a KGB resident in New York, Gennadi Zakharov, was caught with a contact in August 1986. When the FBI arrested Zakharov, the KGB picked up American journalist Nicholas Daniloff on September 7. With its proximity to the Reykjavik summit, the incident enraged Reagan and embarrassed Gorbachev, who came to suspect that the KGB was trying to sabotage his planned arms negotiations. Kryuchkov was also behind a plan to present Reagan with advance knowledge about what subsequently turned into the Iran-Contra scandal, in the hope of blackmailing the American president. The move was confounded by Gorbachev, who assured Reagan that the USSR would not fan the flames of the controversy, leaving Kryuchkov more determined than ever to derail the new general secretary (Shvets 1994, 144–45, 161–62; Andrew 1995, 446; McCauley 1998, 82; Doder and Branson 1990, 158; Bearden and Risen 2003, 188–91).

Many hard-line civilian leaders shared the misgivings of the military and the KGB, especially as NPT threatened to jeopardize the integrity of the external empire. In June 1985 a leading article in *Pravda* written under a pseudonym complained about the dangers of too much heterogeneity and individualism in Eastern Europe. These and other hard-line sources repeated the KGB line that Western "provocateurs" were causing Eastern Europeans to "choose bourgeois democracy" over "reformed socialism." More to the point, Shevardnadze revealed that East European leaders who were reluctant to embrace the reforms urged on them by Gorbachev found allies among Soviet officials and "emissaries" (Remnick 1994, 234; Schmidt-Hauer 1986, 148; Shevardnadze 1991, 115).

Public displays of differences between Gorbachev and hard-liners continued for most of 1985 and 1986, indicating an intense behind-the-scenes power struggle. Gorbachev was able to purge the armed forces by retiring a large number of senior officers. In an unprecedented development, Minister of Defense Marshal Sokolov was not promoted to full membership of the Politburo. Purges also took place in the Ministry of Foreign Affairs, where Shevardnadze tried to flush the allies of the rigidly orthodox Gromyko. Ambassador Dobrynin replaced the stalwart Ponomarov in the International Department of the Central Committee and Vadim Medvedev, the head of the Central Committee's Academy of Social Sciences and a key NPT architect, was slated to head the Socialist Countries Department of the Central Committee. Dobrynin was mandated to develop a more West-friendly policy while downgrading support for revolutionary movements, and Medvedev's appointment signaled the Kremlin's growing detachment from its socialist satellites. Undoubtedly, Gorbachev scored an important victory when his chief hard-line rivals Romanov and Grishin were expelled from the Politburo and the latter was also relieved of his duties as the party secretary of Moscow and replaced in December 1985 with Yeltsin (Brown 1996, 213–20; Hazan 1987, 169; Doder 1988, 300–301).

Still, the opposition remained entrenched in the army, party, and state bureaucracy. To use Zaslavskaya's (1990, 186) terminology, they ranged from "conservatives" to "reactionaries" and were determined to undercut Gorbachev. Following the 27th Party Congress, during which the original anti-Brezhnev coalition broke up, orthodox elements coalesced around Ligachev, whose relatively young age and clean image made it harder for the reformers to dismiss him as part of the corrupt kleptocracy or doddering gerontocracy. The apparent strength of the opposition convinced Gorbachev that reforming the Soviet system would have to go beyond the relatively modest *uskorenie* policies. In the meantime, though, he had to scrap his plan to dismantle the privileged status of the military. Indeed, the budget for 1985–86 showed no signs of reduction in the rate of growth in military expenditure (Holloway 1989–90).

Such power struggles and the resultant confusion in public policy are not unusual during periods of transition. However, the mixed signals in Moscow made it harder on Soviet watchers in the United States to evaluate Gorbachev's political debut and, more important, agree on where the Soviet Union was headed.

Making Sense of Gorbachev: The Politics of the Predictive Process in Washington

The ascendancy of Gorbachev deepened the simmering tensions between the squeezers and the dealers in the Reagan administration. Adept at playing the bureaucratic game, both factions tried to imprint the official Soviet estimate with their own interpretation of the developments in Moscow. Gates (1996, 335) alluded to this struggle by noting that "how people . . . viewed Gorbachev in his early days . . . depended on where they worked, their own political philosophy, and how much they knew about Russian and Soviet history."

True to form, the squeezers, including Weinberger, Casey, and Perle, were highly skeptical of Gorbachev and his agenda. In his first evaluation of Gorbachev in June 1985, Casey wrote that neither the new leader nor those around him were "reformers and liberalizers" (Fitzgerald 2000, 329; Winik 1988–89). Gates, who was promoted to deputy director of central intelligence in April 1986, tended to side with the hard-liners. Tellingly, Gates (1996, 335–36, 375–77) compared Gorbachev to an "uncertain trumpet" and chose to focus on Soviet policies that indicated continuity rather than change.

Describing the reforms as "rhetoric," Gates pointed out that much of the Moscow praxis was essentially orthodox in nature. As for NPT, Gates considered it to be a clever trick aimed at reviving détente without changing "basic Soviet positions" on strategic upgrade, arms control, or limiting the amount of money pumped "into Nicaragua, Angola and Afghanistan." To the extent that hard-liners acknowledged change, they argued that this was merely a *peredyshka*, a breathing space for communism to regroup and achieve its avowed goal of world domination. In the words of Gates, it was "war by another name," a "war without declaration, without mobilization, without massive armies" (quoted in Andrew 1995, 495).

George Shultz and other dealers strongly disagreed with this assessment and argued that Gorbachev was sincere in his effort to reform the Soviet system and improve international relations. Shultz (1993, 527–29, 703, 724) formed a positive impression of Gorbachev during Chernenko's funeral and was further confirmed in this belief by a number of meetings with Shevardnadze. According to the secretary of state, a number of other observers, including Charles Wick from the Information Agency, shared his opinion. An article by a senior Soviet analyst in the State Department published in *Foreign Policy* described Gorbachev as an "organic reformer" who sincerely wanted to liberalize the Soviet Union (Ploss 1986). However, Shultz had a hard time persuading Casey and Gates, who continued, in his words, to insist that the "Soviets wouldn't change and couldn't change." In order to fashion a coordinated response to Gorbachev, in the beginning of 1986 a "steering committee" of senior officials was created that met in the State Department on Saturdays. But the Saturday seminars did not settle matters. As Gates (1996, 377), who attended along with Casey, put it, "there was no meeting of the minds between me and the Secretary."

With Reagan seemingly in the middle, both sides had a large stake in their version of Soviet reality. Finding it hard to imagine that the Soviet Union would ever collapse, the dealers saw Gorbachev's ascendancy as an opportunity to conclude the START and INF agreements and solve a number of regional conflicts. For the anticommunist crusaders in the administration, Gorbachev's real or apparent change of course was unwelcome news. Casey and other true believers were as determined as ever to vanquish the Soviet Union, a scenario that would have been impossible if Gorbachev managed to improve the economy. The July 16, 1986, report of the Committee on the Present Danger stated that the real goal of American foreign policy should be "peace in a pluralistic world" rather than arms negotiations. The report also noted that such negotiations should be a "means to an end" rather than an "end itself" (Rostow 1987, 26). This was a roundabout way of implying that by making overtures to Moscow, the administration "has sacrificed most of the momentum and many of the principles and initiatives that marked its early years." At the very least, the crusaders urged the administration to beef up the American military arsenal first and then negotiate with the Soviet Union from a position of undeniable strength (Rostow 1987, 26; Eberstadt 1988, 45).

Much to the disappointment of right-wing critics, President Reagan sided with Shultz on the issue of negotiations even though he found Gorbachev to be a dedicated communist who believed that the system was "managed poorly" and could be fixed. The "Soviet economic tailspin" helped to convince him that the new leader would "come around" to an arms reduction agreement palatable to the United States (Reagan 1990, 612, 660, 707; Andrew 1995, 494–95). The president also refused to abandon the nuclear arms treaties in spite of the fact that the Soviet Union had continued to violate the 1972 ABM treaty. According to Shultz (1993, 522, 728, 749), Reagan also resisted the efforts of Casey and Weinberger to use the Daniloff incident to scuttle the Reykjavik summit.

Even though right-wing critics decried Reagan's apparent "defection" from the anticommunist crusade, the administration did not abandon its plans to destabilize the Soviet system and further increase Moscow's imperial cost. Largely driven by the indefatigable Casey, these efforts included a further restriction on transfer of Western technology and a disruption of international markets in order to confound the centrally planned Soviet economy, which had relied on a relatively stable international supply and demand network (Persico 1990, 522). Acting upon the same rationale, Washington also rejected Shevardnadze's plea to reach a face-saving deal on Afghanistan. On the contrary, the CIA had used the war to destabilize the Soviet Muslim republics by, among other things, radicalizing the population, which was encouraged to demand more local and religious autonomy, thus testing Gorbachev's credibility (Rashid 2002, 44). In another attempt at subversion, the CIA used the growing resistance to the war among Soviet citizens to foment more political unrest. In a parallel move, the quasi-governmental National Endowment for Democracy intensified its activities in Poland and other satellites by funding a host of initiatives. The Institute for Democracy in Eastern Europe was charged with monitoring workers' rights, and the NED-financed Center for Democracy run by a Soviet dissident was tasked with pressing for human rights in the Soviet Union (Gates 1996, 427; Coogan and Vanden Heuvel 1988; Muravchik 1988; Puddington 1988, xi). Speaking in 1986, Casey asserted that these tactics were highly effective in delegitimizing communism. In his words, "a progressive withdrawal of domestic support for a government accompanied by nagging military pressure . . . is what helps bring down or alter a repressive regime" (quoted in Menges 1990, 7).

Conservatives had also intensified efforts to expose Soviet machinations against the United States, which were given a detailed hearing in a 1985 conference entitled "Contemporary Soviet Propaganda and Disinformation." Utilizing material obtained from defectors and other sources, they accused the KGB of creating forgeries that purported to show American conspiracies against Third World leaders and blamed it for spreading rumors that Washington had masterminded the spread of AIDS in Africa and the kidnapping of South American babies to harvest their parts. Conservatives asserted that such disinformation practices had actually intensified after Gorbachev came to power (Bittman 1985; Andrew 1995, 496; Gates 1996, 358; Laqueur 1985, 247). An even more effective tool involved publicizing Soviet human rights abuses, including slave labor practices in the Gulag. A CIA report, which put the number of Gulag prisoners at 4 million, had been widely disseminated, and Reagan (1990, 606–7) was fond of recalling that women prisoners in a Soviet labor camp smuggled out a poem congratulating him on his reelection and praising his anticommunist campaign. Shultz (1993, 503) strongly suspected that the slave labor issue was used to sabotage the State Department's negotiations, especially as such practices were said to continue under Gorbachev. These tactics also irritated liberal observers like Cohen (1986, 27), who accused the CIA of using "prejudicial language" when discussing slave labor on the grounds that "prisoners in most American penitentiaries must also work." But prominent dissidents like Solzhenitsyn (1985) counteracted by blasting Western liberals for obfuscating the extent of Soviet coercion.

Keenly attuned to symbolism in public discourse, the hard-liners were opposed to any gesture of the State Department that would legitimize communist leaders. Gates (1996, 358) admitted that the CIA "pulled out all the stops to make Gorbachev unwelcome in Geneva." Visits of U.S. diplomats to East European countries whose leaders—Jaruzelski in Poland, Erich Honecker in East Germany, and Nicolae Ceausescu in Romania—were viewed as vulnerable by the NED were strenuously discouraged. Secretary of State Shultz (1993, 877) bitterly resented this strategy. As he would later sarcastically describe it, the hard-liners urged him to avoid visits to all "evil empire" leaders since it "would enhance their credibility." Frustrated by the opposition, on August 5, 1986, he submitted his resignation, but the president rejected the offer. Although Shultz gained control over contacts with the Soviet bloc, the squeezers retained a fair measure of influence in the administration.

With the factional struggle raging, the CIA's Soviet estimate, already strained by years of methodological disagreements and ideologically motivated suspicions, struggled to retain a modicum of objectivity and impartiality. On the whole, SOVA analysts managed to convey the performance crisis in the Soviet Union, with a special emphasis on technologically "antiquated industrial base." They also became more attuned to the softer indices of legitimacy crisis, going as far as to discuss "societal malaise" (CIA Documents, SOV85–10165, SW85–10038, SOV85-10175, SOV85–10005, SWM-86–20051, SOV85–10141).

Gorbachev's modernization process, which was said to be ambitious in scope but not revolutionary, prompted a large number of studies. CIA analysts described in great detail the new reforms, ranging from agriculture policies to a more relaxed public discourse. They also listed the numerous obstacles faced by the new leadership, including bureaucratic resistance and pressures from the military sector (CIA Documents, SOV 86–10042, GI-86–10083X, SOV 85–10141, SOV 86–10023; MacEachin 1996, no. 17).

However, the Agency had no detailed knowledge of the budding antireformist alliance between Ligachev, military leaders, and the KGB's rising star, Kryuchkov. There was also no awareness that Kryuchkov's increased stature stemmed from the fact that, in 1985, he was managing the American spy Aldrich Ames, a CIA counterintelligence branch chief of Soviet operations. Ames supplied the KGB with the names of twenty-five agents and Soviet officials who were working for U.S. and British intelligence. His betrayals, compounded by those of FBI counterintelligence officer Robert Hanssen, would effectively destroy the CIA's human intelligence capabilities within the Soviet Union (Carlisle 2004, 27–29). According to a Soviet defector, Kryuchkov's success with Ames emboldened him to believe that he could manipulate and ultimately replace Gorbachev (Andrew 1995, 499; Shvets 1994, 162). Oleg Kalugin (1994, 241), a high-ranking KGB official, later revealed that he had warned Gorbachev's aide Yakovlev about Kryuchkov's intentions and ambitions.

Lacking deep knowledge of the complexities of the Soviet power struggle and unable to use the fuzzy concepts of NPT, the CIA had to rely on hard data to gauge Soviet defense spending and, by extension, Gorbachev's commitment to reform. But the focus on the bottom line revealed a deep split in the Agency between Casey partisans and some SOVA analysts. In a June 1985 testimony to Senate, Gates and Lawrence Gershwin, the National Intelligence Officer (NIO), predicted a 5–7 percent growth of Soviet defense expenditures until the year 1990; a 7–10 percent growth was projected if a more ambitious deployment strategy was to take place. However, in March 1986, a SOVA paper claimed that unless Gorbachev succeeded in modernizing the economy, the coming crunch would make such increases impossible. SOVA's conclusions were welcomed by Shultz, who could argue that economic difficulties would compel Moscow to engage in more vigorous arms control. But Weinberger and other hard-liners were reluctant to accept the notion that "economic constraints would impinge seriously on Soviet defense programs" (Firth and Noren 1998, 95–96).

With both sides entrenched in their positions, the CIA and the rest of the administration had to wait for the next phase of Gorbachev's reform to determine the direction of change. It was left to the academic community, less encumbered by research protocols and boasting of powerful predictive paradigms, to make an early assessment of Gorbachev and the direction of change.

The Revisionist Paradigm Vindicated? Gorbachev and the Reformability of the Soviet System

Gorbachev's ascension to power galvanized Sovietology. The predictive endeavor became especially valued, prompting academics and pundits alike to speculate on Gorbachev's "real intentions" and creating in the process a thriving "Soviet studies industry" (Rutland 1993, 109; Ulam 2000, 256). Since, as noted, predictions are shaped by scholarly paradigms, the rush to analyze the future of change in the Soviet Union refocused attention on the core assumption of the revisionist-pluralist and totalitarian schools of thought.

Mainstream Sovietologists had to make a major adjustment in order to explain the Gorbachev phenomenon. After years of underestimating the social malaise and economic decay, some leading scholars admitted that the Soviet system was in deep crisis. Describing the Brezhnev legacy as "harsh," one of them wrote that "the weight of ineffectual and archaic political and economic institutions conspires to deny the country access to the global and third revolution" (Bialer 1986b, 57–80; Bialer and Afferica 1985, 643; Hough 1985; Lapidus 1986b). Political scientists also became less optimistic about problems of ethnicity and nationality (Lapidus 1986a). Olcott (1982; 1986, 73), who in 1982 showed little apprehension about Muslims, was now describing them as Moscow's "troublesome minority." Still, an expert who analyzed center–periphery relations as part of "demand articulation in the Soviet Union" found that an "asymmetrical but genuine exchange" and "licensed demandingness" existed. In the language of comparative politics still favored by pluralists, this finding implied an orderly exchange in Moscow–republic relations (Breslauer 1986, 651, 679).

Though finally admitting to Soviet distress, liberal scholars were convinced that the crisis of performance and legitimacy was far from terminal. Responding to Marshall Goldman (1983) and other samples of "crisis literature," Hough (1986, 283–84) warned against what he described as the "comfortable feeling that the Soviet Union is in irreversible decline." He predicted that the young Gorbachev was determined to reverse the decline and might even "usher the new century in triumph." Another scholar argued that "the emphasis upon crisis in the communist system is premature," adding that the "economic difficulties [the Soviets] may face may be mediated by political action" (White 1986, 470). Still another contended that "economic stress provoking political failure is conceivable," but not "very likely." He went on to assert that in the "final analysis stability depends on legitimacy" and that the "legitimacy of the Soviet regime in the eyes of its people and elites is much stronger than many Western analysts assume" (Bialer 1986b, 36, 335, 345).

As the promise of reforms turned into reality, the revisionists felt increasingly vindicated in their long-standing belief that the Soviet system was capable of reforming itself. Revisionists were first to assert that Gorbachev was a genuine reformer and predicted significant change in the system (Cohen 1986, 78–95; Hough 1986; Schmidt-Hauer 1986, 151). There was less certainty as to what a reformed communist system would look like, triggering a broad discussion on regime transition. With models such as "hesitant modernization" and "centralized rationality" bandied around, the formula of market socialism, first developed by the noted Polish economist Oskar Lange in *On the Economic Theory of Socialism* (Lange and Taylor 1938) and given a hearing in the work of Alec Nove (1983) on viable socialism, created much excitement. The then nascent Chinese model of market liberalization, working in tandem with strong political controls, was also mentioned as a possible contender. According to one survey, about 60 percent of the "Sovietological output" reflected the belief that Soviet communism would evolve into a more progressive form, with market socialism becoming a favorite bet. The promise of change in the Soviet Union had even resurrected faith in the convergence theory popular in the 1960s, with the leading futurologist Olaf Helmer forecasting a meeting of the Soviet and American systems (Amann 1986; Pakulski 1986; Brown 1985a; Colton 1986, 4; Rutland 1998, 45; Helmer 1986).

As in the past, revisionist Sovietologists utilized contemporaneous changes in the Soviet Union to revisit the historical legitimacy of the communist regime. Leading the way was Stephen Cohen (1985, 33, 15), who urged "rethinking the Soviet experience" and accused Pipes and other like-minded scholars of practicing "missionary scholarship" in their zealous propagation of the belief that the Soviet Union was a totalitarian society incapable of progressive evolution. Although Cohen admitted that some revisionist scholarship overemphasized "progressive developments" while "minimizing or obscuring the colossal human tragedies and material losses caused by Stalin," he credited the revisionist paradigm with a broader vision of Soviet reality and the ability to discern impending change. Complaining about "totalitarian" biases in American perceptions, Cohen (1986, 36) argued that "the official ideology [in the Soviet Union] still professes lofty values" and the word "conscience has profound meaning." Ironically, the revisionist scholars whom Cohen criticized chose the first two years of Gorbachev's tenure to defend communist legitimacy by further downplaying the scope of Stalin's terror. Ignoring the new reports on Stalin's atrocities published under glasnost, J. Arch Getty, Sheila Fitzpatrick, and others described as highly exaggerated the accounts of terror and fear during the Great Purges and put the number of those killed in the thousands rather than millions (Thurston 1986; Getty 1985; Fitzpatrick 1984).

If for the revisionists the Gorbachev phenomenon was an unpredicted but highly positive occurrence, the developments in Moscow posed a conundrum for the totalitarian paradigm and its conservative and neoconservative followers. After insisting that the party would never give up power, such scholars found it hard to fathom a communist leader bent on shaking up the highly centralized power structure. Reflecting this line of thinking, one observer wrote that "Gorbachev spent 30 years getting to the top" and he "will consider his major duty" to broaden and consolidate the party's power. Another contended that "Gorbachev and his peers have so far shown every sign that their main interest is preserving the domestic status quo and especially the political structure through which they have risen" (Heller 1985; Simis 1985, 4; Kaiser 1986–87; Elliot 1985).

Even those who were willing to consider that Gorbachev might go beyond what Brzezinski (1985, 31) called the KGB formula of "modernization, regimentation and rejuvenation," were skeptical that communism could be reformed, a theme that had been long emphasized by Brzezinski, Pipes, and Soviet dissidents. Echoing Pipes's (1984a) article, two scholars noted that "whatever the scope" of Gorbachev's reform, he would have to confront the "basic incompatibility between modernization and authoritarianism" (Mitchell and Gee 1985, 317). The émigré economist Igor Birman (1985, 115) was even more blunt about Gorbachev's prospects. Noting that economic "decentralization can be effective only if those who make the decisions and those who implement them are ruled by their own selfish interests," Birman asserted that "market socialism makes no more sense than socialism with a human face." The dissident Vladimir Bukovsky (1986, 20) concluded that, regardless of the strategy that Gorbachev will pursue, the "implacable logic of Marxist-Leninist analysis predicts the inevitable demise of socialism." Brzezinski (1986, 127) affirmed his belief that the existence of non-Russian nationalities would prevent the evolution of Soviet Union into a more "modern state."

As always, academic analysis of Soviet trends was closely linked to efforts to influence U.S. foreign policy. Revisionists, pointing to NPT, argued that Gorbachev would move Soviet foreign policy in a more progressive direction. Hough (1985) was among the first to argue that Gorbachev's economic reforms would significantly influence his foreign policy. Simes (1986, 478, 491) maintained that Gorbachev's preoccupation with modernization "warrants a peaceful environment" and that under its new leader the Soviet Union "demonstrated a new sense of purpose, a new realism and a new creativity." Valkenier (1986, 415) found a new "somberness" in Soviet Third World policies and a "predisposition to seek disengagement from risky ventures" there. A noted social psychologist wanted the American intelligence community to "empathize" with the Soviet Union and declared that, though Moscow wanted to hold on to Eastern Europe and Afghanistan, it did not "want to dominate the world" (White 1986, 67). These and other observers urged the Reagan administration to help Gorbachev by removing military threats and expanding economic ties (Schmidt-Hauer 1986, 169; Taubman 1986; Bialer 1986b, 373).

Other academic commentators seized on the liberal signals emanating from Moscow to denounce the administration's continuous military buildup. In a much discussed book, Garthoff (1985, 596) accused Reagan's foreign policy team of exaggerating the Soviet military buildup in order to justify its own aggressive foreign policy. Further to the left was the IPS scholar William Arkin, who co-authored a book charging that the U.S. nuclear structure was "out of control" (Arkin and Fieldhouse 1985). Another author accused the administration of creating a "myth" of Soviet military superiority and denied that the Soviet Union violated SALT II or engaged in chemical warfare in Afghanistan and elsewhere (Gervasi 1986, 45, 75, 237–44). The futurologist Olaf Helmer scolded the United States for a "somewhat hysterical aversion" to any form of Marxism and advocated a total elimination of nuclear weapons (Helmer 1986, 485).

Unpersuaded by Gorbachev's intentions and skeptical of his chances, adherents of the totalitarian model urged the U.S. government to use the contradictions of communism to destroy rather than help to reform the Soviet system. In a forceful restatement of Reagan's anticommunist crusade, Brzezinski (1986, 184, 230–31, 237) offered a "game plan" to undermine the Soviet empire. He contended that the United States should use the "internal contradictions" of the "modern-day Great Russian empire" to promote "national assertiveness" of Muslims, Ukrainians, Baltic peoples, and other minorities as well as pluralization of Eastern Europe and, eventually, of the Soviet Union itself. Brzezinski also counseled against relaxing trade and technological restrictions, stating that the United States should exploit and protect its major asset, technological superiority, which, in his opinion, included SDI.

In staking out early positions on the true character of Gorbachev and the degree of reformability of communism, both the revisionists and the totalitarians relied on the inner logic of their respective paradigms. As Gorbachev was preparing to abandon the limited "acceleration" program for a more radical restructuring of the Soviet system, both his policy and the paradigms of his watchers in the United States were about to be tested in the uncharted territory of a communist regime change.

6

Perestroika

Systemic Change, 1987–1989

With little to show for the *uskorenie* effort, the reformist leadership decided to take the reforms to the level of *perestroika*—loosely translated as restructuring. However, the intense struggle over the desirable limits of systemic restructuring forced Gorbachev to pursue an incoherent and indecisive policy that achieved little success in reforming communism. The mixed signals from Moscow made it harder for American Soviet watchers, already split along ideological and paradigmatic lines, to analyze the fast-paced events and predict the future.

Experimenting with a New Legitimacy Formula: From Gramsci to "Socialist Democracy" and "Socialist Market"

By early 1987 the Kremlin leadership came to realize that the limited *uskorenie* reforms had failed. More important, hope that the Soviet Union could duplicate the much-vaunted Chinese example of liberalizing the economy without changing the political system all but evaporated. Unlike Deng Xiaoping, a hardened revolutionary leader who did not hesitate to use terror to enforce his vision, Gorbachev was psychologically and intellectually committed to a more consensual, Gramcsian style of politics. Unable to compel the vast bureaucracy to support the economic reforms, Gorbachev and his advisers decided to undermine the authority of the party by mobilizing the people. They let it be known that the party replaced commitment to Marxism with a "corrupt network of personal alliances" and, as Gorbachev put it, formed a "braking mechanism" that needed to be overcome in order to achieve progress (Gorbachev 1996, 203; Mlynar 1990, 21; Boyes 1990, 36).

Gorbachev chose the January 27, 1987, plenum to launch a bitter attack on the party and unveil a more radical change of the system, which he dubbed perestroika. Using for the first time the term "crisis" to describe the situation, he warned that without a radical restructuring of the system the Soviet Union would continue its slide into internal decay and international irrelevance. But finding a way to put political pressure on the party was not easy. At the end of 1985, Gorbachev's chief adviser, Aleksandr Yakovlev, wrote a memorandum suggesting that the Communist Party be split in two to promote competitiveness and accountability. If implemented, such a move might have dramatically affected the trajectory of change. However, Gorbachev rejected Yakovlev's idea in favor of a more vague formula of "socialist choice" or "socialist pluralism of opinion." The new formula relied on a fairly free public discourse aimed at keeping the party accountable to the new leadership and more pliant in implementing economic reforms (Boldin 1994, 73; Brown 1996, 105; Robinson 1995, 123–24).

Following the plenum, Gorbachev utilized glasnost revelations to wage a further campaign against the party's legitimacy. In what one observer described as an act of "desacralization of the old order," the general secretary delivered a savage attack on Brezhnev and his "sham" military and literary accomplishments. Brezhnev's name was erased from city streets, and his monuments were removed. Detailed revelations about Brezhnev-era corruption and his high-living family and other officials were made public on a daily basis. The already disgraced Brezhnev son-in-law Yuri Churbanov was sentenced to twelve years in a harsh-regime labor camp and his daughter Galina stripped of her remaining state allowances. The privileges of the nomenklatura were drastically curtailed, including the elimination of the chauffeured Volga sedans, the vehicle of choice of the top elite. Even more significant was Gorbachev's very public admission of the role of violence in the party's ascendance to power. Using the occasion of the seventieth anniversary of the October revolution in 1987, Gorbachev described Stalin's crimes as "enormous" and "unforgettable" (Breslauer 1989; White 1990, 62; Doder and Branson 1990, 182, 297).

With the apparent blessing of Gorbachev, a flood of revelations poured forth. In January 1987, Avtandil Makharadze's film *Repentance*, a powerful condemnation of Stalinism, was released, followed by Vasily Belov's book *The Last Day*, which detailed the destruction of the peasantry during the collectivization drive. Yuri Afanasyev, head of the State History and Archives Institute, wrote that the Soviet regime had been "brought into being through bloodshed, with the aid of mass murder and crimes against humanity" (Sakwa 1990, 93; Doder and Branson 1990, 182). Some argued that the 1932–33 Stalin-induced famine in the Ukraine in which some 5 million died was an example of genocide equaling the Jewish holocaust. In 1988 Gorbachev appointed a Commission for the Additional Study of the Materials Related to Repression of the 1930s, 1940s, and Early 1950s. But the commission, which rehabilitated many of Stalin's victims, failed to keep up with the growing unofficial accounts. Most prominently, Roy Medvedev's new estimate of some 35 million victims of Stalinism, half of whom were either executed or starved to death, was published in the *Moscow News*. The Week of Conscience sponsored by *Moscow News* and the magazine *Ogonyok* fleshed out these statistics with a visually powerful exhibit about the Gulag (Sakwa 1990, 93; Doder and Branson 1990, 182; Aron 2000, 287; Shane 1994, 124, 131, 135).

By delegitimizing the party, Gorbachev hoped to garner enough public support to push through the reforms that comprised the economic dimension of perestroika. To further bolster the reformist cause, the Kremlin released a number of highly sensational revelations about disasters such as the 1953 explosion of plutonium waste in the Ural Mountains and other environmental problems to illustrate what Gorbachev called "our barbaric attitude toward nature." The malfunctioning of the economic system was also given front-page press. By 1988, Abel Aganbegyan and Nikolai Ryzhkov admitted to hidden inflation and to a steady decline of economic growth from a peak of 8 percent in the 1960 to a virtual standstill in the 1980s. It was subsequently revealed that the state budget had been running a deficit since 1976 (Gorbachev 1996, 24; Goldman 1991, 129–30; Doder and Branson 1990, 364; Andrew and Mitrokhin 1999, 557; Lee 1995, 180; Rumer 1989).

An article entitled "Lukavaya Tsifra" (A Cunning Figure) by the journalist Vasily Selyunin and the economist Grigory Khanin in the journal *Novy Mir* in February 1987 included an even more stunning disclosure of the practice of systematic statistical dissimulation and fabrication. The authors asserted that since 1928, Soviet statistics had grossly overstated actual economic performance, efficiency, and price stability, and they claimed that the actual national income had multiplied by only 6.6 times since 1928 and not by 84.4 times as officially posted. Khanin, who became an instant celebrity, noted that this disparity explained the gap between official data and anecdotal evidence of the shabbiness of daily life in the Soviet Union (Smith 1990, 101; Harrison 1993; Laqueur 1994, 58–59; Rowen and Wolf 1990b). As if to vindicate this claim, the glasnost discourse generated a daily deluge of letters and articles describing the overwhelming national poverty topped by an acute crisis in the health system. Even the staunchly ideological newspaper *Komsomolskaia Pravda* complained that before 1917 Russia ranked seventh in world per capita consumption, a figure that went down to seventy-seventh in the 1980s, placing the Soviet Union just below South Africa (Aron 2000, 282–84; Remnick 1994, 202).

While the new team was united in the analysis of past ills, there was, as before, little consensus with regard to the scope of the necessary remedies.

After the disappointment with *uskorenie*, Zaslavskaya, Nikolai Shmelyov, and other radical reformers urged a full transition to a market economy, a step advocated in a June 1987 article. They argued that market mechanisms would rid the economy of the large number of party bureaucrats and their costly privileges and institute a rational price policy for services and goods (Danilov et al., 1996, 327; Doder and Branson 1990, 242). Although by now Gorbachev was persuaded that the command economy was at the root of corruption and stagnation, he and Ryzhkov were unwilling or unable to make a radical transition to a market economy. Further to the left, Ligachev and orthodox cadres were vehemently opposed to any significant liberalization. As a result, the compromise formula of "market socialism" adopted at the June 1987 meeting of the Central Committee featured a patchwork of market and socialist remedies. At its core was the Law on Socialist Enterprises, which imposed *khozraschet*, profit and loss accountability, on enterprises. Central planning was partially dismantled by a provision that removed mandatory plan targets. The Central Committee also approved finance-and-credit mechanisms that allowed more independence to enterprises and facilitated wholesale trade among them. In August, Gorbachev promised agrarian reforms, including leaseholding, a form of private ownership, in order to reverse what the reformers deemed as the ravages of collectivization and "depeasantization" (Arbatov 1992, 259; Aslund 1989, 32–33; Sheehy 1990, 258; Lockwood 2000, 121).

If Gorbachev hoped to use the relatively cautious middle course to navigate perestroika without unduly destabilizing the system, he was bound to be disappointed. The vigorous public discourse had produced a number of unintended consequences. Perhaps the most worrisome from the Kremlin's perspective was the nationalist turmoil in the non-Russian periphery. Starting with the May demonstration of 300 Crimean Tatars who demanded a return to their ancestral homeland from which Stalin had expelled them, 1987 saw a growing wave of nationalist protest. In Central Asia ethnic grievances were inflamed when glasnost revealed widespread genetic deformities in the population caused by underground nuclear testing and the use of chemical defoliants. Tension between Azeris and Armenians, who demanded the return of Armenian-populated territory of Nagorno-Karabakh from Azerbaijan, was running high, and the Baltic republics took steps toward creating national fronts. In September, KGB chief Chebrikov denounced the ethnic conflagration and accused Western intelligence agencies of stirring up trouble (Matlock 1995, 175; d'Encausse 1993, 8–13; Doder and Branson 1990, 373).

Still, Gorbachev, who believed that his reforms would solve the nationality problems, rejected the use of force urged by the KGB. As a result, more nationalist unrest in Central Asian republics followed, fueled, among other things, by perestroika reforms that cut down on subsidies to large families and pressured women to use birth control, policies that many interpreted as deliberately anti-Muslim. The Azeri-Armenian confrontation exploded into a full-scale armed conflict, and the Baltic republics moved toward asserting independence. According to some sources, the KGB actually fostered some of the local conflagrations in order to discredit Yakovlev, who tried to mediate between Moscow and the Baltics (Goldman 1991, 123; Oberdorfer 1992, 397–98; Hill 1993; Azrael 1989, 39; d'Encausse 1993, 77, 78–79).

Yet another consequence of perestroika was the rapid growth of *neformaly*, informal grass-roots organizations that represented an array of interests ranging from the environment to the disabled and pensioners. According to some accounts, by 1988 their number reached some 30,000. As one observer noted, in a few short years the civil society in the Soviet Union, which Gramsci once described as "gelatinous," hardened to the point that it threatened Gorbachev. As if to underscore this point, on August 20–23, 1987, Boris Yeltsin, who emerged as the unofficial leader of the civic movement, convened a conference of about 300 delegates, ostensibly to support perestroika. But Yeltsin used the conference and the October 21 plenum of the Central Committee to harshly criticize the slow pace of reforms and the orthodox Marxists under the leadership of Yegor Ligachev (Mlynar 1990, 27; Galeotti 1997, 73–74; White 1999, 154–84; Remington 1990).

What Yeltsin and other radical reformers viewed as Gorbachev's unduly slow progress greatly alarmed Ligachev and the orthodox elements in the party bureaucracy and the KGB. Topping the list of their concerns were perestroika's destabilizing effects on the republics, which the KGB detailed in a series of highly classified documents. Ligachev and his allies were adamantly opposed to many of Gorbachev's economic reforms, including plans for land leasing and privatization. The hard-liners had also tried to curtail the activities of the civic groups in general and Yeltsin in particular. According to Yeltsin, after he was fired from his post as Moscow's party secretary in November, the KGB made an attempt on his life. In February 1988, Yeltsin, who was subjected to continuing KGB harassment, was dropped from the Politburo (Ligachev 1993, 138; Yeltsin, 1990, 199–202; McCauley 1998, 72; Boldin 1994, 236–37; Azrael 1989, 38).

Hard-liners also bitterly objected to Gorbachev's efforts to delegitimize the party and de-emphasize the class struggle. In an August 1987 meeting, Ligachev chided representatives of the media for showing a "disrespectful attitude toward the generations who constructed socialism." A year earlier, during an intellectual forum where Gramscian "universal human values" were discussed, Ligachev protested against "throwing out" class interests. Ligachev's chief ideological ally, R.I. Kosolapov, the dogmatic editor-in-chief of the party organ

Kommunist and a leader in the neo-Stalinist United Workers Front, founded as a response to Gorbachev, made much the same point (Sheehy 1990, 252; Gorbachev 1996, 200; Arbatov 1992, 296; Dobbs 1997, 196).

By early 1988, Ligachev, the KGB, and other hard-liners became alarmed that the class perspective was disappearing from Soviet politics. During the February Central Committee plenum, Ligachev emphasized that "young people" should be taught "a class vision of the world." Worse, the conservative group became convinced that perestroika had gotten out of control. Ligachev (1993, 91) took to warning that "under the guise of democracy" a new form of dictatorship of anarchy, of "anything goes," had taken root. Matters came to a head when *Sovetskaia Rossiia* published, on March 13, a letter by a Leningrad party activist, a teacher named Nina Andreyeva, that attacked Gorbachev and urged a return to a class-based legitimacy and Communist Party hegemony. Although Ligachev denied involvement, he and the KGB were implicated in the publication of the letter by revelations following the coup against Gorbachev (Ligachev 1993, 298–311; Pozner 1992, 53; Goldman 1991, 180; Robinson 1995, 134).

The Andreyeva letter, which some commentators described as an attempted putsch against Gorbachev, who was out of the country at the time, took the reformist leadership by surprise. Although Gorbachev was initially reluctant to react, when Ligachev left for a scheduled trip on March 27, the reformers rallied against him. On April 5, Yakovlev responded to the "anti-perestroika manifesto," as the letter became known, with an article entitled "Principles of Perestroika: Revolutionary Nature of Thinking." Gorbachev forced a showdown in the Politburo, which voted to reprimand both the editor of *Sovetskaia Rossiia* and Ligachev. However, both sides understood that the incident just raised the stakes in what became Gorbachev's signature effort, the expansion of perestroika to the realm of foreign policy.

Gorbachev's Foreign Policy: The Architect of Imperial Shrinkage

After more than two years in office Gorbachev had yet to win over the powerful military establishment to his vision of international relations. During a February 1987 conference Gorbachev elaborated upon the doctrine of "sufficient security," which virtually forsook a Soviet offensive posture, and in an April speech Yakovlev described the nature of American-Soviet rivalry as economic rather than military. Even though the generals believed that the economy needed revamping, even the more liberal among them remained skeptical of a world in which capitalism would cease to be an enemy and military strength would be replaced with economic prowess (Doder and Branson 1990, 209–15).

Disregarding this skepticism, Gorbachev set out to negotiate a treaty to reduce intermediate-range missiles in Europe by trading the Soviet SS-20s with a range of 500 to 1,500 kilometers for the Reagan-installed Pershings. When Secretary of State Shultz arrived in Moscow in April, Gorbachev went against the wishes of his general staff and agreed to include in the deal the SS-23 with a range of 400 kilometers. The enraged military commanders vowed to resist what was perceived as Gorbachev's attack on the defense establishment (Dobrynin 1995, 623).

However, in a strange twist of events, Gorbachev's hand was strengthened after a young German named Mathias Rust landed his light plane in Kremlin Square on May 28. Describing the military as incompetent, Gorbachev purged a large number of older-generation officers and dismissed the hard-line defense minister General Sokolov. His replacement, the little-known General Dmitri Yazov, and the newly promoted younger officers were said to be more in tune with the Kremlin leader (Larabee 1988; Odom 1998, 108; Suraska 1998, 80). The reshuffle of the military helped Gorbachev to push through his doctrine of "reasonable sufficiency." The intermediate-range nuclear force treaty was signed during the December summit in Washington. In early 1988, the defense leadership began to flesh out the new doctrine, which was described as the "amount of necessary power to deter strategic attack and repel an aggressor at the border, but not beyond" (Matlock 1995, 142–43; Blacker 1993, 86).

Forging of the new doctrine went hand in hand with a scathing critique of the foreign policy of Stalin and Brezhnev. On May 18, Vyacheslav Dashichev, a scholar at the Institute for the Economy of the World Socialist Systems, published an article in *Literaturnaia Gazeta* that all but admitted that the past Soviet record was expansionist and hegemonic. In his view, it created a "perception" that "the Soviet Union is a dangerous power whose leadership wants to eliminate the bourgeois democracies by military means and to establish a Soviet-type communist system throughout the world" (Mendras 1990, 19; Marantz 1988, 15; Kissinger 1994, 800). To make a clean break with the past, in June Shevardnadze announced that class struggle would no longer be considered the basis of Soviet international relations. One month later he convened a high-profile conference of senior Soviet diplomats and international relations specialists to announce the end of the struggle of "two opposing systems" (Ekedahl and Goodman 1997, 43; Matlock 1995, 143–44).

Cashing in on the Rust incident, Gorbachev moved swiftly to cut defense spending and modernize the economy by initiating a military-to-civilian industrial conversion plan. Ironically, this task was made more urgent when the military discovered that Soviet industry could not manufacture sophisticated components for the guidance system of its medium-range missiles in spite of the fact that Soviet intelligence had acquired the appropriate Western technology. Even officers like General Valentin Varennikov and Lieutenant General Leonid Ivashkov, who considered Gorbachev a traitor and favored a coup, agreed that the military must bear some costs of economic restructuring (Odom 1998, 91–92; Novikov and Bascio 1994, 66).

Even before the Rust incident, the Gorbachev team was working on its plans to shrink the empire. On a number of occasions, Gorbachev aides intimated that the Soviet Union was "against export of revolutions." These and other officials had also made it known that military help to Third World regimes would have to be curtailed, if not cut off. Pursuant of this agenda, on February 8, 1988, Gorbachev announced that Soviet forces would complete their departure from Afghanistan before the end of the year (Doder and Branson 1990, 365; Albright 1991).

More poignant but equally determined was Gorbachev's reaction to the unraveling situation in Eastern Europe. As early as the 27th Party Congress in 1986 Gorbachev and Shevardnadze urged their East European colleagues to emulate the Soviet perestroika or face collapse. The matter was discussed during a plenum of the Central Committee in January 1987 and in November Gorbachev denounced the "arrogance of omniscience" of the Soviet Union toward the Warsaw Pact members. The speech, which also promised that Moscow would cease involvement in the day-to-day decision making of its East European allies, was written by Vadim Medvedev, a key reformer, and Oleg Bogomolov, the director of the Institute for the Economy of the World Socialist System. In his memoirs, Gorbachev explained that the Soviet Union could not afford to spend the large sums of money required to prop up the economically inefficient and politically unpopular regimes. Indeed, according to Western sources, Moscow's annual subsidies to the satellites went up from a quarter of a million dollars in the 1960s to some 10 billion in the 1980s (Ekedahl and Goodman 1997, 157; Gorbachev 1996, 446, 471, 479, 483; Brada 1988).

Gorbachev's East European policy faced resistance both at home and abroad. Behind the scenes, the reformist team tried to force the military and its party allies to loosen their grip on the satellites. However, Shevardnadze disclosed that hard-line party officials were appointed as ambassadors to East European capitals against his wishes. The task was even more complicated when it came to persuading conservative East European leaders, most notably in East Germany, Romania, and Czechoslovakia, to liberalize. According to insiders, the much older East European leaders were "out of sync" with Gorbachev's New Political Thinking. They actively lobbied hard-liners in Moscow to use the Soviet army to quell domestic unrest (Oberdorfer 1991, 357; Shevardnadze 1991, 117; Dobrynin 1995, 632).

Adding to tensions over domestic problems, efforts to curtail the empire had provoked a serious hard-line backlash. By early 1988 Gorbachev learned of unauthorized transfers of military aid to Cuba, Libya, and other Soviet clients. The much-publicized military conversion program had made little progress because of obstruction by the defense establishment. Much to the frustration of the Kremlin, the military and its allies had also stymied the Kremlin's efforts to obtain exact figures on defense expenditure, prompting some Soviet civilian critics to turn to Western sources. When in the spring of 1989 Gorbachev forced the issue, the military first resisted and then provided incomplete and misleading figures (Odom 1998, 149–51, 229).

It was also during 1988 that tensions between foreign policy hard-liners and Gorbachev burst into the open. Military spokesmen began to attack their reformist critics, triggering a ferocious debate about New Political Thinking. Taking advantage of Gorbachev's summer vacation, Ligachev joined the fray. On August 5, in a speech in Moscow, Ligachev insisted that the Soviet Union must base its foreign policy on class struggle. In a speech in Tula on August 31, Ligachev attacked Shevardnadze's policy of universal human rights and insisted that the Soviet Union must return to a class-based view of international relations. Outdoing the others in shrillness, the KGB warned that perestroika was a Western-inspired effort to destabilize and break up the Soviet empire. In a September speech honoring Feliks Dzerzhinsky, the founder of the Cheka, the KGB's forerunner, Vladimir Kryuchkov, the new head of the KGB, warned about efforts of the "imperialist special services to convert Soviet people to the bourgeois understanding of democracy" (Doder and Branson 1990, 340). According to a KGB insider, Kryuchkov despised the "doves entrenched in the Foreign Ministry" and was determined to discredit Gorbachev's newfound friends in the West. To this end, the KGB charged that the United States sold Moscow computers that were specially designed to "fail at times useful to the enemy" (Shvets 1994, 158–59). While hard to prove, such a ploy would not have been out of step with Casey's plans to sabotage the Soviet economy (Azrael 1989, 35; Garthoff 1996, 236).

In spite of his worries about Ligachev and other hard-liners, Gorbachev was determined to pursue his goal of imperial shrinkage (Gorbachev 1996, 261). He forced a reshuffle in the Central Committee whereby trusted reformers, including Vadim Medvedev and Yakovlev, took over key ideological and foreign policy portfolios (Doder and Branson 1990, 348). Growing even bolder, the general secretary pushed through the Politburo a decision for a unilateral reduction of armed forces in spite of the fact that senior military commanders had previously gone on record opposing such a step. Gorbachev chose the December 7 meeting of the United Nations to announce that the Soviet Union would unilaterally cut half a million soldiers from its army of just under 5.3 million. He explained that the new international balance of power would be based on "creative cooperation" rather than military rivalry, and that a "transition from an economy of armament to an economy of disarmament" would take place (Gorbachev 1996, 460; Odom 1998, 145).

Although the UN speech created an international sensation, it had a decisively less enthusiastic reception at home. Marshal Sergei Akhromeyev resigned as the chief of the general staff for "reasons of health" and was replaced by the little known and relatively junior General Mikhail Moiseyev. The army, already demoralized by ethnic unrest, increased desertions, and budgetary cuts, was now forced to restructure under the stiff shrinkage schedule. On balance, the army's ethnic problems seemed to grow more acute, especially as conflicts among rank and file, including brutal hazing, acquired ethnic coloration. Using the army to put down ethnic rebellions contributed to the deterioration in moral. In spite of an affirmative action program that sought to promote indigenous officers, there were calls to establish ethnic armies, a move that was strenuously opposed by Defense Minister Dmitri Yazov, General Varennikov, and others (Herspring 1996, 115–21; Lebed 1997, 283).

Joining forces with like-minded elements in the party and the KGB, military hard-liners became more actively involved in fighting perestroika. This potent combination of forces amounted to an alternative authority system that planned to thwart the reformers in the Kremlin. Gorbachev, to avert the emergence of dual authority, proposed during the 19th Party Conference in July the switch to a presidential system. But for the time being, Moscow's policies promised to remain a confusing hodgepodge of the reformist and the orthodox. Hard as such a state of affairs was on the Soviet actors involved in the struggle, it was even more bewildering for the American watchers of the unfolding drama.

Perestroika and the Overload of the Predictive Process in Washington

Tracking the fast-paced perestroika posed a number of challenges for the Reagan administration. The first problem pertained to the rapid release of a large volume of information in Moscow, a development that had the potential for overwhelming the intelligence community. Most pressing was the need to readjust the CIA's data on Soviet economic performance. Such an adjustment was not easy given the factional divisions in the administration. Although the projected 3.9 percent rate of growth was dropped, in 1987 the CIA still showed the Soviet economy as relatively strong and robust. A closely related problem was the sensitive question of the Soviet defense budget as a percentage of the economy, which was estimated to be some 16 to 17 percent for 1987–88. A 1987 CIA memorandum, allegedly representing the hard-line position, noted that in spite of some problems, the system was "viable" and capable of producing large quantities of goods and services, especially for the military. The document noted that zero growth was not likely, but even with no growth in the GNP, the belief was that Moscow had "the resources and the will" to increase defense outlays in case of a turndown in international climate (Firth and Noren 1998, 96, 130). The bureaucratic inertia was also difficult to overcome. For example, the CIA's 1987 *World Factbook* listed the 1986 GNP per capita of East Germany as higher than that of West Germany (Codevilla 1992, 220).

Ironically, the revelations by Soviet leaders, scholars, and journalists muddied the picture further. Gorbachev contended that Soviet defense spending reached 18 percent of national income in the 1981–85 plan; Ligachev asserted that the figure stood at 18–20 percent in 1989, but Yazov put it at 16 percent. At the high end, Yuri Ryzhov, a Supreme Soviet committee chairman, and economist Grigory Khanin maintained that defense expenditure amounted to some 36 percent of the national income. A comparison of the rival estimates led some CIA analysts to argue that the "Soviet leaders did not know, and perhaps could not know, the real cost of Soviet military programs." Soon after, the rapid decline of the Soviet Union eliminated the rationale for the CIA estimates and the Agency reassigned much of its manpower to monitoring the "unprecedented change in the Soviet Union" (Firth and Noren 1998, 188–89, 96–97).

The second and even more taxing problem was the analysis of the ideological debates between Gorbachev and the hard-liners, often couched in arcane Marxist and Gramscian language. Jack Matlock (1995, 145), the U.S. ambassador to Moscow, who was careful to report these disputes to Washington, commented that for Americans who were pragmatic by nature, these "theoretical questions . . . were like arguments of medieval theologians . . . with no relevance to real life." As already noted, little of the SOVA analysis was geared toward the relatively fuzzy domain of legitimacy crisis. Douglas MacEachin, the SOVA chief, later admitted that the Agency had "never really looked at the Soviet Union as a political entity in which there were factors building which could lead at least to the initiation of political transformation that we seem to see" (Fischer 1999, 6).

Even the less esoteric change in military doctrine reflected in Gorbachev's "strategic sufficiency" was not easy to digest. If true, it would have made much of the American military setup irrelevant, "like building a huge dam but the water was flowing in a different direction" (Bathurst 1993, 99). As one observer noted, "scarred by forty years of Cold War, CIA assessments failed to keep pace with the sea-change in Soviet-American relations" (Andrew 1995,

499). MacEachin affirmed that the Agency was caught off guard by Gorbachev's UN speech. But he noted that, even if there were an early inkling about Gorbachev's intention to cut military forces, the CIA would not have been able to publish it, because "we would have been told we were crazy" (quoted in Fischer 1999, 6).

Additional factors complicated the understanding of the process of change in the Soviet Union. First, the intelligence community had a difficult time following the complicated and largely subterranean power struggle in Moscow. A September 1988 SOVA memorandum listed Ligachev, Chebrikov, and other hard-liners as posing a real danger to the reform. Prior to that, a June 1988 report discussed the growing tension between Chebrikov and Gorbachev and speculated on the possible implications of this conflict. However, the extent of the dual authority system, a faction of which, as noted, defied Gorbachev, was not known, nor did Washington perceive the growing alliance between Kryuchkov and the hard-liners in the military. The intelligence community was taken aback when Kryuchkov accompanied Gorbachev to the Washington summit in 1987, but after he was promoted to head the KGB, his seemingly moderate public stance alleviated any suspicions, a fact reflected in CIA reports. Even less attention was paid to Yeltsin and his growing network of allies among nationalists and democrats. Although the Agency correctly identified ethnic strife as a major challenge to perestroika, there was virtually no understanding of Yeltsin's role in channeling the democratic and ethnic pressure that increasingly confounded Gorbachev. There was also no inkling that the KGB and party hard-liners were agitating for his dismissal (MacEachin 1996, nos. 30, 40; CIA Documents, SOV 88–10045X).

Second, by 1987 the politicization of the CIA took its toll on the estimative process. Although Gates (1987–88) denied "cooking books," Melvin Goodman and other SOVA analysts testified that skepticism of Gorbachev's motives was running high among the squeezers in the CIA (Goodman 1997, 1999; Perry 1992, 422–25). Relations between the CIA and the State Department were also tense. When, in late 1987, the Agency warned that ethnic conflicts "had larger implications for the Soviet Union as a whole," the State Department's intelligence bureau "vehemently disagreed," contending that "there would be no cumulative or contagious effects" (Gates 1996, 509).

The extent of Soviet efforts to shrink the Soviet empire was the subject of a particularly heated debate. In a November 6, 1987, meeting with Soviet analysts, Secretary of State Shultz clashed with Gates over the question of whether the Brezhnev doctrine was dead. After Gorbachev promised to withdraw from Afghanistan, Shultz concluded that Moscow was intent on scaling down its involvement in "regional hot spots." However, Gates made a bet with Michael Armacost from the State Department that the Soviet army would not leave and argued that Gorbachev "poured more weapons into regional conflicts." According to Shultz, Gates still believed that Gorbachev was a Leninist who was trying to get a "breathing space with the West" (Andrew 1995, 498; Shultz 1993, 1002–3, 1009; Oberdorfer 1992, 274). The dual authority system, which enabled the Soviet defense establishment to send aid to Third World clients behind Gorbachev's back, might have played into Gates's notion of continuous Soviet deception. A January 1988 CIA analysis found that the Soviet Union had not decreased its material and military aid to less-developed countries (CIA Documents, GI 88–10011).

But those who took a dim view of Gorbachev were finding themselves in the minority. With the death of Casey and the Iran-Contra affair taking its toll on other hard-liners, the balance of power in the administration shifted toward those who wanted to deal with the Soviet Union. In 1987 Frank Carlucci replaced Casper Weinberger as secretary of defense and William Webster was made the head of Central Intelligence. Shultz obtained Reagan's blessing to negotiate a series of arms control agreements with Moscow. Although the president was still on record as crusading against communism—especially in his June 1987 West Berlin challenge to Gorbachev to "tear down this wall"—privately he was won over by the Soviet leader. Nearing the end of his tenure, and mindful of his role in history, Reagan went to Moscow at the end of May 1988 where he famously strolled with Gorbachev in Red Square. On June 1, the two leaders signed the historic Intermediate Range Nuclear Forces Treaty, which eliminated ground-launched missile systems with the range of 500 to 5,000 kilometers.

As expected, the treaty elated the "dealers" but left those who still hoped to vanquish communism furious. Howard Phillips, chairman of the Conservative Caucus, charged that "Reagan is little more than a speech-reader for the pro-appeasement forces in his administration." He complained that the administration viewed Gorbachev as a "new kind of Soviet leader who no longer seeks world conquest" (Reagan 1990, 683; Shultz 1993, 1007–8). Ironically, Reagan's overtures did nothing to mollify the left, which had long accused the administration of anti-Soviet subversion. In March 1988, the *Nation* magazine charged the NED-funded Center for Democracy with using human rights as a guise for collecting intelligence and fomenting ethnic provocations in the republics (Coogan and Vanden Heuvel 1988). In November, a number of participants in a conference at Harvard University entitled "Anti-Communism and the United States: History and Consequences" decried the anticommunist impulse in American foreign policy (Muravchik 1988; Hollander 1992, 21–22).

Overshadowed by partisan disputes was the question of whether perestroika would work. In fact, in 1988 the CIA published a number of increasingly pessimistic assessments about the ability of Gorbachev to revamp the economy or withstand the centrifugal ethnic turmoil (CIA Documents, SOV 88–10035X, SOV 88–10018, SOV 88–10042; MacEachin 1996, no. 36). Still, Gates (1996, 564) admitted that before 1989 the CIA statistical analysis of the Soviet economy "described a stronger, larger economy" than warranted by reality and that the Agency underestimated the military burden on the system. Also, until 1989 the CIA "did not believe that a Soviet communist apparatchik" would "set in motion forces that would pull props from under an already declining system." All this was about to change in 1989, a year that saw Gorbachev take perestroika to a new and truly revolutionary level.

1989: The Year of Revolutionary Restructuring

Much of the pressure on Gorbachev to change course yet again came from the assessment of the economy. At the beginning of the year Abel Aganbegyan privately admitted that the country had plunged into a deep economic crisis. Gorbachev took the warning public in a New Year's address. The influential journalist Fyodor Burlatsky wrote that collectivization was a giant failure, noting that "American farmers, who account for 2.5 percent of the population, not only feed their country but are selling a huge amount of food abroad." Focusing again on the Chinese experiment, Gorbachev wanted to break up the collective farms and sell or lease the land back to peasants, but a March Central Committee meeting decreed that the collective farms would remain the mainstay of agriculture (Doder and Branson 1990, 361–63).

Other dimensions of the economic reform were equally erratic. The limited privatization of light industry and services, as embodied in the over 77,000 cooperatives, was hampered by mixed signals from the government, including the imposition of high taxes on their earnings. The manufacturing industry was not doing much better. The previously enacted Enterprise Law, which prohibited ministries from dictating to enterprises what to manufacture, was aimed at decentralizing the production system. However, the centralized structure was kept almost intact because the ministries placed some 80 percent of all orders. Since many of the enterprises could not meet the newly mandated quality standards to which salaries were pegged, earnings of many workers had actually plunged. Although the 1989 budget indicated a preference for light industry and consumer goods, the disruption in supply networks had resulted in a shortage of goods, including food staples. The budget deficit, estimated at $161 billion, or about 20 percent of government spending, had spurred inflation, which by 1989 stood at 10.5 percent (Doder and Branson 1990, 364; Kort 1993, 312–13; Moskoff 1993, 89).

The general confusion and economic hardship aggravated the psychological difficulty of adjusting to a less regimented system after seventy years of command and control. Workers resisted the new laws linking wages to productivity, and there was resentment at the fact that the social entitlements of the Brezhnev period, however shabby, were being taken away. The price decontrol that the reformist economists were urging on Gorbachev was also unpopular. According to a December 1988 poll, 61 percent of respondents objected out of fear that it would raise the price of food and other staples. As one observer noted, "if Gorbachev wants to succeed he will have to change the [psychological] system of the largest society in the world free of risk" (Yegorov 1993, 73; Cook 1992; Moskoff 1993, 93).

Gorbachev's strategy of using the political process to reform the economy continued to produce unintended consequences. The March 1989 vote to elect the new Congress of People's Deputies (CPD), in which 5,074 candidates competed for the 2,250 seats, demonstrated that even in a marginally competitive election, the party had lost its hegemony. Echoing preference falsification theory, Gorbachev (1996, 283) would later comment that the authority of the party failed because "people stopped being afraid of it." When the Congress opened on May 25, the contrast with the staged proceedings of the past could not have been greater. The suffering of the Soviet people was highlighted and the "venality and incompetence" of the party was denounced by a procession of deputies (Aron 2000, 295).

The CPD also provided the once disgraced Boris Yeltsin with a powerful political platform. In spite of the party's efforts, Yeltsin, who had run for a seat in the CPD from a Moscow district at-large, garnered 5 million votes, or almost 90 percent of the ballots. He used his popularity to press for large-scale privatization, decentralization of power, political pluralism, and economic independence of the republics. In a powerful speech he linked the issue of poverty and destitution in the Soviet Union to the privileges of the elite. When his proposals were defeated by the Congress, Yeltsin and some 400 deputies formed the Inter-Regional Group of Deputies (IRGD) during a July 29–30 meeting. As befitting the first formal opposition, the IRGD established is own newspaper and networked with like-minded elements across the Soviet Union. By fall, Yeltsin's uncanny grasp of democratic politicking had transformed him into what some described as the "Yeltsin phenomenon." By shunning the privileges of power in his personal life he came to embody the political culture that Gorbachev and his well-dressed wife preached but did not live. At the same time, he helped to lower politics from its "Olympian heights and put it on the doorstep of everyman's house" (Aron 2000, 290).

If the political reforms opened the door to a Russian opposition, they sent an even stronger signal to the republics. During 1989 the ethnic struggle, proceeding along three interrelated axes, had intensified. First, in a number of Asian republics, native populations violently attacked "immigrant" minorities, as epitomized by the bloody Ferghana Valley pogrom of Uzbeks against the Meskhetian Turks, a community that had been resettled there from the Caucasus. There were also clashes between Kazakhs and Caucasians in Novy Uzen, which paralyzed oil production in the Caspian Sea. Second, Ossetian and Abkhazian secession movements created extreme tension in Georgia. On April 9, Soviet troops violently suppressed a Georgian nationalist rally in Tbilisi, killing and wounding scores of people. As a result, anti-Soviet feelings intensified greatly, leading the Georgian Supreme Soviet to declare its sovereignty in September. The demand of the Armenians in the Nagorno-Karabakh region to secede from Azerbaijan triggered a full-scale war between the two republics. When Gorbachev ordered an end to the hostilities, he was ignored. In September both Azerbaijan and Armenia declared their sovereignty (d'Encausse 1993, 92, 98–100).

Third, there was a powerful movement in the Baltic republics to repudiate what was considered their unlawful annexation to the Soviet Union in the wake of the 1939 Hitler-Stalin pact. On August 18, Gorbachev's close adviser Yakovlev "unequivocally" condemned the pact, opening the door to demands for independence. In a development even more worrisome to Moscow, there were considerable stirrings of nationalism in Ukraine, the largest of the non-Russian republics and an important agricultural and industrial base of the Soviet Union (Kort 1993, 101, 308–15). Acting behind the scenes were Yeltsin and the IRGD, who worked with the republics to undermine Gorbachev's central power. Yeltsin's standing with the ethnic movement was already well established. When during the previous summer he gave an interview to an obscure Latvian paper, copies spread rapidly across the Soviet Union and some 140 papers reprinted it (Aron 2000, 251).

The meltdown of the inner empire was outpaced by events in Eastern Europe. During the so-called "year of the people," massive movements in virtually all of the satellites forced the communist authorities on the defensive. In July, Gorbachev told the East European leaders that Moscow would not use force to shore up regimes that resisted political change. Nicolae Ceausescu had urged such intervention upon learning that Solidarity had won the national elections in Poland. But on August 22, Gorbachev called the general secretary of the Polish Communist Party, Mieczyslaw Rakowski, to encourage him to participate in a Solidarity-led government. Gorbachev had also forced out the East German hard-liner Erich Honecker, who resigned on October 7. Soon after, Soviet Foreign Ministry spokesman Gennadi Gerasimov announced the demise of the Brezhnev doctrine and stated that some satellites "are doing it their way," which he jokingly dubbed the "Sinatra doctrine." As if to symbolize the disintegration of the outer empire, on November 9 the Berlin Wall came down, opening the way to the subsequent reunification of Germany (Dobrynin 1995, 632; Andrew 1995, 510; Gorbachev 1996, 523)

Gorbachev's permissiveness with regard to events at home and abroad puzzled many. Reacting to the turmoil, *Literaturnaia Gazeta* published an article which argued that radical reforms could be only carried out through strong authoritarian rule, but the general secretary rejected this view. Gorbachev took an equally principled stand with regard to Eastern Europe, observing that "we followed the principle of freedom of choice and noninterference in other countries' affairs" (Gorbachev 1996, 315, 516). Some observers concluded that Gorbachev had overestimated the capacity of the communist system to reform itself in an orderly way. Once things began to unravel, Gorbachev became "the helpless witness to the consequences of his policy." Shocked by the Tbilisi massacre, he had "no stomach for bloodletting" that was required to suppress ethnic unrest. This feeling was undoubtedly reinforced by a realization that coercion would undermine the very legitimacy of his reforms and discredit New Political Thinking (Dobrynin 1995, 632; Gates 1996, 471).

Such qualms were not shared by Soviet hard-liners, who were greatly alarmed by Gorbachev's handling of perestroika and the imperial disintegration. Ligachev (1993, 170) would later describe nationalism and separatism as the double "tragedy of perestroika." The military was upset because Shevardnadze criticized its role in Tbilisi and allowed American and French doctors to conduct an investigation into the massacre. The KGB, which prepared a report on "plans of the leading circles of the United States" to detach Eastern Europe, was equally vexed. Feelings boiled over when Gorbachev nixed a plan to implement a series of "special measures" designed to prevent the downfall of the regimes in East Germany, Czechoslovakia, and Bulgaria. An embryonic "salvation front" led by Ligachev and Chebrikov in the Politburo, a number of military leaders, and the KGB's Kryuchkov began to form during the summer. According to Yeltsin, the salvation front was designing a "step-by-step" model for a unionwide state of emergency and a blueprint for a future coup (Yeltsin 1994, 24; Ekedahl and Goodman 1997, 93; Garthoff 1996, Andrew 1995, 510).

Boosting the salvation front was the growing alarm of a considerable number of party members whose interests were threatened by the reforms. When Gorbachev left in August for a five-week vacation in the Crimea, there were rumors of an effort to oust him from the Politburo. Leningrad activist Nina Andreyeva resumed her attacks on Gorbachev, and Chebrikov delivered a tough law-and-order speech demanding a crackdown on the mounting dissent. Ligachev demanded repression against "those people who are forever attacking the Party, the Soviet Union, our glorious army, and the security organs" (Smith 1990, 504; Kort 1993, 318).

Although the hard-liners apparently failed to oust Gorbachev during a Politburo meeting on September 8 or 9, the pressure chastened the general secretary. Starting in the fall, Gorbachev moved perceptibly to the side of his communist critics. As one observer summed it up, "he became the Party's defender instead of its attacker." The Soviet leader also displayed signs of stress and anxiety, at one point publicly complaining about the rumors of a coup and attempts to destroy perestroika. He was equally bitter about Yeltsin and his followers, with whom he openly clashed at the second Congress of People's Deputies in December 1989 over a demand to repeal Article VI of the Soviet Constitution, which guaranteed the monopoly of the Communist Party. Gorbachev described the IRGD as a "gangster group" and called for the resignation of an editor who published polls showing him trailing behind Yeltsin (Smith 1990, 503–5).

Buffeted by the rapid pace of events and rumors of a coup, political life in the Soviet Union had lost all its customary orderliness and predictability. Both Soviet journalists and the foreign press stationed in Moscow filled reams of paper speculating on the balance of power in the country and the possible path of change. The unsettled situation posed a special challenge to the new administration of President George H.W. Bush, who had taken office in January 1989.

The Bush Administration: Problems of Forecasting in a Revolutionary Whirlpool

During his presidential campaign, Vice President Bush sought to project a hard-line position toward the Soviet Union in general and Gorbachev in particular. However, unlike President Reagan, the newly elected president, his secretary of state James Baker, and national security adviser Brent Scowcroft were practical men who would rather deal with the Soviet Union than crusade against it. To prevent any hasty decisions and to get its bearing, the new administration ordered a national security review by the State Department. When the review was finally made available on March 14, 1989, Bush criticized it as "old thinking" and asked for more "imaginative" reporting. Meanwhile, the administration adopted a "think piece" prepared by Condoleezza Rice, the Soviet specialist on the National Security Council (NSC). It outlined a fairly cautious policy of disarmament deals with the Soviet Union and a somewhat more energetic effort to help the East European countries "to exercise greater control over their own affairs" (Bush and Scowcroft 1998, 9, 40; Halberstam 2001, 60; Beschloss and Talbott 1993, 46–47).

Still, the new road map depended on an assessment of Gorbachev's motivation. By spring, many in the administration were convinced that the Soviet leader was genuine in his desire to reform the system and espouse a new foreign policy, a fact attested to by two CIA reports in February and March (CIA Documents, SOV 89–10012X, SOV89–10021X). Secretary of State Baker, who formed a close relationship with his Soviet counterpart Shevardnadze, was among the major proponents of this position. He was seconded by Jack Matlock (1995, 178), the U.S. ambassador in Moscow, who lobbied for American investment and other forms of support for perestroika. This so-called "activist group" was persuaded that "glasnost" and "new thinking" could be used effectively with Gorbachev to "push him in directions that advanced our interests" (Baker 1995, 69).

The "activists" were opposed by the "status quo plus" school of thought espoused by Secretary of Defense Dick Cheney and other hard-liners who felt that rather than help Gorbachev, the United States should capitalize on Soviet weakness to squeeze more concessions. Gates (1996, 474), who became Scowcroft's deputy, argued that Gorbachev did not have the capacity to "build a new structure based on democratic values and a market economy" because of his conviction that communism could be fixed. Gates's public skepticism—expressed in an April speech in Brussels and a May article in the *Washington Post*—exasperated Baker, who was already ruffled by Cheney's statement in April that Gorbachev would ultimately fail and would be succeeded by a Soviet leader hostile to the United States (Andrew 1995, 506).

With so much riding on Gorbachev's success, the CIA analysis was not encouraging. In April, the Agency warned for the first time about the possibility of a coup "involving a minority of Politburo members supported by elements of the military and the KGB." It stated that the Soviet Union was "less stable than at any time since 1930s." A May 1989 estimate gave Gorbachev a fifty-fifty chance of survival over the next three to four years. More significantly, a number of outside experts, and especially Brzezinski, took the more radical view that the communist experiment was on the verge of collapse and predicted the dawn of the "postcommunist era" (National Security Archives, 00600; Andrew 1995, 506, 509).

Such a possibility notwithstanding, Bush and Scowcroft decided to adopt the "activist" philosophy of betting on Gorbachev. On May 12, 1989, the president spelled out the new policy during a commencement speech at Texas A&M University. He proclaimed that the United States would move beyond containment to "actively promoting the integration of the Soviet Union into the international system," pending changes in its foreign policy. Listing the changes, the president called for sovereignty of Eastern Europe and the tearing down of the Berlin Wall. Given the rapid unraveling of the communist hold on the satellites, such demands were far from daring. Indeed, during a mid-July trip to Poland and Hungary, Bush found out for himself how advanced this process was (Bush and Scowcroft 1998, 53; Beschloss and Talbott 1993, 69–70).

While acknowledging the events in Eastern Europe, the administration was careful not to appear too enthusiastic for fear of undermining Gorbachev in the eyes of his hard-line opposition. The same restraint was shown with regard to the turmoil in the inner empire. Gates admitted that the force of nationalism caught the CIA by surprise because of "inadequate" capabilities in non-Russian republics and among ethnic groups. After being informed by Shevardnadze about the extent of the nationalist turmoil on July 29, Baker promised that Washington would show understanding for Moscow's need to "put down strikes and other forms of political activity." A few weeks later, on September 11, the State Department outlined a number of possible future scenarios, listing authoritarian modernization, military coup, post-Gorbachev paralysis, and post-Gorbachev collapse. Baker noted that the paper "reinforced our conviction" to support Gorbachev. Cementing their friendship, the secretary of state hosted Shevardnadze at his retreat in Jackson Hole, Wyoming, at the end of September. All throughout the fall Baker worked hard to persuade the president and others on the foreign policy team to stand by the embattled Soviet leader. Robert Blackwell, the National Intelligence Officer for the Soviet Union, supported this position in a highly classified report (Gates 1996, 466, 510; Beschloss and Talbott 1993, 95, 141; Baker 1995, 143).

But in a testimony to the continuous division over the Soviet estimate, this approach was questioned by a number of SOVA analysts, including Grey Hodnett, who in September submitted a paper titled "Gorbachev's Domestic Gambles and Instability." The paper, which was supported by SOVA director George Kolt, Fritz Ermarth of the National Intelligence Council, and Gates, concluded that Gorbachev's quasi-reforms "were the worst of all possible worlds—all pain and no gain." Hodnett warned that the social unrest could result in a hard-line effort to impose orthodox totalitarianism or an "Ottomanization" of the Soviet Union, with republics breaking away and hard-liners trying to depose Gorbachev. Although CIA director William Webster tried to downplay the disagreements, the implication of Hodnett's report was radical in the sense that it recommended a switch from Gorbachev to Yeltsin. Hodnett felt that Yeltsin's program of democratization and market reforms might cause short-term disruptions, but would ultimately "have a better chance of creating a 'social equilibrium'" than Gorbachev's half-measures to fix communism (National Security Archives, 00602; Beschloss and Talbott 1993, 141–42; Gates 1996, 514).

Given the rising stature of Yeltsin, Hodnett's recommendation should have received a serious hearing. However, a number of factors conspired against it. Perhaps the most important one was the impression formed by the administration during Yeltsin's visit to the United States in September 1989. The trip, sponsored by the New Age Esalen Institute in California, got bad press coverage, with many articles taking the cue from an Italian journalist who portrayed Yeltsin as an inebriated buffoon. Yeltsin intimated that the KGB had manipulated coverage of the visit and that someone had slowed the tape of his speech to make him appear drunk (Yeltsin 1990, 256–57). Yeltsin's visit to the White House was a huge failure. Matlock (1995, 247–51) described the White House as "skittish" about receiving the head of Gorbachev's opposition, and Bush's aides were taken aback when Yeltsin tried to force a meeting with the president. During Yeltsin's presentation Scowcroft dozed off and subsequently described him as a "devious two bit headline grabber." The general impression was that Yeltsin "was a bombastic political lightweight who would soon fade from the scene" (Matlock 1995, 247–51). Baker, who met Yeltsin in the State Department, was said to have referred to the Russian leader as a "flake" (Beschloss and Talbott 1993, 104; Aron 2000, 334; Gates 1996, 478).

The president's unease with unorthodox political figures who had strong and passionate beliefs may have compounded Yeltsin's problems. Although Bush denied this, other observers noticed that the president had exhibited the same reaction to Polish leader Lech Walesa, whose "manners and aspirations," like those of Yeltsin, "seemed exotic." As one commentator put it, "anyone emerging from the hot and messy kitchen of history instantly looked out of place in the cool *bon ton* of the Bush White House" (Beschloss and Talbott 1993, 86). In fairness to Bush, others shared his view. Ambassador Matlock reported that many of his diplomatic colleagues felt that Yeltsin was "prone to exaggerations." Former presidential contender Gary Hart accused Yeltsin of embracing nationalism, which he described as a threat to "stability and predictability" (Bush and Scowcroft 1998, 120–21; Aron 2000, 334; Matlock, 1995, 113; Hart 1991, 179).

Even if Yeltsin had made a better personal impression, it is doubtful whether the administration would have moved to embrace him. As in other revolutionary situations, political power in the Soviet Union was too fluid for anyone to determine where the center of gravity was at any given time. Although some observers later criticized Bush for preferring Gorbachev, "the mask of Russia," over Yeltsin, who was "its true face," this was the kind of hindsight wisdom that was absent when Hodnett's report was discussed (Beschloss and Talbott 1993, 47, 141). In any event, Bush's priority was to negotiate arms control agreements rather than destroy communism, making it imprudent to undermine Gorbachev by supporting his opponent, who preached the as yet untested virtues of democracy and market economy. The White House was especially keen on avoiding the perception that it exploited internal Soviet problems, thus exposing the vulnerable Gorbachev to a hard-line backlash. To this end, Baker and Scowcroft squashed in October a speech in which Gates intended to repeat some of Hodnett's warnings about Gorbachev's fragility (Aron 2000, 334; Gates 1996, 480).

The same considerations were behind Bush's low-key reaction to the unraveling of communism in Eastern Europe. When pressed to react to the fall of the Berlin Wall in November 1989, he described himself as not "an emotional kind of guy" so as to avoid, in the words of two commentators, "rubbing Gorbachev's nose in the defeat of world communism" (Bush and Scowcroft 1998, 148; Beschloss and Talbott 1993, 135, 175). The turmoil in the internal empire posed an even greater challenge to the Bush administration. During his September visit with Baker, Shevardnadze inquired whether the White House would be opposed to a Soviet crackdown against the Baltics and other rebellious republics. This and other matters were discussed extensively during Bush's preparation for the Malta summit in December. Although by then intelligence reports described the economic problems as "near-crisis proportions" and portrayed Gorbachev's control as increasingly shaky, the administration decided to support his reforms in exchange for considerable progress on START (which replaced SALT), Conventional Forces in Europe (CFE), and other arms control deals. The White House was also keen to end Moscow's aid to Cuba and a handful of other revolutionary regimes that were still on the Soviet payroll. Bush, who developed an excellent rapport with Gorbachev, assured the Soviet leader that the United States would respond "with restraint" to Soviet use of force in the republics. The same message was conveyed to the Soviet ambassador in Washington, Yuri Dubinin (Gates 1996, 441, 482; Bush and Scowcroft 1998, 154; Eisenhower 1995, 225).

By casting its lot with Gorbachev, the administration hoped to demonstrate its confidence in perestroika and prevent a violent disintegration of a nuclear-armed Soviet Union. The unforeseen consequences of such a development alarmed even the most seasoned practitioners on Bush's team. As Gates (1996, 484) put it, "we shot the rapids of history, and without a life jacket." Still, the decision was taken despite the fact that internal deliberations leading up to Malta revealed less than robust confidence in Gorbachev's long-term survivability. But even the "Gorbachev's pessimists" were surprised by the speed of events that would lead to the collapse of the communist empire almost two years to the date after the summit. Gates (1996, 461) captured this feeling well. He wrote that in "boarding the roller coaster" in 1989, "experts all, we had no idea what lay in store for us sooner than we could imagine." The extraordinary events that culminated in 1989 had also tested the academic paradigms, already working overtime to discern the future.

Paradigmatic Reconfigurations: Changing the View
of the Past as a Way to Predict the Future

Unlike the intelligence services, which dealt with immediate events, the academic community used Moscow's disclosures about the true state of its economy and society to reexamine the underlying precepts of Soviet analysis. With its emphasis on the high performance of the Soviet system, the revisionist paradigm stood to lose the most from Gorbachev's admission of its many failings. One historian was elated that glasnost provided a "fascinating opportunity" to study "all sorts of pathologies formerly denied" (Powell 1988, 302). A special issue of *Survey* entitled "Seventy Years After the Revolution" (1987) listed the numerous ways in which the system had malfunctioned. These were also detailed by Abel Aganbegyan (1988b, 1988c) and by Nick Eberstadt (1988, 10) in his study of poverty in the Soviet Union. Eberstadt's conclusion that communist rule was short on bread as well as freedom challenged the notion of patrimonial legitimacy that was at the core of the revisionist approach. Indeed, even such admirers as John Kenneth Galbraith were now compelled to admit that the Soviet economy had fizzled out in the mid-1970s (Galbraith and Menshikov 1988, 19).

As perestroika revelations mounted, other assumptions of the revisionist paradigm crumpled. The role of a single party as an "effective agent of development" was questioned, and there was an increased acknowledgment of the role of coercion as the major instrument in maintaining regime stability. A 1987 conference organized by Ferenc Feher, a former neo-Marxist associated with the patrimonial model, had actually admitted as much (Gill 1987, 566; Feher and Arato 1989). Using the newly available data on the Gulag system, Laqueur (1989, 241) criticized revisionist historians like J. Arch Getty and Sheila Fitzpatrick for underestimating Soviet terror. The ever outspoken Aleksandr Solzhenitsyn (1988) condemned Western Sovietologists for ignoring the oppressive quality of the regime and for failing to admit that communism could not survive without state terror.

Farther afield, this criticism triggered a move to reexamine the revisionist history of U.S. foreign policy. A new textbook argued that there was no evidence to support the "fashionable" view that the United States was at least equally responsible for the Cold War. On the contrary, it found that the "Soviet state and its leaders bear primary responsibility for the Cold War" (Nogee and Spanier 1988, ix). Others used the occasion to criticize the excessive focus on comparative methodology and ahistoricism in the study of international relations to the neglect of the history or ethnic composition of the Soviet Union (Gaddis 1987; Nye and Lynn-Jones 1988).

Still, some revisionist scholars continued to defend their paradigm. Hough restated his position that "in 1917 Leninism received the support of the majority of the Soviet workers" and that the "Soviet system delivered on its implicit promises to its main supporters." He also criticized those Western observers "who speak incessantly about elite privilege," adding that the real problem was "too much egalitarianism" and "excessive coddling of workers." As for national legitimacy, Hough asserted that ethnic turmoil would not obstruct liberal reforms and called it a mistake "to exaggerate the potential instability in the Soviet Union in the near future." He expressed the belief that "non-Russians will benefit greatly" from the reforms and thus be "reluctant to participate in major riots that may curtail the reforms." Hough continued to maintain that Gorbachev was exaggerating the amount of upheaval and even manufacturing some of the rumors about his vulnerability in order to persuade the intellectuals that "excessive pressure on their part would only produce a conservative reaction." After establishing that Gorbachev "deliberately painted himself into the corner," Hough proceeded to express confidence in the reformablity of the Soviet system under the guidance of the Communist Party, arguing that the hard-liners in Moscow had been defeated and that "Western talk about bureaucratic opposition is grossly overdone" (Hough 1987; 1988a, 25, 27; 1988b, 9, 92, 104, 178, 181). Outdoing Hough's optimism was Ed A. Hewett, a leading expert on Soviet economy. In a book published by the Brookings Institution, the flagship of revisionist scholarship, Hewett (1988, 2) emphasized that the serious problems "should not be allowed to obscure the massive economic security enjoyed by Soviet citizens."

While less assertive, others shared this view. One leading historian argued that "the party was the only institution that could preside over the overhaul of the system" (Lewin 1988, 131, 133), and another claimed that, since 1985, "Soviet political life" was a "multiparty system in a one party system" (Cohen 1988, 287). Motyl, an expert on Soviet ethnic relations, saw little chance that the non-Russians would rebel "as long as the KGB remains intact." Motyl took issue with the notion that the Soviet multi-national structure was "on the verge of collapsing like a house of cards" (1987, 170). In line with revisionist logic, these authors predicted that Gorbachev would successfully transform the system without losing the multinational empire.

But the adherents of the totalitarian paradigm drew a very different conclusion from the same developments. To begin with, they rushed to proclaim themselves vindicated by perestroika's disclosures. In the words of one observer, those who were denounced in the West for describing the Soviet system as inhumane and inefficient, now "find that their arguments are being confirmed by leading [Soviet] journalists and academics" (Elliot 1988, 2). More important, they argued that Gorbachev's difficulties were one more indication that the system could not be reformed. The dissident Vladimir Bukovsky (1987, 39) contended that the system was in terminal crisis and that even if reforms could prolong its life in the short term, Gorbachev would learn that the "marketplace is stronger than socialism." In his work *The Grand Failure: The Birth and Death of Communism in the Twentieth Century*, completed in August 1988, Brzezinski (1989c) reiterated his long-standing argument about the internal contradictions of communism and pronounced the system essentially dead. In order to expedite its demise, Brzezinski urged continuous pressure on Moscow, a call that was also taken up by Bukovsky (1989, 234), who warned Washington against "bailing out" of the anticommunist crusade.

Brzezinski (1988a, 680), always mindful of the larger historical picture, used the occasion to claim victory for capitalism. He took issue with the then-much-debated thesis of the historian Paul Kennedy (1987) that American capitalism was on the decline because of imperial overreach. He called such rumors "fashionable . . . in some intellectual circles" but somewhat premature and an example of "Spenglarian handwringing" over the alleged decline of the West. Brzezinski (1988b, 141) pointed out that the Soviet model had become "irrelevant" in much of the developing world. Another commentator stated that "capitalism is increasingly the only ballgame in town" (Muller 1988, 23). In a sign of the times, the economist Robert Heilbroner, a sometime cheerleader for socialism, agreed with this diagnosis, declaring in January 1989 that capitalism had won (Connor 1991, 3).

As the dramatic events of 1989 unfolded, even some longtime Soviet boosters were shaken. Richard Falk (1989, 142) was compelled to note that "the brutality of the Soviet approach to establishing hegemonic rule was not entirely expected," and that "the immense burden" placed on the people of the communist bloc was not "widely appreciated." An article in the *New Left Review* noted that the experience of the communist regime "forces upon Western socialists the need for further and deeper reflection on the exercise of power" (Miliband 1989, 32). But neither Falk nor the revisionists were ready to admit that the Soviet Union might unravel. Hough (1989, 4), who called Gorbachev's economic reforms "successful," argued that the country was "far from anarchy or a failure of perestroyka." Motyl (1989, 269, 273, 278) described as "faulty" the assumption that the Soviet Union was "not capable" of reforming itself and thus was sliding toward collapse. He argued that the communist system was going through a cyclical crisis comparable to the crises of capitalism and would be able to right itself. He warned that "projections of Soviet decay" were no less fallacious than predictions of

American capitalist growth and echoed Paul Kennedy's prediction that the "prospects for continued [American] ascendancy in an increasingly multipolar word may be too sanguine." All this led Motyl to conclude that the "USSR is sure to remain a formidable world actor for a long time." Breslauer (1989), who gave Gorbachev high marks for leadership, felt that the general secretary had strengthened his hand in dealing with the communist hard-liners and entrenched bureaucracy.

Rejecting such optimism, conservative observers increasingly voiced their opinion that communism was a "failed utopia," as one of them put it (Puddington, 1988; 1989, 32). This notion received a wide hearing when Francis Fukuyama (1989) published an article with the eye-catching title "The End of History." Partially restating the Reagan position that economic prowess rather than military might is a marker of the new international relations, Fukuyama proclaimed that liberal democracy and the market economy had triumphed over communism. Brzezinski (1989a) reiterated his view that "both the ideology and the system had failed."

While sharing this forecast, observers were divided on the specifics of the communist endgame. In an edited volume entitled *Can the Soviet System Survive Reform?* Bukovsky (1989) foresaw a "quiet exit from communism" through ethnic and economic disintegration and even predicted a Russian federation. Brzezinski repeated his long-standing opinion that the "national question" would be the catalyst of disintegration, implying that the multinational empire would revert to its constituent parts (1989b). Shelton (1989) and Aslund (1989) saw the "coming crash" mostly in economic terms. The Lithuanian émigré scholar Alexander Shtromas (1988) surmised that the Soviet system would collapse when, bereft of their central planning power, the partocrats would lose out to the reformist elite. Others predicted that the developing civil society would bring an end to communism. But even the most optimistic of these observers assumed that the systemic breakdown would take between five and ten years to materialize (Beisinger 1988; Timofeyev 1988; Staar 1988; Burks 1988). All were thus caught by surprise when the communist system unraveled within two.

7

The Unintended Consequences
of Radical Transformation

*Losing Control of the Revolution and
the Collapse of the Soviet Union, 1990–1991*

By 1990 the dynamics created by the accelerated pace of perestroika had turned into a chaotic revolution that undermined the last tenets of communist legitimacy. The change was especially profound with regard to membership in the Union, bringing the internal empire to the brink of collapse. As Gorbachev struggled to salvage the Soviet Union, the Bush administration, faced with the unexpected prospect of the demise of the historical enemy of the United States, chose to support the status quo. In the end, both Gorbachev's resolve and American cautiousness were not enough to save the first communist system and the last European empire.

Group Legitimacy and the Soviet "Spring of Nations"

By 1990, after three years of glasnost, which all but refuted the validity claims behind an inclusive Soviet identity, the republics were poised to challenge the institutional framework of the Union. On December 20, 1989, Lithuania made its first move toward achieving sovereignty, bringing Gorbachev to Vilnius in early January on a futile mission to calm nationalist passions. While the Soviet leader was still in Vilnius, the simmering tension between the Armenians and the Azeris escalated into a full-fledged conflict. The Soviet military was ordered to occupy Baku at a cost of more than sixty lives. Soviet intervention unleashed tremendous anger against the Union, followed by demands of Azeri nationalists for full independence. In February, riots broke out in Dushanbe, where Tajiks tried to expel Armenian refugees and other migrants. After Gorbachev imposed a truce, Tajiks started an insurrection against Moscow and the internal ministry troops that patrolled their capital. In March 1990, local elections in Lithuania, Ukraine, and Belorussia resulted in huge victories for the national fronts, which almost wiped out the republican communist parties.

On March 11, the newly elected president of Lithuania, Vytautas Landsbergis, declared his intention to seek independence. Estonia declared its independence from the Soviet Union on March 25, and Latvia served its independence proclamation on May 4. On July 16, Ukraine declared its sovereignty, and on July 27 Belorussia followed suit; on August 23, Armenia declared independence, followed on August 23 and 24 by proclamations of sovereignty by Turkmenistan and Tajikistan. Before the end of the year, all fifteen republics joined the independence bandwagon, with Kyrgyzstan taking the plunge on December 12.

While the dramatic events in the republics were front page, the real paradigmatic change in imperial legitimacy was taking place in Russia. As already noted, glasnost initiated the first comprehensive discussion on the costs and benefits of maintaining an internal empire. A growing number of academics and journalists argued that Russia, which held 92 percent of oil reserves, 85 percent of coal reserves, and was the only producer of diamonds, platinum, and other rare metals, had no need for the republics. Indeed, as a group of scholars pointed out, the Union "represented a tool of redistribution" that took away from Russia its vast resources. Economist Vladimir Kvint contended that the question of "whether the republics should be allowed to leave the Union" should be changed to "whether they should be allowed into the Union" (Gorbachev 1996, 346; Sheehy 1990, 289).

Such thinking was at the core of the arguments espoused by Boris Yeltsin and Demrossiya (Democratic Russia), a group dedicated to gaining independence from the Soviet Union for Russia. Persuaded that neither Gorbachev nor his hard-line communist opponents could be undermined within the framework of the Union, Yeltsin was resolved to devolve power to the republics. In spite of Gorbachev's strenuous opposition, on May 29, 1990, Yeltsin, who campaigned on a platform of independence, became the popularly elected chairman of the Russian republic Supreme Soviet, effectively making him the president of Russia. Two weeks later, on June 12, Russia declared its independence from the Union.

Bolstered by his newly acquired authority, Yeltsin redoubled efforts to help the republics. In June he met with Lithuanian president Landsbergis, who had emerged as a major irritant to Gorbachev. The two leaders agreed to conclude a treaty between their respective republics. A month later Yeltsin traveled to Latvia, where he consulted with the leaders of the three Baltic republics about ways to challenge Moscow. The Russian president followed up with an open letter to the Baltic people urging them to seek independence. In a series of equally intensive contacts, Yeltsin encouraged other republics to resist Soviet plans to slow down the independence movement (Aron 2000, 392).

Indeed, with Russia and Ukraine, the second largest republic, aboard the nationalist wagon, Gorbachev was fighting an uphill battle to halt the imperial meltdown. His cherished belief that the nationalities would choose to stay in the Union on a voluntary basis because "the real benefits of a federation" would nullify the obsession with the "idea of full independence" was all but dispelled. However, recourse for force in Vilnius and Azerbaijan, an economic embargo against Lithuania, and efforts at political manipulation were equally unhelpful. Gorbachev's denunciation of Demrossiya as "isolationists" fell on deaf ears, as Yeltsin's electoral triumph demonstrated. With power ebbing out of the Union, procedural maneuvers of the federal structure became an exercise in futility. When, at Gorbachev's urging, the Soviet legislature declared the supremacy of its laws over those of the republics and tightened the conditions for secession, it was simply ignored. Gorbachev would later describe as a failure his belief that "the development of economic and political reforms would outpace the secessionist process" (Gorbachev 1996, 346, 573).

Even if the citizens of the republics were willing to trade their national identity for economic benefits, Gorbachev had little to offer in terms of improved standard of living. In fact, after almost five years of perestroika the economy was on the verge of collapse.

Economic Legitimacy and the Limits of Market Socialism

The economic indicators at the beginning of 1990 were highly inauspicious. Due to shortages of goods and local hoarding, the consumer market collapsed, inflation increased, the ruble lost value, and unemployment ballooned. According to one estimate, the number of unemployed on January 1, 1990, stood at 6 million, out of which 4.5 were considered permanently unemployed. According to one poll, 73 percent of respondents characterized the shortage of food products as "constant" or "quite often." Panic buying and hoarding added to the psychological uncertainty and the specter of "mafia" was resurrected to explain the economic chaos. Alternative rumors had it that Yegor Ligachev and other hard-liners had created the shortages in order to undermine the reformers (Moskoff 1993, 130–31; McCauley 1998, 183; Aron 2000, 354–60, 396; Pozner 1992, 178–79).

Many insiders blamed the situation on Gorbachev's persistent failure to grasp the principles of economics and his tendency to take often-contradictory advice from assorted academics and political figures. Former ambassador Dobrynin (1995, 635), who had worked closely with Gorbachev, testified that the Soviet leader had no coherent plan and tended to change or improvise solutions, sometimes after a trip abroad. General Volkogonov (1998, 434) added that Gorbachev had "no grand plan" and acted "ad hoc," with ideas often coming in "rapid succession." The dynamics of a transitional system were another source of chaos. Changes in institutional and legal practices often lag behind the operational practices and social ontology, a fact that was reinforced in the Soviet Union by bureaucratic obstructionism. Moreover, the disintegrating Union undermined whatever little coherence Moscow could muster. Some republics ceased supplying food and others raised prices, contributing to inflation. Gorbachev's efforts to challenge decisions by republics that had interrupted delivery of goods and supplies were ignored. To the historically minded in Moscow, all this presented an "ominous parallel" to the situation in 1917 that doomed the moderate Kerensky government and ushered in the Bolshevik revolution. There were food riots in a number of cities and increasing industrial unrest, including strikes by miners, an important mainstay of communist legitimacy (Sergeyev 1988, 53; Moltz 1993; Aron 2000, 354–60, 396–97; Schroeder 1991).

Under tremendous pressure, Gorbachev authorized Prime Minister Nikolai Ryzhkov to work on a new economic plan. The plan, which was announced on May 24, 1990, promised a transition to a market economy by 1996, but received little public credibility because of its vagueness. In the meantime, Yeltsin used his new position to push for an ambitious market economic plan for Russia. Yeltsin (1990, 255) had become a convert to capitalism during his ill-fated visit to the United States in 1989. He confessed that the full shelves in the supermarkets made him recoil at the fact that "such a potentially rich country as ours has been brought to a state of such poverty." Gorbachev, who sought an opportunity to cooperate with Yeltsin, agreed to create a joint Russian-Union committee, which included such prominent economists as Stanislav Shatalin and Nikolai Petrakov, both members of Gorbachev's Presidential Council, and Grigory Yavlinsky, an aide to Yeltsin. Unveiled in August, the plan called for a 500-day transition to a market economy. The 500-Day Plan, also known as the Shatalin-Yavlinsky Plan, envisaged private property, price liberalization, and a massive sell-off of state assets. Most important, the plan, by allocating most economic rights to the republics, would have required a radical reorganization of the government and the abolition of Soviet ministries, effectively turning the Soviet Union into a European Union–style confederation.

Such prospects alarmed hard-line communists, but also concerned Prime Minister Ryzhkov and Leonid Abalkin, the minister responsible for economic reforms. They countered with a third plan that sought both to dilute privatization and to maximize the economic power of the Union. After weeks of temporizing, on October 16 Gorbachev came out in favor of a compromise plan that would have allowed only limited privatization, and postponed price liberalization for two years. Moreover, under the so-called "October choice" plan most economic rights were to be retained by the Union (Lockwood 2000, 126; Jones and Moskoff 1991, 348; Khasbulatov 1993, 80).

That the architect of perestroika should choose a cautious status quo plan that preserved the "socialist market" and the rigid centralization of the Soviet Union embittered his erstwhile supporters. His one-time economic mentor Tatyana Zaslavskaya (1990, 105) repeated her charge that there would be no economic progress without repealing the Marxist principles of social leveling that had severed the connection between contribution and remuneration. A Soviet journalist wrote that "like Lot's wife, Gorbachev looked back at the Staraya Square [the location of the headquarters of the Central Committee] and turned into a pillar of salt." Yavlinsky bemoaned that "the old system was dying and its poisons affected the new that was still in the womb." Shatalin, who resigned from the Presidential Council, called the new proposals an "unintended suicide" (Aron 2000, 405–6).

There is little doubt that Gorbachev was psychologically unwilling or incapable of going the extra mile to reach a market economy. Yeltsin accused him of clinging to a bankrupt socialist system in spite of the fact that it was repudiated by the "people." Dobrynin (1995, 635) noted that, in discussing the economy, the Soviet president never mentioned the word "capitalism." General Volkogonov (1998, 443) suggested that in spite of his reformist impulse, Gorbachev was emotionally "wedded to Leninism." U.S. ambassador Matlock (1995, 554) reflected that "Gorbachev could not psychologically bring himself to make the transformation which would have destroyed communism." Indeed, Gorbachev (1996, 381) would confirm these observations in his memoirs. He explained that the difference between the plans was not economic but rather "about the future model of our society" and that the government plan "was based on the retention of the single Union state" and, equally important, "the fundamentals of the socialist system" (Aron 2000, 406).

However, in making the "October choice" Gorbachev was also prompted by the increasing pressure of his hard-line communist opponents. Greatly alarmed by the speedy unraveling of the empire, by the fall of 1990 the hard-liners had decided to roll back perestroika.

Rolling Back the Revolution: The Communist Backlash, the August Coup, and the Collapse of the Soviet Union

Outmaneuvered and sidelined by Gorbachev, orthodox communists could do little but watch as the fundamentals of the Soviet system were being dismantled or swept away by the perestroika-turned-revolution. The armed forces and the military-industrial complex stood to lose the most. The military, which still struggled to develop the "reasonable sufficiency" doctrine, was faced with large troop cuts mandated by Gorbachev's promise to the United Nations. Even more painful were the Gorbachev-sanctioned reunification of Germany and the pending dissolution of the Warsaw Pact. Things at home were equally bleak. Glasnost exposed the harsh conditions of military service, and desertions were at an all-time high, a development compounded by the increasingly assertive republics, which either sheltered deserters or refused to participate in the draft. Subsequent interviews with senior military officials revealed that by early 1990 the army began showing signs of disintegration, turning it into "a house of cards," as one of them put it. Perhaps most demoralizing was the end of the Cold War. As the liberal Volkogonov noted, the Soviet system and its military backbone "could exist only by watching its opponents through the cross hairs of a gunsight" (Odom 1998, 301–40; Fischer 1999, 18).

The KGB and communist stalwarts like Ligachev were equally aggrieved. They blamed Gorbachev for ethnic violence in the republics, demonstrations, and strikes, and accused him of failure to restore law and order. Ligachev (1993, 113, 143) claimed that by the spring of 1990 "the threat of an all-encompassing crisis hung over the country," but that the "perestroika crowd" did little to remedy the situation. Ligachev complained that he was ignored when, on March 14, he demanded to convene a Central Committee plenum to discuss the situation in Lithuania, which in his view had "spun out of control."

The ever-widening scope of democratization along with the media and artistic freedoms that eroded the last vestiges of Soviet legitimacy were particularly alarming to old-fashioned communists. Indeed, during the first half of 1990 there was a virtual deluge of revisionist renditions of Soviet history, ranging from plays like *Brest Peace* and *Onward, Onward, Onward* to books and articles that accused Stalin of mishandling foreign policy, especially during World War II. There were more revelations about persecution of political prisoners, returning soldiers, and other atrocities, including the testing of biological agents on inmates and the murder of thousands of Polish officers in the Katyn Forest, a fact long denied by the Soviet Union. The media gave extensive coverage to Memorial, a group dedicated to commemorating the millions of victims killed by the state security services during Stalin's reign of terror. Under public pressure, the Politburo approved a monument to the "memory of the millions of victims of the totalitarian regime" to be erected not far from Lubyanka, the headquarters of the secret police. To top all this, in June, Oleg Kalugin, a former general in the KGB, called for the regime to dismantle the security services and "rip out its communist roots" (Dobbs 1997, 311; Kort 1993, 309; Shane 1994, 143; Aron 2000, 286–87; Bagley 1991, 63; Birstein 2001, xvii, 300).

Acting on these and other grievances, in March 1990 an anonymous group of KGB officers circulated an appeal to the Soviet parliament protesting the attack on the name of Lenin and expressing alarm about the "fate of the socialist fatherland." On June 22, Ivan Polozkov, a strident opponent of the free market, was elected leader of the Russian Communist People's Party on an antireform platform. At the 28th Party Congress in July 1990, he and other hard-liners tried to mount a challenge to what Ligachev called Gorbachev's "blind radicalism." Gorbachev managed to repeal the initiative by forcing the retirement of Ligachev and electing his own loyalists to a new Politburo and Central Committee. But in any case, the central organs of the party had little influence under the new presidential system. On February 27 the Supreme Soviet passed a draft law greatly expanding presidential power. On March 13, 1990, the Congress of People's Deputies gave Gorbachev strong presidential powers while also repealing Article 6 of the Constitution, which enshrined the leading role of the Communist Party (Shane 1994, 247; Kort 1993, 324; Robinson 1995, 181).

Facing an alarming loss of control, hard-liners in the KGB led by Vladimir Kryuchkov, the armed forces, the military industry, and the party apparat restructured the amorphous national salvation front into the more visible and energetic Soiuz, a faction boasting more than 500 members in the Supreme Soviet. Among its most activist elements were the "national patriots" representing some 80,000 political officers in the armed forces as well as Russians residing in the republics, who were gravely threatened by the independence movement. Soiuz blamed New Political Thinking and its emphasis on "universal human values" for undermining the raison d'être of the Soviet state. Reflecting the resurgent power of the military, Soiuz accused Gorbachev of making too many concessions in arms negotiations and threatened to reopen or even circumvent the INF and CFE treaties. All throughout the summer and into the fall there were persistent rumors of a military coup. In early September a paratrooper regiment and other units were suddenly deployed to Moscow; according to conflicting Defense Ministry explanations they were sent to either help with the potato harvest or to participate in the November celebrations of the revolution. A subsequent commission of inquiry claimed that the troops were intended as a show of force during a prodemocracy rally scheduled for September 16 (Lebed 1997, 265–68; Fischer 1999, 14; Blacker 1993, 178).

In whatever form, the increasingly shrill protest of the hard-liners was aimed at intimidating Gorbachev. Already unhappy with the "spring of nations" and the capitalist leanings of the Shatalin-Yavlinsky plan, the Soviet president became apprehensive about falling victim to the "Khrushchev syndrome," a reference to the removal of Khrushchev by his antireformist Politburo colleagues in 1964. But the conservatism of his "October choice" did not go far enough to mollify the communist opposition. In a November 2 meeting representatives from Soiuz complained about nationalist attacks against Russian expatriates and the army in the republics and demanded that Gorbachev fire the liberal interior minister Vadim Bakatin. On November 7, during a parade on Red Square, there was an assassination attempt against Gorbachev that was allegedly staged by the KGB to demonstrate that the country was out of control. A few days later, Gorbachev met with more than a thousand military officers for what turned out to be a highly acrimonious debate. It was followed by a public call from Soiuz to remove Gorbachev and transfer power to a Committee for National Salvation (Pozner 1992, 116–18, 119; Fischer 1999, 13; Matlock 1995, 422; Aron 2000, 408).

All along, Kryuchkov was sending Gorbachev reports warning about a plot by Yeltsin and other "democrats" to seize power. Indeed, in 1989 the KGB had established surveillance on Yeltsin and others in the Interregional Group with the aim of proving a CIA plot to dismantle the Union. The KGB also asked FBI agent Robert Hanssen to report on the CIA's plans for unraveling the Soviet Union (Dunlop 1993, 193; Bearden and Risen 2003, 469). Echoing Soiuz, Kryuchkov made his conspiracy theory public in a number of speeches in the fall and winter. On December 11, the KGB chief accused Western intelligence services of planting sleeper agents among the "reformers" in the 1970s in order to dismantle communism from within. In his "doomsday speech" at the Congress of People's Deputies on December 22, 1990, Kryuchkov accused the West of creating a brain drain, of sending contaminated shipments of grain and foodstuffs, and of accumulating billions of rubles to destabilize the economy. Kryuchkov also alleged that some of those who held "radical tendencies" had received "lavish moral and material support from abroad" and demanded the imposition of law and order. Apparently, some of these assessments had been passed on by Aldrich Ames, the CIA official who supplied intelligence to the KGB from 1985 until his arrest in 1994 (Pozner 1992, 128, 135; Dobbs 1997, 330; Ebon 1994, 17; Andrew 1995, 527).

Whether persuaded by these allegations or fearing a coup, Gorbachev made a major effort to accommodate the hard-liners on a number of issues. On November 17, Gorbachev dissolved the reformist Presidential Council, which included Yakovlev, Shevardnadze, and Shatalin, and replaced it with the hard-line Security Council. He tried to appease the military by allowing them to use weapons against "hostile behavior" in the republics. More important, contravening the CFE Treaty, which limited the number of Soviet troops and weapon systems in Europe, Gorbachev allowed the military to either redesignate some troops and weapons slated for reduction or move them into Asia. On December 2, Gorbachev replaced Interior Minister Bakatin with the hard-liner Boris Pugo, who, together with Minster of Defense Dmitri Yazov, authorized joint KGB-army patrols to enforce order. Soon after, Gorbachev ordered the republics to enforce the all-Union draft. When Prime Minister Ryzhkov suffered a heart attack at the end of December, Gorbachev nominated Valentin Pavlov, a staunch opponent of market reforms. In an even more surprising move, Gorbachev appointed another orthodox communist, Gennadi Yanaev, to the newly created post of vice-president of the Soviet Union. Warning that "dictatorship is coming," Shevardnadze tendered his resignation on December 20, followed, on January 19, 1991, by the economist Nikolai Petrakov, the last of the 500-Day Plan holdovers (Ekedahl and Goodman 1997, 45, 47; Foye 1995; Aron 2000, 409; Beschloss and Talbott 1993, 295).

The new team wasted no time in rolling back perestroika. On January 11, 1991, KGB and Interior Ministry troops brutally attacked independence targets in Vilnius, followed, on January 20, by equally bloody reprisals in Riga. Airborne troops were also ordered into Armenia, Georgia, Moldova, and western Ukraine. Reacting angrily to allegations that he had sanctioned the raids in the Baltics, Gorbachev proposed to suspend the law guaranteeing freedom of the press. To implement the new restriction, Kryuchkov was charged with the task of bringing television and other media under control. In fact, the KGB chief created a brand-new center for international propaganda, which, under the leadership of Nikolai Leonov, was designed to reverse liberal reforms. Soon, Leonov's line that the United States was out to destroy the Soviet Union flooded the public channels of communication (Bearden and Risen 2003, 471–72). Most telling was the change of course on the economy. On January 22, Pavlov carried out a decree withdrawing all fifty- and hundred-ruble notes, billed as a blow against "black-marketeers." Four days later Gorbachev gave the police and KGB unlimited authority to search domestic enterprises and foreign ventures suspected of "black-marketeering," Pavolov's euphemism for free enterprise. These and other steps were part of the new prime minister's "anti-crisis plan" to stabilize the economy and return it to a socialist mode.

Even Gorbachev's cherished foreign policy course suffered a reversal. Long unhappy about New Political Thinking, military leaders became extremely embittered by Soviet acquiescence in the Gulf War, reversing decades of Moscow's support for the Iraqi regime. The weakness of Soviet weaponry, which was no match for American technological superiority, added humiliation to the sense of betrayal. According to Defense Minister Yazov, the Gulf War, together with the CFE Treaty, spelled the end of Soviet status as a superpower. Even some former perestroika supporters blamed Gorbachev and Shevardnadze for squandering Soviet foreign policy and security assets in negotiations with the Americans. A high-ranking Foreign Ministry official described Gorbachev's position during the Gulf War as "craven" (quoted in Fischer 1999, 16). Dobrynin (1995, 627) complained that during Gorbachev's short tenure, the "political frontiers of the European continent were effectively rolled eastward to the Russian borders of 1653, which were those before Russia's union with the Ukraine." He added that, "flattered by the Western media, Gorbachev and Shevardnadze were often outwitted and outplayed by their Western partners." With Shevardnadze gone, Aleksandr Bessmertnykh, Gorbachev's new foreign minister, took a cool line toward the West while Gorbachev tried to stop the ground war against Iraq. On a more symbolic level, on March 7 the Central Committee fired General Volkogonov, the official military historian, for writing a history of World War II that was critical of Stalin (Remnick 1994, 401; Herspring 1996, 129).

If Gorbachev hoped to improve his chances by an alliance with traditional communists, the situation in the first quarter of 1991 would dash such hopes. In spite of Pavlov's measures, or maybe because of them, the economy had spun out of control. Due to the collapse of the central distribution system, there were widespread shortages of goods, including food staples, inflation increased, production fell in key sectors, and national income dropped by 10 percent. Following Leningrad, which adopted a rationing system modeled on that used during the Nazi siege of the city in 1941, Moscow and scores of other localities began rationing meat, grain, vodka, and other staples. The cold winter of 1990–91 compounded the difficulties, prompting a Western humanitarian aid effort (Kort 1993, 326–27; Matlock 1995, 438–39).

Taking a hard-line approach to the republics was also of questionable value. The series of bloody clashes between demonstrators and Soviet special forces in the early winter had failed to suppress nationalist agitation and gave Yeltsin yet another opportunity to increase his influence. In January 1991 Yeltsin traveled to the Baltics and appealed to Russian soldiers "to disobey orders to fire on civilians." He implied that the Russian republic would be forced to create its own army and concluded a mutual security treaty with the Baltics. Yeltsin also disclosed that Russia was working on a "quadripartite treaty" with Belorussia, Ukraine, and Kazakhstan. In a televised interview in February, Yeltsin called on Gorbachev to resign and warned about the emerging "fascist" National Salvation Front of Stalinist communists, reactionary trade unions, and "black shirt" nationalists (Yeltsin 1994, 24; Palazchenko 1997, 237; Aron 2000, 410–11; Foye 1995, 83–84).

Even more damaging was the international reaction to Gorbachev's alliance with what looked like some of the more regressive elements in the Soviet system. The United States and other Western countries rebuked the Soviet Union for the bloodshed in the republics and threatened to suspend financial aid. On March 15, Secretary of State James Baker told Gorbachev that Washington was worried about these developments and warned that they would impede Soviet integration into the Western economy, a goal that the Soviet leader had pursued with great zeal. It was apparently as a result of this and similar appeals that Gorbachev decided to break his alliance with the hard-line elements and return to a more democratic and market-oriented posture. As a reward, he was invited to a G-7 meeting in London, where the Soviet Union was promised an associate membership in the International Monetary Fund (IMF), and was encouraged to hope for a large Marshall Plan–style financial rescue effort (Gorbachev 1996, 609–11; Foye 1995, 85–86).

Indeed, the idea of a Soviet "Marshall Plan" had become highly appealing to the increasingly desperate Gorbachev. As Ambassador Matlock noted, bereft of any politically feasible cure for the collapsing economy, Gorbachev "began to dream of a deus ex machina" in the form of a Western bailout, which was put at $100 billion. According to Yavlinsky, who went on to head an economic institute in Moscow, on five different occasions in the spring Gorbachev was overheard making "stinging comments" about Pavlov's "anticrisis" program. Yavlinsky, together with Graham Allison and Jeffrey Sachs from Harvard University, worked out the details of a plan dubbed the "Great Bargain." Also known as the "Window of Opportunity," the plan tried to help Gorbachev establish democracy and a market economy in exchange for a sizable bailout; it had the support of, among others, then British prime minister Margaret Thatcher (Matlock 1995, 531, 535).

In order to curry favor with the West, Gorbachev renewed his efforts to peacefully redefine the relations with the republics. The draft of a new Treaty of Union that was published the previous November served as the basis for a new round of negotiations with Yeltsin and other republican leaders. On April 23, at the official summer residence in Novo-Ogarevo, Gorbachev and leaders of nine republics—Russia, Ukraine, Belorussia, Uzbekistan, Kazakhstan, Azerbaijan, Kyrgyzstan, Tajikistan, and Turkmenistan—unveiled a Joint Declaration, which acknowledged the sovereignty of the republics. The so-called Nine Plus One agreement promised to create a new entity to be called the Union of Sovereign Republics, with a new constitution and democratic elections to the states' representative bodies. Even for those who were not privy to the negotiations, the agreement indicated the growing power of Yeltsin and his followers.

Coming on top of Yeltsin's growing authority, Gorbachev's apparent re-entry into the "reform camp" rattled the hard-liners. Their fears were confirmed when, during his Nobel Prize acceptance speech on June 11, 1991, the Soviet president effectively forswore socialism. Gorbachev's political zigzagging and chaotic decision-making habits confirmed to the hard-liners and even some less partisan members of the inner circle that their leader was as erratic as Khrushchev had been before his ouster (Fischer 1999, 12). One commentator claimed that the Soviet leader, described as "suspicious and erratic, insulting and dismissing people," had undergone a personality change (Boldin 1994, 260–61). Galvanized into action, the hard-liners tried to use the political process to undermine Gorbachev, Yeltsin, and other reform advocates. On May 9, the newspaper *Den* featured a roundtable discussion with some of their leaders, including General Valentin Varennikov and Oleg Baklanov, the head the military-industrial complex, who insinuated that the military could do a better job at governing the Soviet Union than civilians. The party apparatus in the military, the Main Political Administration, became active in the June 12 election for the newly created elected presidency of Russia, but Yeltsin soundly defeated the communist candidate, Nikolai Ryzhkov. Ironically, efforts to politicize the military backfired when Yeltsin managed to garner considerable support among the garrisons stationed in the Russian republic (Dobrynin 1995, 627, 631; Remnik 1994, 435; Matlock 1995, 559; Foye 1995).

Rebuffed at the ballot box, the would-be conspirators took their fight to a meeting of the Supreme Soviet. On June 17, during a closed session, Kryuchkov read parts of a report entitled "On CIA Plans to Recruit Agents Among Soviet Citizens," which he had originally presented to the Politburo in 1987. Kryuchkov repeated his allegation that the CIA recruited "sleeper agents of influence" in the Soviet Union to sabotage the system and that some of them used the vehicle of perestroika to achieve "certain results." Prime Minister Pavlov echoed this theme, adding that the Great Bargain was part of the conspiracy "to sell the motherland to the West." He and other hard-liners such as Pugo and Yazov accused Gorbachev of failing to recognize the danger and asked the Supreme Soviet to give the prime minister additional authority (Andrew 1993, 64; 1995, 528). Since Gorbachev was not informed beforehand, most political observers and foreign embassies in Moscow concluded that the move amounted to a "constitutional coup" (Ebon 1994, 20–21; Beschloss and Talbott 1993, 393).

On June 20, Gavril Popov, the popular mayor of Moscow, told U.S. ambassador Matlock of a pending coup against Gorbachev. Popov listed Pavlov, Kryuchkov, Yazov, and Anatoly Lukyanov, chairman of the Supreme Soviet, as leading conspirators. When informed of the plot by President Bush, Gorbachev replied that "he had given those officials a good telling off." The following day Gorbachev managed to reassert his authority in the Supreme Soviet, but failed to fire the plotters, prompting Ambassador Matlock to wonder about the Soviet leader's "political deafness" (Matlock 1995, 539). Others described his passivity as "insouciance" or "recklessness" (McCauley 1998, 216). A more appropriate explanation was denial; despite his misgivings, Gorbachev repeated Khrushchev's mistake by refusing to believe that Kryuchkov would try to depose him. Even the astute Shevardnadze apparently did not foresee that the KGB chief could organize a conspiracy. In any event, given the fluid balance of power, Gorbachev might have been reluctant to sever his links with the hard-liners. Alternatively, he might have hoped for a "national reconciliation" between the hard-liners and the reformers, with him serving as a center, a balancing act that he had performed before (Palazchenko 1997, 261; Taubman 2003, 3–17; Beschloss and Talbott 1993, 397).

Gorbachev (1991, 15) seemed to have put all his faith in the new Union Treaty, which was finalized on July 23, 1991, and was scheduled for signing on August 20. But it was the prospect of devolving power to the republics, including the fear that Yeltsin would nationalize the Russian oil and gas industry, that prompted the hard-line coalition to act. After months of trying without success to persuade Gorbachev to declare a state of emergency, Kryuchkov and other conspirators apparently decided to forestall the treaty signing by removing the Soviet president. On July 23, *Sovetskaia Rossiia* published an open letter signed by, among others, General Varennikov and Deputy Defense Minister General Boris Gromov, who called for resistance to the "chain-reaction of disastrous disintegration" (Slater 1995, 70). On July 30, the KGB, which had placed a surveillance device in Gorbachev's summer residence outside Moscow, recorded a conversation between Gorbachev, the Kazakh president Nursultan Nazarbayev, and Yeltsin, who suggested that following the signing of the new treaty, "some of the most odious members" of the old regime, topped by Kryuchkov, needed to be replaced. The transcript persuaded Kryuchkov and others that urgent action was needed. Gorbachev confirmed this account in an interview with Radio Free Europe on August 19, 1996 (Dobbs 1997, 372; Dunlop 1993, 194–96).

On August 5, a day after Gorbachev departed for a vacation at Foros in the Crimea, the conspirators, including Yazov and Pugo, met in a KGB sanatorium where they formed the State Committee for the State of Emergency, known by its Russian acronym GKChP. Teams of KGB officers were ordered to produce plans for a state of emergency, which included, among other things, preparations of 300,000 arrest warrants and 250,000 handcuffs. On August 16, the decree for the state of emergency was ready; the next day it was presented to Pavlov, Yazov, Gorbachev's chief of staff Valeri Boldin, Baklanov, and central committee secretary Oleg Shenin. Pavlov, as well as other conspirators, including Yanaev and Lukyanov, joined after some hesitation. Yazov, Varennikov, and other military co-conspirators were to play a key role by ordering elite units to Moscow (Andrew and Mitrokhin 1999, 393; McCauley 1998, 233–34; Foye 1995; Pozner 1992, 11–47; Matlock 1995, 581).

On August 18 the GKChP sent a delegation to Foros to pressure Gorbachev to declare a state of emergency; failing that, he was placed under house arrest. The following day the Emergency Committee announced that Gorbachev was "too ill" to perform his duties and named Vice-President Yanaev as acting president. The leaders of the coup declared that the "authority at all levels has lost the confidence of the population." They pledged to "save the economy from ruin and the country from hunger, to prevent the escalation of the threat of a large-scale conflict with unpredictable consequences for the peoples of the USSR and the entire international community" (Andrew and Mitrokhin 1999, 561; Felshman 1992, 15; Gorbachev 1991, 15).

However, in spite of months of preparation, the coup failed on the third day. The public appearances of the conspirators, some of them evidently drunk or shaky, inspired little public confidence, and many prominent figures denounced the coup. The military, reflecting the general split in the country, fragmented along national and partisan lines. General Evgeni Shaposhnikov, the commander of the air force, and General Pavel Grachev, the commander of the airborne forces, came out against the junta. The elite Taman Motorized Rifle Division, the 106th Airborne Division, and the Kantemirov Tank Division went over to Yeltsin, who was barricaded in the White House, the Russian parliament building in Moscow. The Alpha special forces failed to storm the White House as ordered due to fear on the part of their commanders that this would provoke fighting with opposing military forces. Other units, unwilling to choose sides, stayed on the sidelines. According to Shaposhnikov, by August 21 the entire high command urged Yazov to withdraw the troops and outlaw the GKChP. None of those on the KGB list were arrested, and Yeltsin's communications with the outside world were not cut (Yeltsin 1994, 87; Foye 1995; Blacker 1993, 144, 179–80; Odom 1998; Miller 1992; Ebon 1994, 7; Slater 1995).

Going beyond the behavior of the military, the failure of the coup could be attributed to the changing political culture in the Soviet Union. As the theoretical discussion made clear, once coercion is eliminated and individuals can stop practicing preference falsification, a chain reaction of freely expressed opinions and beliefs leads to a stage of liminality where all previous validity claims are subject to a reevaluation. Indeed, in a poll taken before the August events only 4 percent of the respondents were willing to give complete credence to the claims of the party. Although it is impossible to prove statistically, by August cascading liminality had apparently reached a tipping point. As Gates (1996, 439) noted in less theoretical language, "the Communists who had run the country from behind Oz's curtain for so long were exposed to the entire country and the world as a venal, petty, squabbling bureaucracy." To restore such a badly delegitimized old regime would have required a level of bloodshed that the conspirators could not or would not sanction. Kryuchkov had hoped to engineer a bloodless takeover modeled on Khrushchev's ouster, but according to an August 20 memorandum prepared by KGB analysts for their chief, there was a possibility of mass civil disobedience and bloodshed. Indeed, after a number of protesters were killed in a clash with a military unit, Yazov ordered the withdrawal of troops from Moscow. Throughout, Muscovites used the "people power" techniques perfected during the fundamentalist revolution in Iran to "disarm" soldiers, for example, by stuffing flowers in their rifles; a huge sign near Yeltsin's headquarters proclaimed "Don't Shoot Your Mothers." In spite of emergency regulations, newspapers carried results of hastily conducted polls indicating that only a fraction of Muscovites supported the Emergency Committee (Kort 1993, 328; d'Encausse 1993, 153; Taubman 2003, 3–17; Yeltsin 1994, 99–100).

Equally important was the presence of a well-organized opposition led by Yeltsin. By spending the previous year networking with the military, Yeltsin was able to "peel off" Grachev, Shaposhnikov, Aleksandr Lebed, and other sympathetic commanders, and neutralize still others. Leaders of other republics with whom the Russian president had worked closely lambasted the conspirators, and miners went on strike in protest. By fashioning himself as the leader of the people, Yeltsin was able to deny the Committee whatever legitimacy it had hoped to muster. The well-televised events outside the White House, with Yeltsin standing on top of a tank rallying resistance, made it easier for Western countries to condemn the coup. Even the insular Kryuchkov understood that the emergency government needed some international legitimacy, which the group tried but failed to drum up by securing the support of Foreign Minister Bessmertnykh (Ebon 1994, 7; Lebed 1997, 297).

With the plot in disarray, on August 21 Gorbachev regained control and returned to Moscow on a special flight, but his victory seemed tenuous. As the Soviet president would later comment: "I arrived in a different country"

(Gorbachev 1991, 43). In hindsight, the coup accelerated the collapse of the three pillars that held up the Soviet system: the party, the secret police, and the army. By Gorbachev's (1996, 603) own admission, even before the August plot the Communist Party suffered "extreme hemorrhage," with millions of members quitting; by 1991 only some 15 million were left. Shortly after the coup Yeltsin banned the party from Russia as part of a comprehensive program of decommunization, a step followed by other republics. With Kryuchkov and his top lieutenants arrested, the KGB fared even less well and was subsequently dissolved. Yeltsin, who overruled Gorbachev and appointed Shaposhnikov as defense minister, embarked on a "house cleaning" that elevated a group of commanders sympathetic to the republican cause. Moving fast, the Russian president and his republican counterparts transferred important functions from the Union to the states (Aron 2000, 466–69; Foye 1995, 88; Blacker 1993, 181–82).

In spite of all these setbacks, Gorbachev still hoped to salvage perestroika and the Union. As one observer noted, Gorbachev could not give up on the belief that "the system was reformable—a belief which he continued to hold after the coup," but one that increasingly looked like a quixotic quest (Slater 1995, 60). Gorbachev's personal popularity was at an all-time low, plummeting from a 52 percent approval rating in December 1989 to 21 percent in October 1991. In the month following the coup, rumors and press articles appeared implicating Gorbachev in the conspiracy, a view held by some American scholars as well. At minimum, critics blamed Gorbachev for exercising poor judgment by appointing the would-be conspirators (Matlock 1995, 447; Miller 1992; Yegorov 1993, 56; Knight 1996, 12–37; Dunlop 1993, 202–6).

Adding to the grim picture was the economy, which had virtually collapsed in the last quarter of the year. The budget deficit stood at 30 percent of GDP, and the printing of rubles by the USSR State Bank caused the currency to lose 86 percent of its value against the dollar. At the end of October the Union's central banking authority requested a rescheduling of external debt and defaulted on payments of some $5.4 billion; the hard-currency reserve stood at a catastrophic low of $100 million. There were widespread shortages of food and other goods, reflecting the fact that production had dropped to 79 percent of the 1990 level. With empty stores, standing in lines became even more of a forced national pastime. One survey estimated that Soviet citizens spent between forty and sixty-eight hours a month in queues (Aron 2000, 481–83).

Under these conditions, Gorbachev's efforts to resurrect the Union treaty did not look promising, and although the Soviet leader made more concessions to the republics, a move that brought Yeltsin aboard, the November 25 agreement to approve the treaty did not last. Working on a parallel track, on December 7–8, Yeltsin and the republican leaders of Ukraine and Belorussia met secretly in Belovezhskaia Pushcha in Belorussia to negotiate a new compact, which resulted in the loosely structured Commonwealth of Independent States (CIS). Ignoring Gorbachev's protestations that the agreement was dangerous, illegal, and portended "anarchy and chaos," on December 21–22 eleven former Soviet republics agreed to join the CIS. On December 25 Gorbachev resigned and the Russian flag replaced the Soviet flag over the Kremlin. The USSR officially ceased to exist on the last day of 1991.

In retrospect, perestroika harbored the logic that led this unprecedented experiment to destroy the system it had set out to repair. But as the tumultuous last two years of the reform-turned-revolution unfolded, the participants in the drama could not have predicted the outcome with anything resembling the determinism born out of hindsight wisdom. Making sense of events and predicting the future was even harder on the American watchers.

The Washington Watch: A Guide for the Perplexed

With the momentous events of 1989 behind it, at the beginning of 1990 the Bush foreign policy team faced a novel challenge, which one observer described as "too much success rather than too little success in wrestling concessions from Moscow" (Fischer 1999, 12). Given the declining economy and the increasing boldness of nationalistic advocacy, Gorbachev's future seemed far from secure. Some in the White House worried that Gorbachev was turning into a "desperate sorcerer's apprentice, unable to manage the runaway upheaval his politics had unleashed" (Beschloss and Talbott 1993, 181). A rumor about Gorbachev's imminent political demise reported by CNN on January 30, 1990, caused a sharp drop in the New York Stock Exchange. During his visit in Moscow on February 7–8, Secretary of State Baker was shaken by Shevardnadze's bleak account of the state of the economy and the ethnic strife in the republics (Kort 1993, 322; Matlock 1995, 310–12; Baker 1995, 202).

In a series of meetings starting in early January, the Bush administration enumerated its Soviet policy goals. High on the agenda was German reunification without jeopardizing NATO, a further reduction of arms and troops, and propping up the vulnerable Gorbachev, who, as Bush put it, needed "face and standing" (Fischer 1999, 12). To this end, it was decided that Washington would soft-pedal its reaction to the crisis in Lithuania and other republics. The Lithuanian nationalistic ardor presented the administration with a real dilemma. On the one hand, as the nominal heir to Reagan's anticommunist crusade, Bush had to show a commitment to the self-determination of the republics. On the other hand, the president was apprehensive that pressure from Washington would play into the hands of Gorbachev's hard-line opponents. One of Bush's aides noted that the president was "afraid to light a match in a gas filled room" (Beschloss and Talbott 1993, 205; Gates 1996, 485–89; Andrew 1995, 516).

Indeed, domestic considerations demonstrated that the president's efforts to tread lightly on the Lithuanian issue required some artful footwork. Outraged Reagan conservatives in Congress applied heavy pressure on Bush to recognize Lithuania and rebuke Gorbachev. Even though Bush and Scowcroft described the congressional posturing as "reckless," the administration was forced to warn Gorbachev, a message that was delivered by Ambassador Matlock in a meeting with Shevardnadze on March 8, 1990. The White House also delayed the signing of a trade pact with the Soviet Union until Moscow agreed to lift the embargo against Lithuania and resolve the situation peacefully (Bush and Scowcroft 1998, 216; Matlock 1995, 328).

With stakes this high, the White House was anxiously monitoring the stability of the Soviet Union. A CIA report in March 1990 warned that perestroika was "at a critical junction" and speculated about a possible response by Gorbachev. A May analysis noted that the "Soviet economy stumbled badly," a theme elaborated upon in a series of reports. The potential for mass unrest and ethnic strife was the subject of a number of papers, with a special focus on the Baltic and Asian republics. Other assessments dealt with political changes, including the role of the newly reinvigorated Supreme Soviet and the position of Gorbachev. Still others analyzed his motives for moving to the side of the hard-line opposition (CIA Documents, SOV SEG-9–001, SOV 90–10004, SOV 90–10015, DDB-19000–161, SOV 90–10020, SOV 90–10029, SOV 90–10053, GI 90–10043, SOV 90–10042).

The question of how much pressure the White House could apply without provoking a hard-line backlash against Gorbachev loomed large over the preparations for a May summit in Washington. It was there that Bush hoped to push for German reunification in spite of the fact that a February CIA estimate considered the chances of such an outcome to be virtually nil. Ambassador Matlock (1995, 383) was equally pessimistic, noting that "we . . . had little hope that Gorbachev [could] agree to . . . a united Germany in NATO and survive politically." Robert Blackwell, the National Intelligence Officer (NIO) for the Soviet Union, wrote on March 1 that the German question was "a visceral one for the Soviet population." When, on May 31, Gorbachev agreed in principle to the American demand, observers described it as a "surprise, a miracle, or a mystery that still eludes a convincing explanation." The deal was clinched when Gorbachev dropped virtually all preconditions for reunification during a mid-July meeting with West German chancellor Helmut Kohl. Like Bush and Scowcroft, Kohl was reported to have been "stunned," prompting Baker to comment later that the deal was "too good to be true." As a small concession, West Germany agreed to limit the size of its army and provide the Soviet Union with some $8 billion in aid. The formal reunification agreement was signed on October 3, 1990 (Baker 1995, 234; Fischer 1999, 12; Gates 1996, 493).

The president pushed equally hard for "boldness" in negotiating the CFE Treaty, which started on March 9 under the auspices of the Conference on Security and Cooperation in Europe. The foreign policy team was split on the wisdom of pursuing the ambitious goal of equalizing Western and Soviet military force in Europe, with Baker expressing the most caution. However, the Americans and their NATO allies were surprised by Gorbachev's reasonableness. The treaty, which favored the Western alliance by setting equal conventional force ceilings in Europe, was signed on November 1990 in Paris. Two days later the Charter of Paris that ended the Cold War was signed (Gates 1996, 485–86).

Saddam Hussein's invasion of Kuwait on August 2, 1990, made Gorbachev even more vital to the national security of the United States. In preparation for a war, the Bush administration sought to build a large coalition of European and Middle Eastern countries. Although not part of the coalition, Gorbachev decided to support Washington in spite of strong internal opposition. On August 3 Shevardnadze and Baker issued a joint statement condemning the Iraqi invasion, and on November 27 the Soviet Union supported a UN resolution that authorized the use of force against Iraq to liberate Kuwait. As already noted, coming after the decision on German unification, Gorbachev's Iraq policy fueled accusations that the Soviet leader was "erratic."

With the ground war scheduled to begin early in 1991, worries about perestroika intensified. A number of CIA estimates in January and February painted a bleak picture of the economic situation, ethnic unrest, and social instability. After the bloodshed in the Baltic republics, Gorbachev's future was questioned by the White House anew. In early March even the normally cautious Scowcroft observed that "the window of opportunity appeared to be closing" and Baker commented that "the stock market was heading south; it was time to sell" (quoted in Fischer 1999, 13, 16; Baker 1995, 478). Using the same market metaphor, Condoleezza Rice urged the administration to "diversify" by reaching out to Yeltsin and his fellow republican leaders (Beschloss and Talbott 1993, 345). On April 25, SOVA's George Kolt wrote in "The Soviet Cauldron" that in an atmosphere of "economic crisis, independence aspirations . . . even a putsch is not likely to prevent the pluralistic forces from emerging in a dominant position before the end of the decade." In May 1991, the Agency argued in "Gorbachev's Future" that the Soviet president was losing control over the political process, a fact observed firsthand by Bush, who noted that Gorbachev's team was in a "virtually open rebellion against a Soviet leader." CIA analysts also issued a number of warnings of a possible coup, but the chances of a hard-line success were not rated highly. Still, the May report added darkly that "no matter what happens, the current political system is doomed" (CIA Documents, SOV-91–20177M, SOV M 91–20070X).

Given these uncertainties, with the exception of arms negotiations the White House was cautious in responding to other Soviet initiatives, especially the financially onerous Grand Bargain. Although negotiations on granting Moscow financial aid continued up to the July meeting of the G-7, to which Gorbachev was invited as a price for rejoining the reformist camp, there was more than a little hesitation in the White House. A CIA analysis at that time stated that the Soviet leader's "domination of the Soviet political scene had ended." The report also noted that the Soviet Union "is now in a revolutionary situation . . . a transition from the old order to an as yet undefined new order" (Bush and Scowcroft 1998, 502–3; Matlock 1995, 549–50; Beschloss and Talbott 1993, 376–77, 382; Gates 1996, 520).

Indeed, in spite of Bush's public commitment to Gorbachev and the territorial integrity of the Soviet Union, these and other reports turned the question of how to deal with the Soviet leader into a hotly contested issue. Gates (1996, 503, 515), who had all along rated Gorbachev's chances as poor, found more support for his position. He used the occasion to lobby again on behalf of Yeltsin. Nearly a year earlier, in a memo dated June 6, 1990, Gates warned, "we might have underestimated Yeltsin as a result of the 1989 meeting" and urged the administration to avoid "further negative comments about him." Gates's stand was in line with a series of CIA assessments, wherein both George Kolt and Fritz Ermarth supported Yeltsin. A March SOVA analysis made clear that the Russian leader was a major player and that the "future of the Russian reforms depends on Yeltsin." Pressure also came from Ambassador Matlock, who opened Spaso House, his Moscow residence, to an informal gathering of the reformist circles. Matlock had also urged planning of transition scenarios for a post-Gorbachev period. Richard Nixon, who met Yeltsin in March, tried to influence Bush to embrace the democratic opposition during a White House dinner in April (Matlock 1995, 438–39). Secretary of Defense Cheney had also increased his pro-Yeltsin lobbying (Gates 1996, 503, 515; Bush and Scowcroft 1998, 283; SOV 91–10013X; Horelick 1989–90; Beschloss and Talbott 1993, 345–46, 359–60).

Still, a number of factors conspired against Yeltsin's plan to replace Gorbachev as America's new "best hope" in Moscow. None of the CIA scenarios in 1990 and the first half of 1991 predicted a virtually peaceful dissolution of the Soviet Union by Russia. Lingering doubts about Yeltsin's character and judgment were reinforced by his aggressive championship of the Baltic states' independence. Indeed, the White House, reflecting the judgment of most Western observers in Moscow, considered Yeltsin's February televised call for Gorbachev to step down as yet another example of posturing and self-promotion (Aron 2000, 414). Yeltsin's boorish behavior was a problem for Scowcroft, along with the national security adviser's distrust of "romantic nationalism," which, in his view, threatened to destabilize the Soviet Union. Scowcroft took it quite personally, writing, "it was painful to watch Yeltsin rip the Soviet Union brick by brick." Gates blamed Scowcroft for writing off the CIA as "hopelessly pro-Yeltsin," for disregarding "any CIA assessment on Yeltsin," and for fighting efforts of Matlock and the new Soviet expert on the NSC, economist Ed Hewett, to initiate contacts with the Russian leader (Beschloss and Talbott 1993, 345–46, 359–60). While better disposed toward Yeltsin, the president was reluctant to think about the succession, noting in his diary on March 17 that "you dance with who is on the dance floor" (Bush and Scowcroft 1998, 500, 556). In any event, according to Nixon, Bush was too much of a gentleman to abandon Gorbachev. More important, conditioned by years of watching a highly centralized regime, the CIA, which supplied political assessments, could not fathom the seismic shift in the legitimacy discourse that favored Yeltsin over Gorbachev. As Gates put it, for a long time the Agency "still thought of politics in the Soviet Union as taking place within the walls of the Kremlin" (Berkowitz and Richelson 1995; Gates 1996, 360–61, 430, 504).

But even a better understating of the discursive dynamics would not have trumped the administration's interest in backing Gorbachev and preventing the disintegration of the Soviet Union. The administration was working very hard on completing the Strategic Arms Reduction Treaty (START) that Bush and Gorbachev were due to sign during a July 1991 summit in Moscow. This imperative became more urgent after Gorbachev switched temporarily to align with the hard-liners, a development acknowledged by a CIA report, which also noted that the round of bloodshed in early 1991 was sanctioned by the Soviet president (Matlock 1995, 438–39; Beschloss and Talbott 1993, 287; Gates 1996, 498–99).

With the benefit of hindsight, Scowcroft acknowledged that the administration underestimated the growing power of Yeltsin and his strategy of using Russia to undermine the Union. He noted that "we did not pay close attention" to Yeltsin's Baltic maneuver; "we viewed him as "just one of the

presidents of the republics." Scowcroft also admitted that it was not understood that without Russia, the ability of the Union to function was dim (Bush
and Scowcroft 1998, 498, 497). In fact, the White House was not alone in
misreading the Russian leader. Commenting on Yeltsin's February attack on
Gorbachev over Lithuania, the *New York Times* warned that Yeltsin was "an
unknown quality and could lead to anarchy." During an April 15 meeting of
the European Parliament in Strasbourg, Yeltsin was described as a "provoca-
teur" and a "deliberately irresponsible demagogue" (Yeltsin 1994, 23; Aron
2000, 421).

After Yeltsin's persuasive win in the Russian presidential election in June
1991, the reluctant U.S. administration could no longer ignore the new democratic political reality. On June 20 Bush welcomed the Russian president to
the White House and an intelligence team was dispatched to Moscow to help
with Yeltsin's security (Pozner 1992, 177; Andrew 1995, 529). Secretary of
Defense Cheney, who had been previously restrained by the White House,
came out full throttle in support of Yeltsin. Speaking on "Meet the Press,"
Cheney declared that the Russian leader "represents a set of principles and
values . . . that we hold for the Soviet Union—democratization and demilita-
rization" (Ackerman and Foer 2003, 18).

Still, Bush and his senior policy advisers had a hard time letting go of the
preference for Gorbachev and a stable Soviet Union, which, in their view, only
he could deliver. After the meeting with Yeltsin, Bush promised that "the United
States would continue to maintain the closest possible official relations with
the Soviet Government and President Gorbachev." Such public reassurances
were also necessary because the White House scheduled a high-profile summit meeting in Moscow for July 29–August 1, 1991. In the words of one observer: "it was Gorbachev, not Yeltsin who controlled the mighty Soviet nuclear
arsenal." But Bush seemed to go the extra mile to placate Gorbachev during
the summit; he downplayed the nationalist dynamics that were sweeping the
republics and rebuffed Yeltsin's brand of nationalist leadership. In a speech in
Kiev, he told the Ukrainian audience that the United States supported the Union
and its leader, adding that Americans will not support those who seek independence in order "to replace a far-off tyranny with local despotism." The speech,
dubbed "Chicken Kiev" by critics, was widely derided in the United States,
prompting Gates to admit that "the result was an unhappy one." To make matters worse, during an official dinner in Moscow Yeltsin created an embarrass-
ment by breaking protocol and trying to upstage Gorbachev. Ambassador
Matlock commented that Yeltsin's behavior was "boorish and childish," a view
shared by others in the American delegation (Andrew 1995, 528, 529; Gates
1996, 506; Beschloss and Talbott 1993, 412; Palazchenko 1997, 301; Matlock
1995, 584; Bush and Scowcroft 1998, 512).

The administration's worries about an ethnically driven disintegration of the Soviet Union were balanced by anxiety over a communist coup. As noted, on June 20, Moscow's mayor Popov told Ambassador Matlock of a pending coup. The CIA did not have political assets in Moscow to independently verify the information, but after returning from a Moscow visit, Colin Powell, the chairman of the Joint Chiefs of Staff, reported on July 29 that the Soviet military "detested the political pluralism . . . [and] view it as a loss of order and control" (Bush and Scowcroft 1998, 509, 515). A July intelligence report entitled "Implications of Alternative Soviet Futures" listed a hard-line coup and "regression" as one low-probability scenario. Others featured a chronic crisis, a pluralistic transformation under Gorbachev, and a chaotic and violent fragmentation (Fischer 1999, 16).

On August 10, Matlock had a dinner conversation in Moscow with Shevardnadze, who worried about a "right-wing attack." Seven days later, on August 17, the CIA included a strong warning about the possibility of a coup within the next few days in the President's Daily Briefing. But the CIA's Moscow station chief David Rolph found out about the coup only from the radio on the morning of August 19 (Bearden and Risen 2003, 490). In the United States, CNN carried the news around midnight on August 18; Scowcroft, who accompanied Bush on his vacation in Kennebunkport, was watching the broadcast. Scowcroft (Bush and Scowcroft 1998, 514) realized that a coup was afoot and informed the president. Around the same time, Baker, who was in Wyoming, received a call from the State Department's Operations Center (Matlock 1995, 575; Andrew 1995, 529; Gates 1996, 521; Bush and Scowcroft 1998, 518).

Attempts to draft an official American response were hindered by the split in the Bush team. SOVA's Kolt and Ermarth argued that the coup was poorly executed; Ermarth produced a report that gave the coup a 45 percent probability of "early fizzle." CIA deputy director Richard Kerr and Matlock, who had returned home after his tenure in Moscow, shared this view, which was also supported by Milt Bearden, who was in charge of anti-Soviet clandestine operations. However, Scowcroft felt that based on historical experience, the conspirators might be successful and advised not to "burn bridges" with them. According to Matlock (1995, 587–88), Scowcroft dismissed the CIA analysis as a mixture of speculation and wishful thinking. When Bush gave a statement on the morning of August 19, he refrained from defining the Emergency Committee as "illegitimate" or "unconstitutional," choosing instead the more innocuous term "extraconstitutional." Throughout the day the president also avoided calling Yeltsin. As events in Moscow exposed the plotters' indecisiveness, the Kolt-Ermarth-Bearden view gained credibility. The National Security Agency, which monitored Soviet communications, reported that the conspiracy was receiving little support from the military. Thus in an evening statement from the White House, the president called the coup "illegitimate and unconstitutional." With Yeltsin's status rising and Gorbachev's standing plummeting, the next two days saw a change in the administration's policy. Gates (1996, 523) noted that "we watched in amazement" as Gorbachev, upon his return from the Crimea, ignored "the courageous resistance" in the Russian White House and asserted that he remained a communist. Baker (1995, 521) described the White House reaction as "shocked," leading the Bush team to conclude that Gorbachev had lost touch with political reality (McCauley 1998, 240; Beschloss and Talbott 1993, 432; Andrew 1995, 530; Bush and Scowcroft 1998, 519–21).

As if to highlight the policy switch, on August 20 an Oval Office session decided to expand support for Yeltsin and the Russian authority. The Voice of America was ordered to broadcast Yeltsin's message across the Soviet Union. By early September, Bush had established a fairly good rapport with Yeltsin, whose move to usurp much of the Soviet Union's authority in the name of the Russian republic was described by Gates as "clever, even brilliant." In changing course, Bush bowed to the inevitable. By shifting to Yeltsin, Bush was also trying to protect himself from criticism in the press that his personal commitment to Gorbachev and his "disdain" for Yeltsin had prompted the White House to disregard the CIA's pre-coup warnings (Gates 1996, 523; Bush and Scowcroft 1998, 536; Andrew 1995, 529; Waller 1991).

Still, the pro-Gorbachev bias in the administration lingered. While watching a broadcast of a meeting of the Russian parliament on August 23, the president found Yeltsin's efforts to humiliate his rival "heavy handed." A September 1 article in the *Washington Post* suggested that senior advisers of the president were "expressing profound anxiety" over the prospect of losing Gorbachev. Around the same time, Scowcroft chose a CNN interview to express his concern about the fact that it was "not clear to what end Yeltsin would use his power." This and similar statements prompted the new American ambassador to Moscow, Robert Strauss, to complain to the State Department about the campaign of "Yeltsin bashing" (Beschloss and Talbott 1993, 444; Bush and Scowcroft 1998, 536; Miller 1992).

In a September 5 debate in the White House devoted to the impending breakdown of the Soviet Union, pro-Gorbachev sentiments surfaced again. Defense Secretary Cheney was most aggressive in insisting that such a breakup was to American advantage. Kolt and Ermarth, whom Scowcroft counted among the so-called "Yeltsin-lovers" in the CIA, predicted that the coup would speed up the "building of Russian statehood" (Beschloss and Talbott 1993, 436). However, Baker was apprehensive about a "Yugoslav scenario" and Scowcroft cautioned that a visible White House effort to side with the independence movement would "guarantee long-term hostility on the part of most Russians." Pointing out that the Russian president was a chief booster of republican independence, some critics seized upon these and other statements to charge that Bush and his national security adviser were reluctant to embrace the political change in the Soviet Union. Matlock (1995, 590), who criticized Scowcroft for undue caution on the day of the coup, suggested that "Bush still seemed to view the political maneuvers . . . in personal terms." Dispensing with diplomatic language, the ambassador went on to say that the president had "never completely freed himself from the instincts that had led to his unfortunate statement on the morning of August 19" (Gates 1996, 526; Bush and Scowcroft 1998, 543).

As if to test the administration's position, Ukrainian leader Leonid Kravchuk visited Washington in late September to seek American support for independence and to establish direct economic ties. The White House was also under tremendous domestic pressure to recognize the independence of the Baltic republics, but the president was reported to be reluctant to offend Gorbachev, who, as noted, was still laboring hard to salvage the Union Treaty. Ironically, it was only the prospect of facing voters of East European extraction who were angry with the administration's stance that convinced Bush to make the final break with Gorbachev and, by implication, the Soviet Union (Beschloss and Talbott 1993, 448–49). On December 1, Ukraine cast a vote for independence and was recognized by the United States. When the Belovezhskaia Pushcha agreement was published, many of the original Reagan crusaders rejoiced, but the administration's response was more sober. Although Baker (1995, 562–63) conceded on December 12 that as a consequence of the Soviet collapse "we live in a new world," there was still some apprehension about "a Yugoslavia with nukes." Bush's reaction was even more ambivalent. Referring to Gorbachev as "my friend," Bush detailed the final and poignant phone call from the Soviet leader on December 25. After hanging up, Bush noted in his diary that "it was the voice of a good friend; it was the voice of a man to whom history will give enormous credit" (Bush and Scowcroft 1998, 559, 561).

The peaceful lowering of the Soviet flag over the Kremlin resulted in what the normally unsentimental Scowcroft called the "greatest transformation of the international system since World War I" (Bush and Scowcroft 1998, 564). Although a highly positive development from the standpoint of American foreign policy, this same momentous event opened the intelligence community to criticism of its estimating and forecasting capacity.

The first step in what turned out to be a long process of scrutiny was taken by the conservative American Enterprise Institute, which in April 1990 convened a conference on the CIA's estimates of the Soviet economy. The conference featured a number of economists from Goskomstat, the Soviet bureau of statistics, and émigré economists, including Igor Birman. They found that the CIA underestimated Soviet military expenditure and overestimated the Soviet economy, seemingly vindicating Birman, William Lee, and Steven Rosefielde (Lee 1995, 210; Codevilla 1992, 223; Schroeder 1995).

The September–October 1991 confirmation hearings for Robert Gates, who was picked by Bush to be the new director of Central Intelligence (DCI), generated a more broad-ranging critique of the CIA. Three former analysts testified that Casey and Gates had politicized intelligence to fit Reagan's foreign policy goals, a charge vigorously denied by Gates and Bush. The acrimonious hearings prompted Kolt to send an internal message rejecting charges that SOVA was a politicized "snake pit" (Excerpts, 1991; Sciolino 1991a; 1991b; Gates 1996, 541–50; Andrew 1995, 531). Although Gates was confirmed, fierce criticism persisted. Senator Daniel Patrick Moynihan called for the Agency to be disbanded altogether. Responding to such misgivings, Congress ordered a panel of scholars to evaluate the Agency's Soviet economic estimates in the two decades preceding the collapse. The eagerly awaited report found that, given the challenges of deciphering Soviet statistics, "the CIA was not significantly better or worse than academic specialists" (Berkowitz et al. 1993, 50). Indeed, although less structured than the scrutiny of the CIA, the ongoing reexamination of the academic paradigms was put into overdrive by the speedy demise of the Soviet system.

The Totalitarian Paradigm Vindicated? The Nonreformability of the Soviet System

To the totalitarian school, 1990 brought a confirmation of their key thesis of the nonreformability of the Soviet system. To begin with, the flood of data released under glasnost had illustrated in graphic detail the extent of systemic decay. In language reminiscent of the claims of the totalitarians, a large number of studies documented the extent of environmental degradation, economic malfunctioning, drug and alcohol abuse, malingering, and other anomic behavior in both the civilian and the military sector (Goldman 1990; Conroy 1990; Gross 1990). Based on interviews with party members, two scholars found that nepotism and corruption played a major role in career advancement (Ra'anan and Lukes 1990). The notion that in exchange for efficiency, the system delivered on equity was undermined by a study that found that some developed countries like Sweden offered more equality, along with much better services (Litwack 1991).

Other glasnost-driven research seemed to support the neoconservative assumption that the Soviet Union could not bear indefinitely the increasing cost of an empire. In what looked like a vindication of Reagan's policy, studies demonstrated that cost–benefit analysis featured prominently in Gorbachev's decision to let go of East Germany and other satellites. One observer found that by forcing Moscow into a guns vs. butter dilemma, the United States pushed the Soviet system beyond the brink, making "the future safe for capitalism rather than socialism." Aleksandr Bessmertnykh, the former foreign minister, told a gathering in Princeton that Gorbachev felt that "any attempt to match Reagan's Strategic Defense Initiative . . . would do irreparable harm to the Soviet economy" (quoted in Charen 2003, 116). Even the prominent leftist scholar Fred Halliday (1990, 18) agreed that, faced with the Reagan offensive, the communist system "could not compete economically, in terms of output and technological change." Jurgen Habermas (1990, 21), whose prediction about the coming legitimacy crisis of capitalism had been so influential in the 1970s, sounded defensive when arguing that "the socialist left still has a place and political role to play" (Stent 1990–91; Mastny 1990, 305).

Seizing on these and other indicators, the adherents of the totalitarian paradigm rushed to proclaim the passing of the Soviet system. In a much-discussed article signed with the pseudonym Z, the historian Martin Malia wrote that, at its height, Sovietism represented a "deviant form of modernity" underpinned by "the power of terror." He asserted that there was no "third way between Leninism and market economy" and predicted the failure of Gorbachev's reforms (Malia 1990, 335). Pipes (1990) felt vindicated for devising the Reagan-era policies that brought the Soviet Union to the verge of collapse, quoting Reagan's 1981 speech about turning communism into a "bizarre chapter in human history." Reddaway (1990) restated the claim that the Soviet bureaucracy was a privileged class that would do its best to subvert perestroika and noted that the political center had already collapsed. He warned that unless Gorbachev adopted the democracy-market platform of Yeltsin, he would soon become a "tragic figure." With its prescience seemingly affirmed, the totalitarian paradigm had also gained new disciples. As one of them declared, "I make no apologies for resurrecting the notion of 'totalitarianism.' I believe that it enables us to understand . . . why radical reform became so urgently needed" (Hosking 1990, 7).

The totalitarians used the glasnost data to chastise their revisionist colleagues for downplaying the role of coercion in the maintenance of the regime's legitimacy. Laqueur (1990, xiii, xiv, 7, 16) affirmed that the "revelations of glasnost constitute an absolute vindication of the views of informed critics" of the Soviet regime. Laqueur was especially critical of the revisionist historians for whitewashing Soviet terror, and wondered why such writings were "treated with respect upon their publication." One book, subtitled "Soviet Genocide and Mass Murder," claimed that there were up to 60 million victims of what it called a "megamurder state" with "lethal politics" (Rummel 1990, 1ff). Pipes (1990, 13) scorned Western "progressive" opinion for assuming that "the world was inexorably moving toward collectivism and egalitarianism."

Hollander (1990, 577) pointed out that the unraveling of communism must be extremely painful for "many American intellectuals" for whom Marxian socialism represented a "respectable belief system" akin to a secular religion. He and others also noted that the comparative model, which tended to "normalize" the Soviet system "by adopting concepts borrowed from the noncommunist world," caused social scientists to overlook the extent of decay in the system (Remington 1990, 163). In a sober reappraisal of his life's work, Gabriel Almond (1990, 13–31, 66–116) accused comparative communist studies of "model fitting," that is, trying to fit Soviet reality into extant comparative theories. A methodologically oriented scholar used nonlinear theories of change to argue that it was "a basic mistake to project Western patterns of incrementalism on a [communist] system prone to abrupt reversals" (Groth 1990, 19).

While the conservatives celebrated, the increasingly chaotic course of perestroika challenged the liberal belief in the reformability of the communist system and triggered a heated debate among its disciples. On the one hand was Hough (1989–90, 36, 39), who stated that the Soviet Union would not follow the path of Eastern Europe. He blamed Western observers for allowing their "analysis to reflect the stream of ever changing rumors in the Moscow intellectual community." He also criticized observers who "have become so obsessed with the potential disintegration inherent in the multinational character of the Soviet Union," and reminded them of the "integrative mechanism in such a system." He defended Gorbachev's leadership, describing it as "controlled chaos." Hough (1990, 642, 651, 655) was also sure that perestroika was still on track, stating that "wishful thinking on the part of Moscow radicals and their American supporters . . . had led them to grossly exaggerate the severity of the Soviet Union's problems." Hough explained that the seemingly chaotic situation was simply "the intended result of policy measures" that are taken for granted in many stable countries like India, adding that some of it was deliberately orchestrated by Gorbachev as part of his sophisticated strategy of controlled chaos. In his view, the Soviet leader decided to "let unrest in the republics . . . go to the extreme" so as to "dampen demands for complete democratization." As for the economic chaos, Hough pointed out that many Western observers "do not understand that goods are being distributed through a rationing system or that a political game was being played that had exaggerated the reports about food shortage and other economic woes."

Hough also criticized what he saw as misperceptions about Gorbachev's character and his relations with the party bureaucracy and the military. Far from considering Gorbachev to be a man "with tragic flaws" and "seized by indecision," he viewed Gorbachev's "hesitation" as a clever ploy to maneuver perestroika. Hough blamed Yeltsin and other "radicals" for exaggerating the party's resistance to economic reform and magnifying the threat of the military. He rejected the notion that the Communist Party reflected "the bureaucratic interests of a retrograde organization" and suggested that the party "was positioning itself to be the social democratic opposition to the radicals," a codename for Yeltsin. As for the army, according to Hough, its major anxiety—the independence movement in the republics—was on the decline, guaranteeing Gorbachev almost a certain chance to stay in power until the 1995 presidential election. Hough used his estimation that the Soviet reform project was on track to challenge Malia and other conservatives, especially with regard to their pro-Yeltsin advocacy. Arguing that embracing Yeltsin was based on a "profound misunderstanding of the Soviet Union," Hough warned the Bush administration that Yeltsin and his radicals would introduce "their version of Thatcherism" and oppose Soviet unity (Hough 1990, 667).

But many revisionists took issue with Hough's thesis that the upheaval was part of Gorbachev's deliberate strategy of controlled chaos. Archie Brown (1990, 142) found it "hard to accept" that Gorbachev "would take a deliberate decision to let unrest in the republics go to the extreme." He also contested Hough's view that Gorbachev had nothing to fear from the hard-liners, although he did not think that the Soviet leader should be written off yet. Bialer (1990, 107) went even further, arguing that Gorbachev had lost control over events in all spheres of life and musing about the "passing of the Soviet order."

By 1991 what was ostensibly a debate about Gorbachev's chances turned into a full-fledged fight over the revisionist paradigm. Hough (1991a, 91b, 92, 105) defended his record and attacked those Western Sovietologists and other observers who felt that the Soviet Union was "immutable to change," blaming Soviet intellectuals and émigrés for "feeding" this image to the West. Responding to Reddaway, Hough claimed that "there is no united, privileged bureaucratic ruling class in the Soviet Union" and that Soviet bureaucrats are "the most underprivileged managerial stratum in the world." He also argued that the "Soviet military has every reason to support Gorbachev" and expressed his belief that "Gorbachev's position will be very strong in the mid-1990s." But Breslauer (1991, 113, 115–16) faulted Hough for attacking those who disagreed with him and for creating an impression that the "Sovietological profession is guilty of the sin of collective misjudgment" and predictive failures. Still, Breslauer rejected Reddaway's argument that the center had collapsed, noting that he was willing to support a "wager on Gorbachev's political longevity," because the Soviet leader was "an indispensable liaison" between right and left.

Even after the August coup, Hough (1991b, 309) objected to the notion that Yeltsin had much public support and implied that his movement might represent "values of populism or even fascism." Hough attributed the failure of the coup to the military, which in his view was not willing to break up the Soviet Union and was prepared to initiate "bloodshed to stop the disintegration."

In attacking Yeltsin and his radical reform program, some of the revisionists were expressing a lack of confidence in the political culture of the Soviet Union. To them, Gorbachev's limited political and economic reforms were more in tune with what, following Stephen Cohen, some described as the "deep-rooted conservatism of Soviet society . . . a preference for tradition and order and fear of innovation and disorder" (Gooding 1990, 217). After analyzing a number of polls, White (1990, 215) found the results "broadly consistent with the views of those who had argued that Soviet political culture, formed over centuries of autocratic rule, provided a relatively weak base for the development of pluralistic politics." Lewin (1991, 134) advocated a "one-party democracy" rather than a Western-style multiparty system. Still others doubted that a market economy as envisaged by Yeltsin and Shatalin could take root in a society where "full employment and equality are cherished social goods" (Aage 1991, 17).

While the revisionists argued about the finer points of Gorbachev's status and the political culture of his country, Pipes and other followers of the totalitarian paradigm proclaimed the Soviet president totally irrelevant and urged the White House to embrace Yeltsin. True to character, Pipes (1990–91) criticized Bush for supporting the territorial integrity of the Soviet Union and warned the administration against extending financial aid to underwrite the Great Bargain plan. Crozier (1991, 19) asserted that "the West would be better served by the breakup of the Soviet Union" and the establishment of a formal relationship with Yeltsin and the republics.

Likewise, the totalitarians expressed full confidence in Yeltsin's vision for democracy and market economy. They relied on opinion polls taken by Soviet social scientists who found that "transitions from a paternalistic mass consciousness to an activist, independent culture" were already in the making

(Zdravomyslov 1991, 239). With things hanging in the balance during the coup, Brzezinski (1991) proclaimed the "putschists" to represent "a bankrupt past, in many respects a criminal past" and urged the White House to cast its lot with Yeltsin and other republican leaders.

Although the collapse of the Soviet Union ended the debate about the reformability of the communist system, it triggered a wider inquiry into the problems of predicting a legitimacy crisis that lay at the core of the demise of the communist empire.

8

Reflections on Predictive Failures

This book has attempted to analyze the extremely complex way in which the American foreign policy system discerned and predicted change in the Soviet Union. With this task now accomplished, it remains the burden of the concluding chapter to sum up this process by isolating its paradigmatic, policy, and intelligence dimensions. This analytic scheme allows for reducing the highly synergistic predictive process to manageable categories and provides some economy to the discussion. To the extent that problems of forecasting political change are comparable, these factors can provide an insight into other situations as well.

Paradigmatic Failure: Totalitarianism vs. Revisionism

The theoretical analysis makes it clear that political change, whether revolutionary or incremental, is rooted in changing norms of legitimacy that underlie the collective belief system of a society. Ideally, any successful effort to predict change in a closed society needs to follow its legitimacy discourses. However, a collective belief system is a theoretical construct that involves numerous highly interactive variables that are embedded in fluid and ill-defined discursive situations. While some of these variables can be approximated through concrete "look-see" measures, others have to be inferred from indirectly observed properties at the individual and collective level. To complicate matters, as was shown, legitimacy itself is a difficult and elusive concept that has divided scholars and lay observers alike.

Reflecting such divisions, the legitimacy of the Soviet Union has been analyzed through the prism of two competing paradigms, the totalitarian-neoconservative and the pluralist-revisionist. Based on different ontological and epistemological assumptions, the paradigms offered a very different view of the legitimacy of the communist system and proffered contradictory trajectories of change. Using the Friedrich-Brzezinski indices of totalitarianism, the former stipulated that the Soviet Union was a "repudiated" political regime with little or no popular legitimacy and with submission exacted by large doses of coercion and some paltry material incentives. The system was said to be vulnerable in all three dimensions of legitimacy—membership/territory, authority, and economy—because of the inherent contradictions embedded in its validity claims. Because of these contradictions, or fatal flaws, the prognosis for the Soviet empire's survival was said to be poor. As first elucidated by Brzezinski, the regime was expected to suffer from progressive degeneration and ultimate collapse.

The pluralist-revisionist paradigm developed by Gordon Skilling, Jerry Hough, and other like-minded scholars asserted that the Soviet system, far from being "repudiated," enjoyed fairly high levels of patrimonial legitimacy; in exchange for egalitarianism and guaranteed lifetime economic security, people voluntarily gave up some of their freedoms. These analysts viewed the Soviet Union as a normal system that in due course would evolve into a pluralistic polity. In anticipating this future, social scientists using comparative methodologies produced a large body of research intended to demonstrate that the Soviet Union operated in ways that made it the functional equivalent of a Western democracy. In fact, according to the then popular convergence theory, the United States and the Soviet Union were expected to converge, with the former adopting many of the features of socialism and the latter becoming more pluralistic.

Propelled by the McCarthy backlash and the war in Vietnam, as well as the diffusion of the prevailing social science methodologies into Soviet studies, by the mid-1970s revisionist approaches came to dominate Sovietology, virtually ostracizing the adherents of the totalitarian model. As Malia (1994, 12) described it, "the T-word was banished from polite academic discourse, its use viewed as virtual incitement to Cold War hostility against the 'Evil Empire.'" Critics contended that the "onset of political correctness" made the "reactionary" totalitarian model highly unpopular with scholars and graduate students. However, a small but vocal group of neoconservatives gave the totalitarianism school a new lease on life by pointing out that Brezhnev's Soviet Union more closely resembled Brzezinski's model of oligarchic degeneration than the revisionist vision of a thriving and pluralistically evolving society. By drawing on émigré research and dissident writing, the neoconservatives were able to point out the anomic condition of communist societies. They were greatly helped by the emerging rational choice theory, which contended that preference falsification practiced in coercive societies can be easily mistaken for legitimacy (Motyl 1992, 306).

If it were not for the fact that the paradigms permeated foreign policy discourse on the Soviet Union, these arcane debates on communist legitimacy would have been confined to a small circle of academic practitioners. As noted, after reaching its peak of influence in Carter's New Internationalism, the revisionist paradigm suffered a setback when Reagan's anticommunist crusade—driven by the precepts of the totalitarian model—became the official policy in Washington. The gradual unraveling of the Soviet Union served as the background to a fierce debate between the contending epistemic communities of scholars, analysts, and political actors. With policy analysis and forecasting at a premium, the discourse became especially intense. At the same time, the radically changing situation provided a real-time check on the validity of both paradigms. In a sense, the Soviet collapse generated a Kuhnian-type "experiment" with its own "grand falsification" built in (Rutland 1998, 48).

By synchronizing the analysis of the developments in the Soviet Union, their perceptions in Washington, and scholarly commentaries, this work is the first attempt to provide a time-based assessment of the performance of the paradigms. Such a framework is essential given the frequent accusations of "twenty-twenty hindsight" leveled by critics on all sides of post-mortem debates (Schroeder 1995; Berkowitz et al., 1993).

By and large, this study bears out the argument that, by normalizing the Soviet system, the revisionists missed its anomic features. The large volume of information that has become available since 1991 makes it clear that the three dimensions of the legitimacy discourse—membership/territory, distributive justice, and authority system—were misunderstood. Most glaringly, the widely accepted view that citizens of the republics embraced a Soviet-centered identity glossed over the depth of "crypto-nationalism." Even if most observers did not go so far as the British historian E.J. Hobsbawm, who credited Brezhnev for saving Soviet citizens from disasters such as nationalism, ethnic discontent passed under the revisionist-pluralist screen (Azrael 1991). In the view of one critic, the Soviet Union was a colonial empire but Sovietologists described it as an American-style "melting pot" society (Pipes 2000b). In contrast, most of the recent literature seems to accept the view that the legitimacy of Soviet identity in the republics was maintained through a mixture of coercing the rank and file and co-opting the ethnic elites. Indeed, work published after 1991 has emphasized the Brzezinski thesis of contradiction between the Soviet multinational state and liberalization, stating that once the threat factor disappeared, the "last empire of the twentieth-century" collapsed (Holmes 1993, xi; Gleason 1992, 1–2; Suraska 1998, 1–3;

Eisenstadt 1992; Rywkin 1994, 6–7). Motyl (1999, 27–118) and others have come to the view that the membership/territory structure was reinforced by the totalitarian features of the system. Fitzpatrick (1999, 208) has admitted, "like most people at the time, I was dismissive of nationalities."

The economic contradictions of the system were also poorly served by the postulate that socialist egalitarianism was not only a viable economic system but also a plausible model for global development. The economic data published since glasnost have all but put these notions to rest. First, disclosures by former Soviet officials and investigative reporting have shed more light on the privileges of the nomenklatura hidden under the "sustaining myth" of the worker state (Barner-Barry and Hody 1995, 120). Second, the notion that a nonmarket economy could be efficient, a popular point with sympathetic observers in the '60s and '70s, has been dispelled, granting Hayek and von Mises a "decisive historical confirmation" (Glasner 1992, 49). The shift is apparent in recent scholarship. As one scholar put it, rather than dwelling on the question of why the communist economies collapsed, economists have attempted to address the issue of "why they happened to survive so long" (Brzeski 2000, 119). Experts have pointed out that the Soviet Union was in effect a rentier state; its vast natural resources were "able to mask its structural shortcomings," keeping the system afloat (Goldman 1991, 49; Odom 1992, 81; Arbatov 1992, 215).

Third, there is a near consensus that, in addition to the most obvious inefficiency of a state-run price-setting system, corruption, mismanagement, failure to nurture human capital, and lack of economic accountability had fatally hobbled the economy. In the words of one insider, the system selected people who "were not very talented, but were obedient" and then proceeded to develop "very sophisticated techniques for shielding even totally incompetent officials from any responsibility for their actions." The same observer also acknowledged that corruption, which according to Marxist theory was a staple of capitalism, was actually systemic in the communist economy (Arbatov 1992, 223, 250).

Whatever hope there was that Marx's Soviet disciples got it right has been dispelled by the twin phenomena of information technology and globalization. By the beginning of the '90s the view was that the USSR, with an "autarkic economy and a population largely isolated from global scientific . . . currents" was like a "mule cart" trying to catch up with a Western "express train" (Weir 1993, 177; Harries 1991, 15). With knowledge becoming the most important factor of production, the old Marxist model could hardly generate the required "ingenuity" edge that has separated the winners and losers in the global economy (Homer-Dixon 2000, 383). Even some leading revisionists were forced to acknowledge that "capitalism has successfully made the transition from the industrial age to the technical-information age," whereas the "hypercentralized" socialist economy kept the Soviet Union isolated from "the technological revolution in capitalist countries" (Legvold 1991, 493; Cohen 1993, xxi).

Finally, the revisionist paradigm was particularly susceptible to the linguistic prevarication and other efforts of the Communist Party designed to create the impression of legitimacy. As already noted, the use of value-neutral "scientific" terminology, the reliance on official statistics, and the use of comparative functional-structural methodology to analyze Soviet institutions had led social scientists to the conclusion that the regime was quite legitimate, even by Western standards. The stability of the system was said to be a reflection of its legitimacy, as manifested in growing pluralism, genuine participation, and regime accountability. In addition to the challenge from Timur Kuran's application of rational choice theory, this picture was called into question by the flood of disclosures on the real working of the regime (McNeill 1998). As revealed by Soviet insiders, policy decisions, supposed to represent the "people," were made behind the people's backs and "representative bodies, including the Supreme Soviet, were simply not allowed to formulate or even discuss real policies" (Shevardnadze 1991, 58; Arbatov 1992, 281). In the words of Malia (1991, 27), when "history at last reached the city of Oz, behind the magic curtain there was only a bogus wizard" manipulating the system with "flame, smoke, and noise."

Numerous as these conceptual errors were, on the positive side of the ledger the dominant paradigm in Sovietology was close to the mark in forecasting the emergence of a reformist impulse. As detailed, revisionist scholars were the first to recognize that Mikhail Gorbachev and his followers fit the bill of a reformist elite and "cheered him on" in the pages of foreign policy journals and the popular press. The personal and scientific stakes in the reformers' success of many of the leading scholars in the revisionist camp could not have been higher. Had Gorbachev succeeded in reforming the Soviet system, it would have provided the type of "grand falsification" needed to finally disprove the degeneration and collapse theory of their rivals. As it turned out, it was the totalitarians who could claim that the collapse of Soviet communism vindicated their hitherto marginalized paradigm.

The time-based analysis in this book illustrates the prescience of many of the totalitarian postulates. Brzezinski's early and consistent warnings about the contradictions built into the system have struck a particularly true note. The blueprint of Richard Pipes to utilize these contradictions in order to vanquish communism, buttressed by the detailed work of Charles Wolf and scholars from the Hoover Institution, fit all the characteristics of a successful forecast. On the negative side, though, the logic of the paradigm virtually ruled out the possibility that change could be generated by a communist elite. Indeed, scholars and intellectuals ranging from Jean-François Revel to Jeane Kirkpatrick argued that the system's coercive features would assure its longevity and that the challenge would have to come from a massive uprising. As Kirkpatrick (1990, 274) confessed, "we mistakenly assumed that the impetus to change must come from below. We never considered the possibility that change would be initiated from the top by a leader who first managed to gain power in this most centralized power structure, then use his power to change the system." Interestingly enough, Boris Yeltsin (1990, 154) was equally puzzled about his own success, writing, "I sometimes wonder how I managed to end up [at the top]. Why is it that the system perfected over the years and specifically designed to select people of a certain type should have so failed so badly as to choose Yeltsin?"

This shortcoming notwithstanding, after the disintegration of the Soviet empire the Kuhnian-style discourse on the merits of both paradigms put the totalitarians on the offensive. They seized the moment to accuse their rivals of intellectual bankruptcy and moral obtuseness. Martin Malia, who gained credibility with his correct diagnosis in the Z article, followed up with another high-profile analysis that described communism as a giant utopia whose collapse left rubble all around. Malia and his colleagues compiled a long list of alleged revisionist failings, including pretentious and misleading methodology, a "pervasive distrust" of nonofficial and émigré sources, "seduction by the pluralistic premise," normalizing the unique Soviet experience, and overlooking the "moral degradation wrought by Communism." They also charged that in a desperate effort to prove that reform communism was more than a mere theory, revisionists misrepresented both Gorbachev and Yeltsin. In Malia's words, Gorbachev was considered the "second coming of Bukharin," a reference to the notion that, had he not been liquidated by Stalin, Nikolai Bukharin might have led the Soviet Union into a viable and humane socialism. On the other hand, Yeltsin was dismissed or derided as a "populist" or a "buffoon," and the true revolutionary nature of his August action all but dismissed by the mainstream (Malia 1992a, 97, 104; 1992b; 1992c; 1993; 1994, 7, 493; Pipes 1993; Conquest 1993, 103; Reddaway 1993, 58; Laqueur 1994, 113; Odom 1993; Weigel 1992, 194).

The totalitarians reserved their harshest rebuke for those who minimized the scope of Soviet terror. They contended that communist use of brutal force undermined socialist claims to the moral high ground. Even if the reign of terror was a "Stalinist aberration," the question still remained how the millions of victims could be part of a progressive history (Besancon 1998; Conquest 1993). As Hollander (2000, 163) put it, "ignorance and denial of facts often combined with dismissing their moral-ethical importance . . . apologists opted for the small numbers [of victims] while simultaneously upholding the necessity of such sacrifice." Malia (1992a, 101) and Laqueur (1990, xiii) pointed out that value-neutral language of comparative politics enabled social scientists to sanitize communist horrors; purges were portrayed as "struggle between center and periphery" and terror was described as "social constraint" (Crozier 2000, 512–13, 163).

That such criticism would come from the leading spokesmen of the totalitarian paradigm was altogether expected. However, in a testimony to the Kuhnian-like decline of the revisionist paradigm's popularity, much of the post-1991 research has adopted the view that the Soviet system was both totalitarian and utopian, and its collapse has been described as a "requiem for Karl Marx" (Shane 1994; Krancberg 1994, 14–16, 24; Gleason 1995; Manuel 1992). Scholars have come to the view that the charge that the models used to normalize the Soviet system had a theoretical bias toward stability, suppressed the widespread anomie in the system, and overstated its legitimacy (Urban and Fish 1998; Remington 1993; Tucker 1992, 1993; Motyl 1992; Bathurst 1993, 7; McNeill 1998). At the extreme, there was the whitewash of terror. Even some who recognized that coercion was a policy tool of Moscow were reluctant to make the comparison to fascist and Nazi terror. As one critic noted, emblematic of this attitude was Reinhold Niebuhr's reference to communists as misguided "children of light" as opposed to fascist "children of darkness" (Janos 1991, 95; Beetham 1991, 142; Weigel 1992, 508).

The reevaluation of the role of coercion in the Soviet system by a new generation of scholars reflected the revived influence of the totalitarian school. Numerous newly published accounts detailed how millions of lives had been destroyed through terror, famine, and other forms of coercion. After reviewing archival evidence, the respected historian John Lewis Gaddis (1994) implied that even the most strident critics of the Soviet Union had fallen short of conveying the real story of terror. Stephane Courtois (1999, 27), the editor of *The Black Book of Communism*, noted that the Soviet archives not only confirmed all previous accounts but took his team of researchers one step further into the "ghastly truth."

More recent research has provided new details about the working of the terror system, refocusing attention on the "central place of terror in the political and social history of the USSR" (Werth 1999, 267; Applebaum 2003, 578–83; Yakovlev 2002). Montefiore (2004, 197–336), in his study of Stalin and his inner circle, argued that personal predilections for sadistic violence might have played a role. These and other studies have also illuminated the decades of persecution of orthodox priests and other groups designated as class enemies, putting to rest what one reviewer called the "leftist myths" of a limited and relatively short repression cycle (Pringle 2003, 500; Bathurst 1993, 38). However, the true extent of the atrocities may never be known, since many perished in transport, in undocumented famines, and other venues that were outside the official "statistics of repression" (Applebaum 2003, 583).

In a further testament to the discrediting of the revisionist view of the Soviet Union, some of its major exponents like Jerry Hough, Sheila Fitzpatrick, Seweryn Bialer, Stephen Cohen, and George Breslauer were personally criticized, sometimes in harsh tones. As before, Hough bore the brunt of the attacks, not the least because of his influence on the discipline, which included a prominent role as a media commentator and reportedly as a consultant to the CIA. He was accused of being an apologist for the Soviet regime and of whitewashing its crimes (Miller and Damask 1993; Suraska 1998, 27; Morewood 1998, Conquest 1993; Berkowitz 1993; Draper 1992; McNeill 1998, 67). The charge of moral obtuseness stung one prominent revisionist who admitted that, in analyzing the Bolshevik revolution, she had underplayed the role of violence (Fitzpatrick 1999).

Conversely, totalitarians like Zbigniew Brzezinski, Richard Pipes, and Walter Laqueur, who all focused on terror, were praised for "getting it right." As one observer put it, "Zbigniew Brzezinski showed extraordinary prescience in spite of his much criticized school of totalitarianism. He maintained steadfastly that the system was not capable of reform" (Rutland 1998, 35; McNeill 1998, 65; Armstrong 1993).

Critics of revisionism seized upon the delegitimation of their rivals to reiterate the accusations of deep-seated leftist bias in academia and the transformation of American higher education into a "center of adversarial culture." In this view, the main attraction of Marxism for intellectuals was that it offered a "comprehensive and intellectually respectable belief system" that purported "to combine moral passion with scientific rigor" (Hollander 1990, 577). Accordingly, the lure of scientific socialism was particularly great because of what Malia called "the perverse genius of Marxism," which could present "an unattainable utopia as an infallibly scientific enterprise" (Malia 2000, 71). While in the West the "Janus like" utopian adventure presented the "hope of socialism," in the East it brought the "terror of totalitarianism" to millions. From a safe distance, the Western left "persisted in the belief in the legitimacy of Marxism-Leninism for other people" (Malia 1994, 1). To illustrate this double standard, one critic quoted John Mack, a Harvard professor of psychiatry, who once explained that Soviet authorities downplayed disasters "to protect citizens from emotional distress" (Hollander 2000, 183; Fukuyama 1992, 10; Manuel 1992; Conquest 1993).

According to the same critics, psychologically the preference for Marxism was a reflection of a deep alienation from the bourgeois capitalist societies of the West. In the extreme, this alienation was said to have "produced a strong tendency towards ethical idealism" and an "urge to redesign the human race." As a result, the favorable views of communist systems were largely based on "imaginative projection of . . . ideals and fantasies of Westerners persuaded that their notions of what makes a good society and exemplary ways of life were being realized in these countries." At the very least, Marxism was used to feed the animus toward capitalism and predict its imminent demise (Hollander 1992, 149; 2000, 186–87). Commenting on the failure of such ideologically based forecasts, Perdue noted that "Ivy League departments are not peopled by those whose predictive record bears the greatest historical accuracy. Ivory Tower intellectual capital is acquired by demonstrating polemical proficiency in thwarting the public acceptance of laissez faire economic theories" (Perdue 1998; Green 2000, 31).

Although much of the post-Soviet discourse in the academic community focused on the performance of the respective paradigms, the collapse of the communist empire has also raised the more general question about the degree to which revolutions can be predicted. Harking back to the 1979 fundamentalist upheaval in Iran, this new round of soul searching reflected the frustration of political science at its failure to forecast events. In an edited volume, Nikki Keddie (1995), a participant in the Iran forecasting debacle, argued that revolutions consist of rare contingencies and thus cannot be foreseen. But others argue that revolutions are predictable and that the Soviet one should have been predicted (Goldstein 1995).

Political science has yet to settle this debate, but is worth repeating that nonlinear theories of change discussed in the theoretical chapter hold that revolutions are low-probability events. To use Kuhnian logic, such events reside outside the realm of the dominant paradigm and thus are likely to be overlooked in what one scholar described as a "failure of imagination" (Rutland 1993, 122). Since paradigms include judgments made by observers about the legitimacy of closed political systems, it was only the belief in the illegitimacy of communism that made it possible for the followers of the totalitarianism theory to imagine the collapse of the Soviet empire. Kuran's (1991, 22, 43) work on preference falsification illustrates this assumption. The rational choice scholar pointed out that key pieces of information necessary to predict regime legitimacy and stability like "private levels of satisfaction of the masses" or revolutionary thresholds are essentially unknown in closed societies. Consequently, it is easier for observers to project their own paradigmatically driven beliefs onto the political reality that they try to chart.

Important as the analysis of the academic paradigms might be, its real significance lies in the fact that scholarship was closely associated with applied foreign policy. As already demonstrated, paradigmatic assumptions were embedded in the discursive practices through which American foreign policy toward the Soviet Union was formulated. It was thus intimately related to the policy-level failure as well.

Policy Level: Vanquishing vs. Coexisting

As long as the Cold War gripped international relations, the totalitarian view of the Soviet Union provided a perfect intellectual background for American foreign policy making. Speaking before Congress in 1947, President Truman warned about the coming struggle between two political philosophies, one based on freedom and democracy and the other involving a self-elected minority that imposed its will through terror and the denial of freedom. Truman was no less clear about the fact that, far from being an ordinary international power, the Soviet Union was driven by a messianic impulse to bring communist salvation to the rest of mankind.

To respond to the communist challenge, Washington adopted a policy of containing communism and ultimately defeating it. At its core were a large military buildup and a stringent application of deterrence, but the policy proved costly, as the war in Vietnam demonstrated. The subsequent switch to détente was an admission that coexistence had replaced the dream of crushing communism, but the underlying view of the Soviet Union as a darkly coercive power engaged in a global crusade was still prevalent in the foreign policy discourse. The revisionist paradigm, with its benign view of the communist system and matching emphasis on peaceful coexistence, made its official debut in the New Internationalism, Carter's blend of a moralistic foreign policy with an emphasis on human rights and a sympathetic view of the egalitarian distribution of resources. New Internationalism reflected the hope that cooperation between the two superpowers, rather than deterrence, would create a more peaceful international environment. Another key belief was an assumption that local conflicts were not necessarily related to Soviet global ambitions but rather authentic expressions of indigenous grievances. In this view, Soviet foreign policy, rather than being driven by ideological zeal, was simply interactionist, that is, a normal expression of Great Power realpolitiking. To recall, this view was stringently opposed by the essentialists, who argued that the ideology played a dominant role in Soviet foreign policy.

As noted, for the New Internationalist approach to succeed, Moscow had to behave as the theory predicted. However, Soviet activities in Africa and Latin America raised serious doubts, and when Afghanistan was invaded by Soviet troops in 1979, the revisionist paradigm was discredited. Unlike President Truman, who put a major emphasis on containment, the Reagan administration would develop a detailed blueprint for an anticommunist crusade.

The mix of policies—military buildup, credible deterrence, economic warfare, and political subversion—was designed with the assumption that the Soviet empire was illegitimate and fragile and could be undermined by manipulating its domestic and international environment.

Reagan's bold plan to vanquish the communist system was not universally shared by his administration. Opposing the array of crusading squeezers—William Casey, Casper Weinberger, and Roger Clark—were dealers like George Shultz and the State Department bureaucracy. Whereas the former saw in the Soviet interregnum an opportunity to push more aggressive policies, the latter cautioned against provoking a hard-line backlash in Moscow and proposed negotiation and other confidence-building measures. Bureaucratic squabbles in foreign policy making are not uncommon and have been amply discussed in the bureaucratic model of decision making. However, in the case of the Reagan administration these difficulties were compounded by the president's decision to give an equal hearing to both Weinberger and Shultz.

The contradictory advocacy undermined Washington's ability to develop a consistent policy and, as is inevitable in such cases, prevented a clear forecast of the consequences of American actions in trying to effect change in the Soviet Union. The Soviet reaction to Able Archer gave credibility to the warnings of the dealers that vigorous deterrence efforts could lead to a belligerent response from Moscow. Confronted with the forecast of a possible nuclear disaster and under attacks by the rejuvenated peace and nuclear freeze camps, by his second term Reagan had abandoned parts of the anticommunist crusade in favor of disarmament negotiations. In the process, the administration developed a vested interest in supporting Gorbachev and his perestroika policy.

With Bush taking up residence in the White House, there was a further shift toward negotiations, making protection of the status quo in Moscow a top priority of the administration. Considerations of the once cherished goal of defeating communism became an exercise in contemplating a "Yugoslavia with nukes" scenario. In spite of some CIA reports, Bush and his top foreign policy advisers never seriously considered the alternative scenario of a peaceful transformation under Yeltsin. As noted, Yeltsin's own behavior was a contributing factor, along with the American president's alleged discomfort with change. However, it is also important to recognize that foreign policy bureaucracies have inherent limitations in dealing with revolutionary change. As one insider in the Iran debacle noted, "the tacit but all pervasive assumption of all governments is that tomorrow will, by and large, be very much like yesterday" (Sick 1985, 39). To envision a Yeltsin-led CIS as the successor regime to the Soviet Union was well beyond the incrementalism associated with routine foreign policy thinking.

Strong intelligence findings can help to overcome foreign policy routines. But as described, the intelligence community had a complex track record in analyzing the Soviet system.

Intelligence Level: Advocacy vs. Objectivity

Historically, the CIA was mandated to provide objective and impartial intelligence. Sherman Kent, a dominant figure in the Directorate of Intelligence in the 1950s, turned this mandate into a binding intelligence doctrine. The so-called Kent doctrine, which reflected many of the assumptions of the then popular developmentalist paradigm, exuded a strong positivist belief in a "rational" political universe that experts could objectively analyze by parsing political reality in a detached and dispassionate way. In yet another important stipulation, Kent argued against mixing of the operational and analytical objectives of the CIA. In the words of one observer, in its ultimate logic, this apolitical intelligence analysis should be conducted "along the lines of a world-class think-tank . . . a kind of living encyclopedia or reference service" (Shulsky 1993, 183).

Such high analytic standards became impossible to follow during the height of the Cold War, especially as the operational branch of the Agency was involved in attempts to remove a series of Third World leaders thought to be sympathetic to the Soviet Union. The Carter administration tried to restore the Kentian ideal of objectivity, only to be accused by neoconservative critics of introducing a leftist bias into the Directorate of Intelligence. In the wake of the fundamentalist revolution in Iran, Carter ordered a high-level interagency task force to suggest ways to improve the CIA's efforts to predict political instability in countries of vital importance to the United States (Seliktar 2000, 186–97).

The Reagan administration set out to overhaul the CIA to suit its new mission of undermining the Soviet regime. Based on the recommendations of Reagan's transition team, the Kent doctrine was modified to incorporate the critique of Kent's intellectual rival, Willmore Kendall. Kendall (1949) disputed the epistemic assumption that predictive "truths" can be separated from the values and outlooks of analysis and doubted whether political reality is neatly packaged or universally rational. Kendell was also skeptical about the wisdom of separating analysis from the political goals of the administration. Richard Pipes (1995b, 39), a later critic of the CIA, emphasized that, while ideally analysis should be separated from policy, "it is not attainable," adding that Nixon, Carter, and other presidents twisted intelligence findings. While the new formula did not support advocacy, Casey's CIA was urged to engage in a vigorous analysis of opportunities.

The history of the Agency's Soviet analysis bears testimony to these doctrinal and political strictures. To assure maximum objectivity, the Soviet estimate reflected a heavy emphasis on numerical data, most notably tracking the Soviet economy as part of the all-important calculation of the military-to-civilian spending ratio. Such exactitude reflected the penchant for quantitative evidence in the American political culture. Nevertheless, as shown, in spite of a tremendous investment of resources, both sides of the political spectrum vilified the Soviet estimate. While left-wing critics claimed that the Agency overestimated Soviet military expenditure to justify an American military buildup, their right-wing counterparts charged that the Soviet GNP was overstated, masking Moscow's huge military outlays. Richard Perle argued (1995, viii) that as a consequence of this distortion, the West was forced into undue concessions during arms negotiations. The CIA's efforts to readjust its estimate placated neither side and increased its credibility problem.

Because of what one scholar dubbed the "culture of exactitude" in Washington, the CIA had continued to use GNP and other statistical measures even when it became clear that the Soviet economy bore little resemblance to a rational Western model. Some scholars referred to it as the problem of false precision, pointing out the futility of trying to determine whether the rate of growth was 2.0 or 2.5 percent (Löwenthal 1993; Berkowitz and Richelson 1995). As detailed in this work, glasnost made it clear that, by concentrating on stringent quantitative indices, the Agency overestimated the strength and health of the Soviet economy. The new data strengthen the claims of Igor Birman, William Lee, Steven Rosefielde, and others who had long argued that the Soviet economy was heavily militarized (Steinberg 1992). Interestingly, Oskar Lange, whose model of market socialism Gorbachev had tried to create, came to a conclusion that the continuous defense expansion had turned the Soviet Union into a "barrack economy" on a par with imperial Germany and other garrison states (Janos 1991, 940). Perhaps more important is the fact that, given the convoluted national accounting system, the true extent of Soviet militarization may never be known.

The emphasis on quantified indices detracted from efforts to analyze the more qualitative aspects of Soviet life that could have alerted the intelligence community to the impending legitimacy crisis. As will be recalled from the theoretical discussion, unlike a crisis of performance, to which it is related, a crisis of legitimacy is difficult to analyze because it is rooted in an ongoing societal discourse. Like the revisionist methodology that it emulated, the CIA's statistically oriented research could not have conveyed the depth of Soviet anomie and malaise. In what turned out to be a prescient warning, a former intelligence official wrote that standard methods and approaches "are inappropriate to assessing emotion driven, political upheavals.

If Americans want to understand the historic political tide shifts, they must ignore their itch for quantification [and] curb their fascination with models that bear minimal relations to reality" (Carver 1990, 148). This, as already described, was also the gist of the long-standing critique of Pipes (1995b). A leading economist would later admit that the CIA's GNP measure "was a progressively meaningless instrument" to discern "the impending social and political upheaval, because it tells us nothing about expectations, satisfaction or disappointments" of the Soviet masses (Becker 1994, 323).

Methodology had limited the ability of the CIA to probe the depth of the legitimacy crisis in more subtle ways as well. In spite of efforts to modify the Kent doctrine, like their academic counterparts, SOVA analysts were most comfortable with things that could be formally defined, put into a Western context, and preferably counted (Codevilla 1992, 199). This type of empiricism, exacerbated by cultural parochialism, ethnocentric projection, mirror imaging, and plain gullibility, made it hard to discern the more amorphous expressions of delegitimation and anomie. Pipes (1995b, 38–39) wrote that, among other things, the CIA did not understand religious or ideological beliefs. Another critic noted that American specialists never took account of the effect of rampant alcoholism in the Soviet Union (Bathurst 1993, 529).

Although the intelligence community bore the lion's share of blame for its estimating practices, the role of policymakers, including Congress, should not be overlooked. First, politicians are generally averse to acting on the basis of long-term projections. Indeed, Gates (1987–88) complained that, unless related to a crisis situation, reporting to politicians on long-range issues was an "exercise in frustration." For busy politicians ambiguity and complexity in analysis are irritants and an impediment to good decision making. There is even less tolerance for theoretically laden concepts such as discourse, legitimacy, or collective belief system. In the view of one critic, "the intellectual propensities of U.S. analysts may well be due . . . to those of the policy makers they serve. There is a demand for certainty," which succinct reports and quantification best serve (Codevilla 1992, 203). Second, the intense partisanship surrounding the Soviet estimate turned it into a playing field on which the liberals and conservatives conducted fierce battles. Such a discursive practice all but precluded the use of softer qualitative estimates that were much more vulnerable to the type of critical scrutiny afforded to quantitative data.

The quantitative approach had an additional implication for intelligence analysis and forecasting. Since the American military budget was linked to estimates of the strength of the Soviet economy and its civilian–defense ratio, Reagan's military buildup would not have been approved had it been advanced under its true goal of competitive strategy, that is, overwhelming

Moscow by forcing it into a costly arms race. The only way to convince Congress to fund the buildup was to present a compelling argument that Moscow was increasing its military expenditure, a strategy made difficult by the CIA's overestimation of the robustness of the Soviet economy. The more subjective, ideologically driven forecasts of the Casey group, which probed systemic vulnerabilities including low morale, alcoholism, and abysmal productivity, would not have been persuasive.

In a related manner, congressional requirements, influenced by the anti-intelligence backlash in the mid-1970s, imposed a high legal standard on intelligence reports. Although less stringent than the evidentiary standard in a court of law, preference for well-documented findings and "smoking guns" was quite prevalent. This posed a major problem for Soviet analysis, especially as it pertained to the murky world of Moscow's assistance to international terrorism. The cool reception of Claire Sterling's detailed study of the communist terrorist network was a case in point, along with the fierce but ultimately inconclusive debate about whether the KGB had attempted to assassinate Pope John Paul II by using the Bulgarian secret service. Ironically, data from the Soviet archives and other evidence proves that, if anything, the CIA underestimated the role of Moscow and its East European proxies in international terrorism (Laqueur 1994, 208; Gates 1996, 565).

Since the public discourse was heavily influenced by the same liberal precepts that permeated the revisionist paradigm, qualitative forecasts derived from the totalitarian model were met with special scrutiny. The case of the much-criticized Robert Gates illustrated this point well. Gates, who along with Weinberger and Cheney argued that Gorbachev would not be able to make the psychological, let alone institutional, transition to a market democracy, was attacked for being an unreconstructed hard-liner. Only in retrospect would this stand, and his early pro-Yeltsin advocacy, earn him a belated respect for prescience when, in fact, his forecasts were all along underpinned by the belief in Soviet nonreformability. Gates (1996, 575) illustrated this proposition, writing that the fight against the evil Soviet empire was "a glorious crusade" driven by belief that the inherent weaknesses of communism "ultimately would bring it down."

The feud between SOVA's Third World division and Gates should be construed as another variation of the same problem. Melvin Goodman's assertions that Moscow cut spending on Third World conflicts in the mid-1980s were correct only to the extent that the formal Soviet government was concerned. As will be apparent from the discussion on the dual authority system, hard-line military and party officials had continued to funnel money and supplies to Cuba, Angola, Nicaragua, and Vietnam long after Gorbachev ordered them stopped. Such machinations were not impossible in the chaotic and Byzantine Soviet bookkeeping system, but the formalistic quantitative model could not acknowledge transactions based on fuzzy, hearsay evidence emanating from a disintegrating empire. Not incidentally, American intelligence had similar problems in following the dual authority system in the wake of the Iranian revolution. In line with the preference for formal structures and processes, the CIA and the State Department devoted most of their attention to the secular government, which was a "Western-friendly" façade constructed by the much more subterranean fundamentalist movement (Seliktar 2000, 73–125).

The fight over the extent of Moscow's involvement in revolutionary conflict also bears on the meaning of politicization in the intelligence community. According to one intelligence insider, politicization is a "complex phenomenon" that can take many forms ranging from outright "cooking of the books" to subtle hints that certain "analytical conclusions" are not welcome (Firth and Noren 1998, 7). Indeed, Gates was accused of rejecting the "Soviet-decline-of-involvement" thesis to legitimate Casey's anticommunist campaign. Goodman (1997, 128–43), Gates's chief antagonist, asserted that "Casey and Gates advocated a confrontational policy toward the Soviet Union and slanted intelligence to support it." Yet, what looked like a clear case of forgoing objectivity in the name of advocacy could also be construed as a clash of two different methodologies. For Goodman, an adherent to the more exacting empiricism of mainstream social science, the softer, anecdotal observations from a variety of formal and informal sources embraced by the totalitarians were an anathema. In the more Kuhnian sense, thus, politicization amounts to a deviation from the norms of the dominant paradigm.

Further aggravating the CIA's problems was the fact that the Soviet demise was one of the most radical changes in modern history because all three dimensions of legitimacy—membership/territory, authority system, and distributive justice—were transformed simultaneously. The panel appointed by Congress to investigate the Soviet estimates pointed out that these low-probability occurrences pose special challenges for intelligence agencies. They require particularly compelling evidence to break through the dominant paradigm, especially in the 1960s and 1970s when "many serious people actually debated the effectiveness of market economy versus socialism" and Soviet territorial integrity was accepted as a given (Berkowitz et al. 1993, 38). Senator Moynihan chided the intelligence community for failing to recognize by the late 1970s, as he had, that "Soviet economic growth was coming to halt" and that the "society as well as the economy was sick," yet such hunches were not enough to qualify as "grand falsification." Ironically, given the standards of discourse in Congress, Moynihan would have had a hard time convincing his own colleagues (Becker 1994, 292).

Even if the CIA had presented a more dramatic case for the imminent demise of the Soviet empire, there is no guarantee that the Bush administration would have adopted a different course of action. In fact, for more than a year before the August coup, Gates and other Soviet experts in the Agency, as well as Cheney and his team, had lobbied hard on behalf of Yeltsin. But as detailed, President Bush and his senior foreign policy team argued that the Gulf War coalition, the unification of Germany, and arms control negotiations would fare better with Gorbachev at the helm. To critics possessed of hindsight wisdom this decision may seem either too cautious or too callous. But as the theoretical chapter suggests, revolutionary change involves a large number of factors that suddenly coalesce in a way that cannot be known a priori. Statistically, forecasting in such a situation amounts to an attempt to relate a stochastic variable (crisis or opportunity) to a dynamically evolving scenario that is composed of a large number of highly correlated events. The probability of any one of these events occurring depends upon whether a number of other events are likely to occur, a calculation that is hard to perform and even harder to "sell" to policymakers. Even so, it was the intelligence community that was blamed for the administration's decision to opt for the relative comfort of the Gorbachev status quo instead of betting on Yeltsin.

What is even more interesting, much of the criticism of the CIA's Soviet estimate came from liberal revisionists who had a long record of lauding the vigor of the Soviet economy. It will be recalled from the preceding chapter that the congressionally appointed panel found little difference between the records of academics and the CIA analysts (Berkowitz et al. 1993). The same group was also highly critical of the Agency for its failure to embrace Yeltsin. But, as noted, prominent revisionists like Jerry Hough were among those who warned the Bush administration against backing the Russian leader. This dramatic shift in position can be understood only in the context of a new struggle between the two contending paradigms. With the outcome of the Soviet empire finally revealed, prediction was replaced by postdiction as the new weapon of choice in the debate over who won the Cold War.

Postdiction: Who Won the Cold War, and the Collapse of Sovietology

Dramatic changes such as revolutions have attracted the attention of political scientists eager to analyze the explanatory and forecasting merits of their theories. But in the Soviet case, as in the debates over who "lost" China and Iran, where paradigms had served as foreign policy prescriptions, the academic discourse has reflected the larger historical question of who won the Cold War.

It should come as no surprise that, in many respects, the struggle to explain the end of the Cold War featured the same protagonists. Those who subscribed to the totalitarian view credited Reagan's foreign policy with accelerating the demise of communism. They pointed out that Reagan's strategy of targeting the soft "moral underbelly" of communism, combined with economic warfare and the SDI-led military buildup, was highly successful (Laqueur 1994, 127; Pipes 1995a, 2000; Malia 1999, 406–7; 2000; Conquest 1993). Observers with no ideological ax to grind have supported this contention. They point out that the "evil empire" speech decried by many in the United States for being provocative in fact galvanized the nascent opposition across the vast stretches of the Soviet bloc. When Reagan visited Eastern Europe after the collapse of communism, many dissidents told him that his speech "gave them enormous hope." Vaclav Havel went so far as to refer to Reagan's oratory as an example of the "power of words to change history" (Edwards 1999, 250). Others have pointed out that the Reagan team plugged into the then new phenomenon of globalization to further destabilize the archaic, semi-autarkic communist economy (Patman 1999; Greenstein and Wohlforth 1994, 10; Mastny 1996, 192; Mastanduno 1985; Deudney and Ikenberry 1991–92).

The developments in the Soviet Union itself seem to confirm these observations. Headlined by SDI, the combined effects of the Reagan crusade nudged the Soviet leadership to reevaluate its defense policy. Ambassador Dobrynin (1995, 609) later wrote that "one of the moments at which strategists in the Soviet Union started to reconsider their position was when Reagan announced his SDI program. . . . Perhaps we overestimated the military significance of Star Wars, but its unveiling made us think about the situation once again and thus brought us closer to arms control." Former foreign minister Bessmertnykh likewise acknowledged that SDI, "as much as anything else," caused the leadership to reconsider its foreign policy, propelling the moderates into positions of power (Greenstein and Wohlforth 1994, 19). What is more, the crisis and frustration among top leaders forced an examination of the tenets of communism, paving the way for Gorbachev's perestroika. As is evident from the previous chapters, the selection of Gorbachev and the acceptance of his remedies by the Politburo would not have been possible without a more general recognition of the legitimacy crisis in the country. American foreign policy did not cause the crisis, but the Reagan policies were carefully chosen and calibrated to turn the chronic irritation into a conflagration.

Giving Reagan credit for dismantling communism was an anathema to revisionists, many of whom, as detailed, had criticized Reagan's policies. In its most radical form, the revisionist critique has denied that the Reagan administration had anything to do with the revolutionary developments in the Soviet empire. The journalist Frances Fitzgerald, who made her name opposing the war in Vietnam, declared that she knows of no "American scholar who believes that the United States ended the Cold War." She scorned "conservative pundits" who advance the argument "that the Reagan administration had played a major role in [the USSR's] downfall" (Fitzgerald 2000, 437, 475). In her view the collapse was related to a continuous deterioration of the Soviet economy, which resulted "from the failures of the system created by Lenin and Stalin—not from any effort on the part of the Reagan administration" (quoted in Charen 2003, 8). Raymond Garthoff (1992, 129), another prominent revisionist, asserted that "the West did not, as widely believed, win the Cold War through geopolitical containment and military deterrence. Nor was the Cold War won by the Reagan military buildup and the Reagan doctrine. . . . Instead, victory came when a new generation of Soviet leaders realized how badly their system at home and policies abroad failed."

As for the president himself, he was described as ignorant, confused, and otherwise lacking in mental capacity. Garthoff (1994, 759) posited that "Reagan was in many ways like a ceremonial monarch, entirely dependent on his viziers and courtiers for his limited knowledge of what was going on in the outside world." A standard textbook depicted Reagan as "vague," "confused," and "ignorant" (LaFeber 1991, 302–3). With some modifications, such depictions have been standard fare in other textbooks (Laqueur 1994, 126). A milder form of revisionism claimed that the correlation between Reagan policies and the events in the Soviet Union was spurious; through sheer "dumb luck" (or "Irish luck") Reagan happened to be in the White House during a generational change in the Soviet leadership (Patman 1999).

In the revisionist interpretation, Reagan policies not only impeded the liberalization in the Soviet Union, but harmed American national interests by causing huge defense budgets and unnecessary confrontations with Moscow (Goodman 1997). According to Gates (1996, 552), the revisionists used his confirmation hearings to popularize the notion that the "CIA had failed catastrophically" by missing the final collapse of the Soviet Union. Liberal critics could claim that the "huge sum of money spent on defense" had been unnecessary because "the Soviet Union was weak and would have collapsed on its own." Condemnation of Reagan's anticommunist crusade took more subtle forms as well. For instance, David Halberstam, in his well-received *War in a Time of Peace*, described the struggle between Reagan's ideologues and the more pragmatic Bush wing of the Republican Party; he praised Bush for conducting a cautious détente-like policy. As one reviewer noted, this was an indirect way of saying that the aggressive Reagan policies were unnecessary and reckless (Kagan 2001).

Not to be outflanked in the struggle for history's judgment, conservatives charged that, in changing their assessment of the Soviet Union, the revisionists were intellectually ingenuous at best and fraudulent at worst (Hollander 2000). Taking the lead was Peter Schweitzer (1994, 282), the author of a book detailing how Reagan's secret strategy hastened the collapse of the Soviet Union. He described as "ironic" the fact that many Western observers "who once insisted that the Soviet economy was comparable to that of the United States . . . now suddenly contend that the decline and fall of the Soviet empire was somehow inevitable." Laqueur (1994, ix, 122) observed that "some of those who thought of the Soviet Union as the wave of the future now claim that it was a mirage from the beginning, lacking ideological appeal, and was in later years a colossus with feet of clay that should never have been taken seriously." Among those whom Laqueur singled out was the IPS scholar Richard Barnet, a leading believer in the legitimacy of the communist system who in the 1970s argued that the Soviet Union was an economic and military "giant" on a par with the United States. Two decades later, and eager to deny any American input, Barnet (1992, 116) used the Brzezinski-like argument that the "system contained the seed of its own destruction," and that the "Cold War ended because of internal failures and disappointments." Critics also pointed out that Barnet and other revisionists were previously on record warning that Reagan policies would provoke a mighty Soviet military response.

Pipes (1990, 15) took issue with another newly floated revisionist argument that the Soviet Union was "such an abomination against basic human aspirations" that it was doomed to wither away. He contended that if this line of reasoning was correct, the "British appeasers of the 1930s could have boasted after Germany's surrender in 1945 that they had been right after all, because a system as abominable as Nazism never presented a serious danger to democracy." He restated this and other themes in his autobiography, which summed up his lifelong struggle to vanquish communism (Pipes 2003). Gates (1996, 106) added that Soviet end-game weakness and collapse has "clouded the memories of many people as to the relentlessness, magnitude and fearsomeness . . . of the Soviet military buildup from 1962 to 1987."

Conservative and neoconservative critics pointed out that the revisionist paradigm should be discredited altogether because of its key claim that the Soviet Union was a functional-rational polity comparable to other states in both domestic and foreign policy. Pipes (1995a) targeted Raymond Garthoff, who was considered the intellectual leader of interactionism, for particular criticism. He noted that the Soviet archives and other revelations made it clear that Moscow's policy, both domestic and foreign, was driven by ideology. He also derided other popular revisionist theories, like the argument that Washington had fomented the conflict with the Soviet Union to keep its economy afloat, or that Americans, responding to some dark psychological needs, had turned the Soviet Union into the "bogeyman." In this view, the bogeyman theory, popular in political psychology in the 1970s and 1980s, was one more example of the intellectual habit of blaming the United States for all international ills. As Conquest (1993, 97) put it, the "fetishism of socialism" and hostility to the West were born when "many second-rate academics" radicalized by the war in Vietnam developed a "Pavlovian reflex rejection of their own system."

This necessarily short review of the literature on who won the Cold War brings the discussion back to broader issues of paradigmatic change. While, as Kuhn asserted, paradigms are resistant to change within a given generation of scholars, the collapse of the Soviet empire altered the field of Soviet studies. The "old Sovietology" of the Cold War collapsed amid mutual recrimination, paving the way for a "new Sovietology." Unlike the old Sovietology, where analysis was based on paradigmatic assumptions with little empirical evidence to support them, the new Sovietologists have used the post-1991 revelations to bolster their conclusions.

As pioneered by John Lewis Gaddis, post-revisionism became the first fruit of the new Sovietology. A moderate revisionist himself, Gaddis (1994, 148) retracted his former stand, stating that "the people of the former Soviet Union appear to have associated themselves more closely with President Reagan's famous indictment of the state as an 'evil empire' than with the more balanced academic assessments." He added: "the archives . . . are providing documentary evidence for such an interpretation." Gaddis (1997, 283, 292–93) declared that "the new Cold War history will take ideas seriously; the way that the conflict ended is bound to reshape our view of how it began and evolved." Moreover, the "new sources suggest that ideology often determined the behavior of Marxist-Leninist regimes," rather than serving as a post-hoc justification. After reviewing the new sources, Gaddis put much of the blame for the Cold War on the Soviet Union and its communist ideology. Echoing Malia, he concluded that the Soviet empire had unraveled because of a "collapse of legitimacy." "The people . . . suddenly realized that the emperors had no clothes on . . . it resulted from a shift in how people thought, not from any change in what they saw."

While it is too early to determine how history will answer the question of who won the Cold War, Gaddis's post-revisionist analysis, which has been followed by other works, is indicative of a Kuhnian shift toward a totalitarian vision of the communist system.

**Understanding the "Great Unknown": The Collapse of the
Soviet Union and Predicting Political Change in the Future**

It is customary in the "summing up" chapter of a work of this type to offer
some suggestions for improving the prediction of political change. Indeed,
the post–Cold War period has presented unprecedented problems in this realm.
The tried and true concepts of the past have been replaced with novel challenges of dealing with Islamic fundamentalism, as the events of September
11 demonstrated. This and other types of international terrorism and the danger of nuclear, chemical, and biological warfare emanating from terrorist
groups or rogue regimes require new conceptual tools.

Last but not least, economic issues have become vastly more important to
national security. In a world of economic interdependence, the economic
stability and prosperity of any given country depends on a series of inter-
locking equations that involve numerous markets. As the co-called "high
politics" of diplomacy and military balance of power are being replaced by
the "low politics" of trade, monetary policies, and movements in global stock
markets, much of the forecasting effort has become diffuse and multifaceted.

To the extent that this study offers more general insight into the predictive
process of closed societies or movements, the implications are sobering. To
be successful, intelligence warnings have to be issued early enough to alert
an administration and enable it to intervene effectively, whether to avert a
crisis or to seize an opportunity. In cases of radical political change, such a
judgment can be made only by following the legitimacy discourse of a given
society and determining whether a normative shift is likely to occur in any of
the three dimensions of the collective belief system, thus affecting the political structure. However, as the Soviet case illustrates and the developments in
Iraq have confirmed, in highly coercive totalitarian systems the crisis of legitimacy can simmer unexpressed and undetected.

The focus on a collective belief system also highlights the linkage between
the legitimacy of the authority system and economic performance. Eudaemonics
are important in maintaining the legitimacy of the authority system, whether it
is totalitarian, authoritarian, or democratic. At the same time the relation is not
deterministic. Highly coercive regimes can survive serious performance crises
by suppressing a challenge to the system and the elites that advocate it. Alternatively, regimes can manipulate nationalist or religious feelings to reinvigo-
rate their support, as the Serbian case demonstrated.

The absence of deterministic relations in the nexus of legitimacy and performance posits a challenge to any linear notions of change. The current
wave of democratization around the globe has been underpinned by the al-
lure of the market economy. But performance failures can erode the legitimacy

of a democratic authority or delegitimize market-oriented norms of distributive justice. The halting progress of market democracy in Russia and other former Soviet republics underscores this problem. The same dynamics explain why Islamic fundamentalism has been on the increase. Prevented by religious norms from embracing the principles of market economy, many Muslim societies are locked in a cycle of poverty and high demographic growth that reinforces the legitimacy of a distinctive non-Western and nonmarket belief system. Indeed, this formula seems to be at the core of the so-called "clash of civilizations" theory, which projected that the twenty-first century would see a titanic struggle between the West and Islam.

While this study cannot confirm this forecast, it draws attention to the legitimacy formulas that drive change in belief systems. This and other issues call for theoretical developments that are at present rarely explored, and therein lie the challenges for future studies of predictive political analysis.

References

Aage, Hans. 1991. Popular attitudes and perestroika. *Soviet Studies* 43: 3–25.

Ackerman, Spencer, and Franklin Foer. 2003. The radical. *New Republic*. December 1, 18.

Adams, Jan S. 1983. Citizens' participation in community discussions in the USSR. In *Politics and participation under communist rule*, ed. Peter J. Potichnyi and Jane Shapiro Zacek. New York: Praeger.

Aganbegyan, Abel. 1988a. Acceleration and perestroika. In *The new stage of perestroika,* ed. Abel Aganbegyan and Timor Timofeyev. New York: Institute for East-West Security.

———. 1988b. New directions in Soviet economics. *New Left Review* 169: 89–96.

———. 1988c. *The economic challenge of perestroika.* Trans. P.M. Tiffen. Bloomington: Indiana University Press.

———. 1989. *Inside perestroika: The future of the Soviet economy.* Trans. H. Szamuely. New York: Harper and Row.

Ajami, Fouad. 1981. *The Arab predicament: Arab political thought and practice since 1967.* Cambridge: Cambridge University Press.

Albright, David E. 1991. Soviet economic development and the Third World. *Soviet Studies* 43: 27–59.

Almond, Gabriel A. 1966. Political theory and political science. *The American Political Science Review* 60: 869–79.

———. 1990. *A discipline divided: Scholars and sects in political science.* Newbury Park, CA: Sage.

Almond, Gabriel, and Sidney Verba. 1965. *The civic culture.* Boston: Little, Brown.

Amalrik, Andrei. 1970. *Will the Soviet Union survive until 1984?* New York: Harper and Row.

Amann, Ronald. 1977–78. Soviet technological performance. *Survey* 23: 61–72.

———. 1986. Searching for an appropriate concept of Soviet politics: The politics of hesitant modernization. *British Journal of Political Science* 16: 475–94.

Andelman, David A. 1982. Economic crisis and Soviet trade. *Washington Quarterly* 5: 82–91.

Anderson, Martin. 1988. *Revolution: The Reagan legacy.* Stanford, CA: Hoover Institution Press.

Anderson, Myrdene. 1986. Cultural concatenation of deceit and secrecy. In *Deception: Perspectives on human and nonhuman deceit*, ed. Robert. W. Mitchell and Nicholas S. Thompson. Albany: State University of New York Press.

Andrew, Christopher M. 1993. KGB foreign intelligence from Brezhnev to the coup. *Intelligence and National Security* 8: 52–67.

———. 1995. *For the president's eyes only: Secret intelligence and the American presidency from Washington to Bush.* New York: HarperCollins.

Andrew, Christopher M., and Oleg Gordievsky. 1990. *KGB: The inside story of its foreign operations from Lenin to Gorbachev.* New York: HarperCollins.

Andrew, Christopher M., and Vasily Mitrokhin. 1999. *The sword and the shield: The Mitrokhin archive and the secret history of the KGB.* New York: Basic Books.

Andropov, Yuri V. 1990. Sixty years of the USSR. In *The Soviet multinational state. Readings and documents*, ed. Martha B. Olcott. Armonk, NY: M.E. Sharpe.

Applebaum, Anne. 2003. *Gulag. A history.* New York: Doubleday.

Apter, David E. 1965. *The politics of modernization.* Chicago: University of Chicago Press.

———. 1974. *Political change.* London: Frank Cass.

Arbatov, Georgi A. 1973. *The war of ideas in contemporary international relations.* Trans. David Skvirsky. Moscow: Progress.

———. 1992. *The system: An insider's life in Soviet politics.* New York: Times Books.

Arkin, William M., and Richard W. Fieldhouse. 1985. *Nuclear battlefields: Global links in the arms race.* Cambridge, MA: Ballinger.

Armstrong, John A. 1971. Communist political systems as vehicles for modernization. In *Political development in changing societies*, ed. Monte Palmer and Larry Stern. Lexington, MA: Heath.

———. 1973. Comments on professor Dallins' bias and blunders in American studies on the USSR. *Slavic Review* 32: 578–87.

———. 1993. New essays in Sovietological introspection. *Post-Soviet Affairs* 9: 171–75.

Aron, Leon. 2000. *Yeltsin: A revolutionary life.* New York: St. Martin's Press.

Ash, Timothy G. 1984. Under the Western eyes: Poland, 1980–1982. *Washington Quarterly* 7: 120–34.

Aslund, Anders. 1989. Gorbachev's struggle for economic reform: The Soviet reform process. Ithaca, NY: Cornell University Press.

Axelrod, Robert. 1986. An evolutionary approach to norms. *American Political Science Review* 80: 1095–1110.

Azar, Edward E., and Nadia N. Farah. 1981. The structure of inequalities and protracted social conflict: A theoretical framework. *International Interaction* 7: 317–35.

Azrael, Jeremy R., ed. 1978. *Soviet nationality policies and practices.* New York: Praeger.

———. 1987. *The Soviet civilian leadership and the military high command.* Santa Monica, CA: Rand.

———. 1989. *The KGB in Kremlin politics.* Santa Monica, CA: Rand.

———. 1991. The Soviet "National Front": Some implications for U.S. foreign policy. In *The rise of nations in the Soviet Union*, ed. Michael Mandlebaum. New York: Council on Foreign Relations.

Bagley, Tennet H. 1991. Treason in the KGB: New facts from inside. *International Journal of Intelligence and Counterintelligence* 5: 63–75.

Bahry, Donna. 1991. The Union republics and Gorbachev's economic reform. *Soviet Economy* 7: 215–55.

Bahry, Donna, and Carol Nechemias. 1981. Half full or half empty: The debate over Soviet regional equality. *Slavic Review* 40: 366–83.

Baker, James A. 1995. *The politics of diplomacy: Revolution, war and peace, 1989–1992*. New York: G.P. Putnam's Sons.

Balzer, Harley D. 1982. The Soviet scientific and technical intelligentsia. *Problems of Communism* 31: 66–72.

Baran, Paul A., and Paul M. Sweezy. 1966. *Monopoly capital: An essay on the American economic order*. New York: Modern Reader Paperback.

Barghoorn, Frederick C. 1966. *Politics in the USSR*. Boston: Little Brown.

———. 1973. Factional, sectoral, and subversive opposition in Soviet politics. In *Regimes and oppositions*, ed. Robert A. Dahl. New Haven, CT: Yale University Press.

———. 1974. Politics in the USSR. In *Comparative politics today*, ed. Gabriel A. Almond. Boston: Little, Brown.

———. 1976. *Détente and the democratic movement in the USSR*. New York: The Free Press.

Barner-Barry, Carol, and Cynthia A. Hody. 1995. *The politics of change: The transformation of the former Soviet Union*. New York: St. Martin's Press.

Barnet, Richard J. 1971. The illusion of security. *Foreign Policy* 3: 71–87.

———. 1977. *The giants: Russia and America*. New York: Touchstone Books.

———. 1983. Preface to "Workers against the Gulag." In *First harvest: The Institute for Policy Studies, 1963–1983*, ed. J.S. Freidman. New York: Grove Press.

———. 1992. A balance sheet: Lipman, Kennan, and the Cold War. In *The end of the Cold War*, ed. Michael Hogan. Cambridge: Cambridge University Press.

Bathurst, Robert B. 1993. *Intelligence and the mirror: On creating an enemy*. London: Sage.

Baylis, Thomas A. 1972. In quest of legitimacy. *Problems of Communism* 21: 46–55.

Bearden, Milt, and James Risen. 2003. *The main enemy: The inside story of the CIA's final showdown with the KGB*. New York: Random House.

Beardsley, Philip L. 1973. *Whose country America?: An introductory reader on American politics*. Encino, CA: Dickenson Publishing.

Becker, Abraham C. 1994. Intelligence fiasco or reasoned accounting: CIA estimates of Soviet GNP. *Post-Soviet Studies* 10: 291–329.

Beetham, David. 1991. *The legitimation of power*. Atlantic Highlands, NJ: Humanities Press International.

Beisinger, Mark R. 1988. Political reform and Soviet society. *Current History* 87: 313–20, 345.

Bell, Coral. 1980. *President Carter and foreign policy: The cost of virtue?* Cambarra: The Australian National University.

Bell, Daniel M. 1976. *The cultural contradictions of capitalism*. New York: Basic Books.

Berki, R.N. 1982. The state, Marxism and political legitimacy. In *Political legitimation in communist states*, ed. T.H. Rigby and F. Feher. New York: St. Martin's Press.

Berkowitz, Bruce D., and Jeffrey T. Richelson. 1995. CIA vindicated. *The National Interest* 41: 36–46.

Berkowitz, Daniel M., Joseph S. Berliner, James R. Millar, Paul R. Gregory, and Susan J. Linz. 1993. An evaluation of the CIA's analysis of Soviet economic performance 1970–1990. *Comparative Economic Studies* 35: 33–57.

Bertsch, Gary K. 1980. West-East technology transfer. *Problems of Communism* 29: 74–78.

Besancon, Alain. 1998. Forgotten communism. *Commentary* (January): 24–27.

Beschloss, Michael R., and Strobe Talbott. 1993. *At the highest levels: The inside story of the end of the Cold War.* Boston: Little, Brown.

Betts, Richard K. 1983. Warning dilemmas: Normal theory vs. exceptional theory. *Orbis* 26: 828–33.

Bialer, Seweryn. 1980a. Poland and the Soviet imperium. *Foreign Policy* 59: 522–39.

——. 1980b. The politics of stringency in the USSR. *Problems of Communism* 29: 19–33.

——. 1981. The harsh decade: Soviet policies in the 1980s. *Foreign Affairs* 59: 999–1020.

——. 1983a. The political system. In *After Brezhnev. Sources of Soviet conduct in the 1980s*, ed. R.F. Byrnes. Bloomington: Indiana University Press.

——. 1983b. The Soviet Union and the West in the 1980s: Détente, containment or confrontation. *Orbis* 27: 35–58.

——. 1984. *Stalin's successors.* New York: Cambridge University Press.

——. 1986a. The question of legitimacy. In *States and societies*, ed. David Held, Oxford: Basil Blackwell.

——. 1986b. *The Soviet paradox: External expansion, internal decline.* New York: Alfred A. Knopf.

——. 1990. The passing of the Soviet order. *Survival* 32: 107–20.

Bialer, Seweryn, and Joan Afferica. 1982–83. Reagan and Russia. *Foreign Affairs* 61: 249–71.

——. 1985. The genesis of Gorbachev's world. *Foreign Affairs* 64: 605–44.

Bialer, Seweryn, and Thane Gustafson. 1982. Introduction. In *Russia at the Crossroads*, ed. Seweryn Bialer and Thane Gustafson. The 26th Congress of the CPSU. London: George Allen and Unwin.

Billington, James H. 1987. Realism and vision in American foreign policy. *Foreign Affairs* 65: 630–52.

Birch, Anthony H. 1984. Overload, ungovernability and delegitimation. The theories and the British case. *British Journal of Political Science* 14: 135–60.

Birman, Igor. 1980a. The financial crisis in the USSR. *Soviet Studies* 32: 84–105.

——. 1980b. Limits of economic measurement. *Slavic Review* 39: 603–9.

——. 1981. *Secret incomes of the Soviet state budget.* The Hague: Martinus Nijhoff.

——. 1985. The Soviet economy: Alternative view. *Survey* 29: 102–15.

Birstein, Vadim J. 2001. *The perversion of knowledge: The true story of Soviet science.* Boulder, CO: Westview Press.

Bittman, Ladislav. 1985. *The KGB and Soviet disinformation: An insider's view.* MacLean, VA: Pergamon-Brassey's International.

——. 1990. The use of disinformation by democracies. *International Journal of Intelligence and Counterintelligence* 4: 243–63.

Blacker, Coit D. 1993. *Hostages to revolution: Gorbachev and Soviet security policy, 1985–1991.* New York: Council on Foreign Relations Press.

Bockmuhl, Klaus. 1986. *The challenge of Marxism: A Christian perspective.* Colorado Springs, CO: Helmers and Howard.

Boldin, Valery I. 1994. *Ten years that shook the world: The Gorbachev era as witnessed by his chief of staff.* Trans. E. Rossiter. New York: Basic Books.

Booth, Ken. 1979. *Strategy and ethnocentrism.* New York: Holmes and Meier.

Borovik, Artyom. 1991. Waiting for democracy. *Foreign Policy* 84: 51–60.

Boulding, Kenneth E. 1962. *Conflict and defense. A general theory.* New York: Harper.

Bova, Russell. 1988. The Soviet military and economic reform. *Soviet Studies* 40: 385–405.

Boyes, Roger. 1990. *The hard road to market: Gorbachev, the underworld and the rebirth of capitalism*. London: Secker and Warburg.

Brada, Josef C. 1988. Interpreting the Soviet subsidization of Eastern Europe. *International Organizations* 42: 639–58.

Braeman, John. 1983. The New Left and American foreign policy during the age of normalcy: An examination. *Business History Review* 57: 73–104.

Braillard, Philippe, and Pierre de Senarclens. 1980. The international system. Limits to forecasting. *Futures* 12: 453–64.

Braley, Russ. 1984. *Bad news: The foreign policy of the New York Times*. Chicago: Regnery Gateway.

Brandsma, Andries S., and A.J. Hughes Hallett. 1984. How vulnerable is the Soviet economy?: The effectiveness of economic sanctions. *Futures* 16: 163–72.

Brennan, John. 1983. A little visit with Yuri Andropov. *American Opinion* (May): 19–38.

Breslauer, George W. 1976. The Soviet system and the future. *Problems of Communism* 25: 66–70.

———. 1978. *Five images of the Soviet future: A critical review and synthesis*. Berkeley: University of California Institute of International Studies.

———. 1980. Political succession and the Soviet political agenda. *Problems of Communism* 29: 34–52.

———. 1986. Provincial party leaders' demand articulation and the nature of center–periphery relations in the USSR. *Slavic Review* 45: 650–72.

———. 1989. Evaluating Gorbachev as a leader. *Soviet Economy* 5: 299–340.

———. 1991. Understanding Gorbachev: Diverse perspectives. *Soviet Economy* 7: 110–20.

———. 1992. In defense of Sovietology. *Post-Soviet Affairs* 8: 197–238.

Brinkley, Douglas. 1998. *The unfinished presidency: Jimmy Carter's journey beyond the White House*. New York: Viking Press.

Brinton, Crane. 1965. *The anatomy of revolution*. New York: Vintage Books.

Brown, Archie. 1979. Governing the USSR. *Problems of Communism* 28: 103–8.

———. 1982. Leadership succession and policy innovation. In *Soviet Policy for the 1980s*, ed. Archie Brown and Michael Kaser. Bloomington: Indiana University Press.

———. 1983. Andropov: Discipline and reform. *Problems of Communism* 32: 18–31.

———. 1984. Political science in the Soviet Union: A new stage of development. *Soviet Studies* 36: 317–44.

———. 1985a. Gorbachev: New man in the Kremlin. *Problems of Communism* 24: 1–23.

———. 1985b. *Political culture and communist studies*. Armonk, NY: M.E. Sharpe.

———. 1990. Gorbachev's leadership: Another view. *Soviet Economy* 6: 141–54.

———. 1996. *The Gorbachev factor*. Oxford: Oxford University Press.

Brown, Michael B. 1985. *Models in political economy: A guide to the argument*. Boulder, CO: Lynne Rienner.

Brzeski, Andrzey. 2000. The end of communist economics. In *The collapse of communism*, ed. Lee Edwards. Stanford, CA: Hoover Institution Press.

Brzezinski, Zbigniew K. 1956. *The permanent purge: Politics in Soviet totalitarianism.* Cambridge, MA: Harvard University Press.

––––––. 1966. The Soviet political system: Transformation or degeneration. *Problems of Communism* 15: 1–15.

––––––. 1968. America in the technetronic age. *Encounter* 30: 16–26.

––––––, ed. 1969. *Dilemmas of change in Soviet politics.* New York: Columbia University Press.

––––––. 1970. *Between two ages: American's role in the technotronic age.* New York: Viking Press.

––––––. 1971. Political implications of the Soviet nationality problem. In *Soviet nationality problems*, ed. E. Allworth. New York: Columbia University Press.

––––––. 1972. How the Cold War played. *Foreign Affairs* 51: 181–209.

––––––. 1976. Soviet politics from the future to the past. In *The dynamics of Soviet politics*, ed. P. Cocks, R. Daniels, and N. Whitter Heer. Cambridge, MA: Harvard University Press.

––––––. 1983a. *Power and principle: Memories of the national security adviser 1977–1981.* New York: Farrar, Straus, Giroux.

––––––. 1983b. Tragic dilemmas of Soviet world power: The limits of a new-type empire. *Encounter* 61: 10–17.

––––––. 1984. *The conduct of East-West relations in the 1980s.* London: International Institute for Strategic Studies.

––––––. 1985. Overview of East-West relations. *Washington Quarterly* 8: 3–38.

––––––. 1986. *Game plan: A geostrategic framework for the U.S.-Soviet contest.* Boston: Atlantic Monthly Press.

––––––. 1988a. America's new strategy. *Foreign Affairs* 66: 680–99.

––––––. 1988b. Sentiments and strategy: The imbalance in America's Third World policy. *The National Interest* (Summer): 140–47.

––––––. 1989a. Ending the Cold War. *Washington Quarterly* 12: 29–34.

––––––. 1989b. *The grand failure: The birth and death of communism in the twentieth century.* New York: Charles Scribner's Sons.

––––––. 1989c. Toward a common European home. *Problems of Communism* 38: 1–16.

––––––. 1990. *The grand failure: The birth and death of communism in the twentieth century.* 2d ed. New York: Collier Books.

––––––. 1991. Scholars see a 'putsch,' a gang of rivals, and analyze the plotters' chance. *New York Times*, August 21.

Brzezinski, Zbigniew, and Samuel P. Huntington. 1971. *Political power: USA/USSR.* New York: Viking Press.

Buchanan, Thompson R. 1982. The real Russia. *Foreign Policy* 47: 26–45.

Bukovsky, Vladimir. 1986. Will Gorbachev reform the Soviet Union? *Commentary* (September): 19–24.

––––––. 1987. The political condition of the Soviet Union. In *The future of the Soviet empire*, ed. Henry S. Rowen and Charles Wolf. New York: St. Martin's Press.

––––––. 1989. The quiet exit from communism. In *Can the Soviet system survive reform?* ed. G.R. Urban. London: Pinter Publishers.

Bunce, Valerie. 1985. The empire strikes back: The transformation of the Eastern bloc from a Soviet asset to a Soviet liability. *International Organization* 39: 1–46.

Bunce, Valerie, and John M. Echols. 1979. From Soviet studies to comparative politics. *Soviet Studies* 31: 43–55.

Burks, Richard V. 1984. The coming crisis in the Soviet Union. *East European Quarterly* 18: 61–71.

———. 1988. The coming crisis in the Soviet Union. In *The Soviet Union and the challenge of the future*, ed. Alexander Shtromas. New York: Paragon House.

Burrell, Gibson, and Gareth Morgan. 1985. *Sociological paradigms and organizational analysis: Elements of the sociology of corporate life.* London: Heinemann.

Burton, Donald F. 1983. Estimating Soviet defense spending. *Problems of Communism* 32: 85–93.

Bush, George, and Brent Scowcroft. 1998. *A world transformed.* New York: Alfred A. Knopf.

Byrnes, Robert F. 1977–78. Moscow revisited: Summer 1978. *Survey* 23: 1–18.

Caldwell, Lawrence T., and Robert Legvold. 1983. Reagan through Soviet eyes. *Foreign Policy* 52: 3–21.

Cardoso, Fernando H., and Enzo Faletto. 1979. *Dependency and development in Latin America.* Berkeley: University of California Press.

Carlisle, Rodney, ed. 2004. *Encyclopedia of intelligence and counterintelligence.* Armonk, NY: M.E. Sharpe.

Carr, Edward H. 1962. *The new society.* Boston: Beacon Press.

Carver, George A., Jr. 1990. Intelligence in the age of glasnost. *Foreign Affairs* 69: 147–66.

Casey, William J. 1989. *Scouting the future: The public speeches of William J. Casey.* Washington, DC: Regnery Gateway.

Chalidze, Valery. 1977. *Criminal Russia. Essays on crime in the Soviet Union.* Trans. P.S. Falla. New York: Random House.

Charen, Mona. 2003. *Useful idiots: How liberals got it wrong and still blame America first.* Washington: Regnery.

Chatfield, Charles. 1992. *The American peace movement.* New York: Twyne.

CIA Documents. 2001. Released as *CIA's Analysis of the Soviet Union 1947–1991.* vol. 1 and vol. 2 (CD-ROMs).

Clayton, Elizabeth. 1980. Productivity in the Soviet Union. *Slavic Review* 39: 446–58.

Clem, Ralph S. 1983. The changing of Soviet nationalities: Socioeconomic and demographic correlates. In *Politics and participation under communist rule*, ed. Peter J. Potichnyj and Jane Shapiro Zacek. New York: Praeger.

Cline, Ray S. 1981. *The CIA under Reagan, Bush and Casey.* Washington, DC: Acropolis Books.

Cline, Ray S., and Yona Alexander. 1984. *Terrorism: The Soviet connection.* New York: Crane Russak.

Cnudde, Charles F. 1973. Stochastic processes and political theory. *Comparative Political Study* 6: 255–60.

Cockburn, Andrew. 1983. *The threat: Inside the Soviet military machine.* New York: Random House.

Cocks, Paul, Robert V. Daniels, and Nancy W. Heer. 1976. *The dynamics of Soviet politics.* Cambridge: Cambridge University Press.

Codevilla, Angelo M. 1988. Is there still a Soviet threat? *Commentary* 86: 23–28.

———. 1992. *Informing statecraft: Intelligence for a new century.* New York: The Free Press.

Coffman, Richard, and Michael Klecheski. 1982. The 26th Party Congress conference: The Soviet Union in a time of uncertainty. In *Russia at the Crossroads: The*

26th Congress of the CPSU, ed. Seweryn Bialer and Thane Gustafson. London: George Allen & Unwin.

Cohen, Stephen F. 1973. *Bukharin and the Bolshevik revolution: A political biography 1888–1938*. New York: A.A. Knopf.

———. 1980. The friends and foes of change: Reformism and conservatism in the Soviet Union. In *The Soviet Union since Stalin*, ed. Stephen F. Cohen, Alexander Rabinowitch, and Robert Sharlet. Bloomington: Indiana University Press.

———. 1983. The Soviet system: Crisis or stability. *The Nation*, August 6–13.

———. 1984. Mikhail Gorbachev as the heir apparent to Konstantin Chernenko. *The Nation*, November 17: 503.

———. 1985. *Rethinking the Soviet experience: Politics and history since 1917*. New York: Oxford University Press.

———. 1986. *Sovieticus: American perceptions and Soviet realities*. New York: W.W. Norton.

———. 1988. Supporters and opponents of perestroika: The second joint Soviet economy roundtable. *Soviet Economy* 4: 275–318.

———. 1993. Introduction. In *Inside Gorbachev's Kremlin: The memoirs of Yegor Ligachev*, ed. Yegor K. Ligachev. Trans. C.A. Fitzpatrick, M.A. Berdy, and D. Dyrcz-Freeman. New York: Pantheon.

Coleman, Fred. 1996. *The decline and fall of the Soviet empire*. New York: St. Martin's Press.

Coleman, Kenneth M. 1977. *Self-delusion in U.S. foreign policy: Conceptual obstacles to understanding Latin America*. Erie: Northwestern Pennsylvania Institute for Latin American Studies.

Collins, Edward M. 1998. *Myth, manifesto, meltdown: Communist strategy 1948–1991*.

Colton, Timothy J. 1986. *The dilemma of reform in the Soviet Union*. New York: Council on Foreign Relations.

Connor, Walter D. 1972. *Deviance in Soviet society: Crime, delinquency, and alcoholism*. New York: Columbia University Press.

———. 1975. Generations and politics in the USSR. *Problems of Communism* 24: 20–31.

———. 1979a. *Socialism, politics, and equality. Hierarchy and change in Eastern Europe and the USSR*. New York: Columbia University Press.

———. 1979b. Workers, politics and class consciousness. In *Industrial labor in the USSR*, ed. Arcadius Kahan and Blair A. Ruble. New York: Pergamon Press.

———. 1991. *The accidental proletariat: Worker, politics, and crisis in Gorbachev's Russia*. Princeton, NJ: Princeton University Press.

Connor, Walter D., and Zvi Y. Gitelman. 1977. *Public opinion in European socialist system*. New York: Praeger.

Conquest, Robert. 1988. *Harvest of sorrow*. London: Arrow.

———. 1993. Academia and the Soviet myth. *The National Interest* 31: 91–98.

Conroy, Mary S. 1990. Abuse of drugs other than alcohol and tobacco in the Soviet Union. *Soviet Studies* 42: 447–80.

Converse, Philip E. 1964. The nature of belief systems in mass publics. In *Ideology and discontent*, ed. David. E. Apter. New York: The Free Press of Glencoe.

———. 1987. Changing conceptions of public opinion in the political process. *Public Opinion Quarterly* 51: 512–25.

Coogan, Kevin, and Katrina Vanden Heuvel. 1988. U.S. funds for Soviet dissidents. *The Nation*, March 19.

Cook, Linda J. 1992. Brezhnev's social contract and Gorbachev's reform. *Soviet Studies* 44: 37–56.

———. 1993. *The Soviet social contract and why it failed: Welfare policy and worker politics from Brezhnev to Yeltsin.* Cambridge, MA: Harvard University Press.

Coser, Lewis A. 1964. *The function of social conflict.* Glencoe, IL: The Free Press.

Courtois, Stephen, et al. 1999. *The black book of communism: Crimes, terror, repression.* Cambridge, MA: Harvard University Press.

Crocker, Chester A., and William H. Lewis. 1979. Missing opportunities in Africa. *Foreign Policy* 35: 142–61.

Crouch, Martin. 1990. *Revolution and evolution: Gorbachev and Soviet politics.* New Delhi: Prentice Hall of India.

Crow, Susan. 1995. 'New Thinking' and the collapse of the Soviet bloc. In *The Demise of the USSR*, ed. Vera Tolz and Iain Elliot. London: Macmillan.

Crozier, Brian. 1979. Power and national sovereignty. *National Review*, February 2.

———. 1991. Getting Gorbachev wrong. *Midstream* (February–March) 17–19.

———. 2000. *The rise and fall of the Soviet empire.* Roseville, CA: Forum.

Crozier, Brian, Drew Middleton, and Jeremy Murray-Brown. 1985. *This war called peace.* New York: Universe Books.

Dahl, Robert A. 1970. *After the revolution? Authority in a good society.* New Haven, CT: Yale University Press.

Dalby, Simon. 1990. *Creating the second Cold War.* London: Pinter Publishers.

Dallin, Alexander. 1980. To the editor. *Foreign Affairs* 59: 192–96.

———. 1992. Causes of Soviet collapse. *Post-Soviet Affairs* 8: 279–302.

Dallin, Alexander, and Gail W. Lapidus. 1987. Reagan and the Russians: American policy toward the Soviet Union. In *Eagle Resurgent? The Reagan era in American foreign policy*, ed. Kenneth A. Oye, Robert. J. Lieber, and Donald Rothchild. Boston, MA: Little, Brown.

Daniels, Robert V. 1978. Whatever happened to the Russian revolution? *Commentary* 66: 48–54.

Danilov, Alexander A. et al. 1996. *The history of Russia: The twentieth century.* New York: The Heron.

Davies, James C. 1962. Toward a theory of revolution. *American Sociological Review* 6: 5–19.

Davis, Christopher, and Murray Feshbach. 1980. *Rising infant mortality in the USSR in the 1970s.* Washington, DC: U.S. Bureau of the Census.

de Borchgrave, Armand, and Robert Moss. 1980. *The spike.* New York: Crown Publishers.

DeJames, R. Benneson. 1994. Managing foreign policy: Carter and experiment toward Africa, January 1977–May 1978. In *Foreign policy and post-presidential years*, ed. Herbert. D. Rosenbaum and Alexei Ugrinsky. Westport, CT: Greenwood.

Dellums, Ronald V., with R.H. (Max) Miller and Lee H. Hamilton. 1983. *Defense sense: The search for a rational military policy.* Cambridge, MA: Ballinger Publishing.

d'Encausse, Hélène Carrère. 1979. *Decline of an empire: The Soviet socialist republic in revolt.* New York: Newsweek Books.

————. 1982. *Confiscated power: How Soviet Russia really works.* New York: Harper and Row.

————. 1993. *The end of the Soviet empire: The triumph of nations.* Trans. F. Philip. New York: Basic Books.

Denitch, Bogdan D. 1979. Legitimation and the social order. In *Legitimation of regimes: International framework for analysis*, ed. Bogdan Denitch. Beverly Hills, CA: Sage.

Deudney, Daniel, and G. John Ikenberry. 1991–92. The international sources of Soviet change. *International Security* 16: 74–118.

Deutsch, Karl W. 1953. *Nationalism and social communication: An inquiry into the foundation of nationality.* Cambridge, MA: MIT Press.

Deutsch, Morton. 1975. *Distributive justice.* New Haven, CT: Yale University Press.

Diggins, John P. 1973. *American left in the twentieth century.* New York: Harcourt Brace Javonovich.

————. 1993. *The rise and fall of the American left.* New York: W.W. Norton.

DiPalma, Giuseppe. 1991. Legitimation from the top to civil society: Politico-cultural changes in Eastern Europe. *World Politics* 44: 49–80.

Dixon, W.J., and B.E. Moon. 1986. The military burden and basic human needs. *Journal of Conflict Resolution* 30: 660–84.

Djilas, Milovan. 1969. *The unperfect society. Beyond the new class.* Trans. Dorian Cooke. New York: Harcourt, Brace and World.

Dobbs, Michael. 1997. *Down with the Big Brother: The fall of the Soviet Empire.* New York: A.A. Knopf.

Dobrynin, Anatoly. 1995. *In confidence: Moscow's ambassador to America's six Cold War presidents.* New York: Times Books.

Doder, Dusko. 1988. *Shadows and whispers: Power politics inside the Kremlin from Brezhnev to Gorbachev.* New York: Random House.

Doder, Dusko, and Louise Branson. 1990. *Gorbachev: Heretic in the Kremlin.* New York: Viking Press.

Douglas, Mary. 1992. *Risk and blame: Essays in cultural theory.* London: Routledge.

Draper, Theodore. 1992. Who killed Soviet communism? *The New York Review of Books*, June 11.

Dugger, Ronnie. 1983. *On Reagan: The man and his presidency.* New York: McGraw-Hill.

Duignan, Peter, and Alvin Rabushka, eds. 1980. *The United States in the 1980s.* Stanford, CA: Hoover Press.

Dumbrell, John. 1993. *The Carter presidency: A re-evaluation.* Manchester, England: Manchester University Press.

Dunlop, John B. 1993. *The rise of Russia and the fall of the Soviet empire.* Princeton, NJ: Princeton University Press.

Dutter, Lee E. 1990. Theoretical perspectives on ethnic political behavior in the Soviet Union. *Journal of Conflict Resolution* 34: 311–34.

Easter, Gerald M., and Ann M. Gruber. 1989. The dynamics of change. In *Toward a more civil society: The USSR under Mikhail Sergeevitch Gorbachev*, ed. William G. Miller. New York: Ballinger.

Easton, David. 1953. *The political system.* New York: Alfred Knopf.

————. 1965. *Systems analysis of political life.* Chicago: Chicago University Press.

————. 1969. The new revolution in political science. *American Political Science Review* 63: 1051–61.

Eberstadt, Mary T. 1988. Arms control and its casualties. *Commentary* (April): 39–46.

Eberstadt, Nick. 1988. *The poverty of communism.* New Brunswick, NJ: Transaction Books.

Ebon, Martin. 1987. *The Soviet propaganda machine.* New York: McGraw Hill.

———. 1994. *KGB: Death and rebirth.* Westport, CT: Praeger.

Edwards, Lee. 1999. *The conservative revolution: The movement that remade America.* New York: The Free Press.

Eidlin, Fred H. 1979. Soviet studies and scientific political science. *Studies in Comparative Communism* 12: 133–43.

Eisenhower, Susan. 1995. *Breaking free: A memoir of love and revolution.* New York: Farrar Straus Giroux.

Eisenstadt, S.N. 1992. Center–periphery relations. In *Thinking theoretically about Soviet nationalities,* ed. Alexander J. Motyl. New York: Columbia University Press.

Ekedahl, Carolyn. M., and Melvin A. Goodman. 1997. *The wars of Eduard Shevardnadze.* University Park: The Pennsylvania State University Press.

Elliot, Ian. 1985. The great reformer. *Survey* 29: 1–11.

———. 1988. How open is 'openness'? *Survey* 30: 1–24.

Elsenhans, Hartmut. 1983. Rising mass income as a condition of capitalist growth: Implications for the world economy. *International Organization* 37: 1–40.

English, Robert D. 2000. *Russia and the idea of the West: Gorbachev, intellectuals and the end of the Cold War.* New York: Columbia University Press.

Epstein, Edward C. 1984. Legitimacy, institutionalization and opposition in exclusionary bureaucratic-authoritarian regimes: The situation in the 1980s. *Comparative Politics* 17: 37–54.

Epstein, Edward J. 1978. The war within the CIA. *Commentary* (August): 35–39.

———. 1982. Disinformation: Or why the CIA cannot verify an arms control agreement. *Commentary* (July): 21–28.

———. 1986. Petropower and Soviet expansion. *Commentary* (July): 23–28.

Erikson, Kai. 1986. On work and alienation. *American Sociological Review* 51: 1–8.

Etzioni-Halevy, Eva. 1985. *The knowledge elite and the failure of prophecy.* London: George Allen and Unwin.

Evangelista, Matthew. 1999. *Unarmed forces: The transitional movement to end the Cold War.* Ithaca, NY: Cornell University Press.

Evans, Rowland, and Robert Novak. 1981. *The Reagan revolution.* New York: E.P. Dutton.

Excerpts from Gates' testimony on his record at the CIA. 1991. *New York Times,* October 2; October 4.

Fagen, Richard. 1978. A funny thing happened on the way to the market: Thoughts on extending dependency ideas. *International Organization* 32: 287–300.

Fainsod, Merle. 1964. *How Russia is ruled.* Cambridge, MA: Harvard University Press.

Falk, Richard. 1989. The superpowers and a sustainable détente for Europe. In *The new détente: Rethinking East-West relations,* ed. Mary Kaldor, Gerald Holden, and Richard Falk. London: Verso.

Faris, Robert E.L. 1955. *Social disorganization.* New York: The Roland Company.

Feher, Ferenc. 1982. Paternalism as a mode of legitimation in Soviet type societies. In *Political legitimation in communist states,* ed. T.H. Rigby and Ferenc Feher. New York: St. Martin's Press.

Feher, Ferenc, and Andrew Arato, eds. 1989. *Gorbachev: The debate.* Cambridge: Polity Press.

Feifer, George. 1973. *Russia close-up*. London: Cape.
————. 1976. *Moscow farewell*. New York: Viking Press.
————. 1981. Russian disorders: Economic disaster and the end of the social dream. *Harper's* (February): 41–55.
Feldbrugge, F.J.M. 1984. Government and shadow economy in the Soviet Union. *Soviet Studies* 36: 528–43.
Felshman, Neal. 1992. *Gorbachev, Yeltsin, and the last days of the Soviet empire*. New York: St. Martin's Press.
Ferguson, Julia. 1983. More on the freezers and Soviet agents. *The Review of News* (June): 51–58.
Feshbach, Murray. 1982. Social maintenance in the USSR: Demographic morass. *Washington Quarterly* 5: 92–98.
Feshbach, Murray, and Alfred Friendly, Jr. 1991. *Ecocide in the USSR: Health and nature siege*. New York: Basic Books.
Festinger, Leon. 1957. *A theory of cognitive dissonance*. New York: Peterson and Co.
Feuer, Lewis S. 1976. What is an intellectual? In *The intelligentsia and the intellectuals: Theory, methods and case study*, ed. Alexander Gella. Beverly Hills, CA: Sage.
————. 1978. University Marxism. *Problems of Communism* 27: 65–72.
Firth, Noel E., and James H. Noren. 1998. *Soviet defense spending: A history of CIA estimates 1950–1990*. College Station: Texas A&M University.
Fischer, Benjamin B. 1999. *At the Cold War's End: US Intelligence on the Soviet Union and Eastern Europe*. Washington, DC: History Staff, Center for the Study of Intelligence.
Fitzgerald, Frances. 2000. *Way out there in the blue: Reagan, Star Wars, and the end of the Cold War*. New York: Simon and Schuster.
Fitzpatrick, Sheila. 1974. Cultural revolution in Russia, 1928–1938. *Journal of Contemporary History* 9: 33–52.
————. 1978. *Cultural revolution as class warfare*. In *Cultural revolution in Russia, 1928–1931*, ed. Sheila Fitzpatrick. Bloomington: University of Indiana Press.
————. 1982. *The Russian revolution 1917–1932*. Oxford: Oxford University Press.
————. 1984. The Russian revolution and social mobility: A re-examination of the question of social support for the Soviet regime in the 1920s and 1930s. *Politics and Society* 13: 119–41.
————. 1999. Cultural revolution revisited. *Russian Review* 2: 202–9.
Fleron, Frederick J. 1969. *Communist studies and the social sciences. Essays on methodology and empirical theory*. Chicago: Rand McNally.
Flint, Jerry. 1980. Welcome to the club. *Forbes*, October 13: 61–64.
Flis, Andrzej. 1988. Crisis and political ritual in postwar Poland. *Problems of Communism* 36: 43–54.
Florig, Dennis. 1986. The concept of equal opportunity in the analysis of social welfare. *Polity* 18: 392–407.
Foye, Stephen. 1995. The demise of the Soviet armed forces. In *The demise of the USSR*, ed. Vera Tolz and Iain Elliot. London: Macmillan.
Frasier, J. 1974. Validating a measure of national political legitimacy. *American Journal of Political Science* 18: 117–34.
French, Julius R.P., and Benjamin Raven. 1959. The bases of social power. In *Studies of social power*, ed. D. Carthwright. Ann Arbor: University of Michigan Press.
Frey, Fredric W. 1985. The problem of actor designation in political analysis. *Comparative Politics* 17: 127–52.

Friedrich, Carl J., and Zbigniew K. Brzezinski. 1956. *Totalitarian dictatorship and autocracy.* Cambridge, MA: Harvard University Press.

Fry, Michael G., and Miles Hochstein. 1993. Epistemic communities: Intelligence studies and international relations. *Intelligence and National Security* 8: 14–28.

Fukuyama, Francis. 1989. The end of history. *The National Interest* (Summer): 3–18.

———. 1992. *The end of history and the last man.* New York: The Free Press.

———. 1993. The modernizing imperative: The USSR as an ordinary country. *The National Interest* 31: 10–18.

Furhman, Peter. 1988. Another stake through Stalin's heart. *Forbes*, December 26.

Gaddis, John L. 1983–84. The rise, fall and future of détente. *Foreign Policy* 62: 354–77.

———. 1987. Expanding the data base: Historians, political scientists, and the enrichment of security studies. *International Security* 12: 3–21.

———. 1992–93. International relations theory and the end of the Cold War. *International Security* 17: 5–58.

———. 1994. The tragedy of the Cold War history: Reflections on revisionism. *Foreign Affairs* 73: 142–54.

———. 1997. *We know now: Rethinking the Cold War history.* New York: Oxford University Press.

Galbraith, John, K. 1967. The new industrial state. Boston: Houghton Mifflin.

———. 1984. Reflections: A visit to Russia. *New Yorker*, September 3: 54, 60–61.

———. 1985. The new industrial state. 4th ed. Boston: Houghton Mifflin.

Galbraith, John K., and Stanislav Menshikov. 1988. *Capitalism, communism and coexistence.* Boston: Houghton Mifflin.

Galeotti, Mark. 1997. *Gorbachev and his revolution.* New York: St. Martin's Press.

Galston, William A. 1980. Justice and the human good. Chicago: Chicago University Press.

Galtung, Johan. 1976. Toward new indicators of development. *Futures* 8: 261–65.

Garson, Mark. 1996. *The neoconservative vision. From the Cold War to the cultural war.* Lanahm, MD: Madison Books.

Garthoff, Raymond L. 1978. On estimating and imputing intentions. *International Security* 2: 22–32.

———. 1985. Détente and confrontation. Washington, DC: The Brookings Institution.

———. 1992. Why did the Cold War arise, and why did it end? In *The end of the Cold War: Its meaning and implications*, ed. M. Hogan. Cambridge: Cambridge University Press.

———. 1994. *The great transition: American-Soviet relations and the end of the Cold War.* Washington, DC: The Brookings Institution.

———. 1996. The KGB reports to Gorbachev. *Intelligence and National Security* 11: 224–44.

Garton Ash, Timothy. 1984. Under Western eyes: Poland, 1980–1982. *Washington Quarterly* 7: 120–34.

Gates, Robert M. 1987–88. The CIA and American foreign policy. *Foreign Affairs* 66: 215–30.

———. 1989. Discussion. In *Intelligence requirements for the nineties*, ed. R. Godson. Lexington, MA: Lexington Books.

———. 1996. *From the shadows: The ultimate insider's story of five presidents and how they won the Cold War.* New York: Simon and Schuster.

Gelman, Harry. 1984. *The Brezhnev Politburo and the decline of détente.* Ithaca, NY: Cornell University Press.

Gershman, Carl. 1978. The world according to Andrew Young. *Commentary* (August): 17–23.

———. 1979. Selling them the rope. *Commentary* (April): 35–45.

———. 1980. The rise and fall of the new foreign policy establishment. *Commentary* (July): 13–24.

Gervasi, Tom. 1986. *The myth of Soviet military supremacy.* New York: Harper and Row.

Getty, John Arch. 1985. *Origins of the great purges. The Soviet Communist Party reconsidered.* New York: Cambridge University Press.

Gibney, Frank. 1960. *The Khrushchev pattern.* New York: Duell, Sloan and Peace.

Gidwitz, Betsy. 1982. Labor unrest in the Soviet Union. *Problems of Communism* 31: 25–42.

Gilison, Jerome M. 1968. Soviet elections as measure of dissent. The missing one percent. *American Political Science Association* 62: 814–26.

———. 1972. *British and Soviet politics: Legitimacy and convergence.* Baltimore, MD: The Johns Hopkins University Press.

Gill, Graeme. 1987. The single party as an agent of development. *World Politics* 39: 566–78.

Gitelman, Zvi. 1983. Are nations merging in the USSR? *Problems of Communism* 32: 35–47.

Gitlin, Todd. 1978. Media sociology: The dominant paradigm. *Theory and Society* 6: 205–55.

Gladwell, Malcolm. 2000. *The tipping point: How little things can make a big difference.* Boston: Little, Brown.

Glasner, David. 1992. Hayek and the conservatives. *Commentary* (October): 48–50.

Gleason, Abbott. 1995. Totalitarianism: The inner history of the Cold War. New York: Oxford University Press.

Gleason, Gregory. 1992. The 'national factor' and the logic of Sovietology. In *The post-Soviet nations: Perspectives on the demise of the USSR*, ed. Alexander J. Motyl. New York: Columbia University Press.

Godson, Roy, ed. 1980. *Intelligence requirements for the 1980s: Analysis and estimates.* New Brunswick: Transition Books.

Goldman, Marshall I. 1983. *U.S.S.R. in crisis: The failure of an economic system.* New York: Norton.

———. 1987. A time to rethink. *Moment* (April): 14–17.

———. 1990. Gorbachev the economist. *Foreign Affairs* 69: 28–44.

———. 1991. *What went wrong with perestroika.* New York: Norton.

Goldstein, Jack A. 1995. Why we could (and should) have predicted the revolution of 1989–99. In *Debating revolutions*, ed. N.R. Keddie. New York: New York University Press.

Gooding, John. 1990. Gorbachev and democracy. *Soviet Studies* 42: 195–232.

Goodman, Elliot R. 1984. The Brezhnev-Andropov legacy: Implications for the future. *Survey* 28: 34–69.

Goodman, Melvin A. 1997. Ending the CIA's Cold War legacy. *Foreign Policy* 106: 128–43.

———. 1999. Who is the CIA fooling? Only itself. *Newsweek* (October).

Gorbachev, Mikhail. 1987. *Perestroika. New thinking for our country and the world.* New York: Harper and Row.

———. 1991. *The August coup: The truth and the lesson.* New York: HarperCollins.

———. 1996. *Memoirs.* New York: Doubleday.

Graham, Daniel O. 1995. *Confession of a Cold Warrior.* Fairfax, VA: Preview Press.

Gray, Colin S. 1981. The most dangerous decade: Historic mission, legitimacy, and dynamics of the Soviet empire. *Orbis* 25: 13–28.

———. 1984. Moscow is cheating. *Foreign Policy* 56: 141–52.

Green, Peter. 2000. Collapsophe. *The New Republic* (March 20).

Greenstein, Fred I., and William C. Wohlforth, eds. 1994. *Retrospective on the end of the Cold War: Report of a conference sponsored by the John Foster Dulles Program for the Study of Leadership in International Affairs.* Princeton, NJ: Princeton University Center of International Studies.

Greenwald, G. Jonathan, and Walter B. Slocombe. 1987. The economic constraints on Soviet military power. *Washington Quarterly* 10: 117–32.

Gross, Natalie. 1990. Youth and the army in the USSR in the 1980s. *Soviet Studies* 42: 481–98.

Grossman, Gregory. 1977. The second economy of the USSR. *Problems of Communism* 26: 25–40.

Groth, Alexander J. 1974. The "isms" in totalaristianism. In *Politics in Advanced Nations,* ed. Norman J. Vig and Rodney Stiefbold. Englewood Cliffs, NJ: Princeton Hall.

———. 1990. Communist (surprise) parties. *Orbis* 34: 17–32.

Gurr, Ted R. 1968. A causal model of civil strife: A comparative analysis using new indices. *American Political Science Review* 62: 1104–24.

———. 1970. *Why men rebel.* Princeton, NJ: Princeton University Press.

———. 1973. The revolution–social change nexus: Some old theories and new hypotheses. *Comparative Politics* 5: 359–92.

Gurtov, Melvin. 1974. *The United States against the Third World.* New York: Praeger.

Haass, Richard, and Melissa Williams. 1988. *Reykjavik Summit: Watershed or washout.* Cambridge, MA: John F. Kennedy School of Government.

Habermas, Jurgen. 1975. *Legitimation crisis.* Boston: Beacon Press.

———. 1990. What does socialism mean today? The rectifying revolution and the need for new thinking on the left. *New Left Review* (September–October): 3–22.

Hahn, Jeffrey W. 1978. Stability and change in the Soviet Union: A developmental perspective. *Polity* 10: 542–67.

———. 1981. Soviet demographic dilemmas. *Problems of Communism* 30: 56–61.

Haines, Gerald K., and Robert E. Leggett. 2001. *CIA's analysis of the Soviet Union: 1947–1991.* Washington, DC: Center for the Study of Intelligence, Central Intelligence Agency.

Halberstam, David. 2001. *War in time of peace: Bush, Clinton and the generals.* New York: Scribner.

Halliday, Fred. 1990. The ends of Cold War. *New Left Review* (March–April): 5–24.

Hanson, Philip. 1992. *From stagnation to catastroika: Commentaries on the Soviet economy, 1983–1991.* New York: Praeger.

Hardt, John P., and Donna Gold. 1983. Andropov's economic future. *Orbis* 27: 11–19.

Harries, Owen. 1991. The Cold War and the intellectuals. *Commentary* (May): 13–20.

Harrison, Mark. 1993. Soviet economic growth since 1928: The alternative statistics of G.I. Khanin. *Europe-Asia Studies* 45: 141–67.

Hart, Gary. 1991. *Russia shakes the world: The second Russian revolution and its impact on the West.* New York: HarperCollins.

Hauslohner, Peter A. 1987. Gorbachev's social contract. *Soviet Economy* 3: 56–60.

Hazan, Baruch A. 1987. *From Brezhnev to Gorbachev: Infighting in the Kremlin.* Boulder, CO: Westview Press.

Hazard, John N. 1960. *The Soviet system of government.* Chicago: The University of Chicago Press.

Heller, Michael. 1985. Gorbachev for beginners. *Survey* 29: 12–18.

Helmer, Olaf. 1986. The future relationship between the superpowers. *Futures* 18: 484–92.

Herspring, Dale R. 1990. *The Soviet high command, 1967–1989: Personalities and politics.* Princeton, NJ: Princeton University Press.

———. 1996. *Russian civil-military relations.* Bloomington: Indiana University Press.

Hewett, Ed A. 1988. *Reforming the Soviet economy: Equality vs. efficiency.* Washington, DC: The Brookings Institution.

Herz, John H. 1978. Legitimacy: Can we retrieve it? *Comparative Politics* 10: 317–49.

Hill, Ronald, J. 1993. Managing ethnic conflict. *Journal of Communist Studies* 9: 57–74.

Hill, Ronald J., Timothy Dunmore, and Karen Dawisha. 1981. The USSR: The revolution reversed? In *The withering away of the state? Party and state under communism,* ed. Leslie Holmes. Beverly Hills, CA: Sage.

Hollander, E.J., and J.W. Julian. 1970. Studies in leader legitimacy, influence and innovation. In *Advances in experimental social psychology,* vol. 5, ed. L. Berkowitz. New York: Academic Press.

Hollander, Paul. 1981. *Political pilgrims: Travels of Western intellectuals to the Soviet Union, China, and Cuba 1929–1978.* New York: Oxford University Press.

———. 1983. Laboring under socialism. *Problems of Communism* 32: 57–61.

———. 1990. The Berlin Wall collapses, the adversary culture endures. *Orbis* 34: 565–78.

———. 1992. *Anti-Americanism. Critique at home and abroad 1965–1990.* New York: Oxford University Press.

———. 2000. Judgments and misjudgments. In *The collapse of communism,* ed. L. Edwards. Stanford, CA: Hoover Institution Press.

Holloway, David. 1982. Foreign and defense policy. In *Soviet policy in the 1980s,* ed. Archie Brown and Michael Kaser. Bloomington: Indiana University Press.

———. 1989–90. State, society, and the military under Gorbachev. *International Security* 14: 5–24.

———. 1988–89. Gorbachev's New Thinking. *Foreign Affairs* 68: 66–81.

Holmes, Leslie. 1993. *The end of communist power: Anti-corruption campaigns and legitimation crisis.* New York: Oxford University Press.

Holroyd, P. 1978. Changes and discontinuity: Forecasting for the 1980s. *Futures* 10: 31–43.

Holsti, Ole R. 1962. The belief system and national image: A case study. *Journal of Conflict Resolution* 6: 244–52.

Holzman, Franklyn D. 1980. Are the Russians really outspending the U.S. on defense? *International Security* 4: 86–104.

———. 1982. Soviet military spending: Assessing the numbers game. *International Security* 6: 78–101.

————. 1989. Politics and guesswork: CIA and the DIA estimate of Soviet military spending. *International Security* 14: 101–31.

Homans, George C. 1961. *Social behavior: Its elementary forms*. London: Routledge and Kegan Paul.

Homer-Dixon, Tad. 2000. *The ingenuity gap*. New York: Knopf.

Hook, Sidney. 1985. How has the United States met the major challenges since 1945? *Commentary* 80: 47–50.

Horelick, Arnold L. 1989–90. U.S.-Soviet relations: Threshold of a new era. *Foreign Affairs* 69: 51–69.

Horowitz, Irving L. 1977. *Ideology and utopia in the United States, 1956–1976*. London: Oxford University Press.

Hosking, Geoffrey A. 1990. *The awaking of the Soviet Union*. Cambridge, MA: Harvard University Press.

Hough, Jerry F. 1972. The Soviet system—petrifaction or pluralism? *Problems of Communism* 21: 25–45.

————. 1973. The bureaucratic model and the nature of the Soviet system. *Journal of Comparative Administration* 5: 134–67.

————. 1976. Political participation in the Soviet Union. *Soviet Studies* 28: 3–20.

————. 1977a. The man and the system. *Problems of Communism* 26: 1–17.

————. 1977b. *The Soviet Union and social science theory*. Cambridge, MA: Harvard University Press.

————. 1978. The cultural revision and Western understanding of the Soviet system. In *Cultural revolution in Russia, 1928–1931,* ed. Sheila Fitzpatrick. Bloomington: University of Indiana Press.

————. 1980. *Soviet leadership in transition*. Washington, DC: The Brookings Institution.

————. 1982a. Issues and personalities. *Problems of Communism* 31: 20–40.

————. 1982b. *The Polish crisis—American policy options: A staff paper*. Washington, DC: The Brookings Institution.

————. 1983a. Andropov's first year. *Problems of Communism* 32: 49–64.

————. 1983b. Pluralism, power and the Soviet Union. In *Pluralism in the Soviet Union. Essay in Honor of H. Gordon Skilling*, ed. S.G. Solomon. New York: St. Martin's Press.

————. 1985. Gorbachev's strategy. *Foreign Affairs* 64: 33–55.

————. 1986. *The struggle for the Third World*. Washington, DC: The Brookings Institution.

————. 1987. The end of Russia's Khomeini period. *World Policy Journal* 4: 583–604.

————. 1988a. *Opening up the Soviet economy*. Washington, DC: The Brookings Institution.

————. 1988b. *Russia and the West*. New York: Simon and Schuster.

————. 1989. The politics of successful economic reform. *Soviet Economy* 5: 3–46.

————. 1989–90. Gorbachev's politics. *Foreign Affairs* 68: 26–41.

————. 1990. Gorbachev's endgame. *World Policy Journal* 7: 639–72.

————. 1991a. Assessing the coup. *Current History* 90: 305-310.

————. 1991b. Understanding Gorbachev: The importance of politics. *Soviet Economy* 7: 89–109.

Hough, Jerry F., and Merle Fainsod. 1979. *How the Soviet Union is governed*. Cambridge, MA: Harvard University Press.

Huber, Robert T. 1989. *Soviet perceptions of the U.S. Congress: The impact on super-power relations.* Boulder, CO: Westview Press.

Hughes, Thomas L. 1981. Up from Reaganism. *Foreign Policy* 44: 24–36.

Huntington, Samuel P. 1983. The defense policy of the Reagan administration. In *The Reagan presidency: An early assessment,* ed. Fred I. Greenstein. Baltimore, MD: Johns Hopkins University Press.

———. 1991. *The third wave democratization in the late twentieth century.* Norman: University of Oklahoma Press.

Hyland, William. 1982. Kto kogo in the Kremlin. *Problems of Communism* 31: 17–25.

———. 1987. Reagan-Gorbachev III. *Foreign Affairs* 66: 7–21.

Ioffe, Olimpiad. 1990. *Gorbachev's economic dilemmas: An insider's view.* St. Paul: Merrill/Magnus.

Isaac, Rael J. 1983. The Institute for Policy Studies: Empire on the left. *Midstream* 26: 7–18.

Isaac, Rael J., and Isaac, Erich. 1983. *The coercive Utopians: Social deception by America's power players.* Chicago: Regnery Gateway.

Jackman, Robert. 1976. Politicians in uniforms: Military governments and social change in the Third World. *American Political Science Review* 70: 1078–97.

Jacobs, Dan N. 1978. The Kremlin and problems of innovation. In *Innovation in communist systems,* ed. Andrew Gregory and James A. Kuhlman. Boulder, CO: Westview Press.

Janos, Andrew C. 1991. Social science, communism, and the dynamics of political change. *World Politics* 44: 81–112.

Jasinska-Kania, Aleksandra. 1983. Rationalization and legitimation crisis: The relevance of Marxian and Weberian works for an explanation of the political order's legitimacy crisis in Poland. *Sociology* 17: 154–64.

Jasso, Guillermina. 1980. A new theory of distributive justice. *American Sociological Review* 45: 3–32.

Jasso, Guillermina, and Peter Rossi. 1977. Distributive justice and earned income. *American Sociological Review* 42: 631–51.

Jeffreys-Jones, Rhodri. 1989. *The CIA and American democracy.* New Haven, CT: Yale University Press.

Johnson, Chalmers. 1966. *Revolutionary change.* Boston: Little, Brown.

Jones, Anthony, and William Moskoff, eds. 1991. *The great market debate in Soviet economics.* Armonk, NY: M.E. Sharpe.

Kagan, Robert. 2001. Why America blinked. *New Republic,* December 3: 29–42.

Kaiser, Robert G. 1976. *Russia: The people and the power.* New York: Atheneum.

———. 1986–87. The Soviet pretense. *Foreign Affairs* 65: 236–51.

———. 1991. *Why Gorbachev happened: His triumph and his failure.* New York: Simon and Schuster.

Kaldor, Mary. 1978. *The disintegrating west.* New York: Hill and Wang.

Kalugin, Oleg. 1994. *The first directorate.* New York: St. Martin's Press.

Kanet, Roger E. 1971. *The behavioral revolution in communist studies.* New York: The Free Press.

Kaplan, Lawrence F. 2000. Fall Guys. *The New Republic* (June 26).

Karklins, Rasma. 1981. Nationality power in Soviet republics: Attitudes and perceptions. *Studies in Comparative Communism* 14: 70–93.

Kassoff, Allen. The administered society: Totalitarianism without terror. *World Politics* 16: 558–75.

Katz, Zev. 1971. Sociology in the Soviet Union. *Problems of Communism* 20: 22–40.

Keddie, Nikki R. 1995. Can revolutions be predicted: Can their causes be understood? In *Debating revolutions,* ed. N. R. Keddie. New York: New York University Press.

Kendall, Willmore. 1949. The function of intelligence. *World Politics.* 1: 540–52.

Kennedy, Paul. 1987. *The rise and fall of great powers.* New York: Random House.

Keren, Michael. 1976. The GDR's economic miracle. *Problems of Communism* 25: 85–91.

Khasbulatov, Ruslan. 1993. *The struggle for Russia: Power and change in the democratic revolution.* London: Routledge.

Kimmel, Michael S. 1990. *Revolution: A sociological interoperation.* Philadelphia: Temple University Press.

Kinder, Donald R., and D. Roderick Kiewiet. 1979. Sociotropic politics: The American case. *British Journal of Political Science* 11: 129–61.

King, Anthony. 1975. Overload: Problems of governing in the 1970s. *Political Studies* 23: 284–96.

Kirkpatrick, Jeane. 1979. Dictatorship and double standards. *Commentary* (November): 34–45.

———. 1990. *The withering away of the totalitarian state . . . and other surprises.* Washington, DC: AEI Press.

Kirsch, Henry. 1982. Political legitimation in the German Democratic Republic. In *Political legitimacy in communist states*, ed. T.H. Rigby and Ferenc Feher. New York: St. Martin's Press.

Kissinger, Henry A. 1981. *For the record: Selected statements, 1977–1980.* Boston: Little, Brown.

———. 1994. *Diplomacy.* New York: Simon and Schuster.

———. 1999. *Years of renewal.* New York: Simon and Schuster.

Kitrinos, Robert W. 1984. International Department of the CPSU. *Problems of Communism* 33: 47–75.

Knight, Amy W. 1988. *The KGB. Police and politics in the Soviet Union.* Boston: Unwin Hyman.

———. 1996. *Spies without cloak: The KGB's successor.* Princeton, NJ: Princeton University Press.

Knorr, Klaus. 1964. Failures in national intelligence estimates: The case of the Cuban missiles. *World Politics* 16: 455–67.

Kolakowski, Leszek. 1971. *Marxism and beyond.* London: Paladin.

———. 1980. The self-poisoning of the open society. *Survey* 25: 5–16.

Kolko, Gabriel. 1969. *The roots of American foreign policy: An analysis of power and purpose.* Boston: Beacon Press.

Kolko, Joyce, and Gabriel Kolko. 1972. *The limits of power: The world and United States foreign policy, 1945–1954.* New York: Harper and Row.

Korbonski, Andrzej. 1983. Conformity and dissent in Eastern Europe. In *Politics and participation under communist rule,* ed. Peter J. Potichnyi and Jane Shapiro Zachet. New York: Praeger.

Kort, Michael. 1993. *The Soviet colossus: The rise and fall of the USSR.* Armonk, NY: M.E. Sharpe.

Kramer, John M. 1977. Political corruption in the USSR. *Western Political Quarterly* 30: 213–24.

Krancberg, Sigmund. 1994. *A Soviet postmortem: Philosophical roots of the "grand failure."* Lanham, MA: Rowman and Littlefied.

Kreisler, Harry. 1996. Conversation with Alexander Yakovlev. *Conversations with History* (November 21). Berkeley: Institute of International Studies, University of California.

Kubalkova, Vendulka, and A.A. Cruickshank. 1989. *Thinking anew about Soviet "new thinking."* Berkeley: Institute of International Studies, University of California.

Kuhn, Thomas S. 1970. *The structure of scientific revolution.* 2d ed. Chicago: University of Chicago Press.

Kuran, Timor. 1991. Now out of nowhere: The elements of surprise in the East European revolutions. *World Politics* 44: 7–48.

———. 1995. *Private truths, public lies: The social consequences of preference falsification.* Cambridge, MA: Harvard University Press.

Kushnirsky, Fyodor I. 1984. The limits of Soviet economic reform. *Problems of Communism* 33: 33–42.

Kux, Ernst. 1984. Contradictions in Soviet socialism. *Problems of Communism* 33: 1–27.

Kuznetz, S. 1955. Economic growth and inequality. *American Economic Review* 45: 1–28.

Kwitny, Jonathan. 1997. *The man of the century: The life and times of Pope John Paul II.* New York: Henry Holt.

Labedz, Leopold. 1980. The politics of survival. *Survey* 25: 41–65.

Ladd, Everett C., Jr., and Seymour M. Lipset. 1971. The politics of American political scientists. *PS* 4: 135–38.

———. 1973. *Academics, politics and the 1972 election.* Washington, DC: American Enterprise Institute.

———. 1975. *The divided academy: Professors and politics.* New York: McGraw-Hill.

LaFeber, Walter. 1991. *America, Russia, and the Cold War 1945–1990.* 6th ed. New York: McGraw-Hill.

Landy, Paul. 1961. What price corruption? *Problems of Communism* 10: 18–25.

Lane, Christel. 1978. *Christian religion in the Soviet Union: A sociological study.* Albany: State University of New York Press.

———. 1984. Legitimacy and power in the Soviet Union through socialist rituals. *British Journal of Political Science* 14: 207–18.

Lane, David. 1979. Soviet industrial workers: The lack of legitimation crisis. In *Legitimation of regimes: International framework for analysis,* ed. B. Denitch. Beverly Hills, CA: Sage.

Lane, Robert E. 1978. Interpersonal relations and leadership in a 'cold society.' *Comparative Politics* 10: 443–61.

———. 1979. The legitimacy bias: Conservative man in market and state. In *Legitimation of regimes: International framework for analysis,* ed. Bogdan Denitch. Beverly Hills, CA: Sage.

———. 1986. Market justice, political justice? *American Political Science Review* 80: 384–402.

Lane, David, and Felicity O'Dell. 1978. *The soviet industrial worker: Social class, education and control.* London: Martin Robertson.

Lange, Oskar, and Fred M. Taylor. 1938. *On the economic theory of socialism.* Minneapolis: University of Minnesota Press.

Lapidus, Gail W. 1984. Ethnocentrism and political stability: The Soviet case. *World Politics* 36: 555–80.

———. 1986a. The Soviet national question. In *The Gorbachev era,* ed. Alexander Dallin and Condoleezza Rice. Stanford, CA: Stanford Alumni Association.

————. 1986b. Soviet society in transition. In *The Gorbachev era*, ed. Alexander Dallin and Condoleezza Rice. Stanford, CA: Stanford Alumni Association.

Laqueur, Walter. 1980. Containment for the 1980s. *Commentary* (October): 33–42.

————. 1981. Pity the poor Russians. *Commentary* (February): 32–41.

————. 1983a. U.S.-Soviet relations. *Foreign Affairs* 62: 561–86.

————. 1983b. What we know about the Soviet Union. *Commentary* (February): 13–21.

————. 1985. *A world of secrets: The uses and limits of intelligence.* New York: Basic Books.

————. 1989. *The long way to freedom: Russia and glasnost.* New York: Charles Scribner's Sons.

————. 1990. *Soviet realities: Culture and politics from Stalin to Gorbachev.* New Brunswick, NJ: Transaction Books.

————. 1994. *The dream that failed. Reflections on the Soviet Union.* New York: Oxford University Press.

Larabee, F. Stephen. 1986–87. Gorbachev: The road to Reykjavik. *Foreign Policy.* 65: 3–28.

————. 1988. Gorbachev and the Soviet military. *Foreign Affairs* 66: 1002–26.

Larson, Thomas B. 1978. *Soviet-American rivalry.* New York: W.W. Norton.

————. 1988. Gorbachev and the Soviet military. *Foreign Affairs* 66: 1002–26.

Leavit, Robert, and Gary Orren. 1983. *Freezing the arms race: The campaign in Washington.* Cambridge, MA: The John F. Kennedy School of Government.

Lebed, Aleksandr. 1997. *My life and my country.* Washington, D.C.: Regnery Publishing.

Ledeen, Michael A., and William H. Lewis. 1981. *Debacle: The American failure in Iran.* New York: Alfred A. Knopf.

Lee, William T. 1995. *CIA estimates of Soviet military expenditures: Errors and waste.* Washington, DC: American Enterprise Institute.

————. 1997. *The ABM treaty charade: A study in elite illusion and delusion.* Washington, DC: Council for Social and Economic Studies.

Legvold, Robert. 1979. The super rivals: Conflict in the Third World. *Foreign Affairs* 57: 755–778.

————. 1980. Containment without confrontation. *Foreign Policy* 40: 74–98.

————. 1991. The revolution in Soviet foreign policy. In *The Soviet system in crisis: A reader of Western and Soviet views*, ed. Alexander Dallin and Gail W. Lapidus. Boulder, CO: Westview Press.

Leighton, Marian K. 1991. Soviet propaganda as a foreign policy. New York: Freedom House.

Lenski, George E. 1966. *Power and privilege: A theory of social stratification.* New York: McGraw Hill.

Leonhard, Wolfgang. 1987–88. The Bolshevik revolution turns 70. *Foreign Affairs* 66: 410–29.

Levesque, Jacques. 1997. *The enigma of 1989: The USSR and the liberation of Eastern Europe.* Berkeley: University of California Press.

————. 1988. *The Gorbachev phenomenon.* Berkeley: University of California Press.

Lewin, Moshe. 1991. *The Gorbachev phenomenon: A historical interpretation.* 2d ed. Berkeley: University of California Press.

————. 1988. *The Gorbachev phenomenon. A historical interpretation.* Berkeley: University of California Press.

Ligachev, Yegor K. 1993. *Inside Gorbachev's Kremlin: The memoirs of Yegor Ligachev.* Trans. C.A. Fitzpatrick, M.A. Berdy, and D. Dyrcz-Freeman. New York: Pantheon.

Linden, Carl A., and Dmitri K. Simes. 1977. *Nationalities and nationalism in the USSR: A Soviet dilemma*. Washington, DC: Center for Strategic and International Studies.

Linton, Ralph. 1945. *The cultural background of personality*. London: Prentice Hall.

Lipset, Seymour M. 1959. American intellectuals: Their politics and status. *Daedalus* 88: 469–86.

———. 1973a. Commentary: Social stratification research and Soviet scholarship. In *Social stratification and mobility in the USSR*, ed. Murray Yanowitch and Wesley A. Fisher. White Plains, NY: International Arts and Sciences Press.

———. 1973b. Social stratification in the Soviet Union. *Survey* 19: 114–85.

———. 1982. The academic mind at the top: The political behavior and values of faculty elites. *Public Opinion Quarterly* 46: 143–68.

Lipset, Seymour M., and Richard Dobson. 1973. The intellectuals as critics and rebels. *Daedalus* 101: 137–98.

Lipset, Seymour M., and Everett C. Ladd, Jr. 1972a. The political future of activist generation. In *The new pilgrims: Youth protest in transition*, ed. Philip G. Altbach and Robert S. Laufer. New York: McKay.

———. 1972b. The politics of American sociologists. *American Journal of Sociology* 78: 77–104.

Little, D. Richard. 1980. Political participation and the Soviet economy. *Problems of Communism* 29: 62–67.

Litwack, John M. 1991. Discretionary behavior and Soviet economic reform. *Soviet Studies* 43: 217–36.

Lockwood, David. 2000. *The destruction of the Soviet Union: A study in globalization*. New York: St. Martin's Press.

Löwenthal, Richard. 1970. Development vs. utopia in communist policy. In *Change in communist systems*, ed. Chalmers Johnston. Stanford, CA: Stanford University Press.

———. 1976. The ruling party in a mature society. In *Social consequences of modernization in communist societies*, ed. Mark G. Field. Baltimore, MD: John Hopkins University Press.

———. 1993. Intelligence epistemology: Dealing with the unbelievable. *International Journal of Intelligence and Counterintelligence* 6: 319–26.

Lukes, Igor. 1989. Great expectations and the last illusions: Soviet use of Eastern European proxies in the Third World. *International Journal of Intelligence and Counterintelligence* 3: 1–14.

Luttwak, Edward N. 1983. *The grand strategy of the Soviet Union*. New York: St. Martin's Press.

McAuley, Mary. 1984. Political culture and communist politics: One step forward, two steps back. In *Political culture and communist studies*, ed. Archie Brown. Basingstoke, Hampshire: Macmillan.

McCauley, Martin. 1998. *Gorbachev*. London, NY: Longman.

McDonough, Peter, Samuel Barnes, and Antonio López Pina. 1986. The growth of democratic legitimacy in Spain. *American Political Science Review* 80: 735–60.

MacEachin, Douglas J. 1996. *CIA assessments of the Soviet Union: The record versus the charges*. Washington, DC: Center for the Study of Intelligence.

———. 2000. *US intelligence and the Polish crisis: 1980–1981*. Washington, DC: Center for the Study of Intelligence.

MacFarlane, S. Neil. 1992. Moscow's 'New Thinking' on Third World liberationism.

In *Moscow and the global left in the Gorbachev era*, ed. Joan B.Urban. Ithaca, NY: Cornell University Press.

McFaul, Michael. The fourth wave: Democracy and dictatorship in the post-communist world. Paper presented at APSA meeting, September 2000.

McNeill, Terry. 1998. Soviet studies and the collapse of the USSR: In defense of realism. In *Rethinking the Soviet collapse: Sovietology, the death of communism and the new Russia*, ed. Michael Cox. London: Pinter.

McWilliams, Wilson Carey. 1971. On political legitimacy. *Public Policy* 19: 429–56.

Majone, G. 1989. *Evidence, argument, and persuasion in the policy process*. New Haven, CT: Yale University Press.

Malia, Martin. [Z]. 1990. To the Stalin Mausoleum. *Daedalus* 119: 295–344.

———. 1991. The hunt for the true October. *Commentary* (October: 21–29).

———. 1992a. From under the rubble—what? *Problems of Communism* 41: 89–106.

———. 1992b. Leninist endgame. *Daedalus* 121: 57–76.

———. 1992c. Yeltsin and us. *Commentary* (April: 21–28).

———. 1993. A fateful logic. *The National Interest* 31: 80-90.

———. 1994. *The Soviet tragedy: A history of socialism in Russia 1917–1991*. New York: The Free Press.

———. 1999. *Russia under the Western eyes. From the bronze horseman to the Lenin mausoleum*. Cambridge: The Belknap Press of the Harvard University Press.

———. 2000. The highest stage of socialism. In *The collapse of communism*, ed. L. Edwards. Stanford, CA: Hoover Institution Press.

Mannheim, Karl. 1955. *Ideology and utopia*. San Diego, CA: Harcourt Brace Jovanovich.

Manning, Bayless. 1976. Goals, ideology and foreign policy. *Foreign Affairs* 54: 271–84.

Manuel, Frank E. 1992. A requiem for Karl Marx. *Daedalus* 121: 1–19.

Marantz, Paul. 1988. *New concepts of East-West relations*. Annual Meeting of the American Political Science Association, Washington, DC.

Marer, Paul. 1974. The political economy of Soviet relations with Eastern Europe. In *Testing theories of economic imperialism*, ed. Steven J. Rosen and James Kruth. Lexington, MA: D.C. Heath.

Marsh, Alan. 1979. The new matrix of political action. *Futures* 11: 91–103.

Maruyama, Magorah. 1973. A new model for future research. *Futures* 5: 435–37.

———. 1974. Endogenous research vs. expert from outside. *Futures* 6: 389–94.

Mastanduno, Michael. 1985. Strategies of economic containment: US trade relations with the Soviet Union. *World Politics* 37: 503–31.

Mastny, Vojtech. 1990. Threat perception on the wane: The 1980s from the perspective of the 1950s. In *The Changing Western analysis of the Soviet threat*, ed. Carl-Chrisopher Schweitzer. New York: St. Martin's Press.

Matheson, Craig. 1987. Weber and the classification of forms of legitimacy. *British Journal of Sociology* 38: 175–98.

Matlock, Jack. F. Interview. In *Conversations with History*. Berkeley: University of California, Institute of International Studies.

———. 1995. *Autopsy on an empire. The American ambassador's account of the collapse of the Soviet Union*. New York: Random House.

Mayer, Alfred G. 1965. *The Soviet political system: An interpretation*. New York: Random House.

———. 1970. Theories of convergence. In *Change in Communist Systems*, ed. Chalmers Johnson. Stanford, CA: Stanford University Press.

Medvedev, Roy A. 1972. *Let history judge: The origins and consequences of Stalinism.* New York: Alfred A. Knopf.

Mendras, Marie. 1990. The Soviet Union and its rival self. *Journal of Communist Studies* 6: 1-23.

Menges, Constantine C. 1988. *Inside the National Security Council: The true story of making and unmaking of Reagan's foreign policy.* New York: Simon and Schuster.

———. 1990. *The twilight struggle: The Soviet Union v. the United States today.* Washington, DC: AEI Press.

Meyer, Alfred G. 1993. Politics and methodology in Soviet studies. In *Post-communist studies and political science. Methodology and empirical theory in Sovietology,* ed. Frederick J. Fleron, Jr., and Erik P. Hoffmann. Boulder, CO: Westview Press.

Michael, D.N. 1985. Thinking about the future. *Futures* 17: 94–103.

Migranyan, Andranik. 1989. Democratization process in socialist society. *Social Science* 20: 105–20.

Miliband, Ralph. 1989. Reflection on the crisis of communist regimes. *New Left Review* 177: 27–39.

Millar, James R. 1977. The prospects for Soviet agriculture. *Problems of Communism* 26 (May–June): 1–16.

Miller, Abraham H., and Nicholas Damask. 1993. Thinking about intelligence after the fall of communism. *International Journal of Intelligence and Counterintelligence* 6: 250–70.

Miller, Stephen. 1992. The Soviet coup and the benefits of breakdown. *Orbis* 36: 69–85.

Mills, Richard M. 1981. The Soviet leadership problem. *World Politics* 33: 590–613.

Misztal, Barbara A. 1996. *Trust in modern societies: The search for bases of social order.* Cambridge, England: Polity Press.

Mitchell, Brian. 1989. Myths of the U.S.S.R.'s strong economy. *Investors Business Daily,* December 10.

Mitchell, R. Judson. 1982. Immobilism, depolitization, and the emerging Soviet elite. *Orbis* 26: 591–610.

Mitchell, R. Judson, and Teresa Gee. 1985. The Soviet succession crisis and its aftermath. *Orbis* 29: 293–318.

Mlynar, Zdenek. 1990. *Can Gorbachev change the Soviet Union? The international dimension of political reform.* Boulder, CO: Westview Press.

Moltz, James C. 1993. Divergent learning and the failed politics of Soviet economic reforms. *World Politics* 45: 301–26.

Montefiore, Simon. S. 2004. *Stalin. The court of the Red Tzar.* New York: Alfred A. Knopf.

Moore, Barrington, Jr. 1966. *Social origins of dictatorship and democracy: Lord and peasant in the making of the modern world.* Boston: Beacon Press.

Morewood, Steven. 1998. Gorbachev and the collapse of communism. *History Review* 31: 33–39.

Morton, Henry W. 1979. Housing problems and policies of Eastern Europe and the Soviet Union. *Studies in Comparative Communism* 22: 300–321.

Moses, Joel C. 1981. Soviet leaders: Roots of behavior. *Problems of Communism* 30: 46–53.

Moshiri, Farrokh. 1985. *The state and social revolution in Iran: A theoretical perspective.* New York: Peter Lang.

Moskoff, William. 1993. *Hard times. Impoverishment and protest in the perestroika years.* Armonk, NY: M.E. Sharpe.

Moss, Robert. 1978. Who's meddling in Iran? *The New Republic* (December 2): 15–18.

Motyl, Alexander J. 1987. *Will the non-Russia rebel? State, ethnicity, and stability in the USSR*. Ithaca, NY: Cornell University Press.

———. 1989. Reassessing the Soviet crisis: Big problems, muddling through, business as usual. *Political Science Quarterly* 104: 269–80.

———. 1992. The end of Sovietology: From Soviet studies to post-Soviet studies. In *The post-Soviet nations: Perspectives on the demise of the USSR*, ed. Alexander J. Motyl. New York: Columbia University Press.

———. 1999. *Revolutions, nations, empires. Conceptual limits and theoretical possibilities*. New York: Columbia University Press.

Mueller, Dennis C. 1979. *Public choice*. New York: Cambridge University Press.

Muller, Jerry Z. 1988. Capitalism: The way of the future. *Commentary* (December): 21–26.

Muravchik, Joshua. 1988. 'Glasnost,' the KGB, and the nation. *Commentary* 85: 47–49.

Naimark, Norman M. 1979. Is it true what they're saying about East Germany? *Orbis* 23: 549–78.

National Security Archives. 1995. Released under FOIA as *The Soviet Estimate: US Analysis of Soviet Union, 1947–1991,* ed. Thomas S. Blanton and Byme. Washington: National Security Archives.

Nimmo, Dan D., and Keith R. Sanders. 1981. The emergence of political communication as a field. In *Handbook of political communication*, ed. Dan D. Nimmo and Keith R. Sanders. Beverly Hills, CA: Sage.

Nitze, Paul H. 1989. *From Hiroshima to glasnost: At the center of decision—a memoir*. New York: Grove Weidenfeld.

Nogee, Joseph L., and John Spanier. 1988. *Peace impossible—war unlikely: The Cold War between the United States and the Soviet Union*. Glenville, IL: Scott, Foresman/Little Brown.

Novak, Michael. 2000. The silent artillery of communism. In *The collapse of communism*, ed. Lee Edwards. Stanford, CA: Hoover Institution Press.

Nove, Alec. 1961. *The Soviet economy*. New York: Frederick A. Praeger.

———. 1980. The Soviet economy: Problems and prospects. *New Left Review* 119: 3–19.

———. 1982. Income distribution in the USSR: A possible explanation of some recent data. *Soviet Studies* 34: 288–289.

———. 1983. *Economics of feasible socialism*. London: Allen and Unwin.

———. 1984. Wither the Soviet economy? *Washington Quarterly* 7: 89–99.

Novikov, Evgeny, and Patrick Bascio. 1994. *Gorbachev and the collapse of the Soviet Communist Party*. New York: Peter Lang.

Nye, Joseph S., Jr. 1984. Can America manage its Soviet policy? *Foreign Policy* 62: 857–78.

Nye, Joseph S., Jr., and Sean M. Lynn-Jones. 1988. International security studies: A report of a conference on the state of the field. *International Security* 12: 5–27.

Oberdorfer, Don. 1991. *The turn: From the Cold War to a new era. The United States and the Soviet Union 1983–1990*. New York: Poseidon Press.

———. 1992. *The turn: From the Cold War to a new era*. New York: Touchstone Books.

———. 1998. *The collapse of the Soviet military*. New Haven, CT: Yale University Press.

Odom, William E. 1976. A dissenting view on the group approach to Soviet politics. *World Politics* 28: 542–67.

———. 1981. Wither the Soviet Union. *Washington Quarterly* 4: 30–49.

———. 1983. Choice and change in Soviet politics. *Problems of Communism* 3: 1–21.

———. 1992. Soviet politics and after: Old and new concepts *World Politics* 45: 66–98.

———. 1993. The pluralistic mirage. *The National Interest* 31: 99–108.

———. 1998. *The collapse of the Soviet military.* New Haven, CT: Yale University Press.

Ofri, Arie. 1983. Crisis and opportunity forecasting. *Orbis* 26: 817–47.

O'Hearn, Dennis. 1980. The consumer second economy: Size and effect. *Soviet Studies* 32: 218–34.

Olcott, Martha B. 1982. Soviet Islam and world revolution. *World Politics* 34: 487–504.

———. 1985. Yuri Andropov and the national question. *Soviet Studies* 37: 103–17.

———. 1986. Moscow's troublesome Muslim minority. *Washington Quarterly* 9: 73–84.

———. 1990. Official Soviet policy and the national problem. In *The Soviet multinational state*, ed. Martha B. Olcott. Armonk, NY: M.E. Sharpe.

Oye, Kenneth A. 1987. Constrained confidence and the evolution of Reagan foreign policy. In *Eagle resurgent? The Reagan era in American foreign policy*, ed. Kenneth A. Oye, Robert J. Lieber, and Donald Rothchild. Boston: Little, Brown.

Packenham, Robert A. 1973. *Liberal America and the third world: Political development ideas in foreign aid and social science.* Princeton, NJ: Princeton University Press.

———. 1992. *The dependency movement: Scholarship and politics in development studies.* Cambridge, MA: Harvard University Press.

Pakulski, Jan. 1986. Ideology and mass compliance: Reflection on Max Weber and Soviet type societies. *British Journal of Political Science* 16: 35–56.

Palazchenko, Pavel. 1997. *My years with Gorbachev and Shevardnadze. The memoir of a Soviet interpreter.* University Park: Pennsylvania University Press.

Parenti, Michael. 1983. *Democracy for the few.* New York: St. Martin's Press.

Parker, John W. 1991. *Kremlin in transition.* Boston: Unwin Hyman.

Parsons, Talcott. 1951. *The social system.* Glencoe, IL: The Free Press.

Parvin, Manoucher. 1973. Economic determinants of political unrest: An econometric approach. *Journal of Conflict Resolution* 17: 271–96.

Patman, Robert G. 1999. Reagan, Gorbachev and the emergence of New Political Thinking. *Review of International Studies* 25: 577–601.

Pemberton, William E. 1998. *Exit with honor: The life and presidency of Ronald Reagan.* Armonk, NY: M.E. Sharpe.

Perdue, John. 1998. Egg-faced economists. Georgia Politics.com. (November 19).

Pereira. N.G.O. 1999. Soviet work attitudes and politics, 1953–91. A preliminary historical sociology. *The Australian Journal of Politics and History* 45: 78–89.

Perle, Richard. 1995. Forward. In William T. Lee. *CIA estimates of Soviet military expenditures. Errors and waste.* Washington: American Enterprise Institute.

Perlmutter, Amos. 1980. The comparative analysis of military regimes: Formation, aspiration, and achievements. *World Politics* 33: 96–120.

Perry, Mark. 1992. *Eclipse: Last days of CIA.* New York: William Morrow.

Persico, Joseph E. 1990. *Casey: From the OSS to the CIA.* New York: Viking Press.

Pettman, Ralph. 1975. *Human behavior and world politics.* New York: St. Martin's Press.

Phillips, James A. 1989. Gorbachev's 'newthink' on the Middle East. *Midstream* (August–September 12–15).

Pilskin, Karen. 1980. Camouflage, conspiracy, and collaborators. Rumors of the revolution. *Iranian Studies* 13: 51–81.

Pipes, Daniel. 1997. *Conspiracy: How the paranoid style flourishes and where it comes from.* New York: The Free Press.

Pipes, Richard. 1975. Introduction: The nationality problems. In *Handbook of major Soviet nationalities,* ed. Zev Katz et al. Riverside, NY: The Free Press.

———. 1976. Détente: Moscow's view. In *Soviet strategy in Europe*, ed. Richard Pipes. New York: Crane, Rusk and Company.

———. 1977. Why the Soviet Union thinks it could fight and win a nuclear war. *Commentary* (July): 21–34.

———. 1980. Soviet global strategy. *Commentary* 69: 31–39.

———. 1981. American perceptions and misperceptions of the Soviet military: Intentions and capabilities. In *Intelligence policy and national security*, ed. Robert L. Pfaltzgraff, Uri Ra'anan, and W. Milberg. Hamden, CT: Anchor.

———. 1984a. Can the Soviet Union reform? *Foreign Affairs* 63: 47–61.

———. 1984b. Survival is not enough. *Survey* 28: 1–33.

———. 1984c. Survival is not enough. *Survey* 28: 1–13.

———. 1986. Team B: The reality behind the myth. *Commentary* (October): 25–40.

———. 1990. Gorbachev's Russia: Breakdown or crackdown. *Commentary* 89: 13–26.

———. 1990–91. The Soviet Union adrift. *Foreign Affairs* 70: 70–98.

———. 1993. 1917 and the revisionists. *The National Interest* 31: 68–79.

———. 1994. *Communism: The vanished specter.* Oslo: Scandinavian University Press.

———. 1995a. Misrepresenting the Cold War: The hardliners had it right. *Foreign Affairs* 74: 154–60.

———. 1995b. What to do about the CIA. *Commentary* 99 (March): 36–43.

———. 1996. A new Soviet era? *Foreign Policy* 62: 46–60.

———. 2000. The fall of the Soviet Union. In *The collapse of communism*, ed. Lee Edwards. Stanford, CA: Hoover Institution Press.

———. 2000b. The fall of the Soviet Union. In Lee Edwards, ed., *The collapse of communism.* Stanford: Hoover Institution Press.

———. 2003. *Vixi: Memories of a non-belonger.* New Haven, CT: Yale University Press.

Ploss, Sidney I. 1986. A new Soviet era? *Foreign Policy* 62: 46-60.

———. 1982. Signs of struggle. *Problem of Communism* 31: 41–52.

Plous, S. 1985. Perceptual illusions and military realities: The nuclear arms race. *Journal of Conflict Resolution* 29: 363–89.

Podhoretz, Norman. 1976. Making the world safe for communism. *Commentary* (April): 31–41.

———. 1981. The future danger. *Commentary* (March): 25–31.

Popplewell, Richard J. 1991. Themes in the rhetoric of KGB chairmen from Andropov to Kryuchkov. *Intelligence and National Security* 6: 513–47.

Porter, Michael E. 1990. *The competitive advantage of nations.* New York: Macmillan.

Posen, Barry R., and Stephen Van Evara. 1980. Overarming and underwhelming. *Foreign Policy* 40: 99–118.

Powell, David E. 1973. Drug abuse in communist Europe. *Problems of Communism* 22: 31–40.

———. 1988. Soviet glasnost: Definitions and dimensions. *Current History* 87: 321–42.

Powell, S. Steven. 1987. *Covert cadre: Inside the Institute for Policy Studies.* Ottawa, IL: Green Hill Publishers.

Pozner, Vladimir. 1992. *Eyewitness: A personal account of the unraveling of the Soviet Union.* New York: Random House.

Prados, John. 1982. *The Soviet estimate: U.S. intelligence analysis and Russian military strength.* New York: The Dial Press.

Prigogine, Ilya, and Isabelle Stengers. 1984. *Order out of chaos: Man's new dialogue with nature.* Toronto: Bantam Books.

Pringle, Robert W. 2003. Russia's killing fields. *Intelligence and Counterintelligence* 16: 499–523.

Pry, Peter V. 1997. *War scare: Nuclear countdown after the Soviet fall.* Atlanta: Turner Publishing.

Puddington, Arch. 1988. *Failed Utopias: Methods of coercion in communist regimes.* San Francisco, CA: Institute for Contemporary Studies.

———. 1989. Life under communism today. *Commentary* (February): 32–38.

Pym, Denis. 1980. Toward the dual economy and emancipation from employment. *Futures* 12: 223–37.

Ra'anan, Uri, and Igor Lukes, eds. 1990. *Inside the apparat: Perspectives on the Soviet system from former functionaries.* Lexington, MA: Lexington Books.

Rakowska-Harmstone, Teresa. 1974. The dialectic of nationalism in the USSR. *Problems of Communism* 23: 1–22.

Ramage, C.S. 1980. Sudden events. *Futures* 4: 268–74.

Ranelagh, John. 1987. *The agency: The rise and decline of the CIA.* New York: Simon and Schuster.

Rashid, Ahmed. 2002. *Jihad: The rise of militant Islam in Central Asia.* New Haven, CT: Yale University Press.

Raskin, Marcus G. 1979. *The politics of national security.* New Brunswick, NJ: Transaction Books.

———. 1983. Introduction to the federal budget and social reconstruction. In *First fruit: The Institute for Policy Studies 1963–1983*, ed. John S. Friedman. New York: Grove Press.

———. 1991. *Essays of a citizen: From national security state to democracy.* Armonk, NY: M.E. Sharpe.

Rawles, Richard. E. 1996. Soviet psychology, perestroika and the human factor: 1985–1991. In *Post-Soviet perspectives on Russian psychology*, ed. Vera A. Kolstova et al., Westport, CT: Greenwood Press.

Rawls, John. 1971. *A theory of justice.* Cambridge, MA: Harvard University Press.

Reagan, Ronald. 1990. *An American life.* New York: Simon and Schuster.

Reddaway, Peter. 1990. The quality of Gorbachev's leadership. *Soviet Economy* 6: 125–40.

———. 1993. The role of popular discontent. *The National Interest* 31: 57–63.

Rees, John. 1983. How and why communists use radical lawyers. *American Opinion* (October): 45–54, 69.

Reich, Robert C. 1989. Re-examining the Team A–Team B experience. *International Journal of Intelligence and Counterintelligence* 3: 387–404.

———. 1993. The role of popular discontent. *The National Interest* 31: 57–63.

Remington, Thomas F. 1983. *Soviet public opinion and the effectiveness of party ideological work.* Pittsburgh, PA: Russia and East European Studies Program, University of Pittsburgh.

———. 1990. Regime transition in communist systems: The Soviet case. *Soviet Economy* 6: 160–90.

———. 1993. Regime transition in communist systems: The Soviet case. In *Post-communist studies and political science: Methodology and empirical theory in Sovietology,* ed. Frederic J. Fleron, Jr., and Erik. P. Hoffmann. Boulder, CO: Westview Press.

Remnick, David. 1994. *Lenin's tomb: The last days of the Soviet empire.* New York: Vintage Books.

Rescher, Nicholas. 1969. A questionnaire study of American values by 2000. In *Values and the future: The impact of technological change on American values,* ed. Kurt Baier and Nicholas Rescher. New York: The Free Press.

Rigby, Thomas H. 1964. Crypto-politics. *Survey* 50: 163–94.

———. 1982. Legitimation: Political legitimacy, Weber and Communist mono-organizational system. In *Political legitimation in communist states,* ed. Thomas H. Rigby and Ferenc Feher. New York: St. Martin's Press.

———. 1983. A conceptual approach to authority, power and policy in the Soviet Union. In *Authority, power and policy in the USSR,* ed. Thomas H. Rigby, Archie Brown, and Peter Reddaway. London: Macmillan.

———. 1984. Dominant and subsidiary modes of political legitimation in the USSR: A comment on Christel Lane's article. *British Journal of Political Science* 14: 219–22.

———. 1990. *The changing Soviet system: Mono-organizational socialism from its origins to Gorbachev's restructuring.* Aldershot, England: Elgar Publishers.

Robinson, Neil. 1995. *Ideology and the collapse of the Soviet system: A critical history of Soviet ideological discourse.* Aldershot, England: Elgar Publishers.

Romerstein, Herbert, and Eric Breindel. 2000. *The Venona secrets. Exposing Soviet espionage and America's traitors.* Washington: Regnery.

Rosati, James A. 1987. *The Carter administration's quest for global community: Beliefs and their impact on behavior.* Columbia: University of South Carolina Press.

Rose, Richard. 1969. Dynamic tendencies in authoritarian regimes. *World Politics* 21: 604–28.

Rosefielde, Steven. 1982. *False science. Understanding the Soviet arms buildup: An appraisal of the CIA's direct costing effort.* New Brunswick, NJ: Transaction Books.

Rositzke, Harry. 1975. The KGB's broadening horizon. *Problems of Communism* 24: 43–45.

Rostow, Walt W. 1965. *The stages of economic growth. A non-communist manifesto.* Cambridge, MA: Harvard University Press.

———. 1987. On ending the Cold War. *Foreign Affairs* 65: 831–51.

Rothman, Stanley, and S. Robert Lichter. 1996. *Roots of radicalism: Jews, Christians and the left.* New Brunswick, NJ: Transaction Books.

Rothschild, Joseph. 1979. Political legitimacy in contemporary Europe. In *Legitimation of regimes: International framework for analysis,* ed. Bogdan Denitch. Beverly Hills, CA: Sage.

Rothstein, Robert L. 1972. *Planning, prediction, and policymaking in foreign affairs: Theory and practice.* Boston: Little, Brown.

Rowen, Henry S. 1989. Political strategies for general war: The case of Eastern Europe. In *Political warfare and psychological operations: Rethinking the U.S. approach*, ed. Frank R. Barnett and Carnes Lord. Washington, DC: National Defense University.

Rowen, Henry S., and Charles Wolf, Jr. 1990a. The future of the Soviet empire. In *The impoverished superpower: Perestroika and the Soviet military burden*, ed. Henry. S. Rowen and Charles Wolf, Jr. San Francisco, CA: ICS Press.

————. 1990b. Introduction. In *The impoverished superpower and the Soviet military burden*, ed. Henry S. Rowen and Charles Wolf, Jr. San Francisco, CA: ICS Press.

Rubin, Barry M. 1980. *Paved with good intentions: The American experience in Iran*. New York: Oxford University Press.

Ruble, Blair A. 1983. Romanov's Leningrad. *Problems of Communism* 32: 36–48.

Rumer, Boris. 1989. Soviet estimate of the role of inflation. *Soviet Studies* 41: 298–317.

Rummel, R.J. 1990. *Lethal politics: Soviet genocide and mass murder since 1917*. New Brunswick, NJ: Transaction Publishers.

Rush, Myron. 1982–83 Guns over growth in Soviet policy. *International Security* 7: 167–79.

Rutland, Peter. 1998. Sovietology. Who got it right and who got it wrong ? And why? In Michael Cox. ed., *Rethinking the Soviet collapse: Sovietology, the death of communism and the new Russia*. London: Pinter.

Rutland, Peter. 1991. The search for stability: Ideology, discipline and the cohesion of the Soviet elite. *Studies in Comparative Communism* 24: 25–57.

————. 1993. Sovietology: Notes for a post-mortem. *The National Interest* 31: 109–22.

Ryavec, Karl W. 1982. The Soviet leadership succession: Change and uncertainty. *Polity* 15: 103–22.

Rywkin, Michael. 1994. *Moscow's lost empire*. Armonk, NY: M.E. Sharpe.

Said, Abdul A., ed. 1971. *Protagonists of change: Subcultures in development and revolution*. Englewood Cliffs, NJ: Prentice Hall.

Said, Edward W. 1978. *Orientalism*. New York: Pantheon Books.

Sakharov, Vladimir, and Umberto Tosi. 1980. *High treason*. New York: G.P. Putnam.

Sakwa, Richard. 1990. *Gorbachev and his reforms*. New York: Prentice Hall.

Schapiro, Leonard. 1982. After Brezhnev: The limits of prediction. *Survey* 26: 169–78.

————. 1984. The end of illusion. In *The Soviet worker*, ed. Leonard Schapiro and Joseph Godson. New York: St. Martin's Press.

Schlesinger, Arthur, Jr. 1983. Foreign policy and the American character. *Foreign Policy* 62: 1–16.

Schmidt-Hauer, Christian. 1986. *Gorbachev: The path to power*. Boston: Salem House.

Schroeder, Gertrude E. 1968. Soviet reality sans Potemkin. *Studies in Intelligence* 12: 43–51.

————. 1991. Perestroika in the aftermath of 1990. *Soviet Economy* 1: 3–13.

————. 1995. Reflections on economic Sovietology. *Post-Soviet Affairs* 11: 197–234.

Schumpeter, Joseph A. 1950. *Capitalism, socialism and democracy*. New York: Harper and Row.

Schwartz, Joel J. 1973. The elusive "new Soviet man." *Problems of Communism* 22: 39–50.

Schweitzer, Peter. 1994. Victory. *The Reagan administration's secret strategy that hastened collapse of the Soviet Union*. New York: The Atlantic Monthly Press.

Sciolino, Elaine. 1991a. In rebuttal to Senate committee, CIA nominee is truthful but incomplete. *New York Times* (October 13).

————. 1991b. Gates takes over CIA, challenged to lift its anxious mood. *New York Times* (November 12).

Scott, James C. 1990. *Domination and the art of resistance.* New Haven, CT: Yale University Press.

Scott, James M. 1996. *Deciding to intervene: The Reagan Doctrine and American foreign policy.* Durham, NC: Duke University Press.

Seliktar, Ofira. 1986. Identifying a society's belief system. In *Political Psychology,* ed. Margaret G. Hermann. San Francisco, CA: Jossey-Bass.

————. 2000. *Failing the crystal ball test: The Carter administration and the fundamentalist revolution in Iran.* Westport, CT: Praeger.

Sergeyev, Victor M. 1988. *The wild East. Crime and lawlessness in post-communist Russia.* Armonk, NY: M.E. Sharpe.

Seton-Watson, Hugh. 1980. The last of the empire. *Washington Quarterly* 3: 41–46.

Sexton, Donald J. 1986. The theory and psychology of military deception. In *Deception: Perspectives on human and nonhuman deceit,* ed. Robert W. Mitchell and Nicolas S. Thompson. Albany: State University of New York Press.

Shabad, Theodore. 1979. Communist environment. *Problems of Communism* 28: 64–67.

Shafer, D. Michael. 1988. *Deadly paradigms: The failure of U.S. counterinsurgency policy.* Princeton, NJ: Princeton University Press.

Shane, Scott. 1994. *Dismantling utopia: How information ended the Soviet Union.* Chicago: Ivan. R. Dee.

Shapiro, Michael J., G. Mathew Bonham, and Daniel A. Heradstveit. 1988. Discursive practice approach to collective decision making. *International Studies Quarterly* 32: 397–420.

Sharlet, Robert. 1974. Gulag; A chronicle of Soviet extralegal history. *Problems of Communism* 23: 65–71.

Sheehy, Gail. 1990. *The man who changed the world: The lives of Mikhail S. Gorbachev.* New York: HarperCollins.

Shelton, Judy. 1989. *The coming Soviet crash: Gorbachev's desperate pursuit of credit in Western financial markets.* New York: The Free Press.

Shevardnadze, Eduard. 1991. *The future belongs to freedom.* New York: The Free Press.

Shevchenko, Arkady N. 1985. *Breaking with Moscow.* New York: Ballantine Books.

Shiraev, Eric, and Vladislav Zubok. 2000. *Anti-Americanism in Russia: From Stalin to Putin.* New York: Palgrave.

Shlapentokh, Vladimir E. 1985. Two levels of public opinion: The Soviet case. *Public Opinion Quarterly* 49: 443–59.

————. 1988. The XXVII Congress—A case study in the shaping of a new party ideology. *Soviet Studies* 40: 1–21.

————. 1989. *Public and private life of the Soviet people: Changing values in post Stalinist Russia.* Oxford: Oxford University Press.

————. 1998. Soviet society and American Sovietologists: A study in failure. In *Rethinking the Soviet collapse: Sovietology, the death of communism and the new Russia,* ed. Michael Cox. London: Pinter.

Shoup, Paul. 1989. Leadership drift in the Soviet Union and Yugoslavia. *Studies in Comparative Communism* 22: 42–56.

Shtromas, Alexander. 1988. How the end of the Soviet system may come about: Historical precedents and possible scenarios. In *The Soviet Union and the challenge of the future: vol. 1. Stasis and change*, ed. Alexander Shtromas and Morton A. Kaplan. New York: Paragon Press.

Shulsky, Abram. 1993. *Silent warfare: Understanding the world of intelligence*. Washington, DC: Brassey's (U.S.).

Shultz, George P. 1993. *Turmoil and triumph: My years as secretary of state*. New York: Charles Scribner's Sons.

Shultz, Richard H., and Roy Godson. 1984. *Dezinformatsia: Active measures in Soviet strategy*. Washington, DC: Pergamon Brassey's.

Shvets, Yuri B. 1994. *Washington station: My life as a KGB spy*. Trans. E. Ostrovsky. New York: Simon and Schuster.

Sick, Gary. 1985. *All fall down: America's tragic encounter with Iran*. New York: Random House.

Simes, Dimitri K. 1979–80. The anti-Soviet brigade. *Foreign Policy* 37: 28–42.

———. 1980. The death of détente. *Intentional Security* 5: 3–25.

———. 1980–81. Deterrence and coercion in Soviet policy. *International Security* 5: 80–103.

———. 1981–82. The military and militarism in Soviet society. *International Security* 6: 123–43.

———. 1984a. America's new edge. *Foreign Policy* 56: 24–43.

———. 1984b. The new Soviet challenge. *Foreign Policy* 55: 113–31.

———. 1986. Gorbachev: A new foreign policy? *Foreign Affairs* 65: 477–500.

Simis, Konstantin M. 1977–78. The machinery of corruption in the Soviet Union. *Survey* 23: 1–18.

———. 1982. *USSR: The corrupt society: The secret world of Soviet capitalism*. New York: Simon and Schuster.

———. 1985. The Gorbachev generation. *Foreign Policy* 59: 3–21.

Simpson, Christopher. 1995. *National security directives of the Reagan and Bush administrations*. Boulder, CO: Westview Press.

Singleton, Fred, ed. 1974. *Environmental misuses in the Soviet Union and Eastern Europe*. New York: Praeger.

Singleton, Seth. 1984. Defense of the gains of socialism: Soviet world policies in the mid-1980s. *Washington Quarterly* 7: 102–15.

Skilling, Gordon H. 1966. Interest groups and communist politics. *World Politics* 18: 435–51.

———. 1970. Group conflict and political change. In *Change in communist systems*, ed. Chalmers Johnson. Stanford, CA: Stanford University Press.

———. 1983. Interest groups and communist politics revisited. *World Politics* 36: 1–27.

———. 2000. *The education of a Canadian: My life as a scholar and activist*. Montreal: McGill-Queen's University Press.

Skilling, Gordon H., and Franklyn Griffith, ed. 1971. *Interest groups in Soviet politics*. Princeton, NJ: Princeton University Press.

Skocpol, Theda. 1979. *States and social revolutions: A comparative analysis of France, Russia and China*. Cambridge: Cambridge University Press.

Slater, Wendy. 1995. The August coup. In *The Demise of the USSR*, ed. Vera Tolz and Iain Elliiot. London: Macmillan.

Smelser, Neil J. 1962. *Theory of collective behavior*. New York: The Free Press.

Smith, Gordon B. 1983. Technology transfer and Soviet innovation. *Problems of Communism* 32: 70–73.

Smith, Hedrick. 1976. *The Russians*. New York: Quadrangle.

———. 1990. *The New Russians*. New York: Random House.

Smith, James A. 1993. *Strategic calling: The Center for Strategic and International Studies 1962–1992*. Washington, DC: The Center for Strategic and International Studies.

Snyder, Alvin A. 1995. *Warriors of disinformation: American propaganda, Soviet lies, and winning of the Cold War*. New York: Arcade.

Solovyov, Vladimir, and Elena Klepikova. 1983. *Yuri Andropov: A secret passage into the Kremlin*. Trans. G. Daniels. New York: Macmillan.

———. 1986. *Behind the high Kremlin wall*. Trans. G. Daniels. New York: Dodd, Mead and Company.

Solzhenitsyn, Aleksandr. 1980. Misconceptions about Russia are a threat to America. *Foreign Affairs* 58: 797–834.

———. 1985. Our pluralists. *Survey* 29: 1–28.

Sorman, Guy. 1985. *The conservative revolution*. Chicago: Regnery Books.

Staar, Richard F. 1980. Soviet Union. In *The United States in the 1980s*, ed. Peter Duignan and Alvin Rabushka. Stanford, CA: Hoover Press.

———. 1988. Soviet Union: A civil society. *Foreign Policy* 70: 26–41.

Staats, Steven J. 1972. Corruption in the Soviet Union. *Problems of Communism* 21: 40–47.

Staniland, Martin. 1991. *American intellectuals and African nationalists 1955–1970*. New Haven, CT: Yale University Press.

Staniszkis, Jadwiga. 1984. The dynamics of a breakthrough in the socialist system: An outline of a problem. *Soviet Studies* 4: 560–73.

Steinberg, Dmitri. 1992. The Soviet defense burden: Estimating hidden defense costs. *Soviet Studies* 44: 237–64.

Steinfels, Peter. 1979. *The neoconservatives: The men who are changing America's politics*. New York: Simon and Schuster.

Stent, Angela. 1990–1991. The one Germany. *Foreign Policy* 81: 53–70.

Sterling, Claire. 1981. *The terror network: The secret war of international terrorism*. New York: Berkeley Books.

Strayer, Robert W. 1998. *Why did the Soviet Union collapse?: Understanding historical change*. Armonk, NY: M.E. Sharpe.

Strumilin, Stanislav G. 1964. *Man, society and the future*. New York: Crosscurrents.

Strumpel, Burkhard. 1972. Economic well being as an object of social measurement. In *Subjective elements of well being, values and social change*, ed. Burkhard Strumpel. Paris: Organization for Economic Co-operation and Development.

———. 1977. The changing face of advanced industrial economics: A post-Keynesian view. *Comparative Political Studies* 10: 299–322.

Sullivan, David S. 1980. Evaluating U.S. intelligence estimates. In *Intelligence requirements for the 1980s: Analysis and estimates*, ed. Roy Godson. New Brunswick, NJ: Transaction Books.

Suraska, Wisla. 1998. *How the Soviet Union disappeared: An essay on the causes of dissolution*. Durham, NC: Duke University Press.

Surazska, Wieslawa. 1986. Normative and instrumental functions of equity criteria in individual choices of the input–payoff distribution pattern. *Journal of Conflict Resolution* 30: 532–50.

Survey. 1987. A special issue. Seventy years after the revolution. 29.

Sutton, Anthony C. 1973. *National suicide: Military aid to the Soviet Union.* New Rochelle, NY: Arlington House.

Szporluk, Roman. 1972. The plight of the minorities. *Problems of Communism* 21: 79–84.

Talbott, Strobe. 1984a. *Deadly gambits: The Reagan administration and the stalemate in nuclear arms control.* New York: A. Knopf.

———. 1984b. *The Russians and Reagan.* New York: Vintage Books.

Tanter, Raymond, and Richard H. Ullman. 1972. *Theory and policy in international relations.* Princeton, NJ: Princeton University Press.

Taubman, William. 1974. The change to change in communist systems: Modernization, postmodernization and Soviet politics. In *Soviet politics and society in the 1970s,* ed. Henry W. Morton and Rudolf L. Tokes. New York: The Free Press.

———. 1986. Sources of Soviet foreign conduct. *Problems of Communism* 35: 47–52.

———. 2003. *Khrushchev: The man and his era.* New York: W.W. Norton.

Teller, Edward. 2001. *Memoirs: A twentieth-century journey in science and politics.* Cambridge, MA: Perseus Publishers.

Theen, Rolf H.W. 1981. The Soviet political system since Stalin. *Problems of Communism* 30: 74–77.

Thomas, John R., and U.M. Kruse-Vaucienne. 1977–78. Soviet science and technology: An introduction. *Survey* 23: 1–28.

Thornton, R.C. 1991. *The Carter years: Toward a new global order.* New York: Paragon House.

Thurston, Robert W. 1986. Fear and belief in the USSR's "Great Terror": Response to Arrest, 1935–1939. *Slavic Review* 45: 213–34.

Ticktin, Hillel H. 1998. Soviet studies and the collapse of the USSR: In defense of Marxism. In *Rethinking the Soviet collapse: Sovietology, the death of communism and the new Russia,* ed. Michael Cox. London: Pinter.

Tiersky, Ronald. 1977. The seduction of Marxism. *Problems of Communism* 26: 65–71.

Tilly, Charles. 1978. *From mobilization to revolution.* Reading, MA: Addison-Wesley.

Timofeyev, Timor. 1988. Social aspects of perestroika. In *New stage of perestroika,* ed. Abel Aganbegyan and Timor Timofeyev. New York: Institute for East-West Relations.

Toffler, Alvin. 1970. *Future shock.* New York: Random House.

Topol, Edward, and Fridrikh Neznansky. 1983. *Red Square.* New York: Quarter Books.

Treml, Vladimir G. 1982. Death from alcohol poisoning in the USSR. *Soviet Studies* 34: 487–505.

Trevor-Roper, H.R. 1988. The lost moments of history. *New York Review of Books* (October 27): 61–67.

Tucker, Robert C. 1961. Toward a comparative politics of movement regimes. *American Political Science Review* 55: 281–93.

———. 1963. *The Soviet political mind. Studies in Stalinism and post Stalinist change.* New York: Frederick A. Praeger.

———. 1981–82. Swollen state, spent society: Stalinist legacy to Brezhnev's Russia. *Foreign Affairs* 60: 414–35.

———. 1992. Sovietology and Russian history. *Post-Soviet Studies* 8: 175–96.

———. 1993. Forward. In *Post-Communist studies and political science,* ed. Frederc J. Fleron, Jr., and Erik P. Hoffmann. Boulder, CO: Westview Press.

Tucker, William. 1996. Complex questions. The new science of spontaneous order. *Reason* January: 34-38.

Turner, R., and L. Killian. 1972. *Collective behavior*. Englewood Cliffs, NJ: Prentice Hall.

Tyler, Tom R. 1990. *Why people obey the law*. New Haven, CT: Yale University Press.

Tyson, James L. 1981. *Target America: The influence of communist propaganda on U.S. media*. Chicago: Regnery Gateway.

Ulam, Adam B. 2000. *Understanding the Cold War: A historian's personal reflections*. Charlottesville, VA: Leopolis Press.

Unger, Aryeh L. 1980. Political participation in the USSR: YCL and CPSU. *Soviet Studies* 33: 107–24.

Urban, Michael, and M. Steven Fish. 1998. Does post-Sovietogy have a future? In *Rethinking the Soviet collapse: Sovietology, the death of communism and the new Russia*, ed. Michael Cox. London: Pinter.

Valkenier, Elizabeth K. 1986. Revolutionary changes in the Third World: Recent Soviet reassessments. *World Politics* 38: 415–34.

Vardys, V. Stanley. 1975. Modernization and Baltic nationalism. *Problems of Communism* 24: 32–48.

———. 1980. Lithuania's Catholic movement. *Survey* 25: 49–73.

Volgyes, Ivan, ed. 1974. Environmental deterioration in the Soviet Union and Eastern Europe. New York: Praeger.

Volkogonov, Dmitri. 1998. *Autopsy for an empire: The seven leaders who built the Soviet regime*. New York: The Free Press.

Von Bertalanffy, Ludwig. 1956. General system theory. *General Systems* 1: 1–10.

Wädekin, Karl-Eugen. 1982. Soviet agriculture's dependence on the West. *Foreign Affairs* 60: 882–903.

Waller, Douglas C. 1991. The CIA called it but nobody listened. *Newsweek* (September 21).

Ward, Michael D. 1983. Things fall apart: A logical analysis of crisis resolution dynamics. *International Interaction* 15: 65–79.

Weigel, George. 1992. *The final revolution: The resistance church and the collapse of Communism*. New York: Oxford University Press.

———. 1999. *Witness to hope: The biography of John Paul II*. New York: HarperCollins.

Weiner, T. 1993. Lies and rigged 'Star Wars" test fooled the Kremlin and Congress. *New York Times* (August 18).

Weir, Fred. 1993. Defining eras: The collapse of the Soviet Union. In *Altered States: A reader in the new world*, ed. Phyllis Bennis and Michael Moushabeck. New York: Olive Branch Press.

Werth, Nicholas. 1999. A state against its people: Violence, repression and terror in the Soviet Union. In *The black book of communism: Violence, repression and terror in the Soviet Union*, ed. S. Courtois, N. Werth, J. Panne, A. Paczkowksi, K. Bartosek, and J. Margolin. Cambridge: Cambridge University Press.

Wesson, Robert G. 1976. *Why Marxism?: The continuing success of a failed theory*. New York: Basic Books.

———. 1980. *The aging of communism*. New York: Praeger.

———. 1984. Totalitarian strength and weakness. *Survey* 28: 186–204.

White, Ann. 1999. *Democratization in Russia under Gorbachev, 1985–91: The birth of a voluntary sector*. New York: St. Martin's Press.

White, Stephen. 1979. Political culture and Soviet politics. London: Macmillan.
———. 1980. The effectiveness of political propaganda in the USSR. *Soviet Studies* 32: 323–48.
———. 1983. Political communication in the USSR: Letters to party, state and press. *Political Studies* 31: 43–60.
———. 1986. Economic performance and communist legitimacy. *World Politics* 38: 462–82.
———. 1990. *Gorbachev in power.* New York: Cambridge University Press.
Williams, William Appleman. 1969. *The roots of the modern American empire: A study of the growth and shaping of social consciousness in a marketplace society.* New York: Random House.
Winik, Jay. 1988–89. The neoconservative reconstruction. *Foreign Policy* 73: 135–52.
Wohlforth, William C. 1998. Reality check: Revising theories of international politics in response to the end of the Cold War. *World Politics* 50: 650–80.
Wohlstetter, Albert. 1974a. Is there a strategic arms race? *Foreign Policy* 15: 3–20.
———. 1974b. Rivals, but no race. *Foreign Policy* 16: 48–81.
Wolf, Charles, Jr. 1982. Beyond containment: Redesigning American policies. *Washington Quarterly* 5: 107–18.
———. 1983. *The cost of the Soviet empire.* Santa Monica, CA: Rand Corporation.
Wolfe, Alan. 1971. Unthinking about the thinkable: Reflection on the failure of the caucus for a new policy science. *Politics and Society* 1: 393–406.
———. 1978. Has social democracy a future? *Comparative Politics* 11: 100–125.
———. 1982. *America's impasse: The rise and fall of the politics of growth.* New York: Pantheon Books.
Wood, Robert S. 1978. U.S. foreign policy as an agent of change in communism. In *Innovation in communist systems*, ed. Andrew Gyorgy and James A. Kuhlman. Boulder, CO: Westview Press.
Wrong, Dennis H. 1980. *Power: Its forms, bases and uses.* New York: Harper and Row.
Wynn, Mark. 1972. Who are the futurists? *The Futurist* 4: 73–77.
Yakovlev, Alexander N. 2002. *A century of violence in Soviet Russia.* New Haven, CT: Yale University Press.
Yanowitch, Murray. 1977. *Social and economic inequality in the Soviet Union.* London: Martin Robinson.
Yanowitch, Murray, and Wesley A. Fisher. 1973. Introduction: The development of Soviet studies on stratification and mobility. In *Social stratification and mobility in the USSR*, ed. Murray Yanowitch and Wesley A. Fisher. White Plains, NY: International Arts and Sciences Press.
Yegorov, Vladimir K. 1993. *Out of a dead end into the unknown: Notes on Gorbachev's perestroika.* Trans. D. Floyd. Chicago: Edition Q.
Yeltsin, Boris. 1990. *Against the grain: An autobiography.* Trans. M. Glenny. New York: Summit Books.
———. 1994. *The struggle for Russia.* Trans. C.A. Fitzpatrick. New York: Times Books.
———. 2000. *Midnight diaries.* Trans. C.A. Fitzpatrick. New York: Public Affairs.
Zamostny, Thomas J. 1984. Moscow and Third World: Recent trends in Soviet thinking. *Soviet Studies* 36: 223–35.
Zaslavskaya, Tatyana. 1990. *The second socialist revolution: An alternative strategy.* Trans. S.M. Davis with Jenny Warren. Bloomington: Indiana University Press.

Zdravomyslov, A.G. 1991. Changes in mass consciousness and outlines of parliamentary activity. *Journal of Communist Studies* 7: 235–56.

Zemtsov, Ilya. 1985. *The private life of the Soviet elite*. New York: Crane Russak.

Ziegler, Charles A. 1997. Intelligence assessments of Soviet atomic capability, 1945–1949. Myth, monopolies and maskirovka. *Intelligence and National Security* 12: 1–24.

Zwick, Peter. 1979. Ethnoregional socio-economic fragmentation and Soviet budgetary policy. *Soviet Studies* 3: 388–400.

Index

Ofira Seliktar earned a bachelor's degree in political science at the Hebrew University of Jerusalem and completed her doctorate in political science at the University of Strathclyde, in Glasgow. She teaches at Gratz College and Temple University and is the author of several books and many articles on the Middle East and predictive failures in intelligence. *Failing the Crystal Ball Test: The Carter Administration and the Fundamentalist Revolution in Iran* (2000) explores the American failure to predict the Khomeini revolution. Seliktar is currently working on a study of the politics of prediction and the war in Iraq.